The Wo

Back to the Future

The Worlds of
Back to the Future

Critical Essays on the Films

Edited by
SORCHA NÍ FHLAINN

McFarland & Company, Inc., Publishers
Jefferson, North Carolina, and London

LIBRARY OF CONGRESS CATALOGUING-IN-PUBLICATION DATA

The worlds of Back to the future : critical essays on the films / edited by Sorcha Ní Fhlainn.
    p.   cm.
    Includes bibliographical references and index.

    ISBN 978-0-7864-4400-7
    softcover : 50# alkaline paper ∞

    1. Back to the future (Motion picture)   2. Back to the future part II (Motion picture)   3. Back to the future part III (Motion picture)   4. Time travel in motion pictures.   I. Ní Fhlainn, Sorcha, 1980–
PN1997.B1935W67   2010
791.43'72 — dc22   2010010463

British Library cataloguing data are available

Front cover: Michael J. Fox as Marty McFly and Christopher Lloyd as
Dr. Emmett Brown with the DeLorean in *Back to the Future Part II*,
1989 (Universal Pictures/Photofest); blue background funnel and foreground fire ©2010 Shutterstock

Manufactured in the United States of America

McFarland & Company, Inc., Publishers
  Box 611, Jefferson, North Carolina 28640
  www.mcfarlandpub.com

For Michéal Ó Flainn

Acknowledgments

This book has become a reality due to the belief, diligence and support of many wonderful people.

To all the contributors, Andrew Gordon, Bernice M. Murphy, Elizabeth McCarthy, Stephen Matterson, Lucy Fife Donaldson, Randy Laist, Michael Williams, Christine Lee Gengaro, Katherine Farrimond, John Exshaw, Christopher Justice, Francis Ludlow and Jennifer Harwood-Smith, for producing such excellent readings, skillful interpretations, insights, criticisms, and explorations of the *Future* trilogy; my sincere thanks to you all.

I also wish to thank the editorial board of *Science Fiction Studies* for its kind permission to reprint Andrew Gordon's essay, "*Back to the Future*: Œdipus as Time Traveler." This article (in an earlier version) was originally published in *Science Fiction Studies*, vol. 14.3 (1987): 372–85.

To my colleagues in the School of English, Trinity College, Dublin, my mentor Dr. Darryl Jones, and close friends; your support has been invaluable.

To everyone involved in making the *Back to the Future* trilogy, especially Robert Zemeckis, Bob Gale, Neil Canton, Alan Silvestri, and the unforgettable cast, Michael J. Fox, Christopher Lloyd, Lea Thompson, Crispin Glover and Thomas F. Wilson; thank you for the magic.

To my mother Léin, and brother Eoghan, who lovingly supported me through the conceptualization, development and realization of this book — from the initial brainwave to the final page — I am forever indebted to you both. With love, to John Gilleese (where's my DeLorean?), who always believed in this book, and in me.

For me, *Back to the Future* continues to endure: from a crystallized moment in my childhood, aged six, watching awestruck and exhilarated as "the biggest lightning bolt in the history of cinema" struck the Clock Tower. As the years went by, the trilogy remained ever present, endlessly re-watched and quoted with my beloved late father Micheál, to whom this book is dedicated.

Table of Contents

Introduction: It's About Time

Sorcha Ní Fhlainn

On December 27, 2007, the Library of Congress' National Film Reg-istry selected *Back to the Future* (1985) to be added to its permanent archive. The film was chosen with twenty-five other films that year, including *Bullitt* (1968), *Close Encounters of the Third Kind* (1977), *Dances with Wolves* (1990), *The Man Who Shot Liberty Valance* (1962), *Oklahoma!* (1955), *12 Angry Men* (1957), and *Wuthering Heights* (1939), all deemed "culturally, historically and aesthetically significant" and to be preserved for future generations for all time.[1] Some critics may have been surprised by the National Preservation Board's selection of Robert Zemeckis' film considering the subject matter of *Back to the Future*: this seemingly "lightweight" film concerns a 1980s teen-ager who inadvertently travels back in time to the 1950s, where he witnesses his parents as teenagers and, because of his disruption to the timeline, must ensure his future existence. To be included among a selection of films that, in broad terms, investigate American history, bigotry, justice, literary adap-tation, the Western genre, science fiction, and the musical, groundbreaking action set pieces and cutting-edge filmmaking techniques, is certainly a mem-orable accolade, and one which, oddly perhaps at first glance, comfortably fits. Indeed, barring the musical and literary genres, *Back to the Future*, as a trilogy, touches upon all of the genres and cinematic developments listed, becoming, in varying degrees, a multi-genre narrative on American culture. Yet, before this accolade was awarded by the Library of Congress, the film (and the trilogy as a whole) had been noticeably absent in film criticism and cultural analyses,[2] largely left to a devoted fan base and film enthusiasts to treasure. Now, twenty five years since its release, *Back to the Future* is finally receiving the cultural and academic attention it richly deserves.

However, despite this lack of academic investigation, *Back to the Future* has achieved a cultural status that precious few other 1980s films could claim. In our digital age, from online communities and fan sites to video websites such as YouTube and Google Video, information is shared and relayed globally and allows the audience access to multiple incarnations of media. The *Future* trilogy, so beloved by fans worldwide, has become suffused with new meanings, readings, and intertextual references beyond the immediate scope of the films. Sites such as YouTube have become cultural platforms for people to share clips from popular films, television shows, bloopers and gag reels, music videos and more, to capitalize upon the potential to share, enjoy, comment on, and (often) parody culturally familiar texts such as the trilogy. Parodies range from the YouTube slash phenomenon that was "Brokeback to the Future"[3]—a cleverly reedited collage of clips from the trilogy to suggest a romantic relationship between Doc and Marty, complete with Gustavo Santoalalla's signature soundtrack from Ang Lee's *Brokeback Mountain* (2005)—to various re-imaginings and "new" versions of scenes and characters from *Back to the Future* in fan videos,[4] cartoons such as *Family Guy*,[5] *American Dad*,[6] and *The Simpsons*,[7] to advertising campaigns,[8] and intertextual referencing in numerous films and television shows.[9] Cultural familiarity is key for these images and "insider" nods to work, and reward us for our assumed knowledge of the trilogy. These references, whether overt or subtle, usually incorporate highly postmodern uses of imagery from the films, images that are instantly recognizable—the DeLorean as a time machine, key lines from the films, skateboarding, and Huey Lewis' theme song "The Power of Love," for example—which, when referenced outside the context of the film, provide modes of reinterpretation and intertextuality that allow the trilogy to live on in cultural memory. Once we are reminded of the trilogy outside of its immediate context, it instills a desire to re-watch, and re-experience the films again and again.

It is unsurprising, then, when we consider its prevalence in our cultural memory, that the *Back to the Future* trilogy is so beloved. Rated by the American Film Institute as #10 in the Science Fiction category of the "10 top 10" (ten categories, ten chosen films) list compiled in 2008, *Future I* was nominated for many awards, winning (among others) three Saturn awards: for acting (Michael J. Fox), special effects (Kevin Pike) and Best Science Fiction Film (1986); an Academy Award for Best Sound Effects Editing (Charles L. Campbell and Robert R. Rutledge), and nomination for Best Song for Huey Lewis' "The Power of Love"; and the People's Choice Award for Favorite Motion Picture of 1985. While *Future II* and *III* were not as well received by critics, *Future II* garnered an Academy Award nomination for Sound Effects Editing, and *Future III* won Saturn awards for Best Supporting Actor (Thomas F. Wilson) and for Best Music (Alan Silvestri).

Furthermore, shortly after the trilogy concluded, its success furthered two subsequent commercial spin-offs. *Back to the Future: The Animated Series*, produced by co-writer and producer Bob Gale, ran for two seasons (26 episodes in total) on CBS, and introduced the time traveling adventures of Doc to new and younger viewers. The storylines largely focused on the adventures of the Brown family (Doc, Clara, Jules and Verne) alongside new characters, following on from *Future III*'s conclusion yet independent from the trilogy's diegesis, and relocated many of its plots outside of Hill Valley in other exotic and remote locations. The second "spin off" was the Universal Studios theme park ride, where new footage starring Thomas F. Wilson and Christopher Lloyd was filmed for an interactive audience experience. While *Back to the Future* as a trilogy remains popular due to fan sites,[10] and cultural referencing, its continued success lies in its very clever and complex script, its memorable performances, generational appeal, and depth. Its cultural legacy is one which summates 1980s America onscreen.

In part, this work facilitates many different readings and approaches to the trilogy. I am myself a scholar, fan and enthusiast of the 1980s, and of the *Back to the Future* trilogy in particular, and the wide-ranging essays collected here reflect my own desire to critically examine the trilogy.[11] The essays span many scholarly disciplines, and critically examine the trilogy in terms of American history, culture, and politics; philosophy, postmodernism and time travel; cinematic landscapes and narratives; representations of femininity and masculinity; and its enduring popularity among audiences. This collection strives to provide a multi-focal representation of the trilogy from differing and interdisciplinary perspectives, and through numerous modes of enquiry. Consequently, it is hoped that this collection will widen the scope of academic writing on the *Back to the Future* films, and that it significantly furthers contributions to the frontier of existing scholarship on the trilogy. To date, scholars and critics have predominantly focused on *Back to the Future* alone, often ignoring and/or disregarding Parts *II* and *III*. While a handful of academic articles exist that merit attention, this collection seeks to overcome this imbalance by exploring the films individually *and* collectively. As further reading of this introduction will illustrate, the *Back to the Future* trilogy can be read through a myriad of prisms which reward the viewer, and the fan, time and again. Presented in five parts, this introduction seeks to investigate the cultural and historical importance of the trilogy, within and beyond its own original timeline (1985, 1989, and 1990). Looking beyond *Future I*, *Future II* is examined not only as a breakthrough film within a film, thus extending the concept of a "sequel," but as a historical incorporation of 1989's turbulent turn of events, which underscore and parallel the narrative.

To briefly contextualize my introductory analysis of the trilogy, I turn to the pervading cultural narratives which dominated the 1980s. In presenting an overview of cinema of the decade, a topic which is covered in detail throughout this work, I focus on the presence of 1980s postmodern signatures in the richly rewarding but critically neglected *Future II*, to situate, analyze and elaborate upon its complex imagery as it looks back (literally and figuratively) at the many facades of the Reagan era. Concluding with a brief overview of the twelve essays which follow, this section invites you to re-contemplate, re-investigate, and return to the trilogy again and again.

Looking Back: 1980s America

Casting a look back to the 1980s, encompassing both terms of Ronald Reagan's presidency and George Bush Sr.'s single term tenure (which concluded in 1992), we can see that the *Back to the Future* trilogy nestles into familiar cinematic patterns of the period: the "coming-of-age" drama, featuring films such as *The Breakfast Club* (1985), *St. Elmo's Fire* (1985), *Pretty in Pink* (1985), and *Say Anything* (1989), which popularized narratives on teenage struggles, while recognizing that teenagers, through the powerful conduit of MTV and specific consumer targeting, had a significant consumer power of their own. Other family films such as *Big* (1988), *Vice Versa* (1988), *Like Father, Like Son* (1987), *Dream a Little Dream* (1989), and *18 Again!* (1988) were among a later phenomenon that tapped into a familiar plot involving the need to reestablish relations (or to trade places) with one's parents or grandparents, and reaffirm one's own personal role within the family unit. While all of these films are chiefly concerned with the "family values" mantra that drove the Reaganite moral code, most of the narratives use "wishing" or "magic" to bring about the youth's necessary transformation, bringing about the moral changes necessary to achieve the coveted status of the "good" family by the film's conclusion.[12] *Future I* was certainly not the only film concerned with this particular plot but, because of its box office success, has furthered the use of this formula well into the latter half of the decade. What permits *Future I* to extend beyond the limits of other similar films is its multiple layering of genre, as a science fiction, action adventure, comedy, family film — a "catch all." By using time travel as a potent plot device, through which both generations of parents and children can relate to their own "time," the film ultimately links both generations, collapsing the inter-generational gaps between them. Sarah Harwood states, "In some respects the eighties were a reprise of trends which surfaced in the fifties ... this period [the 1950s] was also a time of massive upheaval and ideological change which 'threw the family into question.'"[13] Yet this is not how popular culture constructs the nuclear family of the 1950s; "the nature of family life, particularly in suburbia, was far more complicated and tension-filled than the stereotypes of the fifties would have us believe,"[14] illustrating the chasm between images and nostalgia for an era and its political and social history. As critic Andrew Britton notes, "Reaganite space-fiction is there to tell us that the future will be a thrilling replay of the past — with special effects."[15] Certainly *Back to the Future* fits this description, and also fits alongside other 1980s studio productions that largely focused on family narratives and producing sequels.

Robin Wood furthers Britton's conclusion on 1980s cinema, claiming it to be a return, not only to a fictional past, but to a childhood reassurance of comfort and safety — a return to the breast of the mother. Though somewhat scathingly labeling the period as one dominated by Lucas-Spielberg Syndrome, Wood clearly illustrates that the desire to escape the cultural anxieties of the 1980s resulted in Hollywood films that were determined to narratively overcome these fears. Largely looking to the *Star Wars* saga to illustrate, Wood indicates the prominence of the following themes (six in total) which are wholly evident across 1980s Hollywood cinema, some of which can be located in the *Future* trilogy: (1) Childishness or the desired return to childhood by the adult viewer; (2) Special effects — according to Wood, "[Capitalism's] entertainments must become more dazzling, more extravagant"[16]; (3) Imagination and originality that conceals the familiarity of plot and formula — it must be new, but also retain a feeling of the familiar; (4) Nuclear anxiety — wielding this type of power is only safe in American and/or righteous hands: Recall that the DeLorean's time circuits are powered by plutonium and that the secured plutonium used to transport Marty back to 1955 was stolen by the Libyans in order to construct a bomb. Plutonium can be harnessed for good (restoring and improving quality of life for Marty by enabling time travel) or evil (terrorism and destruction)[17]; (5) Fear of fascism — representations of a dystopian future (and a return to questioning America's own past) that must be overcome; and (6) Restoration of the father (be it Darth Vader or George McFly, only by restoring the father can the ideal vision of the future be realized.)[18] These elements, found throughout the popular cinema of the decade, instilled a desire to return to a mythical past, to reinvigorate narratives which reassert and reify the American Dream, and were symptomatic of a decade that wished to forget the realities of the 1980s: unemployment, class inequality, crime, increased drug use, AIDS, and rising levels of poverty.

President Reagan, and the New Right in particular, blamed many of the ills of 1980s society on rising divorce rates, the breakdown of institutions and religion in the public sphere, and the hippie generation — "the allure of the permissive society"[19] — of the late 1960s. Other films in the 1980s also include the breakdown of the nuclear family as a central plot, especially within the horror genre which thrived during the decade, illustrating the pervasive rhetoric on private family life in the public arena.[20] However, the cultural imperative to generate wealth, reestablish the hierarchy within the modern family, and to expand free market capitalism to its fullest extent — the quintessential American Dream according to the New Right — were highly evident within both political rhetoric and popular entertainment. Indeed, one could rightfully hold the view that Reagan wished to invoke the spirit of the 1950s because it would deny that the cultural disruption of the 1960s, or the political backlash of the 1970s, ever took place. In his excellent study of 1980s culture, Graham Thompson succinctly states that the neo-conservatives of the 1980s evidently longed for a return to a mythical American past:

> Part of the neo-conservative agenda of the 1980s was not only a determination to get over the cultural crisis of confidence that Ronald Reagan called the "Vietnam Syndrome" in his First Inaugural Address in 1981, but also a nostalgia for a time before the 1960s, a decade synonymous for many neo-conservatives with "events" — civil rights, multiculturalism, feminism, for instance — that signaled a wrong turn in American history. The attempt to recover the 1950s often formed around a rhetoric of contented domesticity and so called "family values" of respect, monogamy and simplicity.[21]

Reagan's own 1984 campaign slogan "We Brought America Back" summates his desire not only to reverse (or erase, perhaps) the social and political problems that dominated the country during his first presidential campaign in 1980, but also to reiterate and capitalize upon the upturn in the American economy in 1983. This slogan, of economic revivification and a desired reversal of history, boldly captured all that epitomized the incumbent president. And, for a period, the rhetoric worked:

> At the end of the Carter years, 75 percent of Americans said they were no longer confident that the future would be better than the past. Now, after four years of Reagan, more than half had returned to their traditional optimism.... Whatever its initial shortcomings, the Reagan credo had succeeded in winning the ardent support of millions of people inspired with a new faith in themselves and in their country. Even if based on an illusion, this new era of good feelings was one that people wanted to celebrate and savor for as long as possible.[22]

In many ways, *Future I* is a celebration of Reagan's vision of a better America, containing the very essence of the pervading cultural optimism, where anything is possible. By being aware of the audiences' knowledge of the present (1985) and transporting them into a known and desired past (1955), Zemeckis and Gale were able to set up particular references, both local and national, that directly connected both decades (skipping over the turbulent 1960s and 1970s entirely). Illustrating the direct effect of time travel by altering the personal trajectory of fictitious members of the town (such as George and Lorraine McFly and Biff Tannen), it also highlighted the unimaginable truths in modern America (beyond *Back to the Future*'s fictional town of Hill Valley) that were not altered by time travel; Reagan's presidency, as Doc's reaction upon hearing this news in 1955 illustrates, is an unbelievable cultural and political development in the future, a joke Reagan personally loved in the film. According to an anecdote related by producer Bob Gale, "Reagan loved the movie. We [Bob Gale and Robert Zemeckis] heard from the White House that when he ran the movie ... he made the projectionist stop the movie at the reference to 'Who's President of the United States?' and watched it again [because] he was laughing so hard, he missed some of the dialogue."[23] Reagan's own ideology was rooted in the very notion that we can all participate in the American dream, and its benefits were limitless and unimaginable — in sum the plot trajectory of *Future I* when reading the differing versions of 1985 before and after Marty's adventure.

In his State of the Union address on February 4, 1986 (postponed for a week because of the Space Shuttle Challenger disaster on January 28, 1986), Reagan directly quoted the film — "As they said in the film *Back to the Future*, where we're going we don't need roads" — in an attempt to cement the positive sentiments of the film on a national scale. The speech was laden with references to the future, not only concerning the immediate future of the nation — which the State of the Union address seeks to outline — but long term (and often fantastical) future developments for American industry, future landscapes of possibility for the American economy, the future of the Space Race and the Star Wars program, the Cold War, and Reagan's own presidential policies of reduced government size and expenditure. As the future appeared full of possibilities, Reagan often presented his political decisions as optimistic visions for America, glossing over the evident cultural and financial cracks particularly in the latter years of his second term. Reagan's own presence in the *Future* trilogy is both overt and subtle. Not only is he the father of the nation, the restored myth-maker who brought America back from the disillusionment of the Nixon and Carter years, but he is also the grand architect of time itself: bringing his people back to a better time, a better America. Thus, as Susan Jeffords keenly observes, Reagan is constantly with us throughout the entire trilogy, personified in Doc:

> For who is Doc Brown other than Ronald Reagan himself? He has allied himself with technology in the name of progress; survived an assassination attempt (at the hands of Reagan's chief targets, Libyan terrorists!); acted as a surrogate father; turned to science fiction tales for his inspirations (Doc's childhood reading led him to want to build a time machine; Reagan's viewing of *The Day The Earth Stood Still* led him to envision his own "Star Wars" program); fought a future filled with crime, drugs and idleness; enabled a dysfunctional lower class family to improve its wealth and social status; returned an American family to its values of nurturance and success; and found his own personal history not in the hothouse parlors of the east but in the open spaces of the Wild West. Ranging over history, apparently in control of time, Ronald Reagan and Doc Brown come to stand as surrogate fathers, supplying symbolic leadership to a generation of youth whose

futures seemed to have been opened up by their visions of technological wizardry and moral instruction. Both, by the end of the decade, seem to have gone beyond time itself, to have left the limitations of history and entered into the realm of fantasy, glory and dreams.[24]

The references to Reagan's legacy and the transformative and powerful imagery we see in all versions of Hill Valley throughout the trilogy condense the prevailing academic cultural theories at the time. In particular, when exploring the strange and wonderful alternate past, new present, and future permutations of Hill Valley in *Future II* and *III*, we see the full impact of postmodernism come into view. Indeed, that these alternate realities are both familiar and alien proves to be crucial in furthering the diegetic complexities and humor we find in the time travel adventures of Marty and Doc in Hill Valley. Postmodernism is rife throughout the *Future* trilogy and warrants further explanation and exploration.

Postmodern Signatures, or, "There's something very familiar about all this"

In the late 1990s, the term "postmodern" began to shift in meaning within the academic community and in culture at large. Since its inception and proliferation in aesthetic cultural production in the late 1960s, postmodernism has endured a series of phases, during which it has been criticized as a destruction of culture, a commoditization of the arts for capitalism, and, in the 1990s in particular, as an insult — "enter[ing] the public lexicon to signify a loose, sometimes dangerously loose, relativism"[25] — when a "text" is thought to be either vapid or overly complex. "Postmodern" became a word to represent the very best and worst aspects of our cultural experience, depending, of course, on one's own point of view. Perhaps this is why we have very few readings on the *Future* trilogy beyond the criticism of its postmodern construction: all of the films, in varying degrees, unapologetically present culturally aesthetic images synonymous with postmodernism. Postmodernism should be neither feared nor dismissed: the root of its meaning lies in the concept that we have, for better or worse, reached a point in late capitalism where we no longer produce new texts or meanings in isolation. Every text considered to be "postmodern" refers to a broader and shared cultural experience that is widely recognizable; art is no longer produced in isolation or for a private audience — all art forms are bound to a greater dialogue in our understanding of a shared cultural experience. Postmodern imagery, such as those discussed in the following sections, must also refer to an aesthetic construction — it is not new, and plays upon our familiarity with the image. There must be a sense of "knowing" the image in order to replicate it further or to parody it: thus, when we see an image from the past that has been altered to give a new meaning, it becomes postmodern because it relies on our knowledge of the original image to amplify its new altered meaning.

A familiar and effective example can be found in Ridley Scott's award-winning 1984 advertisement for Apple Macintosh: the advertisement sets up images of people entranced by an authoritative man onscreen, recalling George Orwell's frightening "Big Brother" in his seminal novel *1984*. Breaking through the crowds of dazed "citizens" is a young female athlete who spectacularly breaks the screen depicting "Big Brother" with a hammer. The narration concludes the ad with the words "On January 24 Apple Computers will introduce Macintosh. And you'll see why 1984 won't be like '1984.'" Playing upon the knowledge of Orwell's vision of 1984 as a grim dystopian society, the advertisement introduces hope by destroying the "known" image of "Big Brother," and bringing Apple into the ad as a means to break with conformity. The commercial works because it plays upon the viewers' knowledge of the novel *1984*, the year of the ad (also 1984), and the ability to change its meaning, from a dystopian to a free thinking society. Not only does the altered meaning challenge us to think of the brand as radical and different, but it uses familiar images and meanings in order to illustrate the point effectively.

The same ideas are also at work throughout the *Back to the Future* trilogy. The DeLorean DMC12 motor car, which ultimately failed in the American market, has now been altered in the cultural imagination into a recognizable "time machine." It is also the reason why, in *Future III*, Marty's experience of the "Old West" is so familiar to us: not only does it (once again) structure his first encounter with the Tannen clan in the local tavern (reminding us of his previous experiences of Biff and Griff in the local café in the 1950s, and the pastiche-riddled Café '80s in 2015, respectively), but also produces laughter and recognition when Marty introduces himself as Clint Eastwood. In using Eastwood's own name in the script, it instantly recalls Eastwood's iconic Western persona for the audience, and thus begins a memorable collage of images from other famous Westerns, recognizable locations (Monument Valley), music ("Oh My Darlin' Clementine") and actors associated with the genre. Coalesced and condensed into the same world onscreen, the old and the new are collapsed into the same postmodern image. Graeme Turner also locates another pivotal capture of the postmodern in *Future III*:

> [Marty's] avenue to the past is the film screen, a metaphor literalized by his driving the time machine through the movie screen in order to reach the past. The screen, then, is a portal to a nineteenth century that can only exist in a form of images, in the form of cinematic reconstructions, and their very materiality is overtly foregrounded [sic] by the text, a point made especially explicit by the fact

that the drive in happens to be located in Monument Valley. Once back in the Old Western, when the painted image of the Indians gives way to the real Indians(!) who chase the DeLorean across the desert, Marty looks into the rearview mirror to check their location. The point of view shot is perhaps the most representative shot in the film because it synthesizes in a single image the relationship between the past and the present and between genre and postmodern culture. This image, a close up of the mirror, taken from Marty's perspective, frames the approaching Indians perfectly — we see "history," but only as an image from the rearview mirror of the present ... one of the main themes of postmodern historiography is [that] history can exist for us now only in forms of representation, that we can construct the significance of the past only as we frame it in the present.[26]

Returning to *Future I*, we see that the particular method of representing the 1950s onscreen as history, and invoking nostalgia for the past, is precisely what makes *Back to the Future*, and its sequels, so fascinating. History depicted onscreen need not be exactly what has happened, but what has been recorded as happening: "*Back to the Future* is a deliberate and explicit quotation of the Americana of the 1950s that developed on film ... the cinematic 1950s in *Back to the Future* intrudes into the reality of 1950s as recorded history."[27] Thus, the images of the 1950s that we are accustomed to as viewers are also fabrications and constructs in themselves, and are no more "real" for the younger 1980s audience than they are a representation of "reality" for the audience who experienced the 1950s firsthand — we are watching an interpretation of an interpretation, coalesced into one narrative of cultural memory and nostalgia — the very essence of postmodernism. Fredric Jameson describes our understanding of the 1950s onscreen because it is a reimagined period suffused with nostalgia:

> This is clearly ... to shift from the realities of the 1950s to the representation of that very different thing, the "fifties," a shift which obligates us in addition to underscore the cultural sources of all the attributes with which we have endowed the period, many of which seem very precisely derived from its own television programs; in other words, its own representation of itself ... the sense people have of themselves and their own moment of history may have *nothing* whatsoever to do with its reality.[28]

Though we understand that the images presented to us are constructs of fiction, the digested images we watch are representations of the past constructed to provide an idealized version of the period. Postmodernism recognizes that, in the late twentieth century, cultural experience becomes a virtual copy of a copy — Baudrillardian simulacra (where a copy replaces a copy to the extent that we no longer recall the original version or the original source) and self-referentiality. According to Catherine Constable, "Postmodern artists cannot invent new perspectives and new modes of expression; instead they operate as *bricoleurs*, recycling previous works and styles. Thus, postmodern art takes the form of pastiche."[29] Not only does Constable's argument underline the importance of imitation and the borrowing of images to construct new ones (bricolage) in postmodernism, it also highlights that in doing so, we revel in a created world that has never existed. Pastiche crams the images so tightly together that it becomes a new experience in itself, a concentrated imitation creating a desire to experience it all at once, as seen explicitly in the Café '80s. The Café '80s encapsulates many 1980s cultural references through artifacts (video games), crazes (spinning bikes), brands (Pepsi and Nike), politics (Ayatollah Khomeini and Ronald Reagan as simulated waiters), music (Michael Jackson's song "Beat It") and popular culture (the films and programs playing in the background on screens, including *Family Ties*) crammed into one physical space. Once condensed, it is pared down to a set of parodies to work onscreen. Intertextual referencing and simulacra feature extensively in the trilogy to acquaint the audience with other cultural texts (for example, the Western genre in *Future III*), and for the audience to laugh at references to culturally iconic texts/brands not known in the 1950s in *Future I*: Marty's Calvin Klein underwear, and his ordering a "Tab"—a diet soft drink in the 1970 and 1980s, here confused with an open running bill, much like Marty's request for a "Pepsi Free,"[30] which is also misunderstood — at Lou's diner.

Exemplified in *Future I*, Marty references specifically post–1950s cultural texts to convince George to take Lorraine to the dance. Dressed in a radiation suit and brandishing a hairdryer and Walkman,[31] threatening to melt his brain with the music of Eddie Van Halen if he does not comply, Marty addresses George as an alien, resembling the cover art of George's copy of *Fantastic Story* magazine.[32] Marty's three lines in the scene perfectly depict intertextuality: "Silence, Earthling! My name is Darth Vader. I am an extra-terrestrial from the Planet Vulcan." By referencing Darth Vader of George Lucas' *Star Wars* saga (1977; 1980; 1983), Steven Spielberg's loveable alien in *E.T.* (1982), and Mr. Spock's planet of origin in Gene Roddenberry's original *Star Trek* series (1966–1969), and, of course, inspired by the actions of Ralph Kramden (Jackie Gleason) in *The Honeymooners* episode "The Man from Space," seen on television in the 1955 Baines home and as a rerun in the 1985 McFly home, Marty knowingly taps into very significant and successful American science fiction and family texts, inspiring George not only to comply, but eventually to contribute to the genre with his own science fiction novel at the conclusion of *Future I*. The dust jacket of George's novel, *A Match Made in Space*, is illustrated much in the same style as that of *Fantastic Story* magazine, featuring a man in a radiation suit bringing a couple together by way of his visitation to Earth. The cover pinpoints this exact scene between Marty in the radiation suit and George as having a major significance for George's future career as an author. Because the time travel elements of the trilogy allow for such playful referencing, and are set up to significantly pay off and reward the viewer, postmodern interplay is completely incorporated within the *Future* universe, on micro and macro levels.

This interplay also permits Zemeckis and Gale to present Hill Valley as a microcosmic version of America, complete with its Western past, its "idyllic" Eisenhower 1950s and consumption-led Reaganite 1980s, and a potentially consumer-led vision of the future (also starring Reagan as a simulated image onscreen in the Café '80s) in 2015. By leaving a trail of identifiable breadcrumbs throughout the trilogy, Gale and Zemeckis knowingly adapt images of consumerism, product placement, and cinematic intertextual referencing to signpost the shifts between the decades. We subscribe to a visual authenticity of an era via its visual artifacts — the cars, dress, logos, and colloquialisms of the period — which distinctly capture the period from cultural memory onscreen. The artifacts must be recognizable but also distinctly different. Bob Gale explains that this is one method to successfully replicate a period in the past, making it visually "real":

> In terms of creating an image of the past, one of the ways you create the past is through brand names, and we made a conscious effort to find products that had a different logo in the past, so that we could use [them] ... put the brand in there and that makes it real.... Shell gasoline, for example, would have paid more for a placement than Texaco did, but Shell didn't change their logo. Texaco was the perfect gas station because of how different it looked in the '50s compared to the '80s ... the same with Pepsi versus Coke; the coke bottle in the '50s and the '80s were the same, but the Pepsi logo was completely different.[33]

Just as product placement became an essential component in decorating a re-created period onscreen, so too did the promise of continuing that sense of familiarity and identification. No greater reassurance, in serving this need, can be found than in the promise of sequels — familiar characters, scenarios, gags and feelings — recapitulating the magic once more (at least). Indeed the success of *Future I* was its encapsulation of the 1980s mindset onscreen. Its diegetic rewards, in altering Marty's family, financial status and mindset from self-doubt to self-belief, are the product of Reaganite mantra that captivated the nation. And, in true Hollywood studio style, numerous productions of recapitulating sequels to successful box office films appeared, each attempting to re-capture that "feel good" mood, and increasingly becoming a fairly solid financial bet at the box office for the studios. Under Reagan, deregulation and multiplication reigned in generating capital. The box office success of *Future I* ensured a sequel would be made in the decade that nurtured and endlessly recapitulated sequels — a joke captured in the holographic advertisement for *Jaws 19* (including the tagline "This time it's really, really personal" and Marty's reaction to it — "The shark still looks fake") in *Future II*. As Stephen Prince notes:

It seemed as if the industry had been taken over by mathematicians. More and more movies had numbers in their titles: *Superman II* (1981), *Superman III* (1983), *Superman IV* (1987), *Star Trek II: The Wrath of Khan* (1982), *Star Trek III: The Search for Spock* (1984), *Star Trek IV: The Voyage Home* (1986), *Star Trek V: The Final Frontier* (1989), *The Karate Kid, Part II* (1986), *Police Academy 2* (1984), *Lethal Weapon 2* (1989), *Back to the Future Part II* (1989). The imperative to sequelize a successful picture became so all-powerful in the period that ... the studios sought to brand audience loyalty by developing characters and film properties that could be manufactured in perpetuity. As a result, the endings of many films were not really endings, just the postponing of narrative until the next installments.[34]

Just as the sequels of the decade attempted to live up to their first installments (and often failed to do so, especially in the horror genre which was bled virtually dry in the latter half of the 1980s), so too did the new president, George H. W. Bush, attempt to capitalize upon the reputation of his predecessor.

As the era of Reagan came to a close, and the desired idyllic resurrection of the past began to fade from public rhetoric, the mood in America began to shift from one of optimism to one of doubt and inheritance. The election of George H. W. Bush to the White House against Governor Michael Dukakis in 1988 proved to be controversially fought, but ultimately one-sided. The people elected Reagan's vice president for four more years of Reaganite optimism (a political sequel), but this was tinged with doubt over Bush's capability to continue Reagan's legacy. Two major factors contributed to this increasing sense of doubt in the Bush years; the first was the brief but grievous recession known as "Black Monday" in October 1987, which served as an unwelcome reminder that the good times under Reagan could be undone if not kept in check; and second, the reneging of promises made during the election of 1988, in particular, the infamous statement "Read my lips: no new taxes," which Bush later reversed in 1990 with a series of tax increases to attempt to balance the national deficit accrued under Reaganomic policies and military spending earlier in the decade. Hopes for the future began to seem unsteady; unemployment was rising and the White House seemed to be unresponsive to domestic concerns, slow to react and quick to redirect questions on policy. The constructed images of 1980s America under Reagan began to shift and split onscreen, as Bush's political and public persona was revealed to resemble that of his predecessor less and less.

"You know your history": *Future II*

Masculinity onscreen underwent a significant alteration in the late 1980s. Under Reagan, cinematic bodies were split into two distinct groups: the errant body that harbored "disease, immorality, illegal chemicals,"[35] emblems of neo-conservative disgust with the hippie generation; and hard bodies, "the body that was to come to stand as the emblem of Reagan's philosophies, policies, and economies."[36] These hard bodies onscreen were armored with muscle, they were "heroic, aggressive, [and] determined,"[37] as epitomized in films such as Sylvester Stallone's *Rambo* and *Rocky* series; Schwarzenegger's cyborg body in *The Terminator* (1984), and military body in *Commando* (1987); and law enforcement bodies such as Murphy (Peter Weller) in *Robocop* (1987), John McClane (Bruce Willis) in *Die Hard* (1988), and Martin Riggs (Mel Gibson) in *Lethal Weapon* (1987).[38] As physical representations of Reagan idealism, their bodies were projections of American supremacy both at home and abroad.[39] Yet, in 1989, after Reagan left office and the ideologies of the New Right began to dwindle (and would steadily continue to decline during the Bush years), the masculinity that so encased neo-conservative ideology had begun to shift towards doubt, uncertainty, surfacing character flaws, feminized and gentler representations of male role models, and narratives of personal growth. In 1989, Tim Burton's *Batman* was the first of these blockbuster films to incorporate this recent shift in heroic male representation; the second was *Back to the Future Part II*.

The shift away from the extreme Reaganite representation of masculinity can be seen across many films of this period.[40] However, in Burton's *Batman* and Zemeckis' sequel, the split is built in to the characters' very existence onscreen. *Future II* literally splits its lead characters onscreen from their earlier incarnations: Doc circa 1955, and his 1985 self having a brief interaction in the town square in anticipation of the lightning storm; Biff circa 1955 discussing the almanac in his car with his 2015 self ("he says he's my distant relative, I don't see any resemblance"), and Marty, during his first and second bout of time traveling in 1955, specifically at the "Enchantment Under the Sea" dance when seen both on and above the stage.[41] While the splitting is consistent with the use of time travel theory and the threat of paradox in the trilogy, it is also one of many cultural signatures associated with 1989. While Batman (Michael Keaton) spends significant amounts of time masked and costumed, he is, underneath, fundamentally a troubled, flawed and divided character. His onscreen nemesis, Jack Napier (Jack Nicholson), also undergoes a splitting of identity, when transformed into the ever-smiling devious Joker. Linking both films together, both Batman/Bruce Wayne and Marty McFly become split onscreen because of the initial victimization of their parents.[42]

Doubt (personal, national and global) was one of the fundamental issues concerning the Bush presidency — questions were raised on the Cold War and relations with the Soviet Union; how could Bush successfully continue the Reagan revolution that had been cultivated throughout the decade? Further still, in order to maintain this revolutionary legacy, how then could Bush instill his *own* sense of presidential legacy when so dominated and pressured by the New Right to follow in the former president's footsteps? Following the election of 1988, Bush called for a "kinder, gentler" America, initiating a move that was seen by some hard line Republicans as a betrayal of the Reaganite doctrine imbued with tough American supremacy.[43] Despite this call for kindness and compassion, Bush was aware he was not regarded with the trust and affection bestowed upon Reagan, and would soon return to a tactic that served so many presidents seeking re-election before him, a tactic, like Marty's own initial idea of betting on the future — "I can't lose" — that ultimately backfired:

> Bush's aide John Sununu "was telling people that a short successful war would be pure political gold for the president and would guarantee his re-election." ... Bush abandoned sanctions and chose war [with Iraq] because his time frame was a political one set by the approaching 1992 presidential elections.[44]

Marty develops similar flaws, shifting from *Future I*'s Reaganite notion of achieving the good community to one of personal responsibility in order to maintain it. While *Future I* focuses upon the flaws and failures of the McFly family stemming from George McFly's insecurities (and thus, by remolding his father, Marty's lack of self-esteem slowly diminishes over the course of *Future I*'s diegesis), *Future II* introduces two major flaws which Marty must personally overcome. The first is his sense of greed when acquiring the sports almanac in 2015: spurred on by his Reaganite goals in accumulating wealth, Marty attempts to secure a method of betting on future knowledge (sports results) to attain certain affluence, a method that is employed by Biff in the alternate 1985. The second flaw, also introduced in 2015, is his hotheaded response to being called a "chicken"; being unable to rise above this taunt is precisely how he will ultimately end up in the automobile accident with the Rolls Royce, which undoes Marty's dreams of success as a musician in 1985, and, in the future, being "fired" from his 2015 job for participating in a scam, both acts perpetrated by Douglas Needles.[45] While this information is disclosed early on in *Future II* (and perhaps a hidden motivation for Doc to intervene in Marty's family life in 2015 beyond the impending fate of Marty Jr.; for who is Marty truly in 2015 but a generational return to the "failed" version of George McFly in *Future I*?), the flaws raised are finally resolved in *Future III*, illustrating not only the diegetic need to expand and develop upon Marty's flaws, but also to permit a personal growth in both films that results in a maturation of the character overall. A feared inheritance of failure is precisely what makes *Future II* so important when reading the trilogy.

Future II was initially conceived to take place partly in 1967, during the student protests and cultural upheavals against the Vietnam War. Old Biff, rather than travel to 1955, travels to 1967 to give himself the sports almanac. The sections on 2015 and 1985A (an alternate version of 1985 in which Biff Tannen, by stealing the time machine, in 2015, alters history for his own corrupt ends) were present in this draft. The 1960s portion of script was later rewritten and relocated to 1955, because the section was not deemed funny enough ("it was funny in a sad awful way,"[46] according to Zemeckis, especially in reference to the retro clothing) nor significantly different from the plot of *Future I*, as Marty would once again endanger his own existence, this time by interfering with his own conception (recall that Marty, being 17 years old in 1985, was born in 1968). As this divergence to 1967 was considered to compromise the diegetic trajectory of the story, both Gale and Zemeckis decided it would be far more interesting to explore the period "known" from the first film, but to situate the plot of *Future II* at an alternate angle. By re-entering 1955 on the same date as the climax of the original adventure (November 12, 1955, the date of the lightning storm), it permitted Zemeckis and Gale to explore a previously uncharted arena for a sequel to a time travel movie; to re-explore the scope of the previous installment in minute detail, and to look at the paradoxes and alternate permutations of the present (1985A) if time travel is misused. It is interesting to note that, if the 1967 plot had remained, it would tie into the Reaganite concept that the 1960s was the root cause of so many of society's ills in the 1980s, as Marty must restore the correct timeline for the 1980s in 1967.[47]

Despite some initial struggles in development, such as Crispin Glover's refusal to reprise his role as George McFly, the original script having the western narrative appear in the fourth act (making *Future II* an "unfilmable" 260 page script according to Universal Studios president Sid Sheinberg) before opting to enter the West in the third installment, and Zemeckis finalizing his technologically advanced film *Who Framed Roger Rabbit?* (1988) before principle photography on *Future II* had begun, the film generated high levels of anticipation among the critics and the public.

Future II was released on Thanksgiving weekend, November 22, 1989, to mixed reviews. The diverse response ranged from criticism of its complex plotting, an overloaded use of commercial imagery and products, and the "strained credibility" of splitting characters onscreen, to applauding its screwball comedic structure, and its mind-boggling and giddy sense of adventure.[48] Yet, when scrutinized in detail, the film stands up to its critics; not only is it exceptionally aware of its beginnings (remaining faithful to both characters and surroundings) but it is also highly aware of its present, 1989, and illustrates this flux accordingly. For all of its recreation of 1985 as an immediate sequel to the first film, *Future II* refers to the crises in America (and beyond) in 1989, in its representation of 1985A. Much like the postmodern signatures found in *Future I, Future II* was a creation of and for its time: the end of the Reagan revolution that so defined the 1980s culminated in a year dominated by political revolution itself.

For many, the pivotal events of 1989 were seen to be largely "abroad"; in comparison with the upheavals felt in continental Europe, Americans welcomed the fall of communism but predominantly did not participate in the tide of change. With the Reagan legacy at an end, the rhetoric of the Cold War crumbling with the fall of the Berlin Wall on November 9, 1989, and the uprising of students in Tiananmen Square, Beijing, and in Ceausescu's Romania, the appetite for change and dissolution of old and outdated regimes was palpable. Time was ushering in a new and unimaginable future, or indeed a vision of the impending "The End of History?" as Francis Fukuyama wrote in his groundbreaking 1989 article.[49] Though *Future II* was written and developed before 1989's events began to unfold, the signatures of the period, the angst of change and what could become of the country post–Reagan, can be found subtly charted throughout. In 1985A, because of the hyper-imagery of failure it contains, we see a town ravaged by toxic waste, police corruption, gang activity, addiction (drinking and gambling), lacking education and educators, extreme violence and the breakdown of the nuclear family: Reagan's vision of a nightmarish America if left in the wrong hands.

Mirrored in the mood of the nation, the tide of change was uncertain, and seemed capable of swinging in either direction. Indeed, whether it concerned the anger surrounding the *Exxon Valdez* oil spillage in Alaska, "at the time considered to be the worst man-made environmental disaster in U.S. history.... America's last true wilderness had been violated"[50]; the censoring of artwork by Robert Mapplethorpe on display at the Corcoran Gallery as it was deemed to violate moral decency; the scientific strides in researching (and furthering the eventual hope of utilizing) cold fusion, which ultimately failed; and the religious fatwa issued against Salman Rushdie, author of *The Satanic Verses*, resulting in public burnings of his novel, attempts on his life, and bombings of U.S. and British bookstores that stocked his controversial novel; the flux of change evident in 1989 joins the alternate 1985, illustrating the dark underside capable of taking hold within the culture. One can read the cultural nightmares, rippling beneath the surface of the narrative, breaking through in 1985A: the health warning on environmental toxic waste emissions, published under the story of author George McFly's murder in the *Hill Valley Telegraph*; the burning of the Almanac in order to destroy the dangerous and destructive knowledge it contains, restoring and thus reversing the "war" it has initiated by its existence; and the permitted violation of moral decency decorating the backdrop of "*Hell* Valley" with strip clubs, gambling and violence.[51] Postmodern referencing to the crises of the period certainly gave way to a gloomier edge in other film releases of that year, when we consider *Heathers* (kill your friends), *Parenthood* (dysfunctional families), *The War of the Roses* (nasty divorces), *Cinema Paradiso* (censorship and religious power), *Born on the Fourth of July* (traumas concerning Vietnam), *The Fly II* (the continuance of bad science), and *Criminal Law* (legal quagmires and abortion issues) all making an impact onscreen.

Examining the diegesis of *Future II* more closely, we are certainly located in an extremely postmodern text; if viewed by an audience unfamiliar with *Future I*, it becomes a confusing, alienating, and bewildering experience — running virtually backwards in timelines as it furthers the plot (briefly beginning in the "new" 1985 at the end of *Future I*, it begins the plot in 2015, moves back to 1985A, then on to 1955, and concludes with Doc ending up in 1885). As a text on its own terms, it does not work in isolation — it hinges upon our familiarity and our desire to see the familiar patterns established in *Future I* replicated across the entire history of Hill Valley. By being so specifically located within its own world (unlike other film sequels which can usually be viewed separately without knowledge of their origin), *Future II* is a hyper-layering of the narrative of *Future I*, rendered meaningless without its roots. Indeed, if history repeats itself, this is entirely true in *Future II* at an exhaustive level. The depictions of the future, 2015, still star the figureheads of the 1980s — be it the Iranian Ayatollah, digitally presented with hell fire blazing behind him, or Ronald Reagan, declaring a permanent "Morning in America" bedecked in stars and stripes, or Michael Jackson discussing recipes, the "future" is the projected 1980s present thrust forward (albeit in the Café '80s and the antique store, the primary public locations we negotiate in the 2015 where nostalgia for the past is still cultivated) and populated with very familiar faces. It should be noted that, despite its hyper-consumerist landscape, the future is still a positive place to live — unlike the nightmare future-scape presented by Ridley Scott in *Blade Runner* (1982), which shares a deeply post-modern aesthetic of "recycling [images], fusion of levels, discontinuous signifiers, explosion of boundaries, and erosion,"[52] — Hill Valley continues to be "a nice place to live."

We also discover that familiar political faces populate the nightmare present of 1985A in the brief introduction seen at the Biff Tannen Museum, and through newspaper copies of the *Hill Valley Telegraph*. Securing his fortune through gambling (which he later helped to legalize at a national level in 1979), opening nuclear facilities to further his control over state supplies of power, and a toxic waste disposal plant (we can be sure this is an unethical enterprise!), Biff's alteration of the timeline also influences national politics — in a byline under the lead story on Doc being committed to an asylum in the *Hill Valley Telegraph*, it states that Richard Nixon is seeking a fifth term in office violating the 22nd Amendment of the Constitution, which, presumably, has been overturned. It also states that America is still embroiled in Vietnam, with President Nixon vowing to end the war by 1985. Only under the continued presidency of Richard M. Nixon, with the Watergate scandals never uncovered, could this version of America become possible. Furthermore, as Susan Jeffords highlights, other referencing to Vietnam is covert but present, the tombstone of George McFly representing the death of the American spirit with the Vietnam War in 1973.

> George is killed in 1973, the year in which the United States withdrew its final troops from Vietnam. That is the year, this film seems to be saying, in which the nation lost its direction, and was given over to a period of destructive liberal values, the year in which the nation lost its father....
>
> The home [and the nation] has been taken over by a "false" father who was never intended to have a family at all. All of this began in 1973, when the otherwise happy and thriving family/nation was cut off from its source of guidance and leadership by an untimely death. That George McFly was murdered by Biff suggests as well that the nation's troubles were brought about by an unjust assault on the father.[53]

Indeed, the spirit of the nation itself is destroyed in the pursuit of self-interest: only by preserving the unity of the nation can order (and the future as Marty and Doc "remember" it) be restored.

Restoration is central to *Future II*; the fracturing of the nation and of time itself (now "skewed into a tangent") must be repaired at all costs. The theme is also carried across immediately, and unsurprisingly, into *Future III*— famously shot back to back with *Future II*, a feat then unheard of in Hollywood — again to counteract events leading to another unjust death, another tombstone, this time bearing the name of Marty's symbolic father, Doc Brown (a return to an event Marty successfully prevented in *Future I* at the hands of the Libyans). While *Future III* enters the realm of the postmodern through the screen at the drive-in, thrusting us back into the beginnings of Hill Valley and grand displays of famous western narratives, *Future II*, by reentering *Future I*, becomes the ultimate example of inter-textual reflexivity; a postmodern composite of playful, clever bricolage, constructed during a significant period of American self-assessment and cultural re-evaluation.[54] Zemeckis, also self-assessing, concludes: "*Back to the Future II* is probably the most interesting film I have ever made."[55]

Introducing the Chapters

The essays here feature many rich and valuable readings to be gleaned from this groundbreaking and culturally beloved trilogy. In his 1987 essay,

"*Back to the Future*: Œdipus as Time Traveler," now updated to include a reading of the entire trilogy, Andrew Gordon explores the psychosexual oedipal plotting of *Future I*, and the proliferation of sexual symbolism throughout the trilogy. Looking to other time travel films of the 1980s, and highlighting the Capra-esque plotting that has contributed to its sustained success in American culture, Gordon ultimately likens *Future I* to *The Wizard of Oz* in its desired goal to return home from a life-altering adventure. Reading *Future I* as a cathartic response to the prevailing national mood of the period, and the structures of *Future II* and *III* as extended "themes and variations," Gordon's essay pinpoints the reasons *Back to the Future* is beloved by generations of audiences.

In "'You Space Bastard! You killed my pines!': *Back to the Future*, Nostalgia and the Suburban Dream," Bernice M. Murphy posits the suburban landscape, full of dreams and potential nightmares in the 1980s, as a specifically imagined and constructed space in American history, narratively mirrored through the diegetic course of time in Hill Valley. The suburban consumerist ideologies, of both the Eisenhower and Reagan administrations, owe much to the frontier past, and construct 1950s suburban ideals as a dreamscape desired to be returned to, rather than learned from, in the cultural climate of the 1980s.

Stephen Matterson, in "Don't you think it's about time?": *Back to the Future* in Black and White," argues that it is in no way a coincidental choice but, in fact, a necessary development in the cultural preoccupation with the 1950s in the 1980s, that 1955 is the precise year for Marty's first time travel adventure — precisely chosen because it can avoid the cultural shocks registered in the post–'55 era. In looking at the radical changes — literary and historical — that swept through America during that year, including the publication of Allen Ginsberg's controversial poem "Howl" and acts of violence, protest and discontent due to segregation laws, Matterson critically examines the divide in the nation which goes virtually unacknowledged in the film.

Evident in its multiple representations of eras, the *Future* trilogy is largely dominated by, and preoccupied with, generic play (cinematic worlds that play and interact with familiar genres), as cogently argued by Lucy Fife Donaldson in her essay, "'There's something very familiar about all this': Generic Play and Performance in the *Back to the Future* Trilogy." Specifically focusing on the performance of Thomas F. Wilson as Biff/Griff/Buford Tannen, Fife Donaldson explores how performance interacts with the fluidity of genre across the trilogy, culminating in a specific type of viewing pleasure, through the recognition of generic interaction.

Identifying numerous postmodern inter-textual references to the Western genre throughout *Back to the Future Part III*, John Exshaw vividly explores the course of the Western in American cinema in his essay, "Bury My Heart in Hill Valley, or, The Kid who KO'd Liberty Valance." Looking back at the films of John Ford, Sergio Leone, Howard Hawks, and Marty's persona in the Old West, Clint Eastwood, Exshaw skillfully charts the terrain of the West as a genre, considered dead and buried in 1990, revivified and celebrated in the exhaustive recapitulations which decorate the town in *Future III*. Indeed, Hill Valley and its populace are integrated so successfully into the cinematic representations of the Western that it becomes a hyper-spectacle of the genre's most celebrated and iconic films.

Musically, *Back to the Future* is, quite simply, captivating. In Christine Lee Gengaro's essay, "Music in Flux: Musical Transformation and Time Travel in *Back to the Future*," Alan Silvestri's score (the largest orchestral recording at Universal Studios) is examined as the significant glue that binds the films together, and as key to the emotional thrust sustained throughout the entire trilogy. Gengaro highlights specific moments in the film where the score and sourced music fluidly interact, and how the use of sourced popular music successfully transports the audience between the time periods throughout. Including detailed cue sheets analyzing specific motifs and themes featured in all three films, Gengaro's essay underscores the creativity in Silvestri's renowned work.

In Elizabeth McCarthy's essay, "Back to the Fifties! Fixing the Future," the classification of *Back to the Future* as a 1980s teen movie is thoroughly explored alongside issues of class prejudices in the depiction of the McFly family, and the Baines family of 1955. Drawing extensively upon the youth culture of the 1950s, McCarthy argues that the conservative rhetoric of the trilogy posits the cultural developments of the 1950s as the source of social and cultural fragmentation in the 1980s. McCarthy explores how the Reaganite rhetoric of the period coalesces with the films' narrative of upward mobility; covertly lionizing an inherently conservative and acquisitive 1980s culture while masquerading as a celebration of the individual's power to shape his/her destiny. However, as the films' narrative progresses it becomes quite clear that this power, which takes the form of correcting the "mistakes" of the past in order to secure a happy and affluent future for the American family is, in fact, the privilege of the films' chosen few.

Women in the *Future* trilogy fall into specific and rigorous categories of femininity, argues Katherine Farrimond in her essay "'Mom! You look so thin!': Constructions of Femininity Across the Space-Time Continuum." Through her specific study on the differing versions of female representation across the trilogy, through the characters of Lorraine, Jennifer Parker and Clara Clayton, Farrimond reads the trilogy as a space where women must reject, or are rejected because of, any undesirable feminine traits which threaten to destabilize patriarchal order. Achieving future success must combine a balance of desirability and motherhood, and, above all, maintain patriarchal order. It seems that time travel is not meant, in any capacity, for girls.

For Reagan, the final line in *Future I*—"where we're going we don't need roads!"— spoke volumes, and was incorporated into his vision of what America, under his leadership, could achieve. Examining the trajectory and evocative language used by Reagan in his quest to return America to a noble past, Christopher Justice, in his essay, "Ronald Reagan and the Rhetoric of Traveling *Back to the Future*: The Zemeckis Aesthetic as Revisionist History and Conservative Fantasy," looks to the presence of Reagan as an aesthetic creator and presence within 1980s popular culture. Looking to Zemeckis' other historical re-examination of American culture in his Oscar-winning film *Forrest Gump* (1994), alongside a close reading of the president's own ideologically weighted persona, Justice concludes that history is reimagined and reinvented to gloss over the cracks evident in American society since the 1950s. *Back to the Future*, Justice concludes, may be the most significant and enduring relic of 1980s popular culture.

Turning to Lacanian philosophical constructs of master signifiers and generational signification, Michael Williams, in his essay "'This is what makes time travel possible': The Generation(s) of Revolutionary Master Signifiers in *Back to the Future*," charts the layering of generational signification, as described by French psychoanalyst Jacques Lacan, through the specific character developments of George and Marty McFly, and Doc Brown. Looking to the four models of discourse according to Lacan — the discourses of the Master (to achieve mastery), the University (objective knowledge), the hysteric (provoking a desire — to change or alter the projected image of the self— the provoking of the "loser" into acting on his/her desire to be a "winner"), and the analyst (the antagonistic force, person or repression working against the struggle to achieve Mastery of self) — in the diegetic trajectory of *Future I*, the changes brought about by Marty's time traveling ensure future successful signifiers for the entire McFly family.

In Randy Laist's essay, "Showdown at the Café '80s: The *Back to the Future* Trilogy as Baudrillardian Parable," the Baudrillardian concepts of simulacra and hyper-reality are evidenced through the visual construct of the films, as fictional representations of the past, the future, and the cultural present. Because the periods ventured into in the trilogy are simulacral constructs ("artificial" constructs, because the past, present and future are subject to change throughout the films) and eternally repeatable (because the time machine, like a VCR in the 1980s, permits a "playback" of past events), the world of Hill Valley becomes what Baudrillard described as the fourth stage: where the world has become a place of endlessly repeated cycles without origin — copies of copies ad infinitum — and a platform where everything is seamlessly blurred between fantasy and reality. "Reality" becomes "reality by proxy" (we succumb to meanings given to symbols: buy brand X to achieve specific feelings, but these meanings are generated and have no basis in reality). As Laist convincingly reminds us, we are all citizens in Baudrillard's hyper-reality.

Whether it's with a DeLorean, a TARDIS or a phone booth, we are all fascinated by the possibilities of time travel. In the final essay, "'Doing it in style': The Narrative Rules of Time Travel in the *Back to the Future* Trilogy," Jennifer Harwood-Smith and Francis Ludlow investigate and chart the specific use and consistency of time travel concepts throughout the trilogy. Looking back at previous time travel narratives in literature and film, and exploring theories on time travel paradoxes in philosophy and physics, Harwood-Smith and Ludlow present a rich tapestry in which looped timelines, and alternate worlds, are possible explanations and realities in the exploration of the Space-Time Continuum. By comparing other time travel narratives where time is immutable, such as *The Terminator* (1984) and *Bill and Ted's Excellent Adventure* (1989), with the *Future* trilogy, where time is subject to change, Harwood-Smith and Ludlow explore the delicate intricacies, and narrative logic employed in famous time travel texts.

A final note, if I may, on the now immortalized time machine central to the aesthetic legacy of the trilogy: the DeLorean DMC-12. For all of John Z. DeLorean's personal trials and tribulations, his dream sports car's commercial failure and eventual glorification with the success of the films, and its very specific signature as an artifact of the 1980s American Dream, the DeLorean has become the first renowned time machine — a feat John DeLorean could never have imagined. Upon seeing the film in July 1985, John DeLorean wrote a fan letter to Robert Zemeckis and Bob Gale (July 25, 1985), to share his thoughts on seeing his "car of the future" immortalized onscreen. He wrote:

> Dear Gentlemen:
>
> Last week I had the opportunity to see a screening of "Back to the Future" in New York, and want you to know I think it was absolutely brilliant. I was particularly pleased that the DeLorean Motor Car was all but immortalized in the film, and want to thank all those responsible ... for the outstanding job they did in presenting the DMC as the vehicle of the future.... Thanks again for continuing my dream in such a positive fashion.
>
> Sincerely,
>
> John Z. DeLorean

Today, John DeLorean would be proud: with the newly redesigned DeLorean Motor Car available on the market, and avid fans and collectors decorating their own vintage 1980s DMC-12s with replica flux capacitors, OUTATIME license plates, time circuits, and Mr. Fusion power generators, the DeLorean, alongside the *Back to the Future* trilogy, continues to endure, passing from one generation to the next, and beyond. And so it should: after all, it's about time.[56]

Notes

1. The complete list of films selected by the National Film Registry for 2007 may be viewed here: http://www.loc.gov/film/nfr2007.html.

2. Few scholars have actually written with any great depth on *Back to the Future*, and fewer still make significant reference to *Part II* and *Part III*. Of the most in-depth readings on the films, scholars Susan Jeffords, David Wittenberg, and Andrew Gordon have presented different readings on *Back to the Future*, but most concentrate their discussion on the first installment of the trilogy. See Susan Jeffords. *Hard Bodies: Hollywood Masculinity in the Reagan Era*. New Jersey: Rutgers University Press, 1994; David Wittenberg. "Oedipus Multiplex, or, The Subject as a Time Travel Film: Two Readings of *Back to the Future*." *Discourse*, 28.2 & 3, spring and fall 2006, pp. 51–77; Andrew Gordon. "*Back to the Future*: Œdipus as Time Traveler." *Science Fiction Studies*, Vol. 14, No. 3, (Nov. 1987), pp. 372–385. Gordon's essay appears in this collection with kind permission from *Science Fiction Studies* and has been updated and extended to include a discussion on the trilogy.

3. As of November 2009, the YouTube hosted "Brokeback to the Future" clip has garnered 5.5 million hits, illustrating the power of reediting and "fan subversion" that has made YouTube an online sensation in the digital age.

4. Another intertextual example of 1980s time travel narratives cohesively fused together in parody can be found on YouTube. Entitled "Terminator: How it Should End," this excellent animated short video cohesively blurs the plots of *Back to the Future*, *The Terminator* (1984) and *Terminator 2: Judgment Day* (1991), humorously rewarding viewers with its clever repackaging of the texts, interweaving all of the films' most infamous scenes, thus culminating in another form of postmodern bricolage.

5. Seth McFarlane's *Family Guy* has parodied *Back to the Future* more than any other cartoon on network television. The most notable parodies include a scene at the Enchantment Under the Sea dance; Doc's hidden racism; a homage to the opening skateboarding scene of *Future I*; and repackaging *Future I* as a blaxploitation film.

6. In Seth McFarlane's *American Dad*, Stan Smith secretly rebuilds a DeLorean in his garage, freely admitting that he has never seen *Back to the Future*; instead he cites John Z. De-Lorean's work ethic as his sole source of inspiration. There's also an episode of the TV show *Chuck* called "Chuck Versus The DeLorean."

7. "The Simpsons Ride" at Universal Studios, Orlando, which replaced the "Back to the Future Ride" in March 2007, features an animated short starring Doc Brown (voiced by Christopher Lloyd). In the cartoon short, Professor Frink uses the DeLorean to travel back to meet Doc with catastrophic results.

8. Advertisements which tapped into the films' cultural capital include Microsoft, DirecTV, and BMW ("It's not a BMW, it's a time machine"). Promotional tie-ins to coincide with the releases of the sequels included merchandising by KP Crisps (in the UK), Pizza Hut, and the 1989 Nintendo Entertainment System.

9. In *Family Ties* and *Spin City*, both popular television series starring Michael J. Fox, intertextual references to *Back to the Future* were made. In *Family Ties*, a time travel-dream episode entitled "A Philadelphia Story" (season 3; ep. 15) is similar in content to *Future I* as Alex P. Keaton (Fox) wants to boost his father's self-belief, doing so by citing Thomas Jefferson's authorship of the Declaration of Independence. Alex's citation of Jefferson is then reworked into a dream narrative where Alex helps Thomas Jefferson (in the guise of his father Steven Keaton, played by Michael Gross) write the Declaration of Independence, proving that self-belief is necessary to instill change at a personal and national level. The episode aired in January 1985 during the filming of *Future I*; however, *Family Ties* producer Gary David Goldberg had read the

script for *Future I* when Gale and Zemeckis campaigned for Fox to play Marty McFly a year earlier in 1984. In *Spin City*, the episode "Back to the Future IV: Judgment Day" (season 3; ep. 18) reunited Christopher Lloyd onscreen with Michael J. Fox, this time as Fox's political mentor who believes he is Christ reincarnated. Reminding us of their onscreen partnership, Michael Flaherty (Fox) welcomes his mentor Owen (Lloyd) by saying, "This is like stepping back in time" to which Owen replies, "The past is prologue, Michael, men like us keep looking to the future!"

10. A particular website worth mentioning for its attention to detail and forums is www.bttf.com, which continues to chronicle the careers of the actors and filmmakers associated with the trilogy.

11. This book has been gestating in the editor's mind for many, many years. Partly born out of her desire to read critically engaging essays on the trilogy, as articles solely focusing on the films have been noticeably sparse, and also out of a personal love for the films that date back to a *Future* filled 1980s childhood, the editor wishes to sincerely thank all of the contributors and mentors (living and passed on) who made it possible.

12. Films prior to, and since, the 1980s have used this narrative also. For example, both versions of *Freaky Friday* (1976; 2003) use the wish motif to have mother and daughter switch roles for a day. Similar in parts to *Back to the Future*, frustrated father Mike O'Donnell (Matthew Perry) wishes to reclaim his youth and redirect the course of his life in *17 Again* (2009); whereas the opposite occurs in *13 Going on 30* (2004), in which 13-year-old Jenna (Jennifer Garner) wishes to grow up overnight but ultimately returns to her youth to rectify a mistake made evident in her future. Frank Capra's classic film *It's A Wonderful Life* (1946) provides definite inspiration for many of the films listed, especially *Future I* and *II*—where one can easily read Marty's existence proving to be vital for the town of Hill Valley; and 1985A under the grip of Biff Tannen as another version of the nightmarish "Pottersville" sequence in Capra's film.

13. Sarah Harwood. *Family Fictions: Representations of the Family in 1980s Hollywood Cinema*. London: MacMillan, 1997. pp. 4–5.

14. William H. Chafe. *The Unfinished Journey*. Oxford: Oxford University Press, 1999. p. 128.

15. Andrew Britton. "Blissing Out: The Politics of Reaganite Entertainment." 1986. Rpt. in *Britton on Film: The Complete Film Criticism of Andrew Britton*. Detroit: Wayne State University Press, 2008. p. 115.

16. Robin Wood. *Hollywood from Vietnam to Reagan ... and Beyond*. Rev. ed. New York: Columbia University Press, 2003. p. 148.

17. *Back to the Future* has many particular nuclear anxieties attached to it, most of which were written out of the script in later drafts. Not only is the DeLorean fuelled by a nuclear reaction, but the original shooting script began with Marty watching a video on nuclear explosions in school, and situated the climax of Marty's return to 1985 at a nuclear test site in Nevada.

18. While I am briefly summarizing Wood's modes of enquiry on 1980s Hollywood cinema, his treatment of Spielberg/Lucas productions attempts to investigate diegetic trends on a grand scale. Not all of the modes listed feature in the *Future* trilogy, but interwoven commonalities are evident. Wood centralizes his analysis in his chapter "Papering the Cracks: Fantasy and Ideology in the Reagan Era" on the *Star Wars* and *Indiana Jones* series, *E.T.*, *Poltergeist* and *Blade Runner*. Wood, pp. 144–167.

19. The State of the Union Address to Congress by President Ronald Reagan, February 4, 1986. Full video coverage of this address can be found online at The Ronald Reagan Presidential Foundation, http://www.youtube.com/user/ReaganFoundation.

20. While the horror genre (the slasher genre in particular) of the late 1970s/80s is generally populated with teenagers with absent or failed parents, the vampire film in particular, capitalizes on the "broken" or single parent family as a site of weakness, and an effective mode of entry for the vampire to access potential victims. In particular, *Fright Night* (1985), *Near Dark* (1987) and *The Lost Boys* (1987) use this plot device with significant prominence. For more on Reaganomics, single parent families and the Slasher genre, see Sorcha Ní Fhlainn. "Sweet, Bloody Vengeance: Class, Social Stigma and Servitude in the Slasher Genre." *Hosting the Monster*. Holly Baumgartner & Roger David (eds.). New York: Rodopi, 2009. pp. 179–196.

21. Graham Thompson. *American Culture in the 1980s*. Edinburgh: Edinburgh University Press, 2007. p. 104.

22. Chafe, p. 482.

23. Bob Gale interview in "Looking Back to

the Future" on the 2009 DVD Special Edition. *Back to the Future*. Dir. Robert Zemeckis, Universal Studios, 1985. Reagan also claimed to love the CBS television show *Family Ties*, saying it was his favorite show on television in the 1980s.

24. Jeffords, p. 78.

25. Steven Connor. "Introduction." *The Cambridge Companion to Postmodernism*. Steven Connor (ed.). Cambridge: Cambridge University Press, 2004. p. 5.

26. Graeme Turner. *The Film Cultures Reader*. New York: Routledge, 2002. p. 280.

27. Bruce Isaacs. *Towards a New Film Aesthetic*. New York: Continuum, 2008. p. 178.

28. Fredric Jameson. *Postmodernism, or, The Cultural Logic of Late Capitalism*. London: Verso, 1991. p. 281.

29. Catherine Constable. "Postmodernism and Film." *The Cambridge Companion to Postmodernism*, p. 48.

30. This is a slight error in the script, as "Pepsi Free" was not a sugar-free drink but rather a caffeine-free drink in the 1980s (the sugar-free non-caffeine version of Pepsi was Diet Pepsi Free, both of which were launched in 1982). That Marty requests a sugar-free drink, "just give me something without any sugar in it," indicates that this is a minor error in product placement.

31. The use of Eddie Van Halen's music (especially recorded for the film) dates the film very specifically in terms of popular music. Van Halen, the previous year, had a number one hit with its single "Jump" and album *1984*. The reason the tape specifies "Edward Van Halen," as opposed to the band Van Halen, was because full permission from the band was not secured. The hairdryer, initially a prop from a deleted scene where Doc investigates his suitcase full of time traveling supplies in the DeLorean, is used as a physical reminder to George that Marty will melt his brain if he does not take Lorraine to the dance. This scene was cropped in the final edit of the film as the "Darth Vader" line was considered sufficient in itself.

32. George's copy of *Fantastic Story* is dated fall 1954. It was a popular pulp magazine published by Best Books of New York. The cover art was illustrated by renowned artist Jack Coggins, who specialized in illustrating marine life and works of science fiction.

33. Bob Gale and Robert Zemeckis Q&A recorded at the University of Southern California Film School, featured on the DVD version of *Future I. Back to the Future*. [2002 DVD edition of the trilogy]

34. Stephen Prince. "Introduction: Movies and the 1980s." *American Cinema of the 1980s: Themes and Variations*. Stephen Prince (ed.). Oxford: Berg, 2007. pp. 2–3.

35. Jeffords, p. 24.

36. *Ibid.*, pp. 24–25.

37. *Ibid.*, p. 25.

38. Of all the "hard bodies" mentioned, what is perhaps most interesting is the contrast between Riggs and Murtaugh in *Lethal Weapon* (1987). Because being a "hard body" was almost exclusively coded as white onscreen, particular attention is paid to Murtaugh's age and "softness" when compared to Riggs, who is younger, ruthless and more dangerous. For much more on this, see Jeffords, pp. 24–63.

39. Narratives concerning the hard bodied heroes of the 1980s illustrate America's projected power both at home and abroad. While *Rambo*, *Commando*, *Rocky IV* and *Predator* are acutely aware of Reaganite foreign policy and perceptions of unruly "others," hard bodied heroes at home policed against internal enemies: drug dealers, racketeers, organized crime, and corrupt businesses.

40. The "softening" of the hyper-masculine bodies of the 1980s can be seen as early as 1988 in Ivan Reitman's *Twins* (1988). It is interesting to note that Schwarzenegger was softened onscreen again by Ivan Reitman in *Kindergarten Cop* (1990), which was chosen alongside *Back to the Future Part III* to carry the celebratory 75th Anniversary logo of Universal Studios.

41. Jennifer also experiences this "split" in the McFly home in 2015, and, as Doc predicted, faints from the shock of seeing her future self. This does not happen to the other male characters; Marty, Doc and Old Biff being time travelers and aware of their other "selves," and young Biff remaining unaware (or perhaps too stupid to recognize) that his visiting "distant relative" is his future self from 2015.

42. Another split onscreen also concerning doubts on cultural/genetic inheritance from parents was Ivan Reitman's comedy *Twins* (1988). In the Batman universe, the ultimate "split" identity is Two Face.

43. Chafe, p. 500.

44. Howard Zinn. *A People's History of the United States*. 5th ed. New York: Harper Perennial, 2003. p. 595. Zinn quotes Elizabeth Drew of *The New Yorker* and historian John Wiener on Bush's re-election tactics. (No further citation provided).

45. In *Future II*, Needles (Flea from the Red

Hot Chili Peppers) is introduced as a new and unknown character, partly recalling the familiar bully that Biff was in the McFly household at the beginning of *Future I*. By *Future III*, to illustrate Marty's maturation and a full circle resolution, Needles is both the "stinger" (to the audience who knows that Marty has caved into Needles' provocation previously in *Future II*) and the final obstacle for Marty to overcome at the conclusion of the trilogy.

46. Bob Gale and Robert Zemeckis Q&A recorded at the University of Southern California Film School, featured on the DVD bonus disk of the *Future Trilogy. Back to the Future II*. Dir. Robert Zemeckis, Universal Studios, 1989. [2005 4 disc "ultimate DVD edition" of the trilogy]

47. As we conclude that Marty's own birth occurs in 1968, it is tempting to read Marty's own existence representing change (and potential changes in time) as evidenced throughout the "magic" year of 1968. The global landscape was altered through student rioting, cultural upheavals, political assassinations (Dr. Martin Luther King Jr., and Senator Robert F. Kennedy), the Prague Spring, live television images broadcasting the Tet offensive in Vietnam, and the rise of the women's liberation movement, among other significant developments. Many scholars also view 1968 as the pivotal year in the beginnings of postmodernism.

48. These reviews can be found on the film website www.rottentomatoes.com, featuring five reviews on *Future II* (of which three are negative) by critics from *Variety, The Washington Post, The Chicago Sun-Times, The Chicago Reader* and the *New York Times*.

49. 1989 also saw the publication of Francis Fukuyama's article "The End of History" in which he concluded that, with the fall of communism, the world would unite under formations of democracy over time. This does not mean we will cease to have "events" in history, but rather, we will see a broad incorporation of democracy as we have reached the echelon of political representation by having democracy on a global front.

50. Bryan Walsh. "Black Gold on the Last Frontier" *Time Magazine*. Vol. 173, Nos. 26/27. June 29–July 6, 2009. p. 88.

51. While 1985A is obviously fictional, and a highly concentrated version of hell for Marty in our brief time there, it bears some resemblance to the fears expressed by Tipper Gore in her book *Raising PG Kids in an X Rated Society*, in which she articulates that 1980s rock music lyrics, pornographic imagery, and access to violent films and artworks, were becoming increasingly evident trends during the decade. The book's overall message reads as a desire to return America to a constructed, synthetic and sanitized period.

52. David Harvey. *The Condition of Postmodernity*. 1980. Oxford: Blackwell, 2008. p. 311 quoting Giordano Bruno, "Ramble City: Postmodernism and *Blade Runner*." *October*. Vol. 41. 1987. pp. 61–74.

53. Jeffords, pp. 71–72.

54. It is interesting to note that this feeling of self-assessment was also evident in popular music at the time, with the release of Billy Joel's "We Didn't Start the Fire" from the album *Storm Front*, in September 1989. Joel's song is a list, chronicling important events in American history from 1949–1989.

55. Bob Gale and Robert Zemeckis Q&A recorded at the University of Southern California Film School, featured on the DVD bonus disk of the *Future Trilogy. Back to the Future II*. Dir. Robert Zemeckis, Universal Studios, 1989. [2005 4 disc "ultimate DVD edition" of the trilogy]

56. The title of this essay was originally one of the taglines used in advertising the theater release for *Back to the Future Part II* in November 1989.

Works Cited

American Dad. Created by Mike Barker, Seth MacFarlane and Matt Weitzman. 20th Century-Fox Television. 2005.

Back to the Future. Dir. Robert Zemeckis, Universal Pictures, 1985.

Back to the Future Part II. Dir. Robert Zemeckis, Universal Pictures, 1989.

Back to the Future Part III. Dir. Robert Zemeckis, Universal Pictures, 1990.

Back to the Future Part II: Reviews. Online at http://ie.rottentomatoes.com/m/back_to_the_future_2/?critic=creamcrop.

Britton, Andrew. "Blissing Out: The Politics of Reaganite Entertainment." 1986. Rpt. in *Brit-*

ton on Film: The Complete Film Criticism of Andrew Britton. Detroit: Wayne State University Press, 2008.

"Brokeback to the Future" Video Clip. Online at http://www.youtube.com/watch?v=8uwu Lxrv8jY

Bruno, Giordano. "Ramble City: Postmodernism and *Blade Runner.*" *October*. Vol. 41. 1987. pp. 61–74.

Chafe, William H. *The Unfinished Journey*. Oxford: Oxford University Press, 1999.

Chuck. Created by Chris Fedak and Josh Schwartz. "Chuck Versus the DeLorean." Season 2; Episode 10. NBC Universal Television, 2007.

Connor, Steven. "Introduction." *The Cambridge Companion to Postmodernism*. Steven Connor (ed.). Cambridge: Cambridge University Press, 2004. pp. 1–19.

Constable, Catherine. "Postmodernism and Film." *The Cambridge Companion to Postmodernism*. Steven Connor (ed.). Cambridge: Cambridge University Press, 2004. pp. 43–61.

Family Guy. Created by Seth MacFarlane. 20th Century–Fox Television. 1999.

Family Ties. Created by Gary David Goldberg. NBC Television. 1982–1989.

Fantastic Story. New York: Best Books, fall 1954.

Fukuyama, Francis. "The End of History." 1989. Rpt. in *The End of History and the Last Man*. London: Macmillian, 1992.

Gale, Bob. Interview. "Looking Back to the Future." 2009 DVD Special Edition. *Back to the Future*. Dir. Robert Zemeckis, Universal Studios, 1985.

_____, and Robert Zemeckis. Q&A recorded at the University of Southern California Film School, May 2002. Featured on *Back to the Future* trilogy disks 2005 edition with separate Q&As for each film in the trilogy.

Gordon, Andrew. "*Back to the Future*: Œdipus as Time Traveler." *Science Fiction Studies*. Vol. 14, No. 3, Nov. 1987, pp. 372–385.

Gore, Tipper. *Raising PG Kids in an X Rated Society*. Nashville: Abingdon Press, 1987.

Harvey, David. *The Condition of Postmodernity*. 1980. Oxford: Blackwell, 2008.

Harwood, Sarah. *Family Fictions: Representations of the Family in 1980s Hollywood Cinema*. London: Macmillan, 1997.

Isaacs, Bruce. *Towards a New Film Aesthetic*. New York: Continuum, 2008

It's A Wonderful Life. Dir. Frank Capra, RKO Radio Pictures, 1946.

Jameson, Fredric. *Postmodernism, or, The Cultural Logic of Late Capitalism*. London: Verso, 1991.

Jeffords, Susan. *Hard Bodies: Hollywood Masculinity in the Reagan Era*. New Brunswick, NJ: Rutgers University Press, 1994.

Joel, Billy. "We Didn't Start the Fire." *Storm Front*, Columbia Records, 1989.

Library of Congress. National Film Registry 2007. Online at http://www.loc.gov/film/nfr2007.html Accessed on 30/10/2009.

Ní Fhlainn, Sorcha. "Sweet, Bloody Vengeance: Class, Social Stigma and Servitude in the Slasher Genre." *Hosting the Monster*. Holly Baumgartner & Roger David (eds.). New York: Rodopi, 2009. pp. 179–196.

Prince, Stephen. "Introduction: Movies and the 1980s." *American Cinema of the 1980s: Themes and Variations*. Stephen Prince (ed.). Oxford: Berg, 2007.

Spin City. Created by Gary David Goldberg and Bill Lawrence. ABC Television. 1996–2002.

State of the Union Address to Congress by President Ronald Reagan. February 4, 1986. Online at The Ronald Reagan Presidential Foundation www.youtube.com/user/ReaganFoundation

"Terminator: How It Should End." Online at http://www.youtube.com/watch?v=bBBw9 E2Q_aY&feature=PlayList&p=dOWv76j71 Ew

Terminator 2: Judgment Day. Dir. James Cameron, TriStar Pictures, 1991.

The Terminator. Dir. James Cameron, Orion Pictures, 1984.

Thompson, Graham. *American Culture in the 1980s*. Edinburgh: Edinburgh University Press, 2007.

Turner, Graeme. *The Film Cultures Reader*. New York: Routledge, 2002.

Walsh, Bryan. "Black Gold on the Last Frontier." *Time Magazine*. Vol. 173, Nos. 26/27. June 29–July 6, 2009. pp. 86–90.

Wittenberg, David. "Oedipus Multiplex, or, The Subject as a Time Travel Film: Two Readings of *Back to the Future.*" *Discourse*, 28.2 & 3, spring and fall 2006, pp. 51–77.

Wood, Robin. *Hollywood from Vietnam to Reagan ... and Beyond*. Rev. ed. New York: Columbia University Press, 2003.

Zinn, Howard. *A People's History of the United States*. 5th ed. New York: Harper Perennial, 2003.

1. *Back to the Future*: Œdipus as Time Traveler

ANDREW GORDON

Back to the Future was the biggest Hollywood moneymaker of 1985, sur-passing even *Rambo*. Its first run at many theatres was an unprecedented six or seven months straight. What was the secret of its appeal? On the surface it has all the necessary ingredients — comedy, action, suspense, romance, sen-timent, fantasy, special effects, and catchy music — integral to other block-buster SF films of the period, such as *Star Wars* and *E.T.* But these elements alone, or in the wrong mixture, are not enough to guarantee success with a large audience. In addition, *Back to the Future* has a clever plot and the appeal of 1950s nostalgia. The teen hero attracts the young, and the theme of rec-onciliation between past and present, child and adults, attracts their parents as well. Even the critics loved it, taken in by its charm, sentiment, and an ingenious script which was nominated for an Academy Award — another unprecedented achievement for an SF film.[1]

Like *Star Wars, Back to the Future*'s success depends to a great degree upon its ritualistic, celebratory, therapeutic aspects: it is a "clean" family film which attracts all ages, and encourages audience participation (spontaneous clapping and cheering) and repeat viewing (many fans return, bringing friends or fam-ily).[2]

It is this level of the film that most interests me: the paradox of a family comedy which flirts with incest. I would argue that the film succeeds because it deftly combines two connected American preoccupations — with time travel and with incest — and defuses our anxieties about both through comedy.

From 1979 to 1987, there was a proliferation of time travel films, includ-ing *Time After Time* (1979), *Somewhere in Time* (1980), *The Final Countdown* (1980), *Time Bandits* (1981), *Timerider* (1983), *Twilight Zone: The Movie* (1983), *The Philadelphia Experiment* (1984), *The Terminator* (1984), *Trancers* (1985; an imitation of *The Terminator*), *Back to the Future* (1985), *My Science Project*

(1985), the made-for-television movies *The Blue Yonder* (1986) and *Outlaws* (1986), and *Peggy Sue Got Married* (1986), *Flight of the Navigator* (1986), and *Star Trek IV* (1987). According to Wyn Wachhorst, time travel films "increased by more than fifty percent relative to the rise in total science fiction films" during the 1980s.[3]

I believe that this explosion of time travel films in the 1980s represented a pervasive uneasiness about the American present and uncertainty about the future, along with a concurrent nostalgia about the past. These time travel films rarely attempted a vision of the future, and when they did, as in *The Terminator*, the future is bleak and post-apocalyptic. And during the same period (1979–87), in other SF films without a time travel premise, the future was almost always a negative extrapolation from the present: overcrowded, decayed, bureaucratic and soulless, repressive, and either on the verge of destruction or post-apocalyptic. H. Bruce Franklin summarized the negative Hollywood vision of the future from 1970–82[4]; the picture didn't change much in the rest of the 1980s, and the *Star Trek* movies were about the only optimistic cinematic vision of the future, which may account in large measure for their enormous popularity. It also helps to account for the success of *Back to the Future*, which attempted to reassure the audience that, in the words of the movie, "the future is in your hands."

Most 1980s time travel films did not, in fact, concern the future but dealt instead with an escape into an idealized past in a desperate attempt to alter the present and the future. They reflected a growing dissatisfaction with a present that was sensed as dehumanized, diseased, out of control, and perhaps doomed. Somewhere along the line, the unspoken feeling went, something went drastically wrong; if we could only return to the appropriate crossroads in the past and correct things, we could mend history and return to a revised, glorious present or future, the time line we truly deserve. *Back to the Future*, *The Blue Yonder* (about a boy who travels back from 1986 to 1927 to help his grandfather), and *Peggy Sue Got Married* deal with the attempts of individuals to revise their personal time lines by a return to the past; *The Terminator* and *Star Trek IV* concern groups from the future attempting a rescue in our present so that humanity may *have* a future. A similar premise holds in Gregory Benford's novel *Timescape* (1980), where the ecologically poisoned, dying world of 1998 sends a warning back to the prelapsarian world of 1963. The effect of the message is to avert the catastrophe by creating an alternate time line.

Such, then, was the 1980s American preoccupation with time to which *Back to the Future* appealed. But along with anxieties about the future, the film also comically mirrored more accepting popular attitudes about time travel, or rather, "time shifting," and a flattening out of the perspective of time.

Thus Tom Shales notes that, from 1979–85, most time travel movies failed at the box office. "The only one to hit it really big was *Back to the Future*, a phrase that almost sums the Eighties up, and that's partly because the movie made time travel a joke, a gag, a hoot. We are not amazed at the thought of time travel because we do it every day."[5] Shales called the Eighties "The Re Decade," a decade of replays, reruns, and recycling of popular culture, epitomized by videorecorders and videocassettes. "Television is our national time machine."[6]

Back to the Future demonstrated the reciprocity of contemporary image-making, which cuts across all time lines. In the course of the movie, we see video images of the present (Dr. Brown's 1985 experiment) rerun in the past, as well as images of the past (*The Honeymooners*) rerun in the present. The self-reflexivity of *Future*'s use of video points to what Garrett Stewart calls "the 'videology' of science fiction": movies about the technology of the image allow us to observe the ideologies "by which we see and so lead our lives."[7] But this self-reflexivity also illustrates Vivian Sobchack's claim: *Back to the Future* was "a generic symptom of our collapsed sense of time and history."[8]

In fact, past and present are so collapsed in the plot of the movie that the young hero Marty's life threatens to become nothing more than a rerun, like the *Honeymooners* episode repeated during two separate family dinners. The audience gets the eerie comic effect of instant replay when we see gestures, lines, or entire scenes from 1985 echoed almost word for word in 1955. The present reruns the past, or vice-versa. These characters seem subject to a sort of repetition compulsion, doomed to neurotic closed loops until Marty intervenes to rewrite the script.

As SF comedy, *Back to the Future* is more successful than *Time Bandits* or *Peggy Sue Got Married* in playing the incongruities of time travel for laughs. *Time Bandits* is episodic in structure and only fitfully funny, and *Peggy Sue* shifts uncomfortably in tone between farce and melodrama. But *Back to the Future* is consistently funny because it is grounded in the broad humor of television sitcoms and classic Hollywood "screwball comedy."

Harlan Ellison despised *Back to the Future*, complaining that "the lofty time paradox possibilities are reduced to the imbecile level of sitcom."[9] But it seems to me that the use of a sitcom framework was a deliberate strategy on the part of the filmmakers to tame the potentially touchy subject of incest. In the 1970s, sitcom, through such innovative series as *All in the Family* and *M*A*S*H*, became a liberal forum for dealing with controversial social and political issues with a humorous touch. *Back to the Future* offers a popular audience familiarity and reassurance through its stock characters (the Nerd, the Bully, the Nutty Professor) and stock premise (time travel, the subject of so many movies and TV shows) and its star, Michael J. Fox, borrowed from a successful sitcom (*Family Ties*). And the small-town environment it presents is equally formulaic and reassuring to audiences. As Vivian Sobchack mentions, "the mise-en-scène of *Back to the Future* spatializes neither 1955 nor 1985, but the television time of *Leave It to Beaver* and *Father Knows Best*."[10] The filmmakers are aware of the film's roots in television: thus producer Steven Spielberg called *Back to the Future* "the greatest *Leave It to Beaver* episode ever produced" and writer-director Robert Zemeckis described it as "a cross between Frank Capra and *The Twilight Zone*."[11] And I have already noted the homage to Jackie Gleason's *The Honeymooners*.

But the film's comedy is not pure sitcom. Zemeckis, who has directed other comedies (*I Wanna Hold Your Hand, Used Cars, Romancing the Stone*), attributes his success partially to his reverence for "comedy classics" and traditional methods of making comic films.[12] Jack Kroll called *Future* "a true American comedy, with the sweet wit and benevolent bite of Preston Sturges and Frank Capra."[13] Indeed, with its small-town hero, humor, and time travel premise, it bears some comparison with Capra's *It's a Wonderful Life* (the homage becomes explicit in *Back to the Future II*). And Pauline Kael wrote that *Future* "has the structure of a comedy classic."[14] The image of Dr. Brown dangling perilously from the hands of a clock evokes Harold Lloyd. In other words, the film draws on the traditions of both sitcom and classic Hollywood comedy. It has a sure comic sense, employing a whole range of comic devices, including physical humor such as farce and slapstick, situational humor, irony, comedy of character, and verbal wit. The movie exhilarates audiences because it glories in its own outrageousness and plays almost everything for laughs.

So *Back to the Future* makes us laugh at the incongruous possibilities of time travel. But it also makes us laugh at incest, or at least flirts with the possibility of a sexual relationship between mother and son. What is funny about that, especially for a family audience?

In the 1950s Vladimir Nabokov's *Lolita* made the violation of the incest taboo a possible subject for American popular culture. Since then, sociologists and psychologists have been collecting data on incest, and newspaper stories have focused attention on the frequent violations of the taboo and the connections between incest, prostitution, child abuse, and child molestation. Our uneasiness on the subject has not necessarily decreased as our knowledge has increased.[15] In fact, it might be argued that the publicity has perhaps enhanced social anxiety: people may fear that incest is all around them, like AIDS, and that they may be the next to catch it. In any event, in 1985 there was a television movie, *Something About Amelia,* and two feature films on the subject of incest: *The Color Purple* and *Back to the Future*. The most popular of these films, *Back to the Future* makes the (attempted) incest laughable, just as *Lolita* made the subject more palatable by dealing with it through black humor.

But although *Back to the Future* temporarily frees us from some of our anxiety by making incest laughable, it no more renders incest acceptable or guilt free than Woody Allen's *Hannah and Her Sisters* condones adultery. Instead, *Future* distances us from the incest by making both the mother's brazenness and the son's terror laughable. And it teases our fear and desire by a last minute avoidance of the physical act. The desire, guilt, and fear are still attached to the incest taboo, but the audience is comfortable with those feelings because we get a momentary comic bonus from them.

On one level, the film is therapeutic comedy, filled with psychosexual anxiety that is aroused and then relieved. One critic calls it "teenage Woody Allen," and writes that "Marty resolves his sexual crisis by working through his own family romance ... Marty is nothing less than an American Œdipus who learns to conquer his desire for his mother (projected, in the film's key scene, back onto her) and accede to the rule of the father."[16] And other critics assert that "it is on the timeless plane of myth that *Back to the Future* has its finest moments.... In that timeless realm Marty can participate (or rather, almost participate) in that delightful parody of the Œdipus myth...."[17]

I would argue that *Back to the Future* is the first SF film to make explicit the incestuous possibilities that have always been at the heart of our fascination with time travel. Time travel is an unnatural act which is frequently used to allow the fulfillment of œdipal fantasies or family romance. By changing the relative ages of family members and turning the hero into a stranger to his own family, time travel permits the hero to freely romance his own mother or other ancestors or descendants.

Critics have noted that H.G. Wells' Time Traveler comes face to face with a Sphinx and walks with a limp, both of which connect him with Œdipus.[18] And some 20th-century American SF writers have openly explored the incestuous possibilities of time travel. For example, the hero of Robert Silverberg's *Up the Line* wipes himself out by meddling with the past: he defies the time traveler's code by making love to a woman who is his remote ancestor; in the commentary on the DVD of *Back to the Future II*, Bob Gale acknowledges the influence of *Up the Line*. Robert A. Heinlein is the American writer most fascinated with the possibility of violating the incest taboo through time travel. In *The Door into Summer*, the protagonist, through time travel, is able to marry a little girl who is his ward. In *Time Enough for Love* Lazarus Long falls in love with several adopted daughters, including "Llita" (suggesting "Lolita") and "Dora" (suggesting Freud's case study of a woman who loved her father too much), and finally goes back in time to physically consummate his love for his mother. In "All You Zombies," the hero commits the ultimate incest; through time travel and a sex change operation he is able to seduce himself and give birth to himself.[19]

Wyn Wachhorst explains the rise in popularity of time-travel films in psychological terms as "an attempt to reenchant the world, to regain a sense of belongingness, to reinstate the magical, autocentric universe of the child and the primitive — while retaining the reality projected by rational, individualized consciousness."[20] For Wachhorst, the "time travel romance" is a disguised œdipal fantasy. He notes that in movies as *Somewhere in Time*, *Timerider*, and *The Final Countdown*, the omnipotent male time traveler returns to the past (symbolically, Paradise or the world of childhood) where he romances an innocent woman who stands in for the mother (in *Timerider*, she is his grandmother). The variations on this pattern, such as *Time After Time* and *The Philadelphia Experiment*, where the hero goes from the past into the future to find romance with the innocent woman, Wachhorst considers less successful. One could add to his list of 1980s time travel romances involving sublimated incest *The Terminator* (1984), in which a man sends his father into the past to ensure that his father will impregnate his mother.

Back to the Future represents the desublimated form of the time travel romance since the heroine and hero no longer stand in for mother and son but *are* mother and son. Marty McFly is the time traveler as a would-be teenage Œdipus. Like Œdipus, Marty attempts to flee his fate — not to another town but to another time. And like Œdipus, his flight leads him directly into the very predicament he dreaded (and Freud would claim, secretly desired): into his mother's bed. But this is comedy, not tragedy: whereas Œdipus kills his father at the crossroads, Marty rescues his; and whereas Œdipus marries his mother, Marty temporarily endures his mother's sexual attentions for the sake of reuniting his parents. Marty, in other words, is a reluctant Œdipus, an innocent and blameless, comic Œdipus who never consummates the act.

Back to the Future enacts a fantasy of innocent power: Marty is portrayed as innocent victim of circumstances, yet as time traveler he has omnipotent powers. His return to the past enables him to resolve an œdipal crisis and to reshape his life and the lives of his parents for the better. He acts out the "family romance" to which Freud referred: the desire to replace unsatisfactory parents with idealized ones. "It's the story of a kid who teaches his father how to be a man," says Zemeckis.[21]

Marty as omnipotent time traveler goes from the degraded present of 1985 — with its graffiti, x-rated movies, homeless drunks sleeping on benches in littered parks, terrorists stalking the streets — to the prelapsarian 1955; spotless, pristine, virginal. But it is a virginity panting to be deflowered. Our innocent hero now finds himself subject to the sexual terrorism of his own mother, who sees him as the man of her dreams.

Back to the Future, like *It's a Wonderful Life*, is a film about dreams, dreams turned into nightmare and changed back into happy endings. "It's all a dream," Marty tells himself when he arrives back in 1955, "Just a very intense dream." As he walks through the town square, the song that's playing is "Mr. Sandman, Bring Me a Dream." When he first wakes up in his mother's bed, he still believes it is all a bad dream. But his mother, Lorraine, in 1955 considers Marty a "dreamboat" and "an absolute dream."

What exactly is the content of this dream? In "The Relation of the Poet to Day-Dreaming," Freud talks about the kind of "time traveling" which normally occurs in fantasy, dreams, and daydreams:

> The relation of phantasies to time is altogether of great importance. One may say that a phantasy at one and the same moment hovers between three periods of time — the three periods of our ideation. The activity of phantasy in the mind is linked up with some current impression, occasioned by some event in the present, which had the power to rouse an intense desire. From there it wanders back to the memory of an earlier experience, generally belonging to infancy, in which this wish was fulfilled. Then it creates for itself a situation which is to emerge in the future, representing the fulfillment of the wish — this is the day-dream or phantasy, which now carries in it traces both of the occasion which engendered it and of some past memory. So past, present and future are threaded, as it were, on the string of the wish that runs through them all.[22]

Marty's experiences in 1955 and his return to an altered 1985 can be considered an elaborate daydream whose relationship to time corresponds to the pattern described by Freud. His daydream is occasioned by his frustration and failure in 1985, by his personal and sexual insecurity. He retreats to the past, to 1955 — but symbolically he is in the world of infancy, when the bond between himself and his mother was strongest. As Wachhorst says, the time travel romance reinstates "the magical, autocentric universe of the child."[23] In 1955, Marty is both a child overpowered by his mother and, paradoxically, an omnipotent adult who can become the parent to his own parents. After he has indulged and overcome his œdipal fears and desires, and restructured his parents' lives to create the idealized family he desires, he returns to a revised 1985 in which his problems have magically disappeared. In truth, his past, present, and future are threaded "on the string of the wish that runs through them all."

The structure of the film resembles that of the classic Hollywood fantasy, *The Wizard of Oz*: a "realistic" opening sequence establishes a problem for the young protagonist which a "fantastic" second sequence resolves. Characters and scenes from the first sequence recur in the second one, echoed but strangely reshaped by the wish-fulfilling distortions of the dream. *The Wizard* adheres to the conventions of fantasy: the transformation is apparently effected by means of a twister; only at the end is it revealed that the Oz sequence was a feverish dream induced by a blow on the head. *Future* instead uses the conventions of SF: the transformation is effected by machinery (the

DeLorean car/time machine), and the second sequence is presented as real. But it may be significant that the first thing Marty encounters in 1955 is a scarecrow, reminding us of Dorothy in Oz!

Moreover, both Dorothy and Marty are presented as innocents, strangers in a strange land stranded there by accident, not by their own desires, and wishing only to go home. Marty depends upon the bumbling scientist, Dr. Brown, to send him back to his own time, just as Dorothy relied upon the inept Wizard to return her to Kansas. Both films are fantasies of innocent power, in which the protagonist combines the helplessness of a child with the superpowers that the child perceives the adult as having: Dorothy's magical helpers and ruby slippers, or Marty's time machine and other advanced technology from 1985 (skateboard, video camera, and Sony Walkman). Dorothy is acclaimed a powerful witch by the Munchkins, and Marty in 1955 is at first mistaken for an invader from another planet by the paranoid citizens, who have seen too many 1950s SF films and read too many comic books. Later, he takes advantage of their gullibility and happily assumes the role of an extra-terrestrial with superpowers: "Darth Vader from the planet Vulcan."[24]

The opening sequence of *Future*, like the opening of *The Wizard*, is a catalogue of frustration and failure for the protagonist, failures which will all be rectified in the following "dream" sequence. We are introduced to Marty McFly, a 17-year-old living in the California town of Hill Valley in 1985. The chronically tardy Marty first loses his race against time and is late for school the fourth day in a row. There he is put down by a hostile teacher, Mr. Strickland, who accuses him of being a failure like his father George McFly. Then, as Mr. Strickland predicts, Marty loses the school rock band competition. Next, he is frustrated in his attempts to neck with his girlfriend, Jennifer, and arrives home to find the family car wrecked by his father's supervisor, Biff, ruining Marty's hopes for a hot date with Jennifer on the weekend. He sees his father humiliated by Biff and sits down to dinner with a family of nerds and losers, among whom he seems hopelessly out of place. "No McFly ever amounted to anything in the history of Hill Valley," the nasty Mr. Strickland told him, to which McFly cockily replied, "History is gonna change." The second sequence, Hill Valley in 1955, functions as a wish-fulfillment fantasy in which history can be changed, this entire day of defeat canceled and all of Marty's dreams realized.

Marty lacks confidence because he has a weakling for a father and an overpowering mother; thus, he has not yet successfully overcome the œdipal phase. He wishes for a strong father to dominate his threatening mother and help him earn his manhood. Marty's mother in the opening sequence is dissatisfied with her husband and her life: she smokes, eats, and drinks to excess. Her sexual dissatisfaction has made her both repressed and repressing: she denies having any sexuality when she was a girl and disapproves of Jennifer for pursuing Marty. For Marty, this means that she is trying to prevent his sexual development and keep him bound to her.

The father image is split into three stock characters: George the wimp, Biff the bully, and Dr. Brown the nutty professor and kindly "uncle." If George is impotent, then Biff is overly potent (and a rapist), and the celibate Brown is comfortingly asexual (but omnipotent). Biff humiliates the spineless father in front of Marty: in a sense he is as much a representation of Marty's hostility toward his father as he is a symbol of the avenging, sexual, castrating side of the father. Biff bosses the household like the "real man" to whom George's wife and everything else George possesses (job, family, house, refrigerator, and car) belongs. "Say hi to your mom," Biff leeringly tells Marty. Biff's unhealthy intrusion into and destruction of the household, his overturning of the authority of the father, and his symbolic possession of the mother — all these, plus the exaggeration in his depiction, turn him into a symbol of the child's œdipal rebellion against the father. Biff is the unhealthy side of Marty; thus Biff's power must be tamed and restored to its rightful owner, the father, for the film to conclude successfully. Of course, Biff is a stock character, like the rest of the characters: that makes it that much easier for the audience to engage in the same kind of splitting of desires that the film is indulging as a defense. By providing a bully we can hoot at, the film also enables us to cheer for the hero without ambivalence.

As for Dr. Brown the Wizard, he gives Marty the call to adventure and provides him with superscience, the magical tools and the wisdom and confidence he needs to undergo his initiation into manhood. As Zemeckis explains, "The story is anchored in a sort of benevolent Merlin/Arthur kind of relationship between Dr. Brown and Marty."[25] Their relationship also echoes that of Ben Kenobi and Luke in *Star Wars*. Just as Ben Kenobi provides Luke with a light saber and the power of "The Force," so Brown provides Marty with a time machine. And Luke witnesses Ben's death and resurrection (as part of the Force), whereas Marty sees Brown murdered and then return to life; both sequences could be said to do and undo patricidal wishes. Brown also expresses the desires in the film for omnipotence, perhaps as a way to overcome fears of failure, castration, or impotence. The audience roots for both Brown and Marty, for both triumph after a long string of failures and return from near death or apparent death. Finally, since a kid has the power for much of the film, and we are distanced from the parents and other adults, who are made to seem either physically or sexually intimidating, pathetic, or foolish, Dr. Brown serves as a substitute, idealized parent who is wise but funny, and completely asexual.

The father image may be split into three, but the mother image is split into two, which are, roughly, mother-nun and virgin-whore. The repressive mother of the opening sequence in 1985 is transformed into the horny teenager Lorraine in 1955. When Marty rescues his father from an automobile accident, Marty is injured and takes his father's place in his mother's affections. Now he must undo all this, under threat of never being born. What we see here is a simple role reversal or projection of desires: horny Marty and the repressive mother simply switch places, and the mother's lustful pursuit of him expresses both œdipal fears and desires. Throughout, Marty is portrayed as purely innocent, acting only from the noblest of motives and merely the victim of circumstances. This, plus the mother's exaggerated lust and Marty's exaggerated sexual terror, enable us to enjoy it as comedy.

The best that Marty can do is to stage a rescue fantasy in which the father is to save the mother from the pawing of the son, thereby putting Œdipus to rest. Through an ironic (and appropriate) twist of fate, George ends up rescuing Lorraine instead from the molestations of Biff: that is, from innocent Marty's evil stand-in, a sexual beast.

The resolution the film offers is to transform George into a strong father by effectively castrating Biff and transferring his potency to George. Biff's loss of power also represents Marty's abandoning of the desire for the mother. But the desire for omnipotence (perhaps as a defense against the fear of castration) remains at the end: Marty has passed his initiation ritual but he is once again lured into adventure by Dr. Brown. Having rewritten the past and the present, they will now presumably go on to reshape the future. In the exhilarating conclusion, Marty and Jennifer depart with the Professor in the DeLorean (now run by fusion and able to fly), off to the future to rescue their children. The audience leaves the movie on this exhilarating note, feeling a sense of infinite possibilities, feeling that, as a line from the movie goes, "The future is in your hands."

The struggle in the film, then, for Marty and Dr. Brown and George, is to gain power and control over that power, to counter impotence and failure with omnipotence and success. To put it another way, there is a phallic struggle contained within the œdipal one. In the film's opening scene, Marty enters the lab, switches on a machine and turns it all the way up to "Overdrive." He plugs in an electric guitar and stands in front of a monstrously huge amplifier. The first chord he strums destroys the amp and blows him across the room. But Marty makes a soft landing in a chair and is unharmed, despite a bookcase tipping over and dumping its contents on him. The scene prefigures the later scenes when the DeLorean is revved up to Overdrive and blows Marty across time to a safe landing. The film shows the exhilaration of playing around with omnipotence. Marty is the sorcerer's apprentice whose dream comes true, who overcomes all the dangers inherent in possessing fantastic power.

Aside from the electric guitar, the time machine itself is the primary symbol of "phallic" power. It is powerful and intrusive, building up energy and then releasing it in an orgasmic burst. Marty is constantly crashing the car into things. It is difficult for him to control and prone to embarrassing failures to start. The clock tower can be taken as another phallic symbol, particularly in the climactic scene, when it is struck by lightning. And the bazooka with which the Libyan terrorists threaten Marty is made to seem particularly phallic by the camera angle.

The movie also makes comedy out of the exaggerated contrasts between little Marty and the big guys who intimidate him, such as Lou (the owner of the diner) and Biff. These contrasts in size could also be interpreted as phallic. In scene after scene, the camera exaggerates Biff's size as he looms ominously over Marty. Repeatedly, the power balance is restored by cutting Biff down to size, tripping him or hitting him so that he falls down. Biff gets his final comeuppance after he has knocked Lorraine to the ground and forced George to his knees by twisting his arm. At this point, George's fist seems to act independently of him, and he fells Biff with one mighty blow. Afterwards, George pants ecstatically and admires his hand with astonishment and delight before he helps Lorraine to her feet. Because this crucial scene is staged so melodramatically, the sexual symbolism becomes blatant.

Including this scene, I counted 14 instances in which characters tripped, fell, fainted, were knocked down, knocked out, or gunned down. The climactic scenes for all five major characters — Marty, Dr. Brown, George, Lorraine, and Biff— involve their being forced down. We see all of them get up again, though, except for the villain, Biff, who goes down and stays down. When Marty is with his mother in 1955, he is constantly backing away from her or falling over out of sexual terror. There are also six car crashes in the film. These many pratfalls and crashes provide both comedy and action, but they might also suggest an underlying concern with potency, with staying up and crashing through barriers.

Aside from its indulgence in œdipal and phallic fantasies, the film also involves a great deal of voyeurism and exhibitionism. At times, it even seems as if the main pleasure and the main sin is not in incest but in looking, watching, spying, and being looked at. Young Lorraine gazes with longing at Marty, Dr. Brown keeps rerunning the image of himself on videotape, Marty turns his head to gaze at the girls walking by in leotards (and his girlfriend Jennifer forcibly returns his gaze to her), Marty exhibits himself onstage in his guitar performances, Lorraine undresses with the blinds up as George, a "peeping Tom," spies on her through binoculars, and Biff tells Marty repeatedly to stop staring at him ("What are you looking at, butthead?") and tells his buddies to stop staring as he is about to rape Lorraine: "This ain't no peep show." In one of the film's most memorable scenes, we see two Martys: One watches helplessly as Dr. Brown is assassinated while the other, just returned from time traveling, helplessly watches himself watching helplessly.

So *Future* is indeed a fascinating "peep show." Of course, as critics have mentioned, voyeurism and exhibitionism may be an intrinsic feature of making and viewing films, and in most Hollywood films the primary object of the gaze is a woman.[26] This movie is no exception. But the particular emphasis in *Back to the Future* on voyeurism, aside from providing some incidental pleasure for viewers, may be a way of displacing our interest from the overt incest of the plot to the sublimated incest of spying on the parents.[27] In fact, *Back to the Future* might even be considered one extended "primal scene."

The most remarkable primal scene imagery in the film occurs when Marty plays his guitar at the high school dance in 1955. He has just witnessed his parents' first kiss, itself a symbolic primal scene. Marty, who had feared being wiped out of existence if they didn't kiss, has just been reborn, so he plays Chuck Berry's joyous rock anthem "Johnny B. Goode" to celebrate his new lease on life. By a twist of history, his rebirth coincides with the birth of rock and roll. In one of the film's funniest scenes, Marty shows off before this hick 1955 crowd, exhibiting 1985 savvy, as he had done before with his skateboarding. But he overdoes it and embarrasses himself. Marty quickly recapitulates the history of rock and roll and winds up on the floor of the stage, producing heavy metal squeals as he practically copulates with his guitar. Like many rock and roll performances, it is a phallic celebration, with overtones of public masturbation. When Marty opens his eyes, he sees the 1955 audience staring in shocked silence. Shamefacedly, he apologizes: "I guess you guys aren't ready for that yet. But your kids are gonna love it!"

In the context of this film, "it" could stand for either rock and roll or sex (which have always been conflated in the popular imagination, as in "drugs, sex, and rock and roll"). Earlier, Marty's sexuality was repressed by his mother, and his music was repressed by the school. He lost the band contest because his brand of rock was deemed "too darn loud" (read "too sexual"). As I suggested, the entire film is a wish-fulfillment fantasy making up for Marty's disastrous day in 1985 in the opening scenes. So when Marty undoes his failure by playing at the high school dance, he expresses a new confidence both in his music and in his sexuality. After all, he has just rejoiced in witnessing his parents' first kiss, which means that he has accepted their sexuality and so is better able to accept his own.

Thus it is possible to read his guitar playing not simply as masturbatory exhibitionism, which it is, but also as a recapitulation of the primal scene: Marty stands in for both father and mother in the act of conceiving him, and the silent, staring crowd, shocked and puzzled by this violent activity and the strange sounds accompanying it, stands in for the child witness.[28] The scene is pleasurable for an audience in part because it makes primal scene imagery not terrifying but *funny*: the performance is a comic triumph for Marty, who easily shrugs off his embarrassment, showing a new mood of confidence and self-acceptance.

Back to the Future, as I have attempted to demonstrate, appeals on many different psychosexual levels to viewers: it makes comedy out of voyeurism, phallic exhibitionism, incest, and the primal scene. But I should also mention one last level of its humor, which is excremental comedy, a delight in *mess*: the overflowing bowl of dog food, the overturned bookshelf, and the truckload of manure tipped over on Biff. In the final scene, Dr. Brown maniacally rummages through the garbage cans for fuel to power his "Mr. Fusion" generator. It may also be significant that, in such a "clean" comedy, the only vulgarities uttered are "butthead," "serious shit," and "assholes."

Moreover, it is a psychoanalytic commonplace that problems relating to the "anal" phase of development revolve around autonomy and control, cleanliness and order, and time. Not surprisingly, the film concerns all these issues: a struggle for autonomy and control, a revolt against cleanliness and order, and an obsession with time. These conflicts are unconsciously connected, so that the central battle to overcome time also represents Marty's and Brown's struggles for autonomy and control. The opening shot is a long pan of the ticking clocks in Dr. Brown's laboratory, including one with a man dangling from the hands of the clock, just as Dr. Brown will do later. Marty is chronically tardy and, like the Professor, always racing against time. In other words, although an œdipal fantasy is at the heart of the movie, it is connected with and strongly colored by concerns from the stage that Erik H. Erikson called "autonomy vs. shame and doubt."[29]

It is easy enough to dissolve a film into relatively primitive psychosexual levels. But a fantasy of omnipotence will not work for an audience unless it has speed, energy, and style. And *Back to the Future* has these in abundance: its infectious high spirits and restless camera movements catch the viewer up in the action from beginning to end.

The proliferation of Hollywood time travel films in the 1980s, I suggested, spoke to the American nostalgia for the past (evidenced by the entire presidency of Reagan), dissatisfaction with the present, and dread of the future. *Back to the Future* was a therapeutic comedy for the era because it suggests that time and human character is malleable, which is what Americans have always wanted to believe. Granted, it is possible to fault the film for its "blandly positivist" notions of mental health,[30] its antiseptic vision of the 1950s,[31] and its final conversion of Marty's family into yuppies.[32] Nevertheless, these are not fundamental flaws, and they do not detract from the film's power to make us laugh and to reassure us.

The therapeutic nature of *Back to the Future* consists in rendering explicit the incestuous possibilities that have always been at the core of the fascination with time travel and exploiting those possibilities for the purposes of a comic resolution to an œdipal crisis. *Future* allows us to laugh at potentially dangerous material by placing it within the context of classic film comedy and situation comedy and by deliberately using stock character types. Moreover, it distances the œdipal crisis through the fantastic, displaces it from the present to the past and from the child to the parent. Through a fantasy of innocent power, it permits us to identify with an innocent hero, to retreat to the purity of childhood while retaining the power and control of adulthood. The sophistication of the 1980s meets the naïveté of the 1950s, and the film validates both. *Back to the Future* is an ingenious wish-fulfillment fantasy with an upbeat message, a therapeutic family comedy, allowing a rare, momentary reconciliation between past and present and between parent and child.

Back to the Future II and *III*

Although *Back to the Future* was not originally conceived as a trilogy, and the first film stands very well by itself, the sequels display much the same verve, slapstick comedy, action, and romance. In particular, the sequels showcase the clever plotting of Zemeckis and Gale. If the original was Oedipal comedy showing a kind of repetition compulsion — the rerunning of scenes from the present in the past — then the sequels weave ingenious variations on the first film. Zemeckis and Gale can compose on an epic scale, for they have two more movies in which to work out the story. The effect is not mere repetition but theme and variation, like a musical fugue. The sequels demonstrate that overcoming Oedipus is not so easy. The three films together are about the maturation of Marty McFly and his preparation for manhood and a family of his own.

By 2015, Marty has moved from the position of son to father, with a teenage son and daughter with Jennifer. If Marty was cursed with a weak father and a dysfunctional family in *Back to the Future*, then Marty Jr. is in the same position in *Back to the Future II*. The 47-year-old Marty McFly has become a loser like his dad George at the same age at the beginning of *Back to the Future*. We find out the details later in the trilogy: Marty succumbed to his insecurities; never able to bear anyone calling him "yellow" or "chicken," the teenage Marty got in a street race on a stupid dare from the bully Needles. In the resulting car crash, he lost the ability to play guitar and any remnant of his confidence. Now Marty is a middle-aged failure, an office drone living in a bad section of Hill Valley. As the elderly Biff says, in the excremental vision of the series, Marty took his life and "flushed it down the toilet." Lacking a strong father, Marty Jr. has suffered as Marty did, and grown up into a 17-year-old total dweeb, a far worse loser than his father at the same age.

Young Marty, aided by Doc Brown, takes the place of his look-alike son to rescue him from having his life ruined by the bully Griff, grandson of Biff. This sequence reprises the rescue of his father from Biff in *Back to the Future I*, complete with a showdown at the malt shop and a skateboard race through the town square, culminating in a similar defeat of the bully and his gang. The pleasure for the audience is in witnessing the theme with variations: the malt shop and town square dramatically altered from 1955 to 2015, the skateboard changed to a futuristic hoverboard. This is, after all, the essence of Hollywood genre films: the pleasure of recognition, similarity plus difference, repeating a formula with variations. Zemeckis and Gale wink at the audience about the repetitions, so that we're in on the joke. As he witnesses the hoverboard chase, the elderly Biff mutters, "Something very familiar about all this."

In the repetition compulsion of the series, the bullies proliferate: Biff in his various incarnations at different ages; Biff's grandson Griff in 2015; their ancestor in 1885, Buford "Mad Dog" Tannen; and Needles, Marty's nemesis in 1985 and in 2015. Without these villains, the films would lack most of their ingenious plot complications. Although Marty is able to rescue his son from Griff's criminal plans, he is unable to rescue his middle-aged self from yet another stupid dare by Needles. Taunted as chicken, the 47-year-old Marty accepts the offer to participate in his officemate Needles' scheme against the company. Marty is instantly found out and fired. This prompts a desire in the audience to see this undone, in fact, to have the entire future of Marty and Jennifer and their family rewritten the same way that the fate of Marty and his parents and siblings was altered for the better in *I*.

Yet the 2015 sequence is only the first of the three acts that constitute part *II*. Carl Sagan told Zemeckis and Gale that he considered *Back to the Future II* the best movie ever made based on the science of time travel (DVD commentary).[33] And it is a convoluted, sophisticated film that plays on all the paradoxes of time travel. In the second act, an unwitting Marty and Doc and Jennifer return to 1985A, a 1985 altered for the worse. At first, they do not realize it is an alternate timeline caused by the meddling of the elderly Biff, who stole the DeLorean and traveled in time for personal gain. The audience discovers the horrible changes in this time branch only gradually, as Marty does.

In 1985A, thanks to the sports almanac provided by his 2015 self, Biff has become one of the richest men in America and the lord of all he surveys from his penthouse suite atop his skyscraper. Biff's corruption has blighted everything he touched and turned the place into a hellhole of urban decay, complete with sleaze, gambling, violent crime, and toxic waste, so that the town now resembles many declining American cities of the 1980s. Marty's mother Lorraine has been reduced to a weak, drunken bimbo, herself and her children at the mercy of the cruel, abusive Biff.

This sequence is the darkest of the trilogy. Here oedipal comedy descends momentarily into oedipal nightmare, as if fulfilling Marty's worst imaginings. On the one hand, it is a homage to the "Pottersville" sequence in Capra's *It's a Wonderful Life*. On the other hand, it borrows from that oedipal tragedy *Hamlet*, with Marty as Hamlet, Biff as Claudius, and Lorraine as Gertrude. Like Hamlet, Marty returns home to discover that his father is dead and his mother has remarried. Like Claudius, Biff is a superrich and powerful king of his realm, but also a complete villain: a lecher and a murderer. Like Gertrude, Lorraine is a weak woman who has unknowingly wed the man who murdered her husband. Echoing Hamlet's bitter reproaches to Gertrude, Marty says to Lorraine, "Respect? Your husband? How could he be your husband? How could you leave Dad for him?" Like Claudius, having murdered the father and married the mother, Biff must now eliminate the son, who confronts him, knows too much, and threatens his rule.

The unconscious link between Marty and Biff— Biff as Marty's double or anti-self, the expression of his worst desires — becomes explicit in this sequence. Biff of 1985A has merely enacted Marty's wishes. The disaster that has befallen Hill Valley and Marty's family is the consequence of Marty's act in 2015, which gave Biff the idea. Marty tells Doc Brown, "It's my fault. The whole thing is my fault. If I hadn't bought that damn book, none of this would have ever happened." In a sense, then, Marty is responsible for the murder of his father and the sexual degradation of his mother. Moreover, Lorraine in 1985 has had breast implants forced on her by Biff— but in the 2015 sequence, we see Marty. Jr. watching a series of TV programs, one of which seems to be the big breast channel!

The third act of *Back to the Future II* is the most ingenious sequence in the entire trilogy, for it involves Marty and Doc Brown returning to 1955 to retrieve the sports almanac, all the while trying to avoid meeting their earlier selves. We see a reprise of the dance of *Back to the Future I,* in which Marty must weave in and out of the action and insure that events transpire as before, with his parents united, once again undoing the oedipal nightmare. At one point, a girlie magazine called "Ooh La La" is substituted for the elusive sports almanac, suggesting that what Biff and Marty are seeking is actually an object of illicit sexual desire. The climactic *mano a mano* between Biff and Marty involves Biff in his car trying to ram Marty in a tunnel — a kind of symbolic sexual assault.

Back to the Future III repeats an action seen in all three movies: the murder of the father and then the undoing of that act by rescuing the father. Like Luke in the *Star Wars* saga, Marty has a bad habit of losing fathers and father figures. In *Back to the Future I*, Marty in 1985 sees Doc Brown, his surrogate father, gunned down by terrorists. Going to 1985 enables him not only to improve the lives of his parents, his siblings, and himself, but also to rescue Doc. In *II*, in 1985A Marty discovers his father's grave in the cemetery and must return to 1955 to insure that Biff's murder of his father never takes place. And in *III*, Marty discovers not his father's grave but Doc Brown's and must travel to 1885 to prevent Doc's murder by Biff's ancestor Buford "Mad Dog" Tannen.

The incest theme is again deliberately reprised; Marty repeats the now obligatory scene of being knocked out and waking up in the dark in his mother's bed, confused about what year he is in. In *III*, it is the bed of his 1885 ancestors, the farmers Seamus and Maggie McFly (played by Michael J. Fox and Lea Thompson), the first McFlys in Hill Valley, immigrants from Ireland. When Marty awakes, Maggie is quick to tell him, "That's *Mrs.* McFly, and don't you be forgetting it," although he has done nothing to suggest that he is a threat to connubial bliss.

However, Marty's relationship with his ancestors plays only a minor role in *III*; instead, the focus shifts to the romance between Doc Brown and the newly-arrived town schoolteacher Clara Clayton. Whereas in the previous two movies, Doc seemed to be an asexual mentor for Marty, a lifelong bachelor whose romance was entirely with science and who seemed either uninterested in or baffled by women, now, by a plot contrivance, he falls in love at first sight with a beautiful, brainy woman, tailor-made for him by Zemeckis and Gale, for she has his same passion for science and the works of Jules Verne. When Clara comes to Doc to fix her telescope and they share their love for this long, tubular object, one is reminded once again that Zemeckis and Gale's symbolism, although frequently funny, is never subtle!

Doc's romance plays the same role in the plot as Marty's romance with his mother in the first movie; in other words, having exhausted the oedipal complications between Marty and Lorraine in two movies, the oedipal plot now shifts from Marty to Doc Brown. Says Bob Gale, "What we needed to finally have happen at the end was for Marty and Doc to sort of change places, so Marty is the one giving Doc the scientific advice and Doc is acting on his emotions, exactly the opposite of what happened in the first movie."[34] Thus when Clara comes to Doc's barn, repeating the forward behavior of the teenage Lorraine pursuing Marty in *I*, Marty now takes the place formerly occupied by Doc, of the man in the middle, strongly disapproving of the romance and trying to intervene. Marty must discourage the budding love between Doc and Clara to insure his and Doc's return to 1985. Yet, in another sense, Marty is acting like a son intruding between a father and mother, unable to accept their sexuality. In the film's climax, when he gives Doc the hoverboard so that he may rescue Clara, he is finally acknowledging their union, and he returns to 1985 without them.

The last stage in Marty's maturation in the series occurs when he refuses to give in to the taunting of Needles and will not street race with him — just as earlier he had refused to draw his gun against Buford Tannen. Using a gun against Buford would probably have ended with the death of Marty or Doc; racing with Needles would have resulted in the crash that ended his music career. The newly confident, post-oedipal Marty is now ready for manhood.

All the *Back to the Future* films end with a family reunion. At the end of the first film, through his intervention in family history, Marty has transformed them from lower middle-class losers to upscale yuppies. *Back to the Future III*, however, ends with the creation of two new families. Marty will marry Jennifer and no doubt have a successful life. And Doc Brown has married Clara, had two sons, Jules and Verne, and built a new time machine in the form of a flying train (nineteenth-century technology married to the twenty-first century).

Bob Gale mentions that Doc's wardrobe in the final scene of *Back to the Future III* was inspired by that of Professor Marvel in *The Wizard of Oz*.[35] Professor Marvel got to Oz in a balloon; Dorothy got there in a flying house; Dr. Brown travels through time in a flying locomotive which is also his family home. Dorothy brings her dog; Dr. Brown brings his dog and his entire family. We all want to escape into adventure sometimes, but we also yearn for the security of family and the comforts of home: through a fantastic compromise, both Marty and Doc Brown get both. Like Dorothy, Marty McFly runs away from home, but all he ever really wants to do is get back home. Wherever Marty travels in time, from 1885 to 2015, he never leaves Hill Valley, and he always meets his family. The *Back to the Future* trilogy is finally a family comedy with a reassuring message similar to that of *The Wizard of Oz*: "There's no place like home."

Notes

1. For some representative, largely positive, responses to *Back to the Future*, see the reviews by Hoberman, Kael, Kauffman, and Kroll.

2. In 1985-86, I conducted an informal survey of audience response to *Back to the Future*

I. I asked two undergraduate classes at the University of Florida to write their responses, and I taped interviews with some audience members immediately after they viewed the film in a theater. Some of the results were unexpected.

First, entirely without prompting, many praised the film as scrupulously *clean*: "the viewer does not feel dirty"; "good, clean humor ... no sex, gore or profanity"; "not at all offensive"; and "one of the cleanest films, without any type of filth in it." Either these comments are defensive denials, or else this is a sad commentary on the current state of Hollywood films, because *Back to the Future* deals with a peeping tom, attempted rape and attempted incest, and includes three (admittedly mild) vulgarities: "butthead," "shit," and "assholes." Second, based on my limited sampling, this film is apparently very popular with 13-year-old boys, some of whom went first with friends and then returned with their families, including their mothers. You can make of this what you will, but to me it indicates that the film was a therapeutic family comedy.

3. Wachhorst, p. 340.

4. Franklin, "Don't Look Where We're Going."

5. Shales, p. 67.

6. Ibid., p. 68.

7. Stewart, p. 207.

8. Sobchack, p. 274.

9. Ellison.

10. Sobchack, p. 274.

11. Stein, p. 41.

12. Ibid., p. 37.

13. Kroll.

14. Kael, p. 58.

15. See Twitchell.

16. Hoberman.

17. Barksdale and Pace, p. 57.

18. See Scafella, Ketterer.

19. I am indebted to H. Bruce Franklin's discussion of the incest theme in Heinlein in *Robert A. Heinlein*, pp. 120–24, 184–86, and 191–97.

20. Wachhorst, p. 350.

21. *Back to the Future I* DVD commentary.

22. Freud, p. 38.

23. Wachhorst, p. 350.

24. *Back to the Future*, like most SF films since *Star Wars* (1977), is openly intertextual, and our pleasure in the film to a degree depends upon our shared knowledge of twentieth-century American popular culture and the shock of recognition of seeing familiar material reworked in a new context. As Sobchack mentions, "It is only recently that the SF film has so reflexively embraced its own former status as 'schlock' and 'kitsch' and/or embraced the 'whole "degraded" landscape of schlock and kitsch' that represents contemporary American popular culture" (p. 249).

25. Stein, p. 42.

26. On two kinds of voyeurism in film, see Metz, pp. 89–98. On woman as image in film, see Mulvey.

27. Based on my survey, many viewers were fascinated by the idea of spying on the parents: "when the boy finds himself in the past, he seeks the home of his parents" (this response is not strictly true to the plot); "everyone would probably love to go back ... and see what it was like when their parents were young"; "made me wonder about my parents at that age"; "I really enjoyed seeing the main character with his parents as teenagers."

28. For a thorough investigation of primal scene imagery in films, including science-fiction films, see Dervin.

29. Erikson, pp. 251–54.

30. See Hoberman.

31. See Hoberman; Kael, p. 58.

32. Kael, p. 58. Even Zemeckis shamefacedly admits in the DVD commentary that the first film too wholeheartedly bought into 1980s American materialism.

33. *Back to the Future II*, DVD commentary.

34. *Back to the Future III*, DVD commentary.

35. Ibid.

Works Cited

Back to the Future I, II, III. DVD commentary.

Barksdale, E.C., and David Paul Pace. "*Back to the Future.*" *Cinefantastique* (Mar. 1986), pp. 45, 56–57.

Dervin, Daniel. *Through a Freudian Lens Deeply: A Psychanalysis of Cinema*. Hillsdale, NJ: L. Erlbaum Associates, 1985.

Ellison, Harlan. "Harlan Ellison's Watching."
The Magazine of Fantasy and Science Fiction (Jan. 1986), p. 88.

Erikson, Erik H. *Childhood and Society*, 2d ed. New York: Norton, 1963.

Franklin, H. Bruce. "Don't Look Where We're Going: Visions of the Future in Science fiction Films, 1970–82." *Science Fiction Studies*, 10(1983): 70–80.

_____. *Robert A. Heinlein: America as Science Fiction*. New York: Oxford, 1980.

Freud, Sigmund. "The Relation of the Poet to Day-Dreaming" 1908. *Character and Culture*, ed. Philip Reiff (New York: Collier, 1963), pp. 34–43.

Hoberman, J. "Spielbergism and Its Discontents." *The Village Voice*, 9 July 1985, p. 45.

Kael, Pauline. "Back to the Future." *The New Yorker*, 29 July 1985, pp. 57–58.

Kauffman, Stanley. "Traveling to the Past." *The New Republic*, 5 Aug. 1985, p. 24.

Ketterer, David. "Œdipus as Time Traveler." *Science Fiction Studies*, 9 (1982): 340–41.

Kroll, Jack. "Having the Time of His Life." *Newsweek*, 8 July 1985, p. 76.

Metz, Christian. *The Imaginary Signifier: Psychoanalysis and the Cinema*. 1977; Bloomington: University of Indiana Press, 1982.

Mulvey, Laura. "Visual Pleasure and Narrative Cinema," in *Movies and Methods*, vol. 2, ed. Bill Nichols (Berkeley: University of California Press, 1985), pp. 303–15.

Scafella, Frank. "The White Sphinx and *The Time Machine*." *Science Fiction Studies*, 8 (1981): 255–65.

Shales, Tom. "The Re Decade." *Esquire* (Mar. 1986), pp. 67–72.

Sobchack, Vivian. *Screening Space: The American Science Fiction Film*, 2d ed. New York: Ungar, 1987.

Stein, Michael. "Director Bob Zemeckis' Tale of Teen Time Travel." *Fantastic Films* (Oct. 1985), pp. 37, 41–43.

Stewart, Garrett. "The 'Videology' of Science Fiction," in *Shadows of the Magic Lamp: Fantasy and Science Fiction in Film*, ed. George E. Slusser & Eric S. Rabkin (Carbondale: Southern Illinois Press, 1985), pp. 159–207.

Twitchell, James. *Forbidden Partners: The Incest Taboo in Modern Culture*. New York: Columbia University Press, 1986.

Wachhorst, Wyn. "Time travel Romance on Film: Archetypes and Structures." *Extrapolation*, 25(1984): 340.

2. "You Space Bastard! You killed my pines!": *Back to the Future*, Nostalgia and the Suburban Dream

BERNICE M. MURPHY

Back to the Future and its sequels trace the development of the American settlement from frontier to small town to suburb in a manner which ultimately highlights their own innate and problematic (for this critic at least) conservatism. Early in the first film Marty McFly, who, of course, has just traveled back in time thirty years to 1955, tries to return to his family home. The problem is, like Marty himself, that home doesn't actually *exist*, at least not yet. Instead of the dilapidated suburb which will be present in 30 years, Marty finds a green field site and a cheery billboard (illustrated with an image of a Norman Rockwell style nuclear family) which exhorts buyers interested in settling in the forthcoming "Lyon Estates" to "live in the home of tomorrow — today!" The imminence of suburbia's arrival to Hill Valley is emphasized by the fact that bulldozers are framed within the same shot as the billboard: the implication is that at first light tomorrow the workmen will arrive and the peaceful nocturnal vista before us will become a giant building site. Marty has inadvertently returned to a key moment not only in the relationship of his parents, but in the history of Hill Valley itself: the point just before intensive development overruns the countryside and the idyllic small town is superseded by sprawling suburb. The fact that the town itself is literally on the cusp of such significant change is, I would suggest, actually a key, if overlooked element of the film, and one to which the sequels return repeatedly. This isn't just a film about the fate of one teenage boy and his family: it is a series of films which present us with contrasting visions of the American community itself.

That suburban development, and the many other changes which accompanied it, has not necessarily been a good thing for Hill Valley is obvious from the beginning of the film. Marty's high school is litter-strewn, run down and defaced with graffiti. Like Hill Valley's seedy down town area (which comes complete with adult movie theatre, broken clock tower and boarded up windows), Lyon Estates, and the McFly home itself, are untidy, neglected, and decidedly trashy: the ideal architectural corollary to the slovenly, blue collar and un-ambitious nuclear family to which Marty reluctantly belongs.

As the narrative progresses and spills over into the second and third films, it becomes increasingly clear that the fate of the McFly family is also intrinsically linked to that of the wider community of Hill Valley itself: their fortunes (and Marty's attempts to preserve the timeline) determine nothing less than the future, past and present of the town itself. Throughout the series, contrasting versions of the McFly clan, Lyon Estates and Hill Valley battle it out with each other as we get to see the community at key moments of historical importance. These dueling figurations include frontier-era settlement (*BTTF3*); small town on the verge of suburban development (*BTTF1* and *2*); nightmarishly overdeveloped dystopian cityscape (1985A in *BTTF2*); run-down 1980s suburb; utopian 1980s suburb; and the same dynamic set in 2015 and concerning Marty's own future family.

At the heart of the first two films is the placing of 1955 as the year upon which everything somehow depends, for good or for ill: "the temporal junction point for the entire time-space continuum," as Doc Brown declares, before acknowledging the tenuous nature of the entire premise by wryly adding "or maybe it's just coincidence." But it is no such coincidence, as I shall demonstrate during the course of this essay, for the trilogy is indeed fixated with presenting us with a relentlessly sugar-coated, unproblematic and decidedly conservative vision of the 1950s which in fact fits in very well with Reagan-era notions of domesticity and family.

Back to the Future was of course not alone in presenting mid–1980s moviegoers with an inherently nostalgic reimagining of the 1950s. The decade loomed large in eighties cinema, in a trend partially sparked by the success of *Grease* (1978) and *American Graffiti* (1973). On the small screen, the nostalgic sitcom *Happy Days* ran from 1974 to 1984. As in Zemeckis's films, time travel also featured in Francis Ford Coppola's *Peggy Sue Got Married* (1986) in which a heart attack at a high school reunion gives a disenchanted middle-aged housewife (Kathleen Turner) the chance to return to her high school senior year (1960) and relive key moments in her life. *Back to the Future* was of course executively produced by Steven Spielberg, who was originally slated to direct *Peggy Sue Got Married*, and had previously, with both *E.T.* and *Poltergeist* (1984), presented audiences with visions of picket-fence suburban idylls suddenly disrupted by alien (or paranormal) outsiders.

In the Stephen King adaptation *Stand by Me* (Rob Reiner, 1986) a group of young boys are confronted with the realities of life, death and growing up during the course of the summer of '59 (the "best summer of our lives" trope is of course a key conceit of "coming-of-age" stories of this type). Both films utilize a frame structure in which the 1950s sequences are recounted in flashback form and are contrasted with a 1980s present with which the main protagonist is somehow inherently dissatisfied: Gordie La Chance, the narrator of *Stand by Me*, has just learned of the death of one of his childhood friends, news which prompts him to recall epochal events in their lives, whilst Peggy Sue is on the verge of divorce from her feckless and philandering husband, whom she married as a pregnant teenager.

If the examples just mentioned — along with *Back to the Future* itself — could be characterized as "nostalgia films" then one of the most interesting 1950s set 1980s films is Bob Balaban's visually striking and genuinely witty *Parents* (1989) — a viscerally disturbing "anti nostalgia" film which serves as a gory satire of sanitized, nostalgic representations of the decade and of the cultural and consumerist implications of the suburban existence in general. The narrative's focal character, ten-year-old Michael (Bryan Madorsky) is the rather shy, sickly-looking only child of Nick and Lily Laemle (Randy Quaid and Mary Beth Hurt), who, on the surface, seem to be as average a middle-class couple of their time as any other. Michael's sweater-wearing, scientist dad likes to golf and his housewife mom loves to cook: they live in a spacious, luridly furnished tract house in a new neighborhood and drive a brown Oldsmobile. What concerns Michael is the fact that his parents love to consume vast amounts of red meat, the exact source of which they are notably cagey about, and for good reason: they are unrepentant cannibals. Here, the conspicuous consumption of the 1950s, a time when American refrigerators and supermarkets began to contain a wider array of food stuffs at cheaper prices than ever before, literally becomes the stuff of nightmares and the refrain "eat your dinner" takes on deeply disturbing resonances because, in this instance, meat really *is* murder.

Another, similarly macabre take on rose-tinted 1980s "reimagining" of the decade is David Lynch's hyper-stylized and surreal neo-noir *Blue Velvet* (1986) which also begins with an uncannily idyllic looking vision of small-town suburbia and then proceeds to upend this placid image in order to expose the seething tangle of criminal, sexual and psychological neuroses beneath, much as its boyish hero Jeffrey stumbles across a severed human ear whilst strolling across an otherwise idyllic seeming stretch of grass. Even if *Peggy Sue Got Married* ultimately validates the heroine's decision to choose a life of bourgeois domesticity and suburban normality all over again, at least the narrative briefly allows its heroine to briefly flirt with the possibilities of a more bohemian, liberated existence. Similarly, as *Stand by Me* makes clear,

even if the decade was something of a halcyon age for the group friends featured, it was also a time of fear, suffering at the hands of psychotic bullies,
and the loss of innocence (this is, after all, a film which concerns the search
for a little boy's corpse, a macabre plot point which all the nostalgic decade-
appropriate ballads playing in the background cannot quite obscure).

By way of contrast, during the course of the *Back to the Future* trilogy,
there is never any chance at all that Marty McFly might stumble across a dead
body or stray ear, either in the metaphorical or literal sense. The 1955 to which
he repeatedly returns during the series is ultimately depicted as a placid,
upstanding time of good, clean fun: a golden age for the town of Hill Valley,
whose history gradually becomes inextricably linked with that of the McFly
family itself. It stands in stark contrast to the powerful anxieties identified by
Stephen King — the pop lit laureate of the baby-boom generation — in his
semi-autobiographical study of the horror genre *Danse Macabre*:

> We were fertile ground for the seeds of terror, we war babies; we had been raised
> in a strange circus atmosphere of paranoia, patriotism, and national *hubris*. We
> were told that we were the greatest nation on earth and that any Iron Curtain out-
> law who tried to draw down on us in that great saloon of international politics
> would discover who the fastest gun in the West was ... but we were also told exactly
> what to keep in our fallout shelters and how long we would have to stay in there
> after we won the war. We had more to eat than any other nation in the history of
> the world, but there were traces of Strontium-90 in our milk from nuclear test-
> ing.[1]

Yet in *Back to the Future* and its sequels, practically any moment at which
there is a potential frisson of danger or controversy is swiftly defused, usually
by being played for laughs. For instance, small-town bully Biff Tannen (who
would be no match at all for *Stand by Me*'s flick-knife wielding sociopath Ace
Merril) is comprehensively defeated and humiliated in each incarnation he
takes throughout the trilogy and reduced to simple comic relief in each. The
charge created by his attempted sexual assault of Marty's mother in the first
installment is soon eclipsed by the character's relegation to obsequious dog's
body once Marty returns to the newly-utopian present. Similarly, whatever
menace the character carries in the sequels (in which his capacity for murderous activities, and that of his "ancestor" the gun-toting killer "Mad Dog"
Tannen, is made obvious) is similarly dispersed by the end of the trilogy. The
question of race is similarly glossed over with patronizing reference to a single character: Goldie Wilson, whose transition from diner bus boy to long-
time mayor of Hill Valley is obviously meant to epitomize the gains of the
Civil Rights movement. The Cold War goes completely unmentioned (no
bomb shelters here), and the film's approach to sexual politics is perhaps best
summed up by a throw-away comment made by Doc Brown at the beginning

of *BTTF2*, when he renders Marty's girlfriend Jennifer unconscious (even though the plot involves her future as much as Marty's) because "She's not essential to my plan."

The series' notably soft treatment of potentially controversial topics brings to mind comments made by Frederic Jameson at the beginning of his 1989 essay "Nostalgia for the Present" in which he discusses the novel *Time Out of Joint*, also set (at least ostensibly) in an idealized version of small town America during the 1950s:

> There is a novel by Philip K. Dick, which, published in 1959, evokes the fifties: President Eisenhower's stroke; Main Street, U.S.A; Marilyn Monroe; a world of neighbors and PTA's; small retail chain stores (the produce trucked in from outside); favorite television programs, mild flirtations with the housewife next door, game shows and contests; sputniks distantly revolving overhead, mere blinking lights in the firmament.... If you were interested in constructing a time capsule or an "only yesterday" compendium or documentary-nostalgia video film of the 1950s, this might serve as a beginning ... the list is not a list of facts or historical realities (although its items are not invented and are in some sense "authentic"), but rather a list of stereotypes, of ideas of facts and historical realities.[2]

As Jameson goes on to suggest, the idyllic small town setting evoked in the novel — which also functioned as an allegorical expression of Eisenhower America itself— no longer exists in the present day: "the autonomy of the small town has ... vanished. What was once a certain point on the map has become an imperceptible thickening in a continuum of identical products and standardized spaces from coast to coast." Complicating matters considerably is the fact that the setting of Dick's novel ultimately turns out to be a *genuinely* inauthentic space: "a reproduction of the 1950s — including induced and introjected memories and character structures in its human population — constructed in 1997, in the midst of an interstellar atomic war."[3] As Jameson observes, "Dick also takes pains to make it clear that the 1950s village is also very specifically the result of infantile regression on the part of the protagonist, who has also, in a sense, unconsciously chosen his own delusion and has fled the anxieties of the civil war for the domestic and reassuring comforts of his own childhood during the period in question ... the novel is a collective wish fulfillment, and the expression of a deep, unconscious yearning for a simpler and more human social system and a small town utopia very much in the North American Frontier tradition."[4]

In the *Back to the Future* trilogy, the small town, and the suburbs which surround it are also depicted in a nostalgic, essentially inauthentic manner. Indeed, perhaps one of the most interesting aspects of the trilogy is the way in which it serves to chart the transition from frontier to small town to suburban community. As William H. Chafe has put it, "Rarely has a society experienced such rapid or dramatic changes as those which occurred in the U.S.

after 1945."[5] One of the most significant of these changes was the immense housing boom. Millions of soldiers returning from the war in Europe and the Pacific had been promised homes of their own, homes far removed from the crowded, ill-equipped apartments available in the nation's cities. Between 1948 and 1958, eleven million new suburban homes were established. An astonishing 83 percent of all population growth during the nineteen fifties took place in the suburbs. By 1970, they would house more people than either cities or farms.[6] Behind the dry statistics lay the inescapable reality of the situation: that the basic living pattern of American society was undergoing a seismic shift. Almost overnight, a new community could come into being. Bulldozers and construction crews invaded the countryside: the cities saw their populations drop dramatically. Mass production and prefabrication technologies perfected during wartime meant that developers such as William Levitt were able to apply factory style production techniques to the building of family homes and as a result new communities sprang up more quickly than ever before. In a bid to overcome the substantial housing deficit, the government made it easier than ever before for the ordinary citizen to purchase his own home, providing healthy loan guarantees to builders and subsidizing cheap mortgages. As a result, "owning a home became cheaper than renting: an ex–G.I. could realize the American dream in Levittown for $56 a month."[7]

Those who dreamt of the good life fled to the promised land of suburbia: people unwilling — or unable — to afford such a move were left in increasingly poverty stricken and derelict inner cities. Inevitably, as with every other dramatic change, there were those who condemned suburbia and all that it was held to represent. The most common complaint leveled at the new housing developments was that they encouraged mind-numbing conformity in their residents: to many cultural commentators, the suburbs became symbolic of what they imagined to be the most oppressive aspects of 1950s life — sameness, blandness, mindlessness and materialism. Suburbanites were frequently portrayed as the ultimate conformists, and suburbia as a very real threat to the "individualism" of the American people.[8] For critics of suburbia, one of the biggest problems posed by the housing developments springing up all over the countryside was their threat to the integrity of the small town. Suburbia in its modern incarnation had arrived, and not everyone was entirely happy with the changes it would bring.

One of the most obvious ways in which this unease was articulated was in the pop culture of the decade. Alongside the so-called "Creature-Features" of the 1950s and early 1960s, the body-replacement narrative — in which loved ones, friends and neighbors are invisibly "taken over" or "replaced" by threatening, usually alien forces who seek to overthrow everything that God-fear-

2. *"You Space Bastard! You killed my pines!"* (Murphy)

55

ing, freedom-loving Americans hold dear — became one of the most obvious tropes in American horror and science fiction. The type of narrative, which seeks to make the everyday and the "normal" into something somehow alien and threatening derives its visual and emotive effectiveness from the unnerving contrast between a commonplace, ordinary setting and the quietly aberrant behavior of those who wish to subvert normality.[9] After all, what could be more terrifying than suddenly realizing that those around you have gradually been "replaced" by someone, or *something* else? It is for this reason that "the setting of nearly all such films is small town America, a community which is as familiar, predictable, snug and unprivate as a Norman Rockwell magazine cover for the Saturday Evening Post."[10]

In 1950s films such as *Invaders from Mars* (1953), *It Came from Outer Space* (1953), *The Brain Eaters* (1958), *The Brain from the Planet Arous* (1958) and the suggestively titled *I Married a Monster from Outer Space* (1958) it is always small towns, the very heartland of the American psyche, which get invaded first. Like so many of the other 1950s "invisible invasion" films, Jack Finney's *Invasion of the Body Snatchers* (1955) is set in an idealized small town of Mill Valley (note the similarity to "Hill Valley"), which was renamed Santa Mira in the 1956 film. Notably, the insidious onslaught of the emotionless pod-people is characterized in terms which make clear their similarity with the real-life "newcomers" who were "taking over" small towns all over the country: millions of upwardly mobile young suburbanites. We should note here that the original title mooted for *Back to the Future* was "Spaceman from Pluto."

When Marty first arrives back in 1955, driving the "futuristic" looking DeLorean and clad in a yellow anti-radiation suit, the farmer whose land he has arrived on chases after him with a shot gun, yells, "You Space Bastard! You killed my pines!" In a way, he's right. Marty has just come from the asphalt parking lot of the "Twin Pines" mall — the vast commercial development which will soon replace those very pines, built to fulfill the consumerist desires of suburban families like the McFlys. Most malls were built in suburban locations, and the suburbanization of shopping saw the establishment of hundreds of so-called "strip malls," purposely built to facilitate vehicular rather than pedestrian access. Following the opening of the first post-war shopping center in Raleigh, North Carolina, in 1949, succeeding years saw rapid changes: by 1955, there were already 1,000 malls in the country, and by 1956, 1,600, with 2,500 more planned.[11] The opening of the first enclosed mall in 1956 — temperature controlled and designed to be comfortable and exciting — raised the stakes even higher, for "the large scale and well-provisioned shopping centre was to become an important retail feature of post war American suburbia."[12] That Marty should begin his journey from 1985 to 1955 in the parking lot of a mall (complete with huge JC Penney sign lit up in the background) is, I would suggest, no coincidence. It is also interesting that in this same scene, suburbanite and space invader should be considered one and the same, for in *Invasion of the Body Snatchers*, the connection between the two is made obvious in a manner which can also help inform our reading of *Future*.

There is a scene about half way in to Finney's novel when Miles Bennell, the heroic protagonist and his friends (who have also realized that alien invaders have somehow "taken over" their community) silently wander around the Mill Valley's eerily deserted streets, on which even the houses look "withdrawn, resentful and evil," and an indescribable feeling of wrongness fills the air. Businesses are boarded up, windows are dirty, and the little restaurant offers only three entrees, when "for years they'd always had six or eight." The following exchange then takes place: "'Miles, when did all this *happen?*' Becky gestured to indicate the length of the semi-deserted street behind and ahead of us. 'A little at a time,' I said, and shrugged. 'We're just realizing it now; the town's dying.'"[13]

Body snatching alien replicants aside, the decaying, run down portrait of small town America presented here has a great deal in common with that presented to the audience at the beginning of the first film. Nineteen eighties Hill Valley, if not quite dying, is hardly in a healthy state: stark contrast indeed to the relentlessly idealized vision of the town seen by Marty when he goes back to 1955. Fifties Hill Valley is as stereotypically nostalgic as the similarly inauthentic setting of *Time Out of Joint*. As "Mr. Sandman" plays on the soundtrack, Marty views with awe the wholesome scene before him: the adult movie theatre has become a classy cinema playing *Cattle Queen of Montana* starring Ronald Reagan; the streets are bright, clean and filled with thriving small businesses, smartly uniformed attendants stand to attention outside the Texaco station, and the clock tower, yet to be struck by lightning, still works. Even Doc Brown's circumstances are a decided improvement on those seen in 1985: instead of living in a ramshackle lab, he inhabits a swanky family mansion just outside of town. Hill Valley High School is similarly spick and span. It is telling that even though Marty finds that his family's fiscal circumstances have, due to his actions, greatly improved, the first indication that he has successfully returned to the 1980s is his encounter with a homeless man: poverty, it seems, is very much the preserve of the present.

In *BTTF2*, which picks up where the first film stopped (as Doc Brown returns from 2015 to tell Marty and Jennifer that they must do something about their kids) the suburban setting remains important. The lack of professional and fiscal success experienced by the couple in the future is once more brought home to the audience by showing us the run down surroundings in which the protagonists live. As a result of Marty's lifelong inability to back down from a dare, his dreams of musical success have been dashed and he, Jennifer and their dysfunctional children will live in Hilldale, of which it is remarked by the police in 2015 that "they oughta tear this place down." Though Marty succeeds in preventing his future son from becoming a juvenile delinquent (an act which will destroy the family), yet again, his meddling with the timeline has had problematic results. He is unable to resist the temptation to bring back to 1985 a sports almanac listing the result of every major event from 1950 to 2000—but when the book falls into the hands of an aged Biff Tannen, who secretly uses the DeLorean to return to 1955 and give it to his younger self, the fate of both the McFly clan and of Hill Valley itself is decisively and negatively altered.

In fact, Hill Valley has become a city, the seedy, dangerous and trashy personal fiefdom of the immensely rich Biff Tannen, who has become "America's greatest folk hero" thanks to his unprecedented gambling success. The City of Hill Valley comes complete with all the problems associated with the 1980s inner city — crime, organized gambling, biker gangs, drive-by shootings, the high school destroyed in an arson attack — as well a toxic waste plant and a nuclear power plant. In a scene which echoes that in the first film when he comes to home find that the Lyon Estates hasn't even been built yet, Marty returns home to 1985 only to find the streets surrounding the suburb vandalized, a cop car crashed nearby, chalk outlines all over the pavements, and, most suggestively of all, a black family living in his family home. "This has gotta be the wrong year!" he exclaims, as he runs away from the shot-gun wielding father of the house. Because of Marty's momentary weakness of character earlier in the film, the inner city has come to Hill Valley, and his own family has been torn apart as well. Tannen is now his stepfather, George McFly has been murdered, and his Mom is an alcoholic floozy who comes complete with gold chains, a boob job and bad perm. It's understandable then that upon discovering the devastating extent of these changes, Marty cries, "It's like we're in hell or something." Having inadvertently created a utopian version of the present at the end of the first film, by the middle of *BTTF2*, Marty has in turn caused the creation of that utopia's seedy, trashy, and dangerous dystopian flipside.

As in the original, the problems and the positive possibilities of the present are inextricably linked to the year 1955, and Marty must yet again go there in order to sort out the mess he has inadvertently created. It is all, I would argue, further proof of the fact that in this inherently conservative 1980s cultural artifact, the 1950s are seen as someplace to be *returned to* rather than learned from. As Arlene Skolnick has observed of that decade: "President Reagan came to power promising to reinvent the America of the 1950s, with its breadwinner/housewife family, stable economy, and post-war consensus.

But ... what appeared to be great changes in family life in the 1970s and 1980s was actually the resumption of long-term trends that had been interrupted during the deviant 1950s — so the attempt to resuscitate that strange decade was doomed to fail." Similarly, I am of the opinion that Zemeckis's bland, conservative and predictably nostalgic envisioning of the American past throughout the *BTTF* trilogy ultimately renders the films rather less interesting than many of the other family-orientated fantasy blockbusters of the 1980s, several of which — including *Gremlins*, *E.T.*, and *Ghost Busters*— have a genuinely anarchic streak which means they stand up to repeat viewing much better.

In the third film, shot back-to-back with the second, the McFly family fortunes are again inextricably linked to those of the entire town. The year 1955 once more serves as a crucial point of departure for the series: this time, it is the point from which Marty embarks upon his journey back to 1885, when the town of Hill Valley was originally founded, to try and save Doc Brown from death at the hands of the vicious gunslinger "Mad Dog" Tannen. As Marty, with the aid of Doc Brown's younger, 1955 self, prepares for his journey into the town's frontier past, he comes face to face with a very 1950s idea of what the Old West was actually like. Significantly, the mid–1950s saw American culture in the grip of a western-craze. As Karal Ann Marling has noted in *As Seen on TV: The Visual Culture of Everyday Life in the 1950s*, the 1954-55 TV season saw *Davy Crockett* mania at its height, and one of Disney's most popular attractions was the simulated Western experience of "Frontierland." Marling makes clear the connection between this interest in the nation's "heroic" frontier past and the increasingly suburbanized present:

> Like Tomorrowland, Frontierland resonated to powerful themes in the suburban imagination. The ranch house, the knotty-pine den, the outdoor barbecue, the search for an acre of crabgrass beyond the boundaries of urban civilization: these facts of 1950s American life help to explain why the Western Genre accounted for more than a quarter of the movies produced in Hollywood and why the cowboy film of the period was so often domestic in flavor, with the tragic hero — Alan Ladd's *Shane* (1953), John Wayne as Ethan in *The Searchers* (1956) — longing for the stability of home and hearth. Because the footage was cheap and available, television developed a voracious appetite for old Westerns in its early years, but soon demanded more, made to order for the new medium. Disney's *Davy Crockett* episodes — the first one-hour, prime-time Westerns on network television — garnered the highest ratings of the decade (and produced a bonanza of product spin-offs) by validating suburban mobility in the person of the restless frontiersman who waxes nostalgic about home and family as he dies in the wilds of Texas.[14]

Furthermore, the rhetoric which aimed to encourage families to leave the inner cities and build new lives for themselves elsewhere frequently described budding suburbanites as "pioneers" and "settlers," in an effort to link the vast demographic shift currently taking place to the nation's more obviously heroic (and imperialist) past. Harry S Truman even translated the Cold War's national security crisis into the language of pioneer mythology.[15] He compared the situation Americans found themselves in to the days when settlements along the frontier came under attack by hostile Indian tribes (the Soviet's obviously, were the Indians in this instance). The pioneers, according to Truman, responded by forming communities in which every member did their utmost to combat the common danger — the fate of the community therefore depended upon the personal responsibility of each of its members. During the 1950s, then, the link between suburbia and the frontier past was a highly resonant one, exploited by the culture industry, advertisers, and even the government itself.

It is no wonder then that at the beginning of *BTTF3*, Marty accidentally becomes immersed in a very mid–1950s idea of what the Wild West was like. The "period authentic" clothing picked out for him by Doc Brown consists of a lurid pastel pink and blue cow-boy outfit which (in a nice touch) comes complete with an atom motif on the fringed collar — thus neatly linking the *actual* frontier with the scientific frontier which was being expanded at that time. Despite the fact that in the previous two films, Hill Valley has been without a desert, in this installment one suddenly appears on the outskirts of town. Furthermore, it contains a number of pseudo Western adornments, such as the "Pocahontas Snack bar," and an "Indian Village" with concrete tepees.

In order to go back in time to 1885, Marty must drive the DeLorean at top speed towards a drive-in movie screen which is, naturally, showing a Western. As he successfully makes the transition to the past, the Indians which had been galloping towards him on the movie screen are suddenly replaced by real ones, which are then — of course — routed by the cavalry (this victory of colonizer over colonized marks the last point at which the existence of Native Americans is even acknowledged during the narrative). The implication is that the *fake* West had just been replaced by the *real* West. But of course, the vision of frontier life presented to us in *BTTF3* is just as predictable and inauthentic as that found in 1955: the only difference is that this is a thoroughly *1980s* version of the past instead. All that would be somewhat forgivable if the story itself was any good, but unfortunately, this is, as most critics would agree, the weakest of the three films, with a dull and fairly perfunctory narrative which revolves around Marty's attempts to save Doc Brown's life (yet again), defeat Mad Dog Tannen, and find a way back home without the use of gasoline, which has yet to be invented.

However, one element of the film which is of some interest in relation to this article is it's portrait of Hill Valley as a burgeoning town, just beginning to establish itself because of the arrival of the railroad. When Marty arrives, he finds it a place very much under construction, with half erected stores and homes everywhere, and the all-important clock tower still uncompleted. The newness of the town presents a significant counterpart to the newness of the McFly family themselves: Marty soon meets his immigrant Irish ancestor, Seamus McFly (played by Fox), who, along with his wife Maggie — played by Lea Thompson, who had previously portrayed Marty's mother in the earlier films — have just arrived in the United States.

The link between the McFly clan's fate and that of Hill Valley is decisively cemented when Marty's journeys through time finally end as he returns to 1985 once more, this time for good (the DeLorean has been destroyed by a train upon re-entry, which is just as well). As in the first film, a billboard again plays an important role here in establishing the suburban connection. This time, it advertises "Hilldale," future site of "Hill Valley's newest homes" — the place where Jennifer and Marty will live happy ever after, now that Marty has finally straightened out the past (and the future).

Ultimately then, it is my view that the *Back to the Future* films stand as a deeply conservative, conformist and inherently right-wing vision of American history (past, future, and present) of which Alex P. Keaton, the aspiring Republican neophyte played by Fox in *Family Ties*, would surely have approved. "Anyone can make their future what they want it to be" Doc Brown advises Marty (and, by extension of course, us) at the conclusion of *BTTF3*. It is a supposedly heartening proclamation which also carries with it the inherently problematic suggestion that if life doesn't quite turn out as we would like, we have no one to blame but ourselves: social, economic and familial disadvantages are but minor inconveniences to be overcome with a spot of old-fashioned derring-do and self-confidence. After all, it is only when the young, "hip" and adventurous Marty — played of course by Fox, the oldest teenager in the business — accidentally winds up meddling with the past in the first film that the McFly family's decidedly disappointing present is dramatically improved. Indeed, the McFly family have been altered to the extent that the argument could be made that it ultimately ends up as a utopian parallel universe in which true happiness equals a bland girlfriend whose ambitions (as revealed in the sequel) go no further than marriage and motherhood, country-club attending parents, yuppie siblings and, of course, a gleaming Toyota truck standing in the driveway.

Furthermore, it is made clear that during the course of his adventures through time, Marty has finally gained the maturity necessary to make him a successful suburban husband and father. At the very end of the last film, he refuses to participate in a drag race which would have resulted in a crash that would have blighted his future and that of his own future family. True manhood has therefore been achieved by repeated tests of courage, cunning and physical prowess (a model of masculinity which owes much to the Western), but just as important in the final analysis is Marty's climactic willingness to smooth away any rough edges in his character so that he can become an ideal suburbanite. There is no suggestion at all that either Marty or Jennifer will decide *not* to embark upon the road which leads them to a life of conventional domesticity in Hilldale: their future, it seems, has been decisively written, which, given the fact that they're both only seventeen, is rather troubling. It is fitting then that the DeLorean should finally be destroyed on what is literally a one-way track because for Marty McFly, as for the town of Hill Valley itself, all roads eventually go only one way: towards suburbia.

Notes

1. Stephen King, *Danse Macabre*, Warner, 1981, p. 23.
2. Frederic Jameson, "Nostalgia for the Present" (in) *Postmodernism, or, The Cultural Logic of Late Capitalism* (London: Verso, 1991), p. 279.
3. *Ibid.*, p. 282.
4. *Ibid.*, pp. 282–283.
5. William Chafe, *The Unfinished Journey: America Since World War Two* (New York: Oxford University Press, 1999) p. 111.
6. James Patterson, *Grand Expectations: The United States, 1945–1974* (New York: Oxford University Press, 1996), p. 331.
7. Adam Rome, *The Bulldozer in the Countryside: Suburban Sprawl and the Rise of American Environmentalism* (Cambridge University Press, 2001), p. 16.
8. Patterson, pp. 336–338.

9. Vivien Sobchack, *Screening Space: The American Science Fiction Film* (New Brunswick, NJ: Rutgers University Press, 1997), p. 120.
10. *Ibid.*, p. 121.
11. Patterson, p. 334.
12. Eric Avila, *Popular Culture in the Age of White Flight* (Berkeley: University of California Press, 2004), p. 31.
13. Jack Finney, *Invasion of the Bodysnatchers* (London: Sphere, 1956, 1978), p. 97.
14. Karal Ann Marling, *As Seen on TV: The Visual Culture of Everyday Life in the 1950s* (Cambridge, MA: Harvard University Press, 1996), p. 124.
15. Guy Oakes, *The Imaginary War: American Civil Defense and Cold War Culture* (New York: Oxford University Press, 1996), p. 130.

Works Cited

Avila, Eric. *Popular Culture in the Age of White Flight*. Berkeley: University of California Press, 2004.

Chafe, William. *The Unfinished Journey: America Since World War Two*. New York: Oxford University Press, 1999.

Finney, Jack. *Invasion of the Bodysnatchers*. London: Sphere, 1956.

Jameson, Frederic. "Nostalgia for the Present" in *Postmodernism, or, The Cultural Logic of Late Capitalism*. London: Verso, 1991. pp. 279–296.

King, Stephen. *Danse Macabre*. Warner, 1981.

Marling, Karal Ann. *As Seen on TV: The Visual Culture of Everyday Life in the 1950s*. Cambridge, MA: Harvard University Press, 1996.

Oakes, Guy. *The Imaginary War: American Civil Defense and Cold War Culture*. New York: Oxford University Press, 1996.

Patterson, James. *Grand Expectations: The United States, 1945–1974*. New York: Oxford University Press, 1996.

Rome, Adam. *The Bulldozer in the Countryside: Suburban Sprawl and the Rise of American Environmentalism*. Cambridge: Cambridge University Press, 2001.

Sobchack, Vivien. *Screening Space: The American Science Fiction Film*. New Brunswick, NJ: Rutgers University Press, 1997.

3. "Don't you think it's about time?": *Back to the Future* in Black and White

STEPHEN MATTERSON

On the face of it, the choice of 1955 as the year to which Marty McFly travels from 1985 is an obvious and sensible one, in artistic, demographic and financial, terms. For the fiction to work, the gap of thirty years is essential so that Marty can be roughly the same age as his (future) parents in 1955, given the usual rule-of-thumb reckoning that generations are separated by a period of thirty-three years. In commercial terms, the setting of 1955 potentially allows the film to appeal simultaneously (though within different modes of reception) to a middle-aged and a teenaged audience. As Doc Brown says as he plans his ride into the future, 30 is "a nice round number." However, these sensible reasons for choosing 1955 are not the ones given by Robert Zemeckis and Bob Gale in their commentary for the 2002 DVD release of the trilogy. While acknowledging the story's need for the thirty-year gap, they state firmly that their screenplay, which they began work on in 1980, always had 1955 as the destination year. This was because it was the year in which rock and roll music effectively began, and one of the screenplay's key ideas was that Marty brought rock and roll to the 1950s. (Ironically, in the scramble to edit the film for release on the July 4 holiday weekend, Zemeckis and Gale decided to delete the "Johnny B. Goode" scene because it seemed to stall the plot at a crucial point; it was kept in only after favorable audience response at the preview screening.) Nineteen fifty-five is thus represented as the year of innocence, the year before the cultural and historical transformations (such as rock and roll) that were completely to alter the cultural landscape of the United States. To the inhabitants of *Back to the Future*'s 1955, such radical change is as scarcely imaginable as space-travel, visitors from the (then) planet Pluto, and as incomprehensible as Marty's futuristic guitar performance is to the students at Hill

Valley High. Indeed, it is worth remembering that in 1955 space travel was imagined though not yet achieved; the pioneering launch of Sputnik lying two years into the future, in 1957.

But while the film needs to give its audience a 1950s world of stability and comparative innocence, it is itself far from innocent in both the choice of that year and the choice of the 1950s. Historically and culturally, 1955 was a year which initiated radical transformations in the United States, a year that overturns and profoundly challenges the recurring representation of the 1950s as a decade of stability and changes. To juxtapose *Back to the Future*'s 1955 landscape with Allen Ginsberg's is to register both the film's carefully circumscribed terms of representation and the shock that his "Howl" administered to the decade. "Howl" famously begins:

> I saw the best minds of my generation destroyed by madness, starving hysterical naked, dragging themselves through the negro streets at dawn looking for an angry fix, angelheaded hipsters burning for the ancient heavenly connection to the starry dynamo in the machinery of night....[1]

The mid-decade appearance of "Howl" is appropriate for the poem as a pivotal moment of the decade, both in terms of the "poetry renaissance" and in its suddenly making more widely available an increasingly vibrant and increasingly accessible sub-culture. In the 1975 liner notes that he wrote for Bob Dylan's album *Desire*, Ginsberg parenthetically remarks that decades are defined by the year at their center: "every generation-decade flowers in the middle, Poetry Renaissance 1955, Peace Vietnam Berkeley 1965."[2] While he is reflecting in this context on the 1970s, Ginsberg probably also had in mind Dylan's revolutionary partly electric 1965 album *Bringing It All Back Home*. But his comment is particularly illuminating for the 1950s. There is a strong case to be made for 1955 as a defining year for the 1950s in the United States; a year which saw an extraordinary cluster of landmark social, political, literary and musical events, events that would transform the U.S. for decades— to the extent that it is tempting to agree with the hypothesis that the 1960s began in 1955.

In literary terms alone, the year saw a fresh beginning in styles of writing, in new kinds of subjects in writing, and a move away from the so-called academic styles of the 1940s and early 1950s—as Lou Reed puts it in his comic/acerbic song "Sweet Jane" about poets learning rules of verse and ladies rolling their eyes. In poetry this shift was seen most obviously with the first performance of "Howl," with the beginning of the Beat movement, with a radical break from page-based politically aloof writing to performance and political activism. It is also evident in Robert Lowell's starting to write the personal and relatively informal poems that he would collect in 1959 as *Life Studies*, the most influential American poetry book of the second half of the twentieth century. The mid–1950s saw the waning influence of the generation of modernist writers that had dominated the literary scene since the 1920s, as a younger generation sought new and energized forms of continuity or discontinuity from the generation that had included the giants Ezra Pound, T.S. Eliot, Wallace Stevens, William Faulkner and Ernest Hemingway. By coincidence, 1955 saw the centenary of the first publication of Walt Whitman's *Leaves of Grass*, and it is as if the centenary of the defining book of American poetry and of what Whitman stood for as a poet meant a radical reappraisal of his spirit and a renaissance of the energies that he brought to poetry—certainly Ginsberg, with his powerful fusion of poetic energy and social activism, consciously cast himself as a descendant of Whitman. In the meantime, Jack Kerouac criss-crossed the disappearing dark roads of the continent and made 1957's *On the Road* as a coalescing of the experience.

Most importantly in terms of the social and political history of the United States, 1955 is the year in which all kinds of racial segregation start to break down or to be challenged, and when the surge of revulsion at the appalling inequalities of American society will be realized in the Civil Rights Movement and will culminate in the 1964 Civil Rights Act. The year 1954 had seen the Brown v. Board of Education Supreme Court decision which declared segregated education unlawful, and while the process of desegregation was painful, violent and controversial, it became for the most part a significant and realizable aspiration for African Americans and gave a specific focus to the developing Civil Rights Movement. It also made 1955 into a year of violence and confrontation, as African Americans refused to tolerate being cast in the role of the underclass. Nineteen fifty-five begins with the African American opera singer Marian Anderson finally being permitted to perform at the Metropolitan Opera. Autumn sees the stand-off in Little Rock, Arkansas, between federal troops and an unyielding state governor's hostility to desegregation. The year ends with Rosa Parks strategically refusing to give up her seat on a segregated Alabama bus, thereby precipitating the co-ordinated Civil Rights movement. The same year also witnessed the atrocious racial murder of 14-year-old Emmet Till in Mississippi and consequent outrage over the notorious acquittal of the (later) self-confessed killers.

The 1950s are the decade in which relations between black and white undergo seismic transformation, primarily because of protest strategies of occupying superficially or supposedly innocent or neutral spaces such as public transport or Woolworth's lunch counter in order to expose the fact that they are embedded in racial inequalities and social injustice. The counter or the public space is made to lose the appearance of innocence and is changed into an arena of inequality and competing forces. When one invokes the historical facts of what is actually an extraordinarily turbulent decade, it is embarrassingly easy to note and expose the falseness that drives the consistent representation of the 1950s as a decade of innocence. But is also to some extent a facile exercise, and it is more interesting to explore how such modes of nostalgia for the decade rely upon a willed restoration of the supposedly neutral or apparently innocent. Such representations strategically require that the lunch-counter and public transport attain once more the apparent innocence that was simply untenable after 1955. It is also apparent that in choosing 1955 for *Back to the Future*, Zemeckis and Gale are very consciously avoiding the post–1955 landscape. It is not just that, in Philip Larkin's phrase, there was "Never such innocence again" but that this innocence is a kind of shared illusion essential for the sustainability of the film's vision.[3] Certainly, providing a nostalgic 1980s take on the 1950s is a large reason for the film's popularity, and in this regard it can be seen as part of a 1980s film preoccupation, evident also in Francis Ford Coppola's highly successful 1986 film *Peggy Sue Got Married*, set in 1960.

The lunch-counter (Lou's Café) in each of the three *Back to the Future* films is a curious space in which each decade is being located in terms of its artifacts, technology, prices and dietary customs. While the café is repeatedly the scene of violence and confrontation, it is notably not racialized or politicized violence, but aggression (typically between the various incarnations of McFly and Biff) that attempts to lose the connotation of violence, that allows confrontation to be played out in predictable, ritualized and, ultimately, safe ways. That is, it becomes a location that has no potential for violence meaningful beyond itself, beyond the individual act. In this respect, it is not that *Back to the Future* erases aspects of the racially charged and transformative 1950s, but that it relocates conflict so that it may be rendered safe, and thereby, part of its commercial package. African Americans are not quite absent in *Back to the Future*, but their presence is, like the violence, channeled into stereotypical or readily recognizable roles — the café's gullible dancing black staff member Goldie, and Foley, the supportive police officer in *Back to the Future II*. Most notoriously, the African American is a metonym for suburban degeneration when the Lyon Estates McFly home is occupied by a black family in the dystopian world of 1985A in *Future II*. These shorthand appearances are necessary for sustaining the language of the film but they also ensure that there is no discomfort arising either from total invisibility, or from any challenge to clearly assigned circumscribed roles. The film cannot afford to have its audience reflect on the segregated high school, but equally it cannot afford to depart radically from historical circumstance, so it must communicate through a series of signifiers that suggest meaning but which resist plenitude.

It would be wrong to be critical or dismissive of *Back to the Future* because of its racial landscape, because this landscape is after all one of the essential components of its entire rationale as comic entertainment. It is not intended to be a worthy, weighty film about race relations in 1950s California, however much it may actually rely upon a series of stereotypes. But what is interesting is while African Americans are visible only in predictable ways, they are in another sense a continual presence. Further, they are present in a way that relates interestingly to a key aspect of 1950s culture. We all know that in terms of American popular culture it is in music that the revolutionary aspect of 1955 is most clearly evident. The year sees the release of "Rock Around the Clock," of Elvis Presley's first recordings (most notably "Hound Dog") and Chuck Berry composing "Johnny B. Goode." It is the year in which the American teenager is finally fully invented, and James Dean is killed on the road. But what the music tells us most clearly is that for the first time, the segregation between different kinds of music is crumbing as white artists and musicians begin to imitate, utilize and make available what was seen to be exclusively black music. The disappearance of segregated music and the race records obviously has profound implications for popular culture and for the music industry. But in some respects it was part of a much larger revolution. For the first time in American history, the black becomes an object of envy for whites, and whites continually express the feeling that something lost or repressed by white culture is cultivated and available from black culture. In "Howl" it is to the "negro streets" that the "best minds" of Ginsberg's generation must go for their "angry fix" and it is African American jazz to which his "angelheaded hipsters" are listening as they sit up smoking. In white literature, a new and revolutionary apprehension of black identity develops, even in otherwise radically different styles of writing.

> At lilac evening I walked with every muscle aching among the lights of 27th and Welton in the Denver colored section, wishing I were a Negro, feeling that the best the white world had offered was not enough ecstasy for me, not enough life, joy, kicks, darkness, music, not enough night ... I wished I were a Denver Mexican, or even a poor overworked Jap, anything but what I was so drearily, a "white man" disillusioned.[4]

Pausing in Denver on one of his monumental journeys (on a road system that will itself be outmoded before his book is published), Jack Kerouac sees not the whiteness of the streets but their seductive darkness; the streets are lovely, dark and deep. He seeks out the colored section, feeling that it is there that life is truly lived — his own version of Ginsberg's negro streets. The passage from *On the Road* concisely summarizes the set of attitudes that eventually define the meaning of the experience it records — the need to escape what Lowell called the "tranquillized fifties," the dulling conformity of white middle-class America, to trash the gray flannel suit and put on the zoot rigout of the hipster. In his essay "The White Race and Its Heroes" Eldridge Cleaver said this passage from *On the Road* marked a cultural turning point for white America, a moment at which it is acknowledged that white culture has failed, is dying because it lacks something that can only be provided by contact with the other, a moment at which black is "life, joy, kicks, darkness, music" and white is melancholy, depression, harsh light and silence: "There is in America today a generation of white youth that is truly worthy of a black man's respect, and this is a rare event in the foul annals of American history."[5]

It is easy to recognize that "wishing I were a negro" is on one level an abominable statement. It requires the romanticizing of pain, deprivation, poverty and an erasure of a troubled and continuing history of oppression. It turns the black into a spectacle, associating "negro" with stereotyped forms of behavior and attitude. It turns the black once more into a body rather than a mind. Kerouac's is an "artificial nigger," to borrow the title of Flannery O'Connor's celebrated short story, coincidentally published in 1955. Calling the sentiment abhorrent is so easy that to do so may be to overlook the most obvious point, which is that the passage is primarily concerned with whiteness, not with blackness. James Baldwin described this passage from *On the Road* as "absolute nonsense, of course, objectively considered, and offensive nonsense at that." But he went on to point out that "yet there is real pain in it, and real loss."[6] Kerouac is describing whiteness, and as Herman Melville put it, white is here not a color but the absence of color, here the absence of energy, freedom, vitality, belonging. White America is failing in some fundamental way — a way that has condemned the best minds of this generation to the margin, that offers nothing in the way of a vital and vibrant culture. It is not even as though what Kerouac articulates in this passage has changed much. Eminem or white rap artists or the white audiences for hip-hop may not exactly want to be black, but they need the performance that black identity seems to require and they participate in what Hazel Carby has explored as the symbolic construction of blackness. As Eldridge Cleaver says; this is turning point for *white* America, and may have very little to do with the actuality of the black except as metaphor or constructed alterity.

The force of Kerouac's reflection partly comes from its being far from unique in 1950s America; it articulates a longing repeated elsewhere by very different minds. The Beat representation of black culture, the negro streets, depends exactly on the same paradigm. It is there in the intense admiration for African American jazz. The longing is also there in John Berryman's use of blackface minstrelsy in *The Dream Songs* at the points where his malleable persona Henry finds his capacity for self-articulation most in crisis. It is also there most painfully, and expressed most bluntly, in "White Negro," a text Norman Mailer eventually published in 1957.

Mailer's essay is an extraordinary conflux of the middle of the decade. Much more than the primitivism of the 1920s warmed-over, it is a space where pop existentialism meets the angst and repressions of a white Jewish male American, a moment when the possibilities of self-realization seem to depend on the capacity to define and listen to another, when an individual's need for violence as reality and truth is expressed not through violence but through its imagined and urgent reality. "White Negro" is an intense exploration of the need for the negro in the life and culture of white America, a need for black in the white psyche. Mailer equates the hipster's apparent freedom from social conventions with an acceptance of the existential condition of alienation from history. Angel-headed or not, the hipster is acting out the consequences of the need to make yourself, construct an identity, to make something out of nothing. For the hipster identity is fluid, not a social given and it requires the open expression of violence and sexuality, a fundamental centering of *body* in one's existence. The black always was the hipster. For the black to be without a defining sense of personal and cultural history is not deprivation but the true human condition. Blacks have had to live with this for over a hundred years, Mailer asserts, and it is about time whites realized that they can learn something from this. While Mailer articulates these ideas in a robust form that inevitably creates controversy, the core actuality of those ideas was certainly expressed by others. It recurs most typically in the work of Richard Wright, and it is straightforward enough to make the connection that Wright did between African American identity and the existential condition. Baldwin memorably articulated this connection:

> to become a Negro man ... one had to make oneself up as one went along.... The world had prepared no place for you, and if the world had its way, no place would ever exist.[7]

For Mailer this is a liberating condition. Whites have learned to cover up, to disguise this fact, just as whites have learned through culture to cover up, to disguise or deflect an elemental nature. Consistent with the primitivist basis of the essay, Mailer finds in black music — jazz, specifically — something that touches the elemental, something that blacks can access but whites, if they hear it at all, find disturbing.

> Knowing in the cells of his existence that life was war, nothing but war, the Negro ... could rarely afford the sophisticated inhibitions of civilization, and so he kept for his survival the art of the primitive, he lived in the enormous present, he subsisted for his Saturday night kicks, relinquishing the pleasures of the mind for the more obligatory pleasures of the body, and in his music he gave voice to the character and quality of his existence, to his rage and the infinite variations of joy, lust, languor, growl, cramp, pinch, scream and despair of his orgasm.... [Jazz] spoke across a nation, it had the communication of art even where it was watered, per-

3. "Don't you think it's about time?" (Matterson)

69

verted, corrupted, and almost killed, it spoke in no matter what laundered popular way of instantaneous existential states to which some whites could respond.[8]

As with Kerouac, this is superficially an abhorrent and derisory representation of the black. As Baldwin commented, the black is being "penalized for the guilty imagination of the white people who invest him with their hates and longings."[9] And yet, it is here that there is a crucial intersection between what could be dismissed as a personal pathology and a cultural fact. The personal pathology is undoubtedly there. The cultural fact is that 1955 sees the end of the race record business and the entrance of black music into white consciousness, even where, as Mailer suggests, whites are unable to access the meaning of the experience. For all of his revulsion at Mailer's essay, in "The Fire Next Time" Baldwin expressed something very similar regarding white lack and black presence: "White people cannot, in the generality, be taken as models of how to live. Rather, the white man is himself in sore need of new standards, which will release him from his confusion and place him once again in fruitful communion with the depths of his own being."[10]

Having enthusiastically recorded the work of black rhythm and blues artists since 1950, Sam Phillips of Sun records is famously quoted as saying "If I could find a white man who had the Negro sound and feel, I could make a million dollars."[11] We know now that a million dollars is a ludicrous fraction of what was made with such a sound. It was made with Elvis Presley, with dozens of white musicians — American and British — who took the Delta Blues as their starting point, and developed that sound into rock, jazz, folk. In Alice Walker's short story "Nineteen-fifty-five" — a story that, typical of Walker's earlier work which brilliantly fuses fiction and essay — Traynor and his white record producers have taken a performance by Gracie Mae "Little Mama" Still, in much the same way that Elvis Presley took the performance of "Hound Dog" from Willie Mae "Big Mama" Thornton. While bringing him unimaginable wealth and fame, Walker represents Traynor is someone haunted by his inability to understand the song in the way that Gracie Mae does; "I've sung it and sung it, and I'm making forty thousand dollars a day offa it, and you know what, I don't have the faintest notion what that song means." He returns repeatedly to question her as his vast wealth increasingly obscures rather than clarifies the song for him; to echo Baldwin's terms, Traynor needs "release" from his "confusion" in order to be "in fruitful communion with the depths of his own being." Walker expresses the inability of both Traynor and his white audience fully to understand what they hear or to articulate what they do hear, even though the performance thrills and engages them in a way that no other music does. When the bloated Traynor dies in 1977 Gracie Mae reflects on the reaction of his distressed white fans:

One of the children called from Detroit. Them dumb fans of his is on a crying rampage, she said. [Sic] You just ought to turn on the TV. But I didn't want to see 'em. They was crying and crying and didn't even know what they was crying for. One day this is going to be a pitiful country, I thought.[12]

Pitiful in that as with Kerouac and Ginsberg, whites have (perhaps tacitly) acknowledged their lack, and have satisfied it by consuming a commodified alterity that they can now no longer recognize as a borrowing or an imitation.

When she calls her story "Nineteen-fifty-five" Walker, like Ginsberg, suggests that this year as crucial for defining the decade and like Zemeckis and Gale, she locates it as both the start and the end. It is here that the implication of the original pitch for *Back to the Future* becomes intricately entangled with the complex interactions between so-called black and white music since that year. The proposal that Chuck Berry's music was sent back from the future by Marty eventually turns into a lighthearted aside in the completed film, when we see Marvin Berry's band The Starlighters at the Enchantment Under the Sea dance struggling to keep up with Marty's metallic rendition of "Johnny B. Goode," and a frantic Marvin on the telephone to his cousin Chuck. Comic though it is, the scene touches on a debate that would resonate, often with intense anger, during the 1960s, over the perception that white musicians effectively stole black music, which they did not fully understand. This debate has become so complex that even Chuck Berry has changed sides on it several times. At some points Berry refused to acknowledge or play with The Rolling Stones, but also recognizing that the popularity of white musicians enhanced his own recognition and availability, and working often with those white musicians — for instance, triumphantly performing "Oh Carol" with Keith Richards and "Johnny B. Goode" with Bruce Springsteen (in his early twenties Springsteen's band was a support act for Jerry Lee Lewis and Chuck Berry).

Lighthearted though it is, the Enchantment Under the Sea scene raises and yet also tellingly sidesteps issues that would be crucial in the years after 1955. In "Slouching Towards Bethlehem" one of the key texts that articulate the 1960s, Joan Didion gives an account of an awareness-raising exercise performed by the Mime Troupers in the Haight-Ashbury area in the summer of 1967. The group, consisting entirely of whites, wearing make-up in blackface and aggressively taunt the black members of the crowd with a series of slogans. One of these slogans is "Who Stole Chuck Berry's Music?" This provokes a brief discussion:

"Just beginning to get annoyed, are you?" one of the Mime Troupers says. "Don't you think it's about time?" "Nobody *stole* Chuck Berry's music, man," says another Negro who has been studying the signs. "Chuck Berry's music belongs to *every-body*." "Yeh?" a girl in blackface says. "Everybody *who*?" "Why," he says, confused. "Everybody. In America." "In *America*," the blackface girl shrieks. "Listen to him talk about *America*."[13]

The phrase "Don't you think it's about time?" of course has a unique resonance in considering these issues as they surface in *Back to the Future*. In the provocative encounter that Didion records, it means it is about time for anger, for awareness of appalling injustice, for racial consciousness. In the film, being "about time" is both its comic *raison d'être* and an accidental comment on what the film suppresses. In returning us to a reassuring 1955 and determinedly ignoring not only the 1960s but the actuality of the 1950s, the film is far from innocent. Its aspirational innocence relies partly on a suppression of issues such as those raised by the slogan "Who Stole Chuck Berry's Music?" and partly through the sly comic reference to them.

Politically conservative versions of the 1960s that emerged in the late 1980s and mid 1990s represented it as a deeply divisive, conflicting decade in which the seeds of later social malaise were sown. Tellingly, and for some, controversially, Zemeckis himself was to underscore this perception and provide a usable and powerful articulation of it for political purposes with his 1994 film *Forrest Gump*. This extraordinarily popular film has deeply divided critics, and many have seen it as a deeply political film which supports conservative re-visioning of U.S. history. In a trenchant essay Jennifer Hyland Wang explored the use that was made of *Forrest Gump* in the 1994 congressional elections, and focused particularly on the changes made to Winston Groom's 1986 novel to accommodate such politicization. Wang comments:

> Compared with the film's nostalgic view of 1950s ... *Gump* argues consistently for "re-visioning" the 1960s as an era of confusion and conflict. The contrast between these two eras is illuminated most clearly through the bodies of Forrest and his childhood love, Jenny. Sporting a '50s crewcut and crisp gingham shirts throughout the decades traced in the film, Forrest is an eternal representative of the 1950s.... Conversely, Jenny represents the 1960s. As the filmmakers revealed, "in pumping up Jenny's role [from the novel to the film], screenwriter Eric Roth transferred all of Forrest's flaws [in the book] — and most of the excesses Americans committed in the '60s and '70s to her."[14]

Back to the Future performs a similar action not by articulating a revisionist 1960s but by implying this through its silence. As Marty's 1955 grandfather Sam Baines gruffly asks when Marty mentions John F. Kennedy Drive, "Who the hell is John F. Kennedy?" Practicing cultural amnesia is easier if you pretend the 1960s did not happen.

Notes

1. Allen Ginsberg. *Howl.* Harmondsworth: Penguin, 1986, p. 3.

2. Allen Ginsberg. Untitled notes to Bob Dylan, *Desire*, 1975, n. p.

3. Philip Larkin. *Collected Poems*. Victoria and London: The Marvell Press and Faber and Faber, 2003, p. 99.

4. Jack Kerouac. *On the Road*. Harmondsworth: Penguin, 1973, pp. 169–70.

5. Eldridge Cleaver. *Soul on Ice*. New York: Dell, 1970, p. 84.

6. James Baldwin. *The Price of the Ticket: Collected Non-Fiction 1948–1985*. London: Joseph, 1985, p. 298.

7. *Ibid.*

8. Norman Mailer. *Advertisements for Myself*. Cambridge and London: Harvard University Press, 1992, p. 341.

9. Qtd. in *Time*, Friday, May 17, 1963.

http://www.time.com/time/magazine/article/0,9171,830326-2,00.html.

10. Baldwin, *The Price of the Ticket*. p. 375.

11. Elaine Dundy. *Elvis and Gladys*. London: Pimlico, 1995, p. 144.

12. Alice Walker. *The Complete Stories*. London: Phoenix, 2005, p. 147.

13. Joan Didion. *We Tell Ourselves Stories in Order to Live*. New York and London: Alfred A. Knopf, Everyman's Library, 2006, p. 95.

14. Jennifer Hyland Wang. "'A Struggle of Contending Stories': Race, Gender, and Political Memory in *Forrest Gump*." *Cinema Journal* 39:3 (2000): 92–115: 97.

Works Cited

Baldwin, James. *The Price of the Ticket: Collected Non-Fiction 1948–1985*. London: Joseph, 1985.

Cleaver, Eldridge. *Soul on Ice*. New York: Dell, 1970.

Didion, Joan. "Slouching Towards Bethlehem" in Didion, *We Tell Ourselves Stories in Order to Live*. New York and London: Alfred A. Knopf, Everyman's Library, 2006.

Dundy, Elaine. *Elvis and Gladys*. London: Pimlico, 1995.

Ginsberg, Allen. *Howl*. Harmondsworth: Penguin, 1986.

_____. Untitled notes to Bob Dylan, *Desire*, 1975.

Kerouac, Jack. *On the Road*. Harmondsworth: Penguin Books, 1973.

Larkin, Philip. *Collected Poems*. Victoria and London: The Marvell Press and Faber and Faber, 2003.

Mailer, Norman. *Advertisements for Myself*. Cambridge, MA, and London: Harvard University Press, 1992.

Walker, Alice. *The Complete Stories*. London: Phoenix, 2005.

Wang, Jennifer Hyland. "'A Struggle of Contending Stories': Race, Gender, and Political Memory in *Forrest Gump*." *Cinema Journal* 39:3 (2000): 92–115.

4. "There's something very familiar about all this": Generic Play and Performance in the *Back to the Future* Trilogy

LUCY FIFE DONALDSON

Genre is signaled through various strategies employed within the construction of a film's mise-en-scène, a significant portion of which I will argue, is transmitted through performance. The material detail of a performance — incorporating gesture, movement, voice, and surrounding elements such as costume — as well as the way it is presented within a film is key to the invocation, establishment and coherence of any given genre. Attention to the complexity of performance details, particularly in the manner in which they reverberate across texts, demonstrates the intricacy of genre and its inherent mutability.

The *Back to the Future* trilogy represents a specific interest in the flexibility of genre. The films incorporate several different generic elements, including aspects of the fifties teen movie, science fiction, comedy and the western. These different modes playfully intertwine with each other creating a complex world of repetitions, echoes and modulations. To explore this patterning in more detail I will interrogate the contribution of performance to generic play through close analysis of Thomas F. Wilson's performance of Biff/Griff/Buford Tannen in an encounter with Marty McFly (Michael J. Fox) in each film. The moments I will interrogate take place in a fifties diner, a retro 1980s diner and a saloon respectively, each space contributing to the similarities and differences in each repetition. Close attention to Wilson's performance of each related character, which contains both modulations and repetitions used specifically to place each film's central generic theme, demonstrates how embedded the play between genres and their flexibility is within the trilogy. Furthermore, this attention aims to draw out not only the details of his performance, but the way in which we experience them and how our attitudes are shaped.

Generic Worlds

The *Back to the Future* trilogy is centered on the adventures of Marty and Doc Emmett Brown (Christopher Lloyd) as they travel backwards and forwards (from 1985 to 1955, 2015 and 1885) through time. In the first film, Marty's time travel is accidental, a consequence of which means that he is forced to intervene with past events to secure his own future. In the second and third films Marty and Doc actively pursue future and past selves to right future or past paths. The effect of these movements in time is that they inhabit various fictional worlds that are simultaneously familiar and strange (all the films take place in different eras of Hill Valley, Marty's home town), and it is these which are at the root of the films' varied generic modes. Whilst Marty, and Doc to some extent, are the fixed points of the trilogy, other characters are tied to these worlds and thus change from film to film.[1] Thomas F. Wilson embodies a series of characters that operate as the key example of this tendency, all of whom are related to one another and occupy similar roles in each of their worlds, and as such literally echo one another across the trilogy. The first is Biff Tannen, a contemporary of Marty's parents, whom he encounters in 1955, 1985 and 2015.[2] The second is Griff Tannen, Biff's grandson in 2015 (a contemporary of Marty's own son, Marty Jr.). The third is Buford "Mad Dog" Tannen, presumably a distant relation to these two, in 1885. That each permutation of the character exists within each fictional world in significantly similar ways draws continuity between time and space that illustrates the interplay of repetition and modulation that forms the basis of the trilogy.

Despite the potentially schematic connection between time and genre, I would suggest that the films' relationship to genre goes deeper. Each film's generic qualities, be it the teen movie of 1955 (which is fundamentally a romance narrative), the science fiction of 2015 or the western of 1885, are framed in a wider context of science fiction and comedy. Furthermore, within each film, and especially across all three, the aspects of the various genres set in place are interlaced through both visual and narrative details, thus constructing a dense layer of references both within and without the texts. In this way the trilogy reflects the notion of film genres as fluid, rather than rigid. The unraveling of genre as a rigid category is a key concern of Robin Wood who argues that "[o]ne of the greatest obstacles to any fruitful theory of genre has been the tendency to treat the genres as discrete."[3] Wood's writing indicates the extent to which Hollywood's genres are interconnected.[4] Providing a useful way to approach genre in response to its interconnectedness, Douglas Pye observes that "[i]t seems more likely that the outlines of any genre will remain indistinct and impossible to chart and that genre criticism should concern itself with identifying *tendencies* within generic traditions and placing individual works in relation to these."[5] I would like to suggest that the repeated qualities of Wilson's performances significantly embody this complexity, offering us certain tendencies or strategies within the different generic worlds of the films. As a result, attention to his performance is potentially revealing in examination of both the trilogy's relationship to genre, as well as in the wider importance of performance to the inherent fluidity of genre.

Biff Tannen (1955)

The culmination of Marty's confrontations with Biff in his journey to 1955 in the first film takes place on his second visit to the town's diner, which is the meeting place for the local teenagers, including Marty's parents, George (Crispin Glover) and Lorraine (Lea Thompson). The space of the diner represents a common trope of teen movies, from both the studio-era and post–studio Hollywood.[6] Its representation in *Back to the Future*, as with other areas of the town, is particularly focused on an iconographic articulation of small town America of the 1950s, with milkshakes, glass Coca-Cola bottles and advertising placards placed in prominence and popular music of the era played within the diegesis. Even the presence of its African American cleaner underscores the period's differences from 1985 (in which the same character is mayor of the town). The décor is predominantly pastels, which contrast to the brighter colors of 1985, giving the space a sense of nostalgia for the 1950s (1985 Hill Valley seems intended to be more "real" as it has graffiti, homeless people and pornography playing at the local cinema) which is both encouraged and implicitly undercut by the film. Biff and his three companions are in complete harmony with this, specifically in the way they are dressed: white t-shirt, jeans, Biff's buzz cut and the 3D glasses one of the gang wears. Even Biff's name is indicative of his place in this world: along with his name, he bears significant visual and narrative parallels to Buzz (Corey Allen) in *Rebel without a Cause* (Nicholas Ray, 1955).

On Marty's first visit to the diner he witnessed an instance of Biff's intimidation of his father.[7] The second visit is intended as an opportunity for George, after Marty's coaching, to ask Lorraine to the school dance, an event which is designed to secure their relationship and ultimately Marty's existence. The very setting of this moment in the diner frames its importance to the representation of the 1950s. However, whilst in the act of wooing Lorraine George is interrupted by Biff, which prompts Marty to intervene.

After his entrance in the background of the frame, Biff interrupts George's faltering progress, shouting out "McFly," to which George responds by turning around to face Biff. At this moment the film cuts to Marty sitting at the diner's long counter, who also turns quickly round and then back, smacking the counter in frustration. The film returns to George with his back to the camera in the foreground, Biff and his gang in the background. As George turns round again, Biff continues speaking, saying to George "I thought I told you never to come in here." George turns back to Biff, and the camera tracks left to place him at the side of the frame with Biff and his gang in the center. Biff then starts to approach George, demanding money and pushing another kid out of the way as he does so, the others in the diner moving round in the background in order to gain a better position from which to watch their confrontation. The film then cuts back to Marty who sits with his back to the action, his gaze cast behind him. A quick pan down to his foot allows us to see him trip Biff as he walks past, at which point the film cuts to a low view of the floor as Biff lands heavily on it, his face in close-up. As the crowd off-screen collectively gasps Biff clenches his fist and sets his face into a grimace. He gets up and the film cuts to a medium shot of Marty, with a partial view of Biff in the foreground as he draws himself up, his left shoulder rising until Michael J. Fox's eyes are only just visible over it. Marty follows Biff's gaze as he stands up, but once Biff reaches the extent of his height, having almost completely eclipsed our view of Marty, Fox bobs up, his eyes rolling over Biff's shoulder. The film cuts to a low angled shot of Biff from over Marty's shoulder, Fox dwarfed again in the frame as Wilson towers over him. Biff starts to make threats, but Marty interrupts him, his gaze suddenly directed over Biff's shoulder, by exclaiming "whoa, what's that?" As Biff starts to turn his head the film returns to the previous shot of Marty, whose face has changed from mock surprise to a look of desperate determination, his jaw set and eyes widened. Marty straightens up and as Biff turns back, Marty punches him square in the mouth. The film cuts to a medium shot of Biff staggering back and crashing into a table, and then again to a medium shot of George who stands watching, with Lorraine rising to stand behind him, looking over his shoulder at the scuffle. The film cuts back to Marty who reacts with alarm to what he has done and rushes off frame left. The film then cuts to a long shot of Marty running towards the diner entrance, charging through Biff's gang who all tumble to the floor in his wake.

In this sequence Wilson successfully embodies the role of 1950s teen bully. Indeed, it seems significant that in this film we primarily encounter him in spaces that sustain his narrative function: the diner, the school cafeteria and the parking lot on the night of the School dance. His appearance securely supports this role, both through the period detail of his hair and costuming (appropriate to the 1950s, as well as being more plain and overtly masculine than the outfits worn by others such as Marty and George) and the physicality of his presence. The language he uses, such as his address to Marty — "punk" — is not only suitably in tune with the general world of the 1950s, but has specific resonance with his tough image.[8]

The sequence places particular emphasis on his physicality: seen among his contemporaries Biff is both taller and more muscular. Biff's fall to the floor and his recovery from this explicitly foreground his bulk, and the violence implicit in it, signaled by the way he clenches his fist and grimaces.[9] This threat is maintained by his contrast to Marty, the angle of the camera and framing of Fox and Wilson during their confrontation accentuates the difference in their height and physicality. As he stands up Wilson almost completely blocks our view of Fox, whilst in the reverse shot the difference in his size draws the camera higher up, thus reinforcing the extreme contrast in their physicality. In this way the moment illustrates the way in which the intimidating influence of Biff's presence is felt in Wilson's relationship to the camera, which now moves with him. The spatial alignment with Fox (and Crispin Glover) established in the scene so far is thus disrupted by Wilson. On his entrance to the diner, the camera remains with Glover, but attention is drawn to Wilson through his verbal interruption. After the cut away to Marty, the film returns to the set-up which privileges Glover, yet this is soon disturbed further, as the camera tracks to place Wilson more centrally in the frame. The way in which Biff's identity is created through Wilson's costume and physicality, as well as the access granted to him, is primarily focused on his role in the generic world of 1955.

That Marty manages to punch Biff and knock him over operates as a considerable surprise to Biff's construction in this sequence. As such it seems that Marty's victory over Biff is only possible because he is from outside this world. It is significant that it is his future knowledge (that we have been party to in the opening scenes of the film) that prompts him to intervene at all, fearing that if his father is undermined by Biff in front of his mother that she will reject him. It is also suggested that his wider temporal knowledge, and Biff's relatively limited experience, allow him to easily trick Biff into looking the other way. As such the contrast between Biff and Marty is not only physical, but related to their generic position. Wilson's performance at this point is firmly situated in the world of 1955, and more specifically within the iconography of the teen movie. As such he reflects the limited nature of this world, signaled predominantly by his appearance only in certain spaces and the repetitiveness of his concerns (his car, beating up dorks and going out with Lorraine). Marty, on the other hand, is from another era/world, operating outside of the teen drama, and as such has a wider concerns and experience, with the benefit of future, and thus further, knowledge. Their clash is thus implicitly related to the brushing up of familiar and strange, old and new, that pervades the film (and the trilogy). The sequence importantly introduces the conflict between Biff and Marty, and sets the tone for later confrontations.

Play: Generic Pleasures

The clash as represented by Marty and Biff in this scene, and the whole of the first and third films, is significant because it inverts what is old and what is new. The 1950s is made to be new and strange, as dictated by our alignment to Marty's experience. Old becoming new is a key instance of the trilogy's playfulness, as making a science fiction film about the past significantly reverses expectation. Our knowledge from the world of 1985, efficiently set up in the first few scenes, allows the possibility of expectation and pleasure in recognition and repetition, as well as difference, which is an essential part of genre. We recognize Biff from the 1950s because we have seen him behave in the same manner in 1985. We expect Lorraine to be chaste and well-behaved as a teenager because that is what she promotes in 1985, and so are amused by her being the exact opposite in 1955. Douglas Pye notes in his writing on genre:

> [P]leasure and interest are generated by the *interplay* of confirmed expectation and novelty, an interplay which implies on the artist's part an imaginative understanding (...) of appropriate conventions, and on the audience's the necessary experience to enter into the conventional relationship. [My italics][10]

The sequence in the diner is a key example of the pleasure created through the setting up of certain conventions, our experience of Marty's world, and the ways in which these are subverted through his confrontation with Biff. Across the whole of the first film Wilson's performance of Biff corresponds to Pye's observation. He repeats certain gestures and dialogue from the opening scenes (when he is an adult), reusing them later on and employing the same kind of tone. The repetition between younger and older self both provides Biff with a coherent identity (until the ending, in which his character changes, due to changes in the past affected by Marty's presence), and gestures to the wider continuities between Hill Valley of past and present.

Griff Tannen (2015)

Interplay of expectation and novelty is given further depth in the second film, where Marty's encounter with Griff in 2015 vividly repeats and modulates that with Biff in 1985. Traveling forwards to 2015 at the start of part two is motivated specifically to reverse future problems for Marty. Once there he is instructed by Doc to intervene in a meeting between Griff and Marty Jr. (also played by Michael J. Fox) which is due to take place in a retro 1980s café. Whereas the first film subverted the expectation created by its science fiction subject matter, the second film plays into this by taking Marty into a garish, technology-based future. Marty arrives in the 1980s café to be confronted with a jarring future take on his present, which echoes the similarities and differences he found in the diner in 1955. The space has the same layout as its 1955 counterpart, its repetition foregrounded by Fox's placement in the space and his similar position in relation to the camera. The atmosphere of the space, with its bright colors, televised waiters and exercising customers, is significantly different. Griff's immediate response to Marty Jr. within the café — "I thought I told you to stay in here" — acts as an instantaneous example of Pye's interplay. The line frames the following encounter as undertaking the conventions begun by the first film — in which he starts by saying "I thought I told you to never come in here" to George McFly — whilst simultaneously subverting them, gently signaling that our expectations of their meeting will be subverted.

After the initial confrontation between Marty Jr. and Griff (during which Marty has hidden behind the counter) results in Marty Jr. being knocked out, Marty switches places with him in order to ensure that his future son doesn't take part in Griff's plan and thus prevent future problems. As he turns to walk away from Griff, Marty is interrupted by Griff's off-screen taunt "What's wrong McFly? Chicken?" Marty stops in a long shot, the entrance to the café in the background, whilst non-diegetic music builds dramatically on the soundtrack. The film cuts to a medium shot of Griff and the three members of his gang, all dressed in a bizarre array of futuristically deconstructed outfits. Griff grimaces and the foremost member of his group pushes a button on his chest plate that sounds a mechanical chicken noise. The film returns to a long shot of Marty, still stood with his back to the others, with Griff — his back to the camera — in the foreground. As Marty turns his face towards him, saying "What did you call me?" Griff pulls out and extends a mechanized baseball bat behind his back. The film cuts again to the previous shot as Griff squawks "Chicken!" in reply. Marty turns round fully, now shown in a medium shot, stepping towards the camera and throwing his hat aside, exclaiming "Nobody calls me...." Before he can finish his sentence, the film cuts back to Griff who pulls out his bat, bringing it up to the foreground of the frame. The film then returns to Marty who exhales and weakly finishes "...chicken." Cutting back to Wilson, the film shows Griff swinging the bat, his gang all bobbing underneath it as he does so, and lurching forwards. At this point the film cuts back to Marty who cries out and ducks as Griff flies into the frame and forwards into the TV behind Marty, sparks flying out of it. A cut to a medium shot of Griff lent over the counter, reveals his bat is wedged into the TV as he jiggles from an electric shock, whilst Marty reappears behind him in the background, his fists raised. The film then cuts to behind Marty, Griff turning to face him, then growling as he lifts himself off the counter. A reverse field shot shows Griff drawing himself up to full height, his body filling the frame and leaving only the top of Marty's head and eyes in it, as he stares at Griff, his eyes widening in astonishment. A cut to another shot behind Marty accentuates the bulk of Griff in the frame as he towers over him, the low angle of the camera drawing attention to their physical difference. The film returns to a view of Marty over Griff's left shoulder as he shouts "Hey! What's that?" and draws his fists up, pulling a punch as Griff turns away. At this point, the film cuts back to Griff who blocks Marty's punch and catches the other's fist in his own. Another cut back to the previous shot of Fox over Wilson's shoulder gives access to Marty as he watches Griff push his fist down. Griff's pleasure in hurting Marty in this manner is revealed with a further cut back to Griff as he gazes intently at Marty, his arm wobbling slightly with the effort, but his face locked into a satisfied scowl. Shortly after, the film cut back to Marty over Griff's shoulder as he continues to watch his arm being pushed down and exhales with pain, finally looking up at Griff. The film cuts away to a medium shot of them both from the side as Marty kicks Griff in the groin — from which a metallic clanking sound issues — and then pulls Griff, now doubled-over, pushing him back into his gang, who all fall over. The scene ends with a cut to a medium shot of the retro cafe's entrance as Marty rushes out through it.

As with the opening line this entire sequence is constructed from the template of the scene I discussed from the first film, presenting a concentrated instance of the interplay between expectation and difference so important to genre. That Marty performs many of the same actions is appropriate to the fact that he is the same person. He is reliving his encounter with Biff in the most literal sense. Fox's performance furthers the repetition through his maintenance of the same comic tone throughout, indicated by his identical treatment of Biff and Griff, and details of expression such as his look over Biff's/ Griff's shoulder. Our alignment to him, both emotionally and cognitively (and mostly physically) encourages the recognition of its sameness. The similarity of Fox's performance tone is significant to this patterning of events, yet also contributes to its differences through interaction with Griff.

Wilson, on the other hand, demonstrates a very different performance as Griff. Similar attitudes and concerns are indicated through the repetition of dialogue and camera set-ups, such as the shot-reverse shot exchange of their physical confrontation, but they are made materially different by elements of Wilson's performance. Most obviously, his appearance is substantially different, made appropriate to the world he inhabits. His costume is unambiguously futuristic, made up of an assortment of styles and fashioned from various materials: he wears a metal hat, large metal and rubber boots, mis-matched biker-type gloves, a tailored and cropped gold and black striped jacket with rubber ridges on the shoulders, a metal codpiece, metal knee pads and a string t-shirt. The resulting effect is an exaggeration of his already bulky physicality and even his shape, as the hat flattens his head. The costume also affects his movements, which are stiffened and slightly robotic in feel, when compared to Wilson's embodiment of Biff. As with Biff from 1955 this attire signals the type of character he is: he is not only from the future, but is singularly aggressive.[11]

The excessiveness of Griff's appearance relates specifically to the world around him. Marty's brief encounter with 2015 so far reveals it to be a heightened world of intrusive technology and over-the-top jumbling of styles, as demonstrated by the huge 3D hologram of *Jaws*, televised advertising placards and flying traffic. Griff's costume and movement in it exaggerates the aggressiveness of his physicality. As he stands up in front of Marty, blocking him out of the frame momentarily Griff's movements are accompanied by a mechanical noise, thus chiming in with the emphasis on technology in this future world, and suggesting more forcefully that Griff resembles a robot, which elements of his costume and movement already evoke.

Another particularly noticeable change to Wilson's performance is his voice, which adds to the feeling of automaton that the costume and movement offer. The register he adopts as Griff is exaggeratedly stilted, the tone consistently fluctuating from high to low, even within a line of a dialogue. Likewise his expressions and gestures are larger-than-life. In the same way that Biff embodies the generic qualities of the 1950s teen movie, Griff successfully occupies the science fiction as articulated by the second film.

The contrast between Griff and Marty further accentuates these differences, well exemplified by the contact between Griff and Marty Jr. in which Fox adopts a similarly exaggerated style that is more in keeping with Wilson's vocal modulations. Griff and Marty's contrast is embedded into the structuring of the scene, which maintains a shot-reverse-shot patterning almost entirely throughout their confrontation. This is a significant change to the first film which placed Biff as a disruption to the scene, the camera relinquishing spatial alignment to Fox and Glover, in order to allow Wilson to dominate the action. This new splitting of alignment is furthered when we gain access to knowledge that Marty doesn't have — the appearance of the baseball bat behind Griff's back — which unbalances their clash, evoking anxiety for

Marty in a way that Biff didn't. One of the key modulations of the scene is the failure of Marty's repeated formula to defeat Griff. That Griff grabs Marty's punch without even looking round signals in that in this instance *Griff* has the wider knowledge, Marty is now the limited one. Likewise, our experience is limited to recognition of things that have already happened, as well as the differences to them, and as such the interplay chiefly operates between the worlds of the films.

Through the continuity offered by Wilson's embodiment of both Biff and Griff and the differences in their clash with Marty, the past, and the future are shown to have important consistencies alongside their very different qualities. This is chiefly managed in the way that Marty manages to integrate himself more or less successfully. The aggression of Biff and Griff provides a commonality between characters, that offers coherence through their familial link, yet their differing concerns and the way they articulate them ensure each character is securely placed within their worlds, and in this respect their genres. That Wilson's characters embody the generic iconography of their different worlds, as set up in each film, bears significance to the place of performance in the construction of genre. The connections between Wilson's differing embodiments and their worlds places performance as an aspect that explicitly signals genre, an example of Pye's "*tendencies* within generic traditions."[12]

Play: Performance Modes

The notion that performance is an integral aspect of generic iconography, relates to Pye's sense that genre is based on culturally shared experiences: "a wide range of shared experiences of a far less specialized kind — actions, gestures, language, occupations, dress and so on — and the meanings these have accumulated within a culture."[13] It is these material aspects of performance than contribute to the recognition and experience of particular genres.[14] Deborah Thomas usefully complements Pye's claims by suggesting that "a given genre is made up of a range of inflections (through local conventions) of broader narrative modes."[15] Although performance is understood as one of these inflections, I would propose that Thomas' comment is more fully applicable to performance, to which the idea of a narrative mode is particularly important. Fox and Wilson could be seen to be occupying performance modes that whilst different to some extent, bear certain relationships to one another (they both contribute to the interplay and expectation that is working more broadly across all the films).

As I have already gestured towards, this could specifically relate to the concept of tone. Fox maintains the same performance mode — that of comedy — over the two scenes, whilst Wilson's mode changes, alongside other differing temporal and spatial aspects. As such Wilson's performance mode corresponds with and is aligned to the fictional world he resides in, be it of the 1950s (teen movie) or 21st century (science fiction). Nonetheless, because we are so much epistemically and emotionally aligned to Marty and his experiences throughout the trilogy, Fox's performance and its placement in the scene guides the overall tone of the sequence to be comedic. So the genres signaled by Wilson are further contained in the wider genres of comedy and science fiction, the clash between Fox and Wilson is part of the comedy. The complexity of difference and continuity thus establishes a relationship between Fox and Wilson's apparently differing performance modes. Indeed, the pleasure of their clash is precisely held in the different performance mode of Wilson, and the way it contributes to the wider generic mode (as embodied by Fox). It is for this reason that we don't take Wilson's characters, and the threat each offers, as seriously as we could. Biff/Griff becomes ridiculous, rather than truly dangerous. The interplay between them embodies the possibility of one film expressing more than one genre.

The confrontation between the two characters, and the different layering of performance modes this entails, suggests that rather than being discrete categories there are relationships between genres that speak of their wider relevance, their shared concerns and thus the innate mutability of genres in American cinema. Surely if we were to consider different genres as separate, neither of the sequences discussed so far would have any coherence, the clash of different genres pulling the fictional worlds apart, rather than drawing them together. In this sense performance could be seen to contribute to the continuity and development across generic axes, making it possible to draw a line between performances in one genre to another.

Buford "Mad Dog" Tannen (1885)

The interrelationship between performance modes is further exemplified in the first meeting of Marty and Buford "Mad Dog" Tannen in the third part of the trilogy. Soon after Marty arrives in 1885, his purpose in traveling to this time focused on saving Doc's life, he goes to the local saloon to find him.[16] The saloon owes more to the iconography of the western movie — complete with large wooden bar, tables with men playing cards and a barman who only serves whiskey — than that of Hill Valley. As an interior space, it is very different to the diner and café in both décor and layout. Accordingly Marty's relationship to the space is altogether different. This is most obviously achieved in his costume of pale pink western shirt with embroidered patterns on the shoulders and long tassels and red trousers, as well as 1980s sneakers, which stand out in relation to the saloon's other inhabitants. In consequence, Marty is revealed as an outsider more instantly than in either of the other films.

Marty tells the barman that he is trying to find the blacksmith and the film cuts to a long shot of him at the bar with his back to the camera. Someone walks into the saloon and their right hip complete with gun holster enters the foreground of the frame. As a voice off-screen exclaims "Hey McFly" the film cuts to a close-up over Marty's shoulder. Fox turns in the direction of the noise and the camera tracks with him as he comes to face the person off-screen, who continues "I thought I done told you to never to come in...." As the speaker pauses, the film cuts to a long shot revealing Buford Tannen and his three followers in the doorway of the saloon. All four of them are dressed in typical cowboy attire — black Stetson, long dark jacket, neckerchief hanging loosely at the neck, gun belt slung across the hips, long boots — making them seem to be identically dressed. Buford exclaims "you aren't Seamus McFly" and moves forwards, gesturing derisively with the handle of a whip, the film cutting to a long shot from behind the bar, with Marty in the foreground as the others approach him.

Buford's entrance here articulates a further modulation of the pattern built up of his interaction with Marty's relatives (father, son, great-great-grandfather respectively) across the trilogy. In this instance he doesn't even get to finish banning him from the Saloon, but cuts himself off in astonishment at Marty's appearance in Seamus' place. In a playful articulation of the interplay of convention and novelty, it is *Buford's* expectations that are subverted. Whilst this most obviously and appropriately recognizes Marty's marked physical contrast to the world he finds himself in, thus maintaining their central clash of old and new as repeated throughout, the moment and its construction efficiently signals the difference of Wilson's character in this film. His aggressive presence is similar (and thus familiar), yet he is very different again to Biff and Griff, both in appearance and tone.

The relationship between Wilson and the camera is once more modified in accordance with his status in this world. Whilst Biff figured as an interruption and Griff as a clash, Buford's presence supersedes both by invading the frame, just his thigh dwarfing Marty this time. This demonstration of his power chimes directly with the iconography of the western, as his gun and holster are the most prominent aspect of his appearance at this point, clashing significantly with Marty's seemingly garish and inauthentic attire (a western by way of the pastels of 1955 Hill Valley). As I have already stressed, performance is a major articulation of generic iconography, which this moment recognizes and illustrates most clearly. This initial glimpse of Buford is then supported by his and his three companions,' appearance in the next shot. As with the previous two films, Wilson's costume places him firmly in the film's version of 1885, as well as suggesting his place in this world. Here they are presented as more authentic, rather than nostalgic, as their attire is suitably dirty and shabby to indicate their lifestyle as criminal, or at least that of itinerant cowboys. This is further recognized in their difference to Seamus McFly (also played by Michael J. Fox), who is a farmer, and other town-dwelling characters like the Barman.

The change in costume is reflected further in material details of Wilson's performance, through his body and his voice. Wilson's specifically masculine and threatening physicality is enhanced through his bearded — and therefore somewhat inscrutable — face, the darkness of his garments, and the way they make him move through the space. All four men lope into the bar, Wilson at their head, the placement of his right hand on his gun belt and languid gesture with the whip in his left particularly suggestive of his physical power and confidence in their control over the space. So, again, Wilson's character's aggression is clear from the outset, his physicality further emphasized through his placement in the frame. Wilson's voice is also different, his register made deeper and his phrasing appropriate to the role of laconic cowboy. In these ways Wilson's performance, as well as the way it is placed in the sequence, both articulates Buford's difference to Marty, and to Biff/Griff, but further reflects the kind of masculinity more commonly encountered in the western.

The scene carries on as Buford and his gang discusses Marty's oddness, his seeming incongruity to their world (the first moment in the trilogy where this has been fully noticed and commented on by another character in quite such detail). Moving on from their torment of Marty, Buford shifts to his purpose, asking the bartender if he has seen the blacksmith. At this point the scene breaks into the start of a more prolonged confrontation between Marty and Buford, but one which significantly undercuts expectation in its difference to the previous two films.

In response to Buford's question the bartender backs away, the camera tracking forwards with him to put Marty in medium close-up as he looks off-screen at Buford with sudden interest, saying "You're 'Mad Dog' Tannen." The film cuts back to Buford, who looks ahead towards Marty and straightens up from his leaning posture on the bar, squaring his shoulders and holding his right hand poised next to his gun as he does so, the camera tracking slightly backwards to keep him in the frame. As the film returns to Marty, the bartender and any other occupants of the bar run to the back and out of the shot. Marty looks behind him and then forwards as Buford says "Mad Dog?" off-screen. The film cuts back to a medium shot of Buford and the gang as he grimaces "I hate that name" and then again to Marty who closes his mouth and looks worried, the camera tracking in towards him slowly. The film returns to Buford as he says "Nobody calls me 'Mad Dog,'" his right hand open and raised over his gun, the camera tracking slowly towards him as he continues to rant, until Wilson is in medium close-up. Placing Marty in a long shot from between Buford and one of the gang, the camera is positioned near to Buford's gun holster and poised hand, which momentarily block our view of Marty, until Buford draws his gun. The film cuts to a low angled medium shot of Buford and the others, his gun pointing down in the foreground. He shoots the pistol and the film returns to the previous long shot of Marty, Fox yelling and leaping in the air. As the film cuts back to a medium shot of Buford and his gang he shouts "Dance!" and then shoots again in Marty's direction.

The significance of this moment, and its disruption of the pattern of Wilson's characters falling over, asserting their physical difference to Marty and him punching, or attempting to punch them, is specifically related to the generic world of 1885, and Buford's place in it. A great deal of the scene's overall pleasure could be said to be the assertion of the difference in American culture between the two eras (as embodied by details contained in Wilson and Fox's performances) and their apparent incongruity, made comedic through Fox's performance and our physical epistemic alignment with Marty (the scene continues as Marty begins to "moonwalk" in avoidance of Buford's bullets). Nonetheless, there are two other important factors built into Wilson's performance and how it is placed within the mise-en-scène. His relationship to elements around him illustrate how the sequence importantly subverts Wilson's earlier appearances in similar moments across the trilogy, as with the occupants of the bar running away in this instance instead of crowding closer. His spatial dominance over the camera's alignment with Marty continues, as parts of his body are placed in close-up in the foreground of the frame, with Fox's entire body is placed in the background, thus combining the strategies in the previous scenes of shifting alignment and contrasting physicality.

The greatest change to their confrontation, however, is the extent to which these aspects and further details insist on Buford's dangerousness. Unlike Biff he has weapons, which unlike Griff's are revealed to us *and* to Marty. The balance between Wilson and Fox's characters has altered so much that it is no longer appropriate for them to have close physical confrontation. Wilson's presence, the particular differences of his appearance and attitude, is constructed around both the generic iconography of the western and how this genre affects the balance of elements already in place. After Marty runs from the bar to escape Buford, he is followed by the whole gang on horseback, lassoed by Buford and dragged back into town to be strung up to the new court-house by his neck, a modulation that indicates just how dangerous Buford, and by implication the world of 1885, is in contrast to Biff of 1955 and Griff of 2015.

In terms of performance modes this could point to the complete differ-ence between a western and a comedy, thus supporting Richard De Cordova's claims that "performance manifests itself so differently in different genres that it seems to call into question the coherence of the concept itself."[17] Yet, this is not the case either here or in the rest of the film. Again, the (im)balance of their clash could be considered through attribution of knowledge and expe-rience, with Marty's initial understanding of this world demonstrated to be entirely lacking, thus giving Buford the upper hand. Indeed, it is not until he changes his own appearance to be more in keeping with his surroundings and then sees the connectedness of their worlds (through popular culture — the metal pie dish he uses as a Frisbee to disrupt Buford's shot at Doc, and his adoption of a metal breast plate echoing Clint Eastwood's character in *A Fistful of Dollars* [Sergio Leone, 1964]) that he is able to outwit Buford. Although Wilson's performance of Buford takes him seriously, Marty does not entirely and our alignment with him dictates our experience. Despite apparent differences, significant cultural continuities are implied across the worlds and as such the genres are placed together in order for us to enjoy their interaction.

Play: Generic Identities

Consideration of the final part of the trilogy, particularly in the recog-nition of its generic identities bouncing against each other more than others, leads appropriately into thinking more widely about the relationship between differing genres and American cinema. Deborah Thomas argues that genres like comedy and melodrama are too pervasive to be considered distinct gen-res: "[o]ne of the problems in construing them as genres is precisely the fact that many of the most central characteristics attributed to them appear to apply to films of many genres, making their generic identities dissolve in our grasp."[18] In consideration of this, a different vocabulary is required to successfully nego-tiate our responses and characters' responses to these genres, such as those in the title of Thomas' introduction to her book *Beyond Genre: Melodrama, Com-edy and Romance in Hollywood Films*: "structures, moods and worlds." In this she argues for a more complex structure of thinking about genre that allows for a film's ability to move between the comedic and melodramatic, but one that simultaneously recognizes that "a film's generic identity ... tends to be more stable: a western generally remains a western all the way through."[19] The last scene articulates Thomas' point, it is certainly consistently a western, yet there are elements of comedy shifting through it. Through my argument of performance embodying generic tendencies, it could be said that Wilson's performance is tied to the generic structure of a western throughout, the fact of his continued dangerousness (until the end, whereupon the repetition of certain moments across the trilogy — such as Wilson's character's aggression towards Marty ending in him being covered in manure/arrest, or both — becomes more pronounced) ensuring that this remains consistent, whilst Fox's performance maintains a comedic mode, allowing the film to be more broadly experienced as a comedy.[20] Furthermore this applies to the trilogy as a whole, with Wilson's performances articulating the more stable genre (the coherent fictional world), which Marty's contrary entrance into offers a structure of comedy across all three films.

Conclusion

In his suggestion that the films in the trilogy "are eclectic, postmodern, generically self-conscious films that incorporate allusions to many previous films" Andrew Gordon situates their generic playfulness as a specifically temporal aspect, a mark of their place in contemporary Hollywood.[21] Yet to place such an emphasis underestimates to some extent the wider fluidity of genre, which runs across studio-era and post–studio Hollywood. As Robin Wood suggests, genres are part of a wider system — American cinema — and as such their concerns are tied to this: "at best, [genres] represent different strategies for dealing with the same ideological tensions."[22] This is a revealing comment in relation to my discussion of Wilson's performance in the trilogy. As I hope to have illuminated, each of the characters he embodies bears a pervasive generic mode, but one that demonstrates crucial continuities, and thus deals with the same basic tensions between old and new, through interaction with Fox's Marty.

Furthermore, although the trilogy does contain references to other films, I would argue that the distance implied by Gordon's comment doesn't accurately answer the experience of watching the films, of how we are placed in relation to the fictional worlds and their inhabitants. Our experience is aligned with, and importantly sympathetic to, that of Marty's, and as such the majority of the self-reflexivity is tied to him. Many of the conventions evoked are part of his world with specific repetitions across the films, as well as the allusions to the other films (as with his reference to Clint Eastwood in the third film, recalling Biff's viewing of *A Fistful of Dollars* in the second film). The pleasure generated in this kind of playful reference, and the more common interplay of conventions set up within the films themselves, and their subversion, fosters a closer and more involved viewing position. The notion of "ironic hybridity" offered by Jim Collins' reading of the third film, likewise suggests the film works to place the viewer in a superior position to its characters.[23] Paying close attention to the material details of performance demonstrates how intimately the films involve us in the construction of their fictional worlds and the continuities and innovations contained in each. Textual analysis of performance thus fleshes out the experience of genre and its pleasures, but also crucially directs us to the material continuities between modes, the way in which a performer can articulate one genre, but also be operating within another.

Notes

1. In the first film, unlike Marty (who originates from 1985 throughout), Doc involved in the majority of the narrative is his past self (from 1955). In the second and third films both Marty and Doc originate from 1985. Alongside the central character of Marty, Michael J. Fox embodies his future adult self, and his two children in 2015, as well as his ancestor Seamus McFly in 1885.

2. To add further complexity, there are 3 different versions of Biff that Marty meets in 1985. The first, at the beginning of the first film, is his father's aggressive boss, who still bullies his father and flirts with his mother. The second, at the end of the first film, is changed directly through Marty's actions in the past to become a mechanic, subservient to George McFly and his family. The third version, in the second film, is a tycoon who owns Marty's home town of Hill Valley, which he has turned into a nightmarish and polarized place of extreme wealth (his) and street violence. He is married to Marty's mother, having killed his father twelve years ago. This version of Biff is a result of his future self, from 2015, stealing the time machine to give his past self (from 1955) a sports almanac from the future, which will allow him to win every bet placed on a sporting event up until 2000.

3. Robin Wood, "Ideology, Genre, Auteur." *Film Comment* 13:1 (1977): 47.

4. The first part of Kathrina Glitre's first chapter in her book *Hollywood Romantic Comedy: States of the Union 1934–1965* offers a well drawn account of genre along these lines, pp. 10–16.

5. Douglas Pye, "Genre and Movies." *Movie* 20 (1975): 29.

6. For example: *The Wild One* (Laslo Benedek, 1953), *American Graffiti* (George Lucas, 1973), *Grease* (Randal Kleiser, 1978), *American Pie* (Paul Weitz, 1999).

7. This echoes a similar interaction between adult George and Biff at the beginning of the film in 1985.

8. Likewise, Lorraine's use of the word "dreamy" to describe Calvin Klein (actually Marty, her future son) is appropriate, not only to the time period, but to her character's overt interest in the opposite sex. Lorraine is not promiscuous, but she is certainly sexualized and thus her declaration of attraction to Calvin in such terms demonstrates a contradiction to the apparently chaste era (provided by Lorraine herself as an adult in 1985 at the beginning of the film).

9. The violence implied here is significant for the character. His sense of threat he poses must not be underestimated, as later he will almost try to force himself on Lorraine, a possibility which is importantly real in the world of the film.

10. Pye, p. 30.

11. I would argue that there is a difference between Biff and Griff in this singularity. Biff's aggression is directed towards status and control, whereas Griff's seems to be the primary aspect of his character.

12. Pye, p. 29.

13. *Ibid.*, p. 30.

14. I refer the reader to Richard De Cor-

dova's discussion of the specificity of performance in musicals, in particular the idea that these
performances have a particular mode of address,
more direct than in any other type of narrative.
Richard De Cordova, "Genre and Performance:
An Overview." *Film Genre Reader 3.* Ed. Barry
Keith Grant. Austin: University of Texas Press,
2003, p. 131.

15. Deborah Thomas, *Beyond Genre: Melodrama, Comedy and Romance in Hollywood
Films.* Moffat: Cameron & Hollis, 2000, p. 10.

16. Doc (from 1985) accidentally goes back
to 1885 at the end of the second film whilst he
and Marty are in 1955. Stuck in 1955 without
the time machine as a result, at the start of the
third film Marty enlists Doc from 1955 to help
him return to 1985 (prompted by a letter left
to him by Doc in 1885 with instructions of the
time machine's whereabouts in 1955). During
their research into Doc's existence in 1885, in
which they find out that he has become the
town's blacksmith, Marty discovers that he died
some months after his arrival. Ignoring Doc's

orders to leave him in the past, Marty and 1955
Doc fix the machine and Marty travels back to
1885.

17. De Cordova, p. 130.

18. Thomas, p. 10.

19. *Ibid.*, p. 14.

20. Equally, the presence of Doc, and Christopher Lloyd's performance, informs the
comedic nature of the trilogy, as well as articulating its continued relationship to science
fiction throughout.

21. Andrew Gordon, "'You'll never get out
of Bedford Falls!': The Inescapable Family in
American Science Fiction and Fantasy Films."
Journal of Popular Film and Television 20:2
(1992): 7.

22. *Ibid.*

23. Jim Collins, "Genericity in the Nineties:
Eclectic Irony and the New Sincerity," *Film
Analysis Goes to the Movies.* Eds. Jim Collins,
Hilary Radner & Ava Preacher Collins. Lon-
don: Routledge, 1993, 242–264.

Works Cited

Collins, Jim. "Genericity in the Nineties: Eclectic Irony and the New Sincerity." *Film Analysis goes to the Movies.* Eds. Jim Collins, Hilary Radner & Ava Preacher Collins. London:
Routledge, 1993. 242–264.

De Cordova, Richard. "Genre and Performance:
An Overview." *Film Genre Reader 3.* Ed.
Barry Keith Grant. Austin: University of
Texas Press, 2003. 130–140.

Erisman, Fred. "The Night Christopher Lloyd
danced with Mary Steenburgen." *Journal of
Popular Film and Television* 20: 1 (1992): 29–
33.

Glitre, Kathrina. *Hollywood Romantic Comedy:*

States of the Union 1934–1965. Manchester:
Manchester University Press, 2006.

Gordon, Andrew. "'You'll never get out of Bedford Falls!': The Inescapable Family in American Science Fiction and Fantasy Films."
Journal of Popular Film and Television 20:2
(1992): 2–8.

Pye, Douglas. "Genre and Movies." *Movie* 20
(1975): 29–43.

Thomas, Deborah. *Beyond Genre: Melodrama,
Comedy and Romance in Hollywood Films.*
Moffat: Cameron & Hollis, 2000.

Wood, Robin. "Ideology, Genre, Auteur." *Film
Comment* 13:1 (1977): 46–50.

5. Bury My Heart in Hill Valley, or, The Kid Who KO'd Liberty Valance

John Exshaw

In 1990, when *Back to the Future Part III* was first released, the Western had been moldering in Boot Hill for the best part of fifteen years, and nothing, it seemed, was going to bring it back. Since 1976, when John Wayne had gone out in a blaze of glory in *The Shootist* and Clint Eastwood had ridden off at the end of *The Outlaw Josey Wales*, the Western had come to resemble a ghost town of broken dreams, its empty, wind-battered streets providing scant shelter for the few crazy-eyed prospectors either too old or too ornery to change and whose only hope was that the old, worked-out gold mine might still yield the occasional nugget — or at least enough for a grubstake.

Instead, the lean times got leaner and the pickings got fewer, despite there being a real-life, honest-to-goodness movie cowboy in the White House. As Ronald Reagan rode into Washington, the Western, in the bloated shape of Michael Cimino's *Heaven's Gate* (1980), was being carted out of Hollywood in the dead of night and unceremoniously dumped in a ditch. An artistic and financial fiasco which not only bankrupted its studio (United Artists), *Heaven's Gate* also marked the end of the so-called New Hollywood era, in which the first generation of directors who had studied film in college had attempted to incorporate the New Wave *auteur* ethos of European cinema into the Hollywood mainstream — with sometimes successful but often variable results.

Less respectfully referred to at the time as "the movie brats," the New Hollywood directors tended, at least from a Western aficionado's point of view, to display a greater interest in talking about Westerns than in actually making them. Film-makers like Francis Ford Coppola, Martin Scorsese, Steven Spielberg, George Lucas, and John Carpenter could — and did — talk with great reverence and enthusiasm about films such as John Ford's *The Searchers*

(1956), Howard Hawks' *Rio Bravo* (1959), and Sergio Leone's *C'era una volta il West* (*Once Upon a Time in the West*, 1968), often citing them as major influences and referencing them in their own work. Yet the fact remains that none of the afore-mentioned directors, now all in the last sunset of their careers, ever seriously engaged with the Western where it matters — on the big screen. When the time came to saddle up and ride to the rescue of the beleaguered genre, the New Hollywood directors were found to be "all mouth and gutwind" (as Robert Ryan so poetically put it in *Lawman*, 1971), a bunch of tinhorns who talked mighty big in the saloon but lacked the sand to stand in the street when the shooting starts.

There were, it should be noted, some honorable exceptions: John Milius entered the film business in the late 1960s with the laudable (if entirely unrealistic) ambition of making B-Westerns; unfortunately for him, Hollywood didn't make B-Westerns any more, having long since left that particular line of territory to television, and he had to settle for scriptwriting credits on *Jeremiah Johnson* and *The Life and Times of Judge Roy Bean* (both 1972) instead. Walter Hill, whose tenacious adherence to the genre over the course of his career marks him as the only director of his generation even remotely worthy of the title, "Western director," made *The Long Riders* in 1980, but throughout the ensuing decade, was confined to one modern-day Western, *Extreme Prejudice* (1987), in addition to *The Warriors* (1979) and *Southern Comfort* (1984), both of which, like John Carpenter's *Assault on Precinct 13* (1976) and Milius' *Red Dawn* (1984), were, in effect, Westerns in disguise.

The Western-in-disguise was an idea much touted by commentators at the time, who liked to propose that the genre had not so much died with its boots on as been subsumed into the burgeoning science-fiction genre spawned by George Lucas' *Star Wars* (1977) and Steven Spielberg's *Close Encounters of the Third Kind* (1978). The notion of "Space, the Final Frontier" (to quote the opening narration of *Star Trek*, itself sold to television as a space-set version of the long-running Western series, *Wagon Train*) as a metaphor for the West was most obviously rendered in films like *Battle Beyond the Stars* (1980) and *Outland* (1981), space-age remakes, respectively, of *The Magnificent Seven* (1960) and *High Noon* (1952), while the *Mad Max* series (and its many low-budget offspring) were clearly Westerns-in-disguise, with roaming motorbike gangs providing an obvious (and inferior) substitute for Apache war parties.[1]

Unsurprisingly, this proposal was quickly run out of town by Western fans, whose response to the suggestion that they should view Han Solo as simply a space-age Wyatt Earp gunning for alien Clantons in an intergalactic Tombstone can be best summed up by John Vernon's celebrated line from *The Outlaw Josey Wales*—"Don't piss down my back and tell me it's raining."

Nor, as the 1980s unfolded, were they likely to be mollified by such derivative and unnecessary offerings as *The Legend of the Lone Rider* (1981), the 3-D post–Spaghetti Spaghetti Western *Comin' at Ya!* (1981), lame comedies like *Lust in the Dust* and *Rustlers' Rhapsody* (both 1985), the fitfully amusing *Three Amigos!* (1986), or even the worthy but low-key *Barbarosa* and *The Grey Fox* (both 1982), chamber pieces which received only minimal distribution before being sold to television.

Any hopes of a revival in the form's fortunes were firmly invested in the genre's one remaining star, Clint Eastwood. His modern-day *Bronco Billy* (1980), while well-received critically, was a minor effort in what was a creatively fallow period of the actor-director's career, but much excitement was generated by the news that he was returning to the Western proper with *Pale Rider* in 1985. Magazine articles with titles like "How the West Was Won Again"[2] abounded, and the irony of the opening scene, in which the daughter of a mining family beset by bad hats prays for a savior to ride to the rescue, was not lost on most fans of the genre. Alas, *Pale Rider* proved to be a disappointing rehash of both George Stevens' *Shane* (1952) and Eastwood's own *High Plains Drifter* (1972), rather than a trailblazer to new horizons west.

The same year also saw the release of another major Western, Lawrence Kasdan's *Silverado*, which, though a modest box-office success, failed to persuade the studios to "endeavor to persevere" (as Chief Dan George trenchantly put it, also in *The Outlaw Josey Wales*). Speaking of *Silverado*, Kasdan observed that he "didn't want to reinvent the western, just reintroduce it. I wanted to show it needn't be a slow form, there can be as much action as in a space movie,"[3] a remark as illuminating as it was depressing. Nothing could better illustrate the depths to which the Western, arguably the very bedrock of American cinema (and of the country's self-image), had fallen than that a leading director of the day should feel the need to "reintroduce" the form to an audience seduced by space-age sagas and the increasingly mindless and preposterous escapades of the New Action Hero (as personified by Sylvester Stallone, Arnold Schwarzenegger, and Bruce Willis).

In addition to exposing the harsh reality of how Hollywood had come to regard the Western, Kasdan also highlighted one of the major failings of the Western since the 1960s: instead of being a staple of entertainment cinema, adventure stories which might or might not deal with contemporary issues as subtext, the Western had become an often ponderous vehicle for morose reflection and anguished, handwringing liberal guilt. Demythologizing and deromanticizing the Western became a fashionable occupation of the terminally hip Hollywood film-maker, with the irritatingly anachronistic and glib (though undoubtedly entertaining) *Butch Cassidy and the Sundance Kid* (1969) leading to warts-and-all portraits of Doc Holliday (*Doc*, 1971) and Billy the

Kid (*Dirty Little Billy*, 1972) which supposedly showed the "true West" in all its muddy mediocrity ("Billy the Kid Was a Punk," as the latter film's publicity helpfully pointed out), while the genuine plight of the American Indian was trivialized in such ham-fisted satires as *Little Big Man* (1970) and *Buffalo Bill and the Indians, or Sitting Bull's History Lesson* (1976). These changes of emphasis also affected the way Westerns looked, with cinematographers and production designers being instructed to use a somber palette of browns, the better to capture the visual realism of artists like Frederick Remington and Charles Russell (both of whose work, somewhat inconveniently no doubt, also contained strong elements of romance), and old sepia photographs of the time. Costumes evolved from what might be termed the romantic realism of the 1950s and the personal style of the Leone hero to the determinedly grubby, with the well-worn Stetson being replaced by an indeterminate and shapeless slouch hat, and every character seemingly dressed in a dreary combination of browns or Sunday-best, as if colored cloth was an unknown commodity west of the Mississippi.[4]

Whereas John Ford's central theme had been the conquering of the wilderness and the advance of civilization (in which the romantic hero will assist and in which he may find a place), Sam Peckinpah (in particular) and Sergio Leone had focused on the passing of the West (in which the romantic hero will usually die or at least be rendered irrelevant). The term "elegiac" became a commonplace in describing such Westerns, and although their concerns were entirely legitimate, they gave rise to the impression that the Western itself, as well as such doomed heroes, had run out of room, time, and purpose. This impression had been reinforced by the fact that, by the mid–1960s, the principal stars of the sound-era Western were either dead (Gary Cooper), past their prime (John Wayne, James Stewart, Henry Fonda), or retired (Randolph Scott, Joel McCrea). The *Easy Rider* generation (which, of course, included the New Hollywood directors) was unlikely to identify with such antiquated, patriarchal, and (with the exception of Fonda) overwhelmingly conservative figures, and, crucially, there was no one to take their place. As Clint Eastwood's career had shown, the Western was easily able to accommodate the Leone-style anti-hero in place of the more traditional model, but by the mid–1980s, such stars as could convincingly carry a Western, such as Charles Bronson, Lee Marvin, and James Coburn, were in or approaching their sixties, while Eastwood himself was, at the time of *Pale Rider*, fifty-five. Furthermore, the early deaths of both Peckinpah (in 1984) and Leone (in 1989) meant that there were no longer any directors with sufficient authority in the genre to provide fresh impetus.[5]

Kasdan's film demonstrated that it was not enough to cast a group of actors, no matter how talented, in a Western and expect them to be automatically convincing *as Westerners.* While New York actors like Kevin Kline and Jeff Goldblum may not have looked quite so amusingly out-of-place as James Cagney and Humphrey Bogart in *The Oklahoma Kid* (1939), they nonetheless possessed a modern, urban sensibility at odds with the requirements of the Western. In short, the cast of *Silverado* looked like a bunch of actors *playing* at being cowboys, and the same may be said of the stars of *Young Guns* (1988), another version of the Billy the Kid saga which proved less a throwback to the "youth-orientated" Westerns of the Fifties and early Sixties than an attempt to find gainful employment for a group of actors (many of whom were the progeny of movie stars) dubbed "the Brat Pack." With "real" Westerners like Jack Palance, Brian Keith, and Patrick Wayne providing a sense of historical continuity, the result was sufficiently popular to merit a sequel — no mean feat in itself, all things considered, and the first indication since *Heaven's Gate* that a Western *not* starring Clint Eastwood could be a viable box-office attraction. By this time, however, Western fans had largely retreated into nostalgia, circling their wagons round the home video boom, as indicated by a full-page advertisement run by a British retail chain trumpeting the fact that John Wayne was handily outselling (outdrawing?) all other stars in the new market.

* * *

The release of *Back to the Future Part III* in May 1990 was given a qualified welcome by Western enthusiasts. Even those with little personal desire to watch a teen-orientated time-travel movie starring Michael J. Fox felt that, following on from *Young Guns* (the sequel to which was due to open three months later), *any* successful film set in the West, and particularly one aimed at the allegedly all-important teen market, was a step in the right direction and therefore to be encouraged (following the sound Western principle of "Round 'em up, rope 'em, and brand 'em young..."), even if only tacitly.

The plotline of *Back to the Future Part III* may be briefly summarized: following an accidental lightning strike on the DeLorean time machine at the end of *Back to the Future, Part II* (1989), Doc Brown is transported back to the town of Hill Valley as it was in 1885. In Hill Valley in 1955, Marty McFly, accompanied by Doc, discovers a tombstone bearing the legend, "Here lies Emmett Brown. Died September 7, 1885. Shot in the back by Buford Tannen over a matter of 80 dollars. Erected in eternal memory by his beloved Clara." Marty travels back to 1885 to save Doc from the "notorious gunman whose short temper and a tendency to drool earned him the nickname "Mad Dog" (and who is the great-grandfather of the series' villain, Biff Tannen). Arriving back in Monument Valley in the middle of a cavalry pursuit of Indians, Marty is found by his own great-great grandfather, an Irish immigrant named Séamus McFly, who helps him on his way to Hill Valley. No sooner has he arrived than Marty falls foul of Buford Tannen in the saloon. On the point of being lynched, he is saved by Doc Brown, who (ostensibly, at least) works as the town's blacksmith. A quarrel develops between Doc and Tannen over the shoeing of the latter's horse. Marty explains his presence to the startled scientist, but their plan to return to the future in the DeLorean is thwarted by the unavailability of gasoline in 1885. Doc then manages to rescue the new school teacher, Clara Clayton, after her horse has bolted, and is soon romancing her (she is, after all, a fellow enthusiast of author Jules Verne) despite the warning on his tombstone. Will the moonstruck Doc agree to go back to the future? Will Marty be able to thwart Buford Tannen as the clock ticks inexorably towards high noon (or 8:00 A.M., in this case)? And with the DeLorean out of action, *how* will they get back to the future?

Clearly then, the onus on the makers of *Back to the Future Part III* was to provide a successful conclusion to what had developed into a trilogy, and the fact that the film was mainly set in the Old West was largely peripheral to that requirement, as director Robert Zemeckis pointed out during shooting; "*Back to the Future III* [*sic*] isn't necessarily a Western. It's a time-travel movie with our characters that goes to the 1800s. And so we'll have horses and guns and shootouts and steam trains and all that stuff. But it's the West seen through the eyes of a kid from the Eighties."[6] Scriptwriter Bob Gale later recalled the genesis of the project: "Bob [Zemeckis] came up with this climax of the train — that was his inspiration. He had said, 'We can go wherever we want and I want to do a Western.' It was: we can create any time period we want, let's go to the Old West and do the beginnings of Hill Valley."[7]

With the film being shot back-to-back with its predecessor, the opportunity presented itself to anticipate the storyline of *Part III* in *Part II* (the original film, released in 1985, had no Western references — the fact that Allan Dwan's *Cattle Queen of Montana*, which starred Barbara Stanwyck and Ronald Reagan, was playing in the Essex cinema of Hill Valley, 1955, was included only to set up a joke about Reagan being President in 1985). In addition to Doc, having decided he should destroy the time machine, expressing the regret that he will be unable to visit his "favorite historical era, the Old West," we see Marty, in the retro-themed Café '80s of Hill Valley, 2015, demonstrating his skill on the video arcade game, *Wild Gunman* (which involves outdrawing a baddie who rather resembles Buford Tannen, and his gang of Leone-esque Mexican gunmen), to a pair of less-than-impressed "future boys," a skill he will put to somewhat more pointed use in *Part III*. In the hellish version of Hill Valley created by Biff Tannen in *Part II*, Marty, standing in the lobby of Biff's Pleasure Palace casino, sees a trailer touting the Biff Tannen Museum, where folks can "learn the amazing history of the Tannen family, starting with his great-grandfather, Buford 'Mad Dog' Tannen, fastest gun in the West." Later, Marty discovers Biff in his penthouse Jacuzzi, enjoying the final scene of Sergio Leone's *Fistful of Dollars* (1964), in which The Man With No Name (Clint Eastwood) outwits the villain with a metal sheet hidden under his poncho. Biff, whatever his other failings, at least knows a good film when he sees one; as he forcefully, if rather crudely, observes, "Bulletproof vest! Great flick! Great frigging flick! The guy is brilliant." Marty then steps forward in a trademark Leone rear-view, hip-level shot and lifts the remote control as if it were a Colt, turning off the film. In *Part III*, Marty will adopt both Eastwood's name and costume, as well as the "bulletproof vest" ruse for his showdown with "Mad Dog" Tannen.[8]

Being set, however fortuitously, within a specific cinematic genre as well as a specific historical time period, *Back to the Future Part III*, more so than its predecessors, allowed Zemeckis and Gale to include many in-jokes and references to other films, in particular those of John Ford, Howard Hawks, and Sergio Leone. As fellow film students at the University of Southern California, the pair were well-versed in the work of such luminaries, but while their allusions are evident enough to Western aficionados, they stop short of self-indulgence, forming part of the background of the film, rather than intruding into the narrative (though it is safe to assume that all but the most obvious would be completely missed by the average "kid from the Eighties"). Among the Westerns cited by Gale as his favorites are Ford's *Rio Grande* (1950) and *The Searchers* (1956), and Hawks' *Red River* (1948), *Rio Bravo* (1959) and *El Dorado* (1966) — leaving one to deduce that the many Sergio Leone references were contributed by Zemeckis.[9]

When Doc prepares to send Marty back in time from 1955 to 1885, he chooses the (fictitious) Pohatchee Drive-in Theatre in Monument Valley as a suitable launching point, on the grounds that they cannot risk Marty arriving in either a populated area or one that is in the middle of nowhere. As Hill Valley is supposedly in California, making the Mojave the nearest available desert, this, of course, is nothing more than a convenient fig-leaf for the fact that the film-makers *wanted* the iconic imagery of Monument Valley (located on the Arizona-Utah border, and particularly associated with Ford), as Zemeckis himself explained, "When our hero goes back to the 1880s, the first image that the audience has to see is one that is immediately recognizable, that they go, 'Oh, yes, we're in the West,' and it had to be Monument Valley."[10]

As Doc readies the DeLorean, Marty emerges from the drive-in shop in the sort of embarrassing B-movie Western costume worn by series' "fantasy cowboys" like Tom Mix and Roy Rogers (a pale blue-and-pink, patterned shirt with fringes, burgundy-red jeans, and two-tone boots), and asks Doc if he is sure his clothing is authentic. "Of course," says Doc, "Haven't you ever seen a Western?" "Yeah, I have, Doc," replies Marty, "and Clint Eastwood never wore anything like this." (Marty has obviously not seen *Bronco Billy*.) Doc, of course, has no idea who Clint Eastwood is. "That's right, you haven't heard of him yet," says Marty, gesturing vaguely at posters for both *Revenge of the Creature* and *Tarantula* (both 1955, in the former of which Eastwood made his screen début), while in the background a sign announces *Francis in the Navy*, in which Eastwood also appeared that same year. Marty drives the DeLorean straight at a hoarding showing an Indian attack, passing through it as the car hits the requisite 88 m.p.h. for time travel, only to find himself in the middle of a real band of apparently charging Indians in Monument Valley, 1885. Narrowly avoiding said Indians, a pursuing cavalry column, and a disgruntled bear, Marty falls down a slope and knocks himself out.

Marty wakes to find himself in the homestead of his great-great-grand-father, Séamus McFly, his wife, Maggie, and their son, William Séan McFly, "the first of our family to be born in America." The Irish immigrant character was a stock figure in the Westerns of John Ford (himself the son of Irish immigrants), being particularly prominent in the director's cavalry trilogy, all of which feature a boozing, brawling, and frequently maudlin cavalry sergeant played by Victor McLaglen. Settlers in Ford's films, however, tended to be either stern Anglo-Saxons or comical Scandinavians, so it would seem likely that, with the McFly clan, Zemeckis was referencing the decidedly Irish family of Brett McBain in Sergio Leone's *Once Upon a Time in the West*, while at the same time providing a plausible screen ancestry for Fox's character (the actor being of Irish extraction).

Marty follows the railroad into town. (Earlier, at the drive-in, Marty has remarked that "it's going to be a helluva long walk to Hill Valley from here," leading to Doc's unconvincing exposition regarding the choice of Monument Valley — in reality, it would be the best part of 400 miles, as the crow flies, to the nearest point of the California state line.) As he walks round the station, the camera tilts up and over the roof of the building to show the out-skirts of the town, a shot lifted more or less directly (though with rather less style and minus music by Ennio Morricone) from the scene in which Jill McBain arrives in Flagstaff in *Once Upon a Time in the West*.

After passing by various makeshift business establishments (horse dealer, bath house, butcher, etc.) and noting the building of the courthouse (which features so prominently throughout the trilogy), Marty enters the Palace Saloon. His request for ice-water provokes a reaction from the bartender (played by Matt Clark, a familiar face from Westerns of the late–Sixties and the Seventies) similar to that inspired by Jill McBain's demand for bathwater in Leone's film, and Marty is served whiskey instead. The drink spills onto the bar, burning into the wood like acid, a reference to William Wyler's *The Westerner* (1940), in which Walter Brennan's Judge Roy Bean serves hooch strong enough to strip the varnish from his bar.

Playing cards at a nearby table are three old-timers, played by Harry Carey, Jr., Dub Taylor, and Pat Buttram, all cast for their long association, and identification, with the Western. "Dobe" Carey, the son of silent Western star, Harry, Sr., was the most illustrious of the trio, having appeared in Westerns for both Ford and Hawks, and later, those of Andrew V. McLaglen and Italian director Enzo Barboni. Taylor had played a recurring comic character called "Cannonball" in series Westerns of the Forties starring Bill Elliott and Jimmy Wakely before appearing in Peckinpah's *Major Dundee* (1965), *The Wild Bunch* (1973), and *Pat Garrett and Billy the Kid* (1973), while Buttram was best remembered as Gene Autry's comic sidekick on both the big screen and television.

Enter Buford "Mad Dog" Tannen (in a Leone-style, rear-angle, gunbelt-level shot), followed by his gang. The character of Buford Tannen is closely based on that of Liberty Valance, the ultimate Western badman of John Ford's *The Man Who Shot Liberty Valance* (1962) — or, more precisely, the performance of Thomas F. Wilson as Buford is a well-sustained parody of Lee Marvin's memorable characterization in that film, in which the ironically-named Liberty is an emblematic representation of untamed frontier individualism, a swaggering, bellicose outlaw who must be defeated before the values of "civilization" introduced by James Stewart's equally representative Eastern lawyer can take root, thereby bringing an end to the mythical West (in which men were men and women made apple pie) embodied by both Valance and John Wayne's Tom Doniphon.[11]

After initially mistaking Marty for Séamus, Buford roars out, "Hey, what's your name, dude?" "Clint Eastwood," replies Marty, with great significance, as if that totemic name alone will make Buford back off. "What kind of stupid name is that?" scoffs Buford. "You're 'Mad Dog' Tannen," observes Marty. Needless to say, Buford takes this badly ("Nobody calls me 'Mad Dog'!") and proceeds to the time-honored Western ritual of making the "dude" dance, firing bullets into the floor near his feet. Marty ends his "routine" (to which Dub Taylor's astonished exclamation of "Shit!" is the only appropriate response) by accidentally upending a spittoon over Buford. A chase ensues around the streets of the town (a Western variant on the skate- and hoverboard sequences in the previous two films), ending with Marty being roped and dragged through the dirt before being strung up by the neck from the courthouse building.

The impromptu necktie party is interrupted by the arrival of a booted, duster-wearing figure who steps into a low, rear-angle Leone shot while readying what appears to be a customized, long-barreled Henry rifle, complete with an outsize loading lever (as seen on John Wayne's personal, customized Winchester, and that used by Woody Strode in *Once Upon a Time in the West*) and an anachronistic telescopic sight (as employed by Clint Eastwood in *The Good, the Bad and the Ugly*). Doc — for it is he — shoots through the rope suspending Marty (just as Eastwood shoots through those suspending Eli Wallach's Tuco on various occasions throughout *The Good, the Bad and the Ugly*) before turning the gun on Tannen and informing him that it will "shoot the fleas off a dog's back at five hundred yards." A debate concerning the merits of Doc's horseshoeing ability ends with Tannen threatening to kill the blacksmith-scientist.

"There are a lot worse places to be than the Old West," Doc informs Marty, as the latter explains his unexpected arrival in 1885. After Marty has changed into a flat-brimmed hat and poncho more in keeping with his chosen *nom de l'Ouest*, the pair unsuccessfully attempt to restart the damaged DeLorean, which leads to Doc meeting Clara Clayton. The "runaway horse" plot device, in which the manly hero gets to demonstrate his bravery and equestrian skills to the insipid heroine while providing a starting point for their inevitable (and usually pointless, distracting, and utterly conventional) romance was, of course, a staple, of virtually every B-Western ever made. The casting of Mary Steenburgen as Clara opposite Christopher Lloyd's Doc provides a somewhat tenuous continuity with the Western proper — or at any rate, with Jack Nicholson's *Goin' South* (1978), an uneven romantic-comedy Western in which Lloyd's Deputy Towfield unsuccessfully woos Julia Tate (Steenburgen, in her film début), only to see her marry a condemned outlaw, Henry Lloyd Moon (played, with what was soon to become a trademark lack of subtlety, by Nicholson himself).

Doc and Clara attend the Hill Valley festival ("Proceeds to construct the clock tower"), where their dance is interrupted by Buford Tannen, who has smuggled a Derringer pistol past Marshal Strickland (whose appearance is based on that of Wild Bill Hickok, and to whom Buford growls, "Smile, Marshal," in an echo of Gary Cooper's famous line — "You wanna call me that, smile" — from *The Virginian*, 1929), only to have his attempt to kill Doc thwarted by Marty. The communal celebration was a central feature of John Ford's Westerns, most notably in *My Darling Clementine* and *The Searchers*, and its sudden interruption by outside forces (Ethan Edwards and another Marty — Martin Pawley — in the latter film) is recalled by Buford's intrusion, which ends with him calling out Marty for a showdown at 8:00 on Monday morning. Prior to this, Marty has drawn on his mastery of *Wild Gunman* to silence the guffaws of a jeering gun salesman (peddling the allegedly "new, improved and refined Colt Peacemaker"). Doc and Clara then proceed to enjoy a moonlit moment together, following which Doc decides he wants to stay with her in 1885. During a subsequent discussion with Marty, he remarks that, "we all have to make decisions that affect the course of our lives. You've gotta do what you've gotta do, and I've gotta do what I gotta do."

That evening, however, having been persuaded against his inclinations to return to the future with Marty, Doc breaks off his romance with Clara and heads for the Palace Saloon to get drunk; instead, he ends up enthralling the locals with tales of the future. The next morning, as the appointed time for the showdown approaches, Marty arrives at the saloon and tells Doc it is time to be leaving. Doc, who has talked through the night, knocks back his hitherto forgotten whiskey and promptly falls flat on his face, dead to the world. Chester the barman calls for "wake-up juice," a kill-or-cure cocktail of ingredients guaranteed to restore sobriety (though perhaps somewhat less hazardous than the recipe, comprising cayenne pepper, hot mustard, ipecac, asafetida, croton oil, and gunpowder, used to revive Robert Mitchum's habitually soused sheriff in Hawks' *El Dorado*).

As Marty and Chester administer to Doc, Buford Tannen arrives for his early-morning showdown with "Clint Eastwood" (in an obvious reference to both *High Noon* and *Once Upon a Time in the West*, Marty has been keeping an eye on the town clock as it ticks towards the fateful hour). When Buford calls out Marty, the latter at first suggests a forfeit, to which Buford responds by calling him a "gutless, yellow turd." Pressed on the matter, a scared and exasperated Marty throws up his hands, asking "What? What if I don't go out there?," only to be told that "Everybody, everywhere, will say Clint Eastwood is the biggest yellowbelly in the West." A gun is slid along the bar to Marty (much as Cheyenne does with Harmonica's Colt in *Once Upon a Time in the West*). Marty picks it up, then exchanges a glance (from under the brim of his hat, much as the real Eastwood does throughout the *Dollars* films) with Séamus McFly, who has arrived for the showdown. Buford shouts out again, this time calling Marty a "gutless, yellow pie-slinger" (a reference to the pie dish Marty threw to prevent the shooting of Doc at the dance, but also an echo of Liberty Valance's "hash-slinger" gibe aimed at James Stewart's Ransom Stoddard).

Still trying, with Séamus' tacit approval, to avoid a shootout, Marty justifies his position by saying, "He's an asshole! I don't care what Tannen says, and I don't care what anybody else says either!" It is at this point, with Marty's reluctance to do what a man's gotta do, that *Back to the Future Part III* comes nearest to subverting, rather than merely recycling and reaffirming, the conventions of the Western. Indeed, one shudders to think how the course of Western history (to say nothing of the space-time continuum) might have been irrevocably altered if, for instance, Gary Cooper's marshal in *High Noon* had turned to Grace Kelly, kicked a pebble, and gently murmured, "Shucks, hon, let's not worry about that Frank Miller. Ain't nothin' but an asshole anyhow." Or if Shane had saddled up and ridden out of the valley, telling little Joey that Jack Wilson was just a no-good varmint hardly worth the trouble of killing.

As with all reluctant heroes, however, circumstances (or at any rate, the scriptwriter) soon dictate that Marty must make a stand. Having asked if there is a back door to the saloon (and been told that there is indeed, "in the back"), Marty and Doc attempt to escape, only to be fired on by Buford's men. Marty dives into a store, but Doc is captured. Buford snatches Doc's pocket watch and tells Marty he has one minute to come out or he will shoot Doc (the watch and the standoff situation being familiar elements from Leone's films). Marty emerges from the store and, after the customary stare-down in which Buford urges him to draw, removes his gunbelt, saying, "I thought we could settle this like men." "You thought wrong," retorts Buford, drawing his gun and shooting Marty in the chest. A gloating Buford shambles down the street, bowing to the onlookers, but when he reaches Marty, the "corpse" comes to life, kicking the gun out of Buford's hand. Buford throws a body punch at Marty, but only succeeds in breaking his fist. Marty throws back his poncho to reveal a stove door strapped to his chest — "Clint Eastwood" has been saved by Clint Eastwood. He proceeds to beat up Buford in true, two-fisted Western he-man fashion before dumping him in a cart of manure (a recurring comeuppance for members of the Tannen tribe throughout the trilogy). The deputy marshal arrives, and Buford and his boys are arrested for holding up the Pine City stage (perhaps a final, fleeting reference to Liberty Valance, who is first seen holding up the stage to Shinbone).

During the showdown sequence, Alan Silvestri's score, which throughout the film has recalled the big, stirring, and unmistakably Western sound composed by Elmer Bernstein for *The Magnificent Seven* (1960), changes to terse woodwind and percussion reminiscent of Morricone's "settling of accounts" themes for the *Dollars* films, though Silvestri wisely resists the temptation to parody the Italian's unique style. An outtake from the same sequence shows Marty lying on his back, apparently dead, with a fly crawling over his face, another nod to *Once Upon a Time in the West*, in which Jack Elam's gunman, waiting for a train to arrive, is plagued by a pesky insect (in fact, the buzzing of the fly can still be heard on the soundtrack as Buford walks towards Marty's "body"). Earlier, we see Clara, having learned that Doc really does love her, demonstrating a disregard for the niceties of train scheduling (by pulling the emergency cord), similar to that of Colonel Douglas Mortimer ("This train'll stop at Tucumcari") in *For a Few Dollars More* (1965). Another outtake shows Buford backshooting Marshal Strickland in front of his young son (thereby explaining why it is Strickland's deputy, rather than the marshal himself, who rounds up Tannen and his gang). In the accompanying commentary, Bob Gale remarks that, "Once Buford kills somebody, you don't want to see Marty *not* shoot him in the gunfight. Buford deserves to die for this, and since we can't kill him, we cut this scene out. And the movie's better for not having it."[12]

The baddie duly defeated, Marty and Doc embark on a race to "cut off [the train] at Coyote Pass," having hatched a plan to use the train to shunt the DeLorean up to speed for reentry to the future. This, naturally, involves boarding the moving train from galloping horses, running over the carriage roofs, and holding up the startled engineer (played by Bill McKinney, seen to rather better effect in both *The Shootist* and *The Outlaw Josey Wales*), who is informed that the hold-up is not really a hold-up but a science experiment. Equally naturally, the "experiment" is a success. Back in 1985, Marty is visited by Doc, Clara, and their two children (Jules and Verne) in their customized time-travel train.

Although, as suggested earlier, it is debatable to what extent (if any) the film's referencing of classic Westerns would have resonated with the target audience of *Back to the Future Part III*, this aspect certainly struck a chord with reviewers and critics, *Variety* opining, "The fun of this meta–Western is partly the recognition of elements familiar from genre classics, the dance from *My Darling Clementine*, the sobering-up concoction from *El Dorado*, the costume from *Fistful of Dollars*. Fox reexperiences [*sic*] all this, literally flying through the screen (at an incongruous Monument Valley drive-in)[13] into every Western fan's dream of being a character in a 'real' Western,"[14] a view echoed in *The Aurum Film Encyclopedia*: "Using the commercially acceptable Science Fiction super-spectacle as an excuse, the film luxuriates in its Western trappings, with specific film references, like the replay of *A Fistful of Dollars* [*sic*] (1964) in the climax, and the use of such major genre images as the horde of galloping Indians, the Ford-style community hoedown, Monument Valley and the thundering Iron Horse, which is turned in the coda into a flying, steam-driven time machine.... Like most post–Serge [*sic*] Leone, post–Sam Peckinpah, post–*Butch Cassidy and the Sundance Kid* (1969) Westerns, this is essentially a meditation on the Western rather than a Western proper, its many delights arising from its knowingness about the form, transmuting Ford's sense of nostalgia for a vanished and probably mythical past into a feeling for a vanished but actual movie genre."[15]

While it may be obvious from even the most cursory glance that *Back to the Future Part III* is not a "Western proper," the assertion that it constitutes a "meditation on the Western" seems a remarkable overstatement of both the film's ambitions, as well as its achievements. As Randolph Scott would have said, "There are some things a man can't ride around," and though it would be gratifying to record that Gale and Zemeckis harbored some more elevated purpose in setting *Back to the Future Part III* within both the historical and mythological West, there is, unfortunately, nothing in their comments on the film to suggest that such was the case,[16] or indeed that the film's wholesale appropriation of the imagery and conventions of the Western amounts to anything more meaningful than providing "fun" for film buffs. Even allowing for the fact that both men were under pressure from Universal Studios to complete the trilogy, and that therefore the script, with some mitigation, might be expected to be less considered and well-constructed than that of the original film, there seems, from a Western fan's point of view, distressingly little point to sending Marty and Doc back to the Old West. Granted that, having projected the pair forwards in time in the second film, it was obvious that they should go back in time in the third installment, one must still ask, why the Old West, as opposed to any other time period?

An immediate question arising from the premise of *Back to the Future Part III* is why Doc Brown should want to take up apparently permanent residence in the Old West in the first place. While his impulse to visit the period is perfectly understandable, it is hardly credible that any scientist-inventor would actually choose to inhabit a time period more technologically primitive than his own. What exactly is Doc supposed to be doing in Hill Valley, 1885? Given his oft-stated (though highly selective) unwillingness to "interrupt the space-time continuum," it is not as if he might be hoping to beat one of his heroes, Thomas Edison, to the invention of the light bulb or the motion picture camera,[17] or to otherwise benefit from his knowledge of the future (thereby reducing himself to the same moral level as Biff Tannen in *Back to the Future Part II*). In fact, there is no reason to suppose that Doc might not have been just as happy visiting the year 1785 (during the heyday of the enlightened, gentleman amateur-scientist), where he could have swapped notes on clock towers and lightning with another of his heroes, Benjamin Franklin. Plenty of employment opportunities for a blacksmith then too, one would imagine.

If, as Gale correctly asserts, "the West is America's mythology," and that in *Back to the Future Part III* he and Zemeckis wished to show "the beginnings of Hill Valley," it is, from a Western perspective, somewhat disappointing to discover that the Hill Valley of 1885 is simply an embryonic version of the town as seen in the previous films, inhabited by forerunners of the characters from those films. There is, it seems almost superfluous to point out, no sense of the historical reality of the Old West, of the dangers and hardships faced by settlers or the true grit required to overcome them, no sense of Hill Valley as a Californian frontier town, no sign of a Mexican population or influence, and no Indians, bar those seen in the sight-gag charge in Monument Valley — in short, no sense that Hill Valley, 1885, is anything other than the prototype of the bland, WASP enclave it will one day become. The only historical character to appear in the film does so solely by proxy, in the form of Marshal Strickland's Wild Bill Hickok make-up and costume. Such unwillingness to engage with either the historical or cultural reality of the past is, it may be added, symptomatic of the *Back to the Future* series as a whole: just as the first film suggests that a black waiter in Hill Valley, 1955, can one day become mayor of Hill Valley, 1985, if only he believes in the American Dream and works hard to "make his future a good one" (with no need for any disagreeable historical necessities like Civil Rights), so Marty McFly is not only seen to learn nothing from his experiences of the past but also to *need* to learn nothing from them — being already, as he is, that high pinnacle of human evolution and adornment of Western civilization, the Eighties' All-American high-school kid.[18]

On a mythological level too, there is no sense in the film of Manifest Destiny, the Progress of Civilization, or the wilderness-into-a-garden themes which so preoccupied John Ford, or even a foreshadowing of the end of the mythic West as found in both *The Man Who Shot Liberty Valance* and the films of Peckinpah and Leone. As the figure of the settler has never been granted mythic status in the Western (except on a collective basis), it is perhaps appropriate that the character of Séamus McFly should be as vague and insubstantial as he is; left to his own devices, one suspects that he would still be sitting on a barstool back in the Auld Country, boring his pals with brave dreams of the New World. This trait, however, certainly has less to do with any traditional depiction of the settler than with the need to show Séamus as the progenitor of a long line of failures ("No McFly ever amounted to anything in the history of Hill Valley," as Mr. Strickland says in the original film), resulting in that *über*-milquetoast, George McFly, father of Marty. Maggie McFly, on the other hand — pious, superstitious, and sharp-tongued — is clearly the backbone of the family, a not uncommon depiction of the pioneer woman in the Western, and one which also, in juxtaposition with her thoroughly domesticated husband, heralds "the world without balls" referred to by Sergio Leone, which, in turn, gave rise to the Western itself as both literary and cinematic genre.[19] Be that as it may, however, neither Séamus nor Maggie prove to have any great bearing, beyond providing a familial reference point, on the narrative of *Back to the Future Part III*.

The role of romantic hero, of the outsider who will set things to rights, therefore devolves onto Marty, but as this is a function which he not only seeks to avoid but of which he also seems to be unaware (despite his alleged familiarity with Westerns; that is to say, of the requirements of both the genre, and of the role, in which he finds himself), it is next to impossible to view him in this light. Even as nominal hero (though, given his generally reactive behavior, "protagonist" might be a better description), Marty acts from neither a sense of civic duty (the traditional, disinterested Defender of Civilization model) nor personal involvement (the Lone Avenger model), despite the fact that, within both the context of "the Western" in which he finds himself and that of the series (i.e., his own family history), his confrontation and defeat of Buford Tannen is absolutely essential and cannot be avoided. In fact, it can be argued that were Marty to accept the traditional moral imperative of the Western hero and actually kill his enemy, he would not only demonstrate to Séamus the necessity of "doing what a man's gotta do" (thereby, conceivably, injecting a little spine into the male side of the McFly family and making his original return to 1955 unnecessary) but also serve the community of Hill Valley by ridding it of the Tannen line. Instead, Marty rejects the ethos of the Western (and of the West that is America's mythology) by seeking refuge in the tactics of the high-school canteen (the suggestion of a forfeit and his attempt to dismiss Tannen as "an asshole"), in the process not only disqualifying himself, despite his eventual and reluctant showdown with Buford, as an authentic Western hero but also rendering his return to the foundation myth of American manhood irrelevant.[20] Indeed, it could be argued that only Buford Tannen fulfills his appointed role within the traditional Western framework, but as he is played more for laughs than menace, his effectiveness in this regard is minimal at best. In the final analysis, therefore, *Back to the Future Part III*, whatever its claims as entertainment, declines to engage with either the Western or the historical West on any real level; it is not just "the West as seen through the eyes of a kid from the Eighties" but the West as window-dressing, an Eighties' theme-park view of the past stripped of any meaning or mythic resonance. A meditation on the Western? Like the man said—"Don't piss down my back and tell me it's raining."

* * *

The *Aurum Encyclopedia*'s description of the Western as "a vanished but actual movie genre" notwithstanding, in point of fact the Western entered the 1990s in considerably finer fettle than it had been since the mid–1970s. In the immediate aftermath of *Heaven's Gate*, Hollywood had tended to view the Western much like an injured horse in need of a mercy bullet, but the combined success of the *Young Guns* films, the television adaptation of Larry McMurtry's *Lonesome Dove* in 1989 and *Dances With Wolves* the following year, appeared to convince the studios that there might indeed still be the odd nugget to be extracted, and that the old mine should perhaps be reopened, at least on a limited basis. As Clint Eastwood put it, "Every few years, somebody makes that announcement [that the Western is dead], and the studios seem to believe it. But then someone makes a good film, and all of a sudden the Western is alive again."[21] Eastwood himself returned to the genre with the magisterial *Unforgiven* (1992, but originally written, significantly enough, in the mid–1970s), while Kevin Costner emerged as the first film star since Eastwood to be strongly identified with the form, making the aforementioned *Dances With Wolves* (perhaps the epitome of the handwringing, liberal-guilt Western), the gloomy and morose *Wyatt Earp* (1994, which followed the considerably livelier *Tombstone* of the previous year), and, later, the excellent *Open Range* (2003). Walter Hill got back in the saddle with *Geronimo: An American Legend* (1993), *Wild Bill* (1995), the first episode of the successful (if remarkably downbeat) HBO series, *Deadwood* (2004), and *Broken Trail* (2006/TV), while also making another Western-in-disguise, *Last Man Standing* (an unofficial remake of *Fistful of Dollars*— itself, of course, an unofficial remake of *Yojimbo*, 1961).

Throughout the 1990s and up to the present day, the Western has continued to break out of the reservation on a regular basis, sometimes in recognizable form, more often in curious mutations that might well be termed the Hybrid Western. Thus there have been animated Westerns (*An American Tail II: Fievel Goes West*, 1991, *Pocahontas*, 1995), Civil War Westerns (*Ride With the Devil*, 1999), Eastern Westerns (*The Last of the Mohicans*, 1992), feminist Westerns (*The Ballad of Little Joe*, 1993, *Bad Girls*, 1999, *Bandidas*, 2006), historical Westerns (*Grey Owl*, 1999, *American Outlaws*, 2001, *The Alamo*, 2004, *The New World*, 2005, *The Assassination of Jesse James By the Coward Robert Ford*, 2007), horror Westerns (*Grim Prairie Tales*, 1990), kung fu Westerns (*Shanghai Noon*, 2000), modern-day comedy Westerns (*City Slickers*, 1991, and its 1994 sequel), post–Leone Leone Westerns (*Posse*, 1993, *The Quick and the Dead*, 1995), post–Western Westerns (*The Hi-Lo Country*, 1998, *Brokeback Mountain*, 2005), science fiction Westerns (*Wild Wild West*), television Westerns (*Buffalo Girls*, 1995, *Trinità & Bambino ... e adesso tocca a noi*, 1995, *And Starring Pancho Villa as Himself*, 2003, *Into the West*, 2005, among many), wallaby Westerns (*Quigley Down Under*, 1990, *Ned Kelly*, 2003, *The Proposition*, 2005), and weird Westerns (*Dead Man*, 1995, *Tears of the Black Tiger*, 2000, *Dust*, 2001, *Blueberry*, 2004, *Sukiyaki Western Django*, 2007). The Western may not be what it once was, but a vanished genre? As John Wayne's *Big Jake* would have put it, "Not hardly."

There have even been occasional sightings of the traditional Western, in the form of the afore-mentioned *Open Range*, *The Missing* (also 2003), and *Seraphim Falls* (2006), while actor-producers Tom Selleck and Sam Elliott continue to do sterling work in bringing adaptations of Louis L'Amour and Elmore Leonard to television. But perhaps the most encouraging sign of a potential return to the verities of the past (when men were men and the devil take the rest) was the surprise success of James Mangold's remake of *3:10 to Yuma*, which topped box-office charts worldwide in 2007. Though entirely unnecessary as a remake of Delmer Daves' outstanding film of fifty years before, it nonetheless proved that a traditional, fictional Western with no ambitions beyond providing stirring entertainment can still "git them dog-gies rolling" all the way to Sedalia. After all, the basic ingredients of the West-ern — a man, a horse, a gun, a challenge — are not rocket science (or even time-travel science), and it is perhaps within that context, of the Western as entertainment, and by demonstrating that the Almighty American Teenager could be persuaded to embrace stories set in the Old West, that *Back to the Future Part III* may be said to have played its part. Yup, there's still gold in them thar hills, long as folks is prepared to go diggin' for it....

Notes

1. That the New Hollywood-era film-mak-ers should demonstrate such an apparent lack of interest in the Western seems all the more curious given the omnipresence of the genre in cinema, television, and advertising throughout their formative years in the 1950s.

2. *Time Out*, London, 26 September–2 Oc-tober 1985.

3. Quoted by Peter Guttridge in "The west-ern rides again," *Sunday Times*, London, 3 Feb-ruary, 1991.

4. When Kasdan attempted to reverse this trend in *Silverado*, however, the result was less than successful, with the principals' costumes, instead of reverting to the classical mode or the well-balanced combination of style and realism found in the best Italian Westerns, looking ex-actly as though they had been run up by the costume department an hour before shooting: too new, too clean, and too bogus.

5. As late as 1993, it was being reported (*Irish Times*, 26 November) that veteran Western di-rector Budd Boetticher would return to the genre with *A Horse for Mr. Barnum*, to be shot in Spain with Robert Mitchum and James Coburn — a project which, alas, failed to mate-rialize.

6. From interview on *Back to the Future 4-Disc Ultimate Edition*, Universal, 2005.

7. From *Brain Storm*, a 2003 interview con-ducted by Scott Holleran for Box Office Mojo. See http://www.boxofficemojo.com/features/?id=1258.

8. On the end credits of *Back to the Future*

Part II, Leone's film is incorrectly given as *For a Fistful of Dollars*, a direct translation of the Italian title.

9. From *Brain Storm*, a 2003 interview conducted by Scott Holleran for Box Office Mojo. See http://www.boxofficemojo.com/features/?id=1258.

10. From interview on *Back to the Future 4-Disc Ultimate Edition*, Universal, 2005. Not that Zemeckis and Gale need be unduly cen-sured on this point: John Ford himself displayed a remarkably cavalier approach to geographical exactitude, happily transplanting Tombstone virtually the entire length of the state of Ari-zona for *My Darling Clementine* (1946), and blithely allowing Ward Bond's Texas Rangers to charge round Monument Valley in *The Searchers*. That noted, one might well suppose that placing Marty in the middle of a cattle drive in a less less-geographically specific West-ern location would have achieved the same ef-fect, and without the need for unconvincing exposition.

11. Wilson, made up to look like Marvin and capturing much of the actor's loping gait and hyper-aggressive demeanor (as well as car-rying a similar, silver-embossed quirt), clearly spent a lot of time studying Ford's film, as shown by an outtake in which, instead of using Valance's preferred pejorative ("dude"), he calls Marty "pilgrim," the equally dismissive term aimed at Stewart's character by Doniphon.

12. From interview on *Back to the Future 4-Disc Ultimate Edition*, Universal, 2005. Asked,

in the Box Office Mojo interview listed previously, to elaborate on Marty's unwillingness to face down Buford, Gale replied: "You have to face your foe if it makes sense — but not if it's about something really stupid. Bar fights are not heroic. It's not the same thing as facing Darth Vader, who's out to destroy the universe [and it's not as if] people's lives are really at stake. If it's just a macho thing, then it's stupid. It doesn't matter what other people think [of you]." Not, it may be remarked, a point of view likely to be endorsed by a proper Western hero, such as J.B. Books in *The Shootist*, whose credo states, "I won't be wronged, I won't be insulted, and I won't be laid a hand on. I don't do these things to other people, and I require the same from them."

13. The fictitious Monument Valley drive-in uses the English spelling of "theatre."

14. *Variety*. Dated (erroneously, it would seem) 1 January 1990. See http://www.variety.com/review/VE1117788828.html?categoryid=31&cs=1.

15. *The Aurum Film Encyclopedia: The Western*, ed. Phil Hardy, Aurum Press, London, 2d ed., 1991. For a critique of *Back to the Future, Part III* from a science fiction perspective, see *The Aurum Film Encyclopedia: Science Fiction*, ed. Phil Hardy, Aurum Press, London, 2d ed., 1991.

16. Gale, on the genesis of *Back to the Future Part III*: "The West is America's mythology. I mean, it's romantic because we're going back to a time which people think back upon with kind of a 'Wouldn't that've been cool to run around in the West?' I mean, any time you've got guys riding around on horses, let's face it, a guy who [*sic*] looks a lot cooler riding a horse than he does driving a Plymouth." From interview on *Back to the Future 4-Disc Ultimate Edition*, Universal, 2005. Gale, on why *Back to the Future Part III* was the most enjoyable part of the trilogy to shoot: "We were on location so it was nice to be away from the studio. We all got to wear cowboy hats." From *Brain Storm*, a 2003 interview conducted by Scott Holleran for Box Office Mojo. See http://www.boxofficemojo.com/features/?id=1258. These comments, coupled with those of Robert Zemeckis quoted in the text, go some way to illustrating why *Back to the Future Part III* need not be regarded as "a meditation on the Western."

17. An undated draft of the screenplay has the young D.W. Griffith witnessing the events in Hill Valley, 1885. Presumably, the fact that the ten-year-old future Father of Film had, by 1885, been no further west than his native Kentucky accounts for his eventual non-appearance in the film. See the Internet Movie Script Database: http://www.imsdb.com/Movie%20Scripts/Back%20to%20the%20Future%20II%20&%20III%20Script.html.

18. At which point, it may be instructive, and certainly amusing, to consider the following observation from *Variety*'s review of *The Breakfast Club* (1985): "When the causes of the Decline of Western Civilization are finally writ, Hollywood will surely have to answer why it turned one of man's most significant art forms over to the self-gratification of high-schoolers." Indeed. See http://www.variety.com/review/VE1117789506.html?categoryid=31&cs=1&query=breakfast+club. Or as Sergio Leone might have put it, "Where the past had no value, the present, often, had no meaning. That is why the future boys appeared."

19. See *West of Everything: The Inner Life of Westerns* by Jane Tompkins (Oxford University Press, 1992) for a detailed analysis of the emergence of the Western as a reaction to the imposition of Victorian, feminine cultural notions of domesticity, piety, vengeance, etc.

20. It may be mentioned that, even among its target audience, *Back to the Future Part III* is regarded as the weakest of the trilogy due, one gathers, to the writer's decision to reduce the character of Marty McFly, ostensibly the focus of the series, to little more than an onlooker, a literal *deus ex machina*, who (in contradiction of Agathon's dictum) can change the past but whose only dramatic *raison d'etre* is to warn Doc of his impending doom. Certainly, beyond saving the life of his friend, Marty has none of the emotional involvement in events that made *Back to the Future* the most satisfying of the trilogy. And, given that Marty's plan to save Doc involves nothing more daring than spiriting him back to the future in the DeLorean (while in the meantime actively avoiding the dramatically necessary showdown with Buford Tannen), his function as even nominal hero is severely undercut.

21. Quoted in the *Boston Sunday Herald*, 2 August 1992.

Works Cited

Assault on Precinct 13. Dir. John Carpenter, 1976.

Back to the Future. Dir. Robert Zemeckis, 1985.

Back to the Future Part II. Dir. Robert Zemeckis, 1989.

Back to the Future Part III. Dir. Robert Zemeckis, 1990.

Battle Beyond the Stars. Dir. Jimmy T. Murakami, 1980.

Boston Sunday Herald, 2 August 1992. Interview with Clint Eastwood.

Bronco Billy. Dir. Clint Eastwood, 1980.

Buffalo Bill and the Indians, or Sitting Bull's History Lesson. Dir. Robert Altman, 1976.

Butch Cassidy and the Sundance Kid. Dir. George Roy Hill, 1969.

Cattle Queen of Montana. Dir. Allan Dwan, 1954.

C'era una volta il West (Once Upon a Time in the West) Dir. Sergio Leone, 1968.

Close Encounters of the Third Kind. Dir. Steven Spielberg, 1978.

Comin' at Ya! Dir. Ferdinando Baldi, 1981.

Dances with Wolves. Dir. Kevin Costner, 1990.

Deadwood. Created by David Milch. HBO Television Series 2004–2006.

El Dorado. Dir. Howard Hawks, 1966.

Extreme Prejudice. Dir. Walter Hill, 1987.

Fistful of Dollars. Dir. Sergio Leone, 1964.

For a Few Dollars More. Dir. Sergio Leone, 1965.

Gale, Bob, and Robert Zemeckis. *Back to the Future 4-Disc Ultimate Edition,* Universal, 2005.

Goin' South. Dir. Jack Nicholson, 1978.

The Good, the Bad and the Ugly. Dir. Sergio Leone, 1966.

The Grey Fox. Dir. Phillip Borsos, 1982.

Guttridge, Peter. "The western rides again," *Sunday Times,* London, 3 February 1991.

Hardy, Phil (ed.). *The Aurum Film Encyclopedia: Science Fiction.* 2d ed. London: Aurum Press, 1991.

_____ (ed). *The Aurum Film Encyclopedia: The Western.* 2d ed. London: Aurum Press, 1991.

Heaven's Gate. Dir. Michael Cimino, 1980.

High Noon. Dir. Fred Zinnemann, 1952.

High Plains Drifter. Dir. Clint Eastwood, 1972.

Holleran, Scott. *Brain Storm,* Bob Gale interview, 2003. Online at http://www.boxoffice mojo.com/features/?id=1258.

Internet Movie Script Database for Back to the Future Part III. Online at http://www. imsdb.com/Movie%20Scripts/Back%20to %20the%20Future%20II%20&%20III%20 Script.html.

Irish Times, 26 November 1993.

Jeremiah Johnson. Dir. Sydney Pollack, 1972.

The Legend of the Lone Rider. Dir. William A. Fraker, 1981.

The Life and Times of Judge Roy Bean. Dir. John Huston, 1972.

Little Big Man. Dir. Arthur Penn, 1970.

Lonesome Dove. Dir. Simon Wincer. Three Episode TV Mini-Series.

The Long Riders. Dir. Walter Hill, 1980.

The Magnificent Seven. Dir. John Sturges, 1960.

Major Dundee. Dir. Sam Peckinpah, 1965.

The Man Who Shot Liberty Valance. Dir. John Ford, 1962.

The Missing. Dir. Ron Howard, 2003.

My Darling Clementine. Dir. John Ford, 1946.

The Oklahoma Kid. Dir. Lloyd Bacon, 1939.

Open Range. Dir. Kevin Costner, 2003.

Outland. Dir. Peter Hyams, 1981.

The Outlaw Josey Wales. Dir. Clint Eastwood, 1976.

Pale Rider. Dir. Clint Eastwood, 1985.

Pat Garrett and Billy the Kid. Dir. Sam Peckinpah, 1973.

Red Dawn. Dir. John Milius, 1984.

Red River. Dirs. Howard Hawks and Arthur Rosson, 1948.

Revenge of the Creature. Dir. Jack Arnold, 1955.

Rio Bravo. Dir. Howard Hawks, 1959.

Rio Grande. Dir. John Ford, 1950.

The Searchers. Dir. John Ford, 1956.

Seraphim Falls. Dir. David Von Ancken, 2006.

Shane. Dir. George Stevens, 1952.

The Shootist. Dir. Don Siegel, 1976.

Silverado. Dir. Lawrence Kasdan, 1985.

Southern Comfort. Dir. Walter Hill, 1981.

Star Wars. Dir. George Lucas, 1977.

Tarantula. Dir. Jack Arnold, 1955.

Three Amigos! Dir. John Landis, 1986.

3:10 to Yuma 2007. Dir. James Mangold, 2007.

Time Out, London, 26 September–2 October 1985.

Tompkins, Jane. *West of Everything: The Inner Life of Westerns.* Oxford: Oxford University Press, 1992.

Unforgiven. Dir. Clint Eastwood, 1992.

Variety. Jan. 1, 1985. Online at http://www. variety.com/review/VE1117789506.html? categoryid=31&cs=1&query=breakfast+club

_____. Jan. 1, 1990. Online at: http://www.variety.com/review/VE1117788828.html?categoryid=31&cs=1.

The Virginian. Television Series, 1962–1971.

The Warriors. Dir. Walter Hill, 1979.

The Westerner. Dir. William Wyler, 1940.

The Wild Bunch. Dir. Sam Peckinpah, 1973.

Young Guns. Dir. Christopher Cain, 1988.

6. Music in Flux:
Musical Transformation and
Time Travel in *Back to the Future*

CHRISTINE LEE GENGARO

The *Back to the Future* (*BTTF*) trilogy follows Marty McFly's odyssey through the past, present, and future. It is a temporal journey, but it is a musical one as well. Music in the films performs the usual functions of movie music, mirroring actions and easing transitions between scenes, but it also helps to differentiate the timelines and time periods that Marty encounters. Furthermore, it serves as an important link between similar events across timelines. In this paper, I hope to outline some of the prominent musical themes in the *Back to the Future* trilogy and discuss how they help to root the viewer in certain time periods, and how these themes function in the narrative. I also plan to focus specifically on the first film and its particular musical issues. In the original *BTTF*, the fluid boundary between score and sourced music — that is, music that provides underscore to scenes (and appears to be unheard by the characters in the film) and music that originates from an onscreen source — can be viewed as an analogue to the fluid boundary among present, past, and future. There are important places in the narrative of *BTTF* where this fluidity is significant. Alan Silvestri's score provides much of the thematic material for the score, but there are also popular songs — from the 1980s and the 1950s — that help set the scene in a more superficial way.

Director Robert Zemeckis and composer Alan Silvestri have collaborated on a number of films. Two of their greatest successes, *Back to the Future* and *Forrest Gump*, are films whose narratives take place over different decades; music is as much an element of setting as costume and make-up. Popular music is especially important in *Forrest Gump*, as the majority of the score features hits from the decades of Forrest's life. The conscious decision to make popular music so important for the sonic landscape of this film was based on the director's understanding of how music would help to cue the audience members in to time changes, but would also stir in them a feeling of identification with Forrest, especially when they recognized music from their past. When asked about Zemeckis' decision to feature popular music prominently in *Forrest Gump*, Silvestri explained: "On *Forrest Gump*, everything was meant to conjure up time periods, for anyone who had lived through those years.... Bob really felt that the dimension of having the audience hear all of the specific music of the time connected with these events would be a wonderful layer in this film, and he was absolutely right."[1] In *Back to the Future* (which predates *Forrest Gump* by nine years), Zemeckis used a fairly limited collection of popular songs, relying heavily on Silvestri's themes to convey the situations and characters in this narrative. The popular songs that are present, however, are very useful. Huey Lewis's "Power of Love" and "Back in Time" are used to great effect. The presence of "Johnny B. Goode"—clearly a vehicle for Marty's considerable singing and guitar-playing talent—at the dance is anachronistic, but this is played for laughs as Marvin Berry calls up his cousin Chuck and presumably bears witness to the birth of Rock and Roll. Popular music appears in *BTTF II* mostly as scenery. Michael Jackson's "Beat It" plays in the 1980s-themed café, and Sammy Hagar's "I Can't Drive 55" helps introduce Biff's casino in the alternate version of 1985. There are popular songs from 1885 in *BTTF III* as "Oh My Darling, Clementine" and "Turkey in the Straw" are played at the dance. Clara and Doc even dance to the acoustic (and wordless) version of ZZ Top's "Doubleback" at the town's Clock Tower celebration.

The first of the three main time periods in the first *Back to the Future* film is Marty's present in 1985. In this timeline, the McFly family struggles. At the beginning of the film, a tardy Marty is admonished by the school principal, "No McFly ever amounted to anything in the history of Hill Valley." Marty has big dreams of success as a rock star, but lacks the self-confidence to send his demo tape to a record company; rejection at the school band auditions leaves him disappointed, and his girlfriend, Jennifer intimates that Marty's fear of rejection may be stronger than his will to succeed. Marty appears to have a very positive relationship with Jennifer, but he seems somewhat emotionally detached from his family. Marty's mother, Lorraine, is a heavy drinker who has let herself go; Marty's father, George—who has been perennially under the thumb of bully Biff Tannen—has not been a particularly strong influence on Marty. Instead, Marty has found a father figure in Doc Brown. Their friendship forms the emotional core of the story, and the conflict between them about the potential benefits of Doc's invention (i.e., Marty's desire to use time travel for financial gain in *BTTF II* vs. Doc's desire to correct Marty's downward spiral in 2015) draws upon philosophical issues of time travel, including ethics and paradoxes. Although this conflict appears in the first film as Marty attempts to save Doc from his violent death at the hands of the Libyans, the conflict deepens in *Back to the Future*'s two sequels.

The score of the first film is extremely effective in conveying the exhilaration and excitement of Marty's time journey, and in differentiating the three time periods covered in the film. The scores of the two sequels, filmed simultaneously and released in 1989 and 1990, rely on the first for musical source material. The score of the second film has much in common with that of the first film. Similar musical cues offer accompaniment to similar situations across different time periods. Take for example Silvestri's "Skateboard Chase," a cue that accompanies both the skateboard chase in *BTTF* and the hoverboard chase in *BTTF II*. The score of *BTTF III* shares some musical cues with its prequels, but it also explores new sonic territory as Marty and Doc find themselves in the Old West.

The scores of the three films constitute a system of musical cues, some of which appear in all three films, while others are related specifically to events in a single film. There is a good deal of overlap in sequences between the first and second films, and the music echoes this overlap. Unlike other film composers who follow the Wagnerian model of leitmotivs — in which the musical associations are unchangeable and true (a character's theme will only appear when he is on screen or when another character is referring to him) — Silvestri used musical cues for events or characters in a very fluid way. The music for the cue "the DeLorean Revealed," for example, refers specifically to the DeLorean in some instances, but in other situations, the initial thematic idea of "The DeLorean Revealed" refers to some magical effect of time travel. The musical cue "The Letter" appears in one instance as Marty is writing a letter in the first film, but in other scenes it accompanies moments of family closeness or nostalgia. The musical cue "The Libyans" has two main musical elements: a military cadence that appears whenever Doc and Marty decide they have a mission to accomplish, and a spiky motif that appears when characters are in danger, and these two elements appear in all three films. Marty, as the main character, does not have his own theme, per se; Doc doesn't have one either. There are themes associated with them, and there are themes that accompany their actions, but as for cues that "belong" to characters, only Clara in *BTTF III* seems to have her "own" music. The first film (and to a great extent, the second) is populated by perhaps half a dozen musical ideas that are combined and transformed in numerous innovative and creative ways to create the sonic world of Marty's past, present, and future.

Zemeckis and Silvestri chose to open the first film not with the main *BTTF* theme, but with the sound of ticking clocks. Silvestri's score does not figure at all at the beginning of the film. In fact, if this time period had a theme song, it would be Huey Lewis' "The Power of Love." It establishes this version of Marty's present when it first appears. Marty talks to Doc on the phone and realizes that he's late for school. He slams the phone down just as the first chords of the song begin. The songs continue as underscore as Marty makes his way through the town square of Hill Valley on his way to school. After school, the song appears again, this time as an instrumental version played by Marty's band, the Pinheads, as they audition for the dance. It makes its final appearance in when Marty and Jennifer are learning about the Clock Tower. The line between score and sourced music is blurred in this instance because "The Power of Love" appears as very quiet underscore while an unnamed character exposits about the bolt of lightning that stopped the clock. The song gets gradually louder during the scene, especially when Jennifer's father comes to pick her up. It is unclear, but the music could possibly be sourced from his car radio. It is definitely still background music, that is, until Marty and Jennifer kiss; the song then takes prominence in the score. As Marty returns home, the song plays, only stopping when he sees the tow truck in front of his house. "The Power of Love" does not appear again in the film after this point, because once Marty leaves this version of 1985, he will never return. When Marty goes to the parking lot of the Twin Pines Mall to meet Doc, life as he knows it is about to change. The score follows suit. When Doc unveils the time machine for Marty, Silvestri's score suddenly gains prominence.[2]

The first of Alan Silvestri's musical themes we hear is an effervescent, sparkling motif consisting of two arpeggiated triads a half step apart. It appears when the temporal magic of time travel is either realized or revealed, and has therefore aptly been named "The Magic of Time Travel" by film music journalists Jon and Al Kaplan. This music appears in Silvestri's cue, "The DeLorean Revealed" because the theme first occurs when Doc unveils the DeLorean to Marty in the parking lot of the Twin Pines mall (it figures in other cues on the soundtrack as well, like "Einstein Disintegrates," but for clarity's sake I will refer to it as "The DeLorean Revealed" in this paper). It appears again once Marty is in the 1950s, and he realizes Lyon Estates — the housing development he grew up in — has not yet been built, Also, in the same scene, the theme sounds when Marty looks at the DeLorean and sees the date November 5, 1955, on the time display. It appears when Marty unveils the time machine for Doc of the 1950s. At the end of the film, the motif appears once more as Doc of the 1980s — who Marty thinks is dead — opens his eyes after the Libyans shoot him. Variations of the theme, or at least related themes, occur when Marty looks at the picture of his disappearing siblings, and at other points (see the cue sheets for other instances). As the Kaplans have pointed out, this theme outlines an "octatonic" flavor. An octatonic scale features alternating whole and half steps; its unique sound has been the basis of numerous sci-fi scores like *The Day the Earth Stood Still*.[3]

In the second phase of the film — Marty's experiences in the 1950s — we hear a number of tunes that cue us in to the time period. Marty's entrance into Hill Valley is heralded by the Four Aces' "Mr. Sandman" (and no Marty, this isn't a dream). "Mr. Sandman" is sourced, playing from a loudspeaker mounted on the outside of the record store. This is awfully convenient for the viewer, because it plays throughout the main square and follows Marty as he walks through the 1955 version of his town. (The sourced music is eventually overshadowed by Silvestri's "The Town Square" cue.) Fess Parker's "The Ballad of Davy Crockett" plays on the jukebox in the diner. These musical cues stand alongside other cultural artifacts to show Marty that he is out of his own time, like the *Honeymooners* episode he sees at his future grandparents' house, and *Cattle Queen of Montana* (starring Barbara Stanwyck and Ronald Reagan) on the marquee of the Essex movie theater. Music from Marty's present — the 1980s — intrudes upon the 1950s only once in this section; Marty convinces George to ask Lorraine to the dance by wearing his radiation suit, claiming to be an alien from the planet Vulcan named Darth Vader, and playing the music of Van Halen (the piece played on the headphones to wake and disorientate George was sourced from guitarist Eddie Van Halen but was never officially released).

We are firmly in the 1950s when George goes to the diner to ask Lorraine to the Enchantment Under the Sea Dance. A fifties song, "Rolling," is playing in the background. The source of the song is the jukebox in the diner, and it forms the sonic backdrop to a typical afternoon in the lives of these teenagers. When Biff and his minions enter into the scene, the music stops. His presence disrupts the peacefulness of the milieu, and by association, the music. Marty interferes in the confrontation between Biff and George, and when Marty takes off through the streets of Hill Valley, "Rolling" starts back up again, and Silvestri's score takes a prominent role. The percussive writing of Silvestri's theme underlines the pressure of this chase (I will discuss this theme below). The score is interrupted at one point when the scene cuts to the point of view of the café and we see all the teenagers watching Marty's daring escape. Lorraine turns and says, to an unseen companion, "he's an absolute dream," while "Rolling" plays in the background. The score regains prominence and Marty effectively escapes Biff, causing his car to run into a truck full of manure. A similar sequence appears in *BTTF II*, involving Biff's grandson Griff (and minions), as they chase Marty through the town square. When Old Biff says, "There's something very familiar about all of this," he is referring to the chase and Marty's evasive actions, but on a meta-level, he's also referring to the nearly shot-for-shot beginning of the chase, the mirrored actions from the first film to the second, and the music. Although Silvestri made minor changes to the cue, it is similar enough to evoke the same sense of anxiety over Marty's escape and the same elation as he outsmarts Griff. Although Griff does not end up running into a truck full of manure in this scene, Biff does after the tunnel chase (and to the same musical cue as he did in the first film).

There is a main theme that appears throughout the film, and at certain times only its first three notes are necessary to convey the elation and excitement of successful time travel. The three-note phrase can also signal the perils and paradoxes of it. (The entire theme is twenty notes long.) The first three notes outline a descending perfect fifth and an ascending tritone. When Doc's dog, Einstein, becomes the world's first time traveler, Doc celebrates as the initial three-note motif of the main theme appears twice, in sequence. The theme appears in its full form when Marty is escaping from the Libyans in 1985, and doesn't appear again until Biff chases Marty through Hill Valley's town square in 1955. When the theme is fully shown, it is heroic and easily recognizable, and Silvestri only has to suggest it with the first three notes to help the audience remember its sweeping glory. The Kaplans explain, "[the theme] is so catchy that all Silvestri has to do is use a handful of notes at any given moment and we know exactly where he's coming from."[4] When Marty is escaping from the Peabody ranch, we get longer statements of the theme (about half of it with an unresolved ending) with rhythmic variation. The full theme appears in the skateboard chase scene. It is heard twice in sequence before the score is interrupted by "Rolling." The three-note version appears as Marty struggles to start the DeLorean at the end of the film, and when Doc tries to restore the detached cable at the Clock Tower. The whole main theme is almost stated as Doc goes to plug in the cable in front of the clock face, but it's interrupted when the cable won't reach. Sequences of part of this theme, fractured as they are, underline the tension of the scene. There is a full listing of both the three-note version of the theme and the full main theme in the cue sheet at the end of this chapter.

The tritone, used as a structural interval of the first three notes of the main theme, has also been used prominently in other scores, most notably *West Side Story*. The instability of the tritone — it urges resolution either down to the perfect fourth, or more likely, up to the perfect fifth — and its historical significance as a "forbidden" interval in counterpoint writing, makes it an ideal choice for a film whose central theme is the fragility of one's existence, as it is based on a series of seemingly random events that make us who we are. In *West Side Story*, one could argue that the use of the tritone in Tony's yearning in "Maria" or in the Jets' big dance number "Cool" signal the listener or viewer that this love story is doomed from the start. In *Back to the*

Future, the tritone outlines an instability, a fragility, but in the context of the entire theme, the tritone is resolved and is strengthened and solidified by the rest of the theme.

The main theme has a consequent phrase that is sometimes attached to it. This consequent phrase of the main theme outlines a descending minor third, decorating it with neighboring tones above and below it. The "Consequent" theme (as I call it) first appears when Marty escapes from the Peabody ranch right after he runs over a pine tree (resulting in the "Lone Pine Mall" we see in the alternate future), and Peabody blasts his own mailbox to smithereens. The Consequent theme appears again in the skateboard chase scene with Biff. We hear it first when Marty is riding on the ersatz skateboard while holding on to a pickup truck. And then reappears — after some percussive piano passages that first appear in the "Libyans" cue — as Marty lets the skateboard roll under the car while he walks over the top of it. The last note of this "Consequent" theme is unheard; as if it's interrupted by Biff's crashing into the manure truck. The Consequent theme does not always follow the main theme. At the opening of the main title music of the score, the Consequent theme is approached by an ascending triad and acts as a sort of time travel fanfare for the main theme.

The Consequent theme appears later in the film as a symbol of resolution. In its more percussive and heroic form (played by the brass) it accompanies Doc's successful re-attachment of the cable from the clock tower, but it also appears in a more lyrical version, played by oboe and strings. The resolution represented by this version is the one of Marty's family. At the dance, Lorraine asks Marty if he minds George taking her home. Knowing he has set their relationship right, Marty talks to them about their future. The theme very delicately underscores this exchange. The theme comes to represent something of the McFly family as a whole. An alternate version of this Consequent theme is present in the last scene of the film, as Doc explains to Marty and Jennifer, "Something's gotta be done about your kids!" And with this final inkling of some possible resolution that Doc is going to set in motion, the film ends. The DeLorean flies straight at the audience while a low rumble in the orchestra sets off Huey Lewis' "Back in Time."

At certain points in the narrative, moments of significance are set off with a short chord progression found in the "1.21 Gigawatts" cue. This particular musical cue occurs when Marty shows Doc the time machine in 1955. As the two characters return to Doc's house to discuss how to get Marty home, the chord progression from "1.21 Gigawatts" plays under the scene. It is especially apt when Marty realizes the chance meeting with his mother has thrown his existence, and that of his siblings, into jeopardy. As Doc warns Marty that his actions in 1955 could have repercussions in his present, this theme punctuates his point.

As mentioned above, Silvestri did not give specific themes to Marty or to Doc. The majority of musical cues seem to rely on the interactions between the characters and the situations. Since Doc spends most of the film explaining things to Marty, Silvestri devised a spiky cue to underscore his exposition. Mirroring Doc's frenetic energy, the music for Doc's exposition — found first in the "Einstein Disintegrates" cue — leaps all over the place. It appears first after Doc has sent Einstein one minute into the future, and he explains to Marty what has happened. This theme works in tandem with the "DeLorean Revealed" cue. The result is a punchy, fun theme with rhythmic energy and an insistent urgency. The theme appears again as Doc realizes the bolt of lightning that hits the Clock Tower can effectively send Marty back to 1985. It also underscores Doc's impatience when Marty is late to meet him the night of the storm. The scene at Twin Pines Mall at the beginning of Marty's odyssey is notable because it represents the fusion of four elements of the score: the three-note main theme, "the DeLorean Revealed" motif, Doc's "Einstein Disintegrates" exposition theme, and the chord progression from the "1.21 Gigawatts" cue.

Whenever the characters are in danger, during the flight from the Libyans, the skateboard chase with Biff, or the clock tower scene, the underscore is a disjunct rhythmic motif. It is essentially an eight-note ostinato. This element first found in the "Libyans" cue is especially prominent near the end of the film as Marty and Doc struggle to make use of the bolt of lightning about to hit the Clock Tower. The steadiness of the motif is often punctuated by brass interruptions and other syncopated elements. Another theme that appears is a percussive military cadence that underscores scenes in which characters prepare for time travel. In the Twin Pines Parking lot, this military cadence underscores Doc's comment to the video camera that he's "about to embark on an historic journey." The appearance of the Libyans soon after causes the theme to become even more percussive and combative. "The Libyans" cue appears again at the end of the film when Marty is about to return to 1985 and Doc is explaining what he must do when the alarm in the DeLorean rings.

If Marty's original present, the one at the beginning of the film, is represented by "The Power of Love," the alternate timeline caused by his time travel is represented by Huey Lewis' "Back in Time." It is interesting to note that the two versions of 1985 are each represented by a Huey Lewis song, but each version gets a different song. "Back in Time" appears when Marty wakes up in the morning in the alternate version of 1985. While the song plays on his clock radio, he reasons that the whole time travel adventure must have been a dream (incidentally, a poster for the Huey Lewis and the News album, *Sports*, can be seen on the wall behind Marty). The song appears again, just after the DeLorean flies towards the audience and it also accompanies the credits.

Finally, there is a bittersweet theme introduced when Doc of 1955 explains his excitement about time travel to Marty. He talks about how wonderful it will be to see "beyond [his] years." Doc also finds the presence of the time machine (Marty's use of which goes unquestioned by Doc) very encouraging; Doc is pleased to know he will succeed in building something that works. Marty is visibly distressed by this conversation because he knows Doc will never use his own invention; the Libyans will kill him in 1985. Underscoring this scene is this "The Letter," a variation of the initial three-note phrase of the main theme. It changes the ascending tritone to a perfect fourth, thus making it a more stable-sounding phrase. The Kaplans describe this theme (which they call the "Americana Theme") as having a "more noble and rested quality."[5] This motif underscores the special relationship between Marty and Doc. Doc has been like a father to Marty, perhaps more of a father than the George McFly of the original 1985 has been. It is Doc who has told Marty, "If you put your mind to it, you can accomplish anything," and now Marty must — at Doc's behest — keep the news of Doc's murder to himself, and do nothing about it. Marty decides to write Doc a letter explaining the situation with the Libyans, and while he writes, "the Letter" plays in conjunction with the resolution version of the Consequent Theme. It is clearly Marty's hope that this letter will resolve the problem: Doc will read the letter, take precautions, and remain alive and well.

There are two scenes in the film that blur the line between score and sourced music in very effective ways. One is a scene I have already discussed: the skateboard chase scene through the main square of Hill Valley. In this scene, Silvestri's score is interrupted by the sourced music of the diner. The changing music underlines the change in point of view from the participants in the chase, to the onlookers. At the end of the film, Marty must play with Marvin Berry and the Starlighters in order to keep the dance going. Since it has already been established (in the very first shots of the film, and at the dance auditions) that Marty plays guitar, he is the logical choice to replace the injured musician. As he strums rather conspicuously the chords for "Earth Angel," he watches helplessly as an unnamed bully separates his parents. Things look bleak for Marty, and indeed, he begins to fade from existence. As this happens, the score overtakes the sourced song, and Marty collapses. George, however, decides to fight for Lorraine, and with a firm restatement of the initial three-note phrase from the main theme, and a fateful kiss, Marty is back on his feet. He instantly begins playing again, but the most extraordinary thing happens as Silvestri's score meshes with the sourced song. Sweeping string orchestration raises "Earth Angel" from a simple ballad to the fateful moment of Marty's rebirth. The combination of score and sourced music in this instance underlines the blurred line between present and past that Doc's time machine has created. It is also a moment of surging emotion that is a memorable movie moment. It was named by *Film Score Monthly* as a "Magnificent Movie Music Moment." The authors describe the scene:

> This is a unique case where source music and original score fuse together to create a whole that actually *is* greater than its parts. As "Earth Angel" (performed live at the Enchantment Under the Sea dance) fades into the background, Alan Silvestri's pounding percussion, swelling brass and churning strings sweep through at the seams — Marty McFly is fading from existence. But as George returns to kiss Lorraine, the *Back to the Future* theme emerges as the voice of fate. The theme rises with two five-note statements, before pulling back and allowing the chorus of "Earth Angel" to take over. Only now it's backed by Silvestri's string underscore, creating an unparalleled dramatic weight.[6]

The first film stands alone in its narrative. Even Doc's appearance at the end in which he tells Marty, "Something's gotta be done about your kids!" does not have to be viewed as the literal beginning to a new story. However, the considerable financial and critical success of the original *BTTF* made sequels inevitable.

Back to the Future II uses many of the same motifs and adds a few new ones, like the "My Father!" cue and the "Alternate 1985" music. But even these themes bear thematic similarities to those of the original score. It is only in the third *Back to the Future* film that Silvestri (and Zemeckis) begin to develop a new musical landscape in which to work. There is a lot of new musical material in *Back to the Future III*, including a love theme for Doc, and a theme for Clara. Although neither sequel was as critically well received as the original, these films allowed Silvestri to create a universe of musical cues that have served the franchise well.

The strength of Silvestri's original score is undeniable. He crafted tunes that sound majestic and noble, while being flexible enough to match comedic action, exposition, or action sequences. He created a musical language of motifs, and then used them either in whole or in fragments, effectively evoking emotion and excitement. *Back to the Future* is a modern classic, an enjoyable adventure whose storylines fit snugly together at the resolution. Through the middle of the film, Alan Silvestri's score manages to mirror the fragmentation Marty's time travel journey has caused, and by the end, it is the glue that seals up the seams of the repaired present.

Back to the Future Cue Sheet

00:25   Clocks ticking

03:24   the electric hum of Doc's amp

04:14   Marty plays one chord on the amp

05:53   "The Power of Love" begins (introduction and verse 1) as Marty takes his skateboard to school through the streets of Hill Valley

06:56   Music stops as Marty arrives at school

08:17   The Pinheads' version of "The Power of Love"

08:41   The Pinheads are told they are "too darn loud"

08:54   Hail to the Chief played from a campaign van

09:12   End of Hail to the Chief

10:03   "Power of Love" starts as a very quiet underscore

10:58   "Power of Love" continues to play, sound gets louder as Jennifer's father drives up; change of volume suggests the music could be sourced

11:17   "The Power of Love" moves to the foreground as Jennifer and Marty kiss (chorus and verse 2), song continues as Marty rides his skateboard home

12:00   Music stops as Marty sees the tow truck in front of the house

17:26   Song playing on the radio; Marty's alarm clock

18:01   Song stops at the scene change

18:41   DeLorean emerges to "The DeLorean Revealed" theme

18:56   Low fanfare as the DeLorean appears

19:14   A three-note theme (related to the main three-note theme used in the rest of the film) is heard/music stops as Doc steps out of the DeLorean

22:02   The first three notes of the main theme appear (descending perfect fifth and ascending tritone). The three-note phrase is imitated three times; "The DeLorean Revealed" theme appears with Doc's exposition theme in "Einstein Disintegrates"

22:58   The music stops

26:58   Chords in the high strings accompany plutonium insertion (beginning of "The Libyans" cue)

27:26   Drums cadences as Doc prepares for his "historic mission"

28:42   Drum cadences become more insistent as the Libyans appear

29:17   Tremolos as Libyans prepare to shoot Doc

29:31   Xylophone tremolo as they prepare to kill Marty

29:50   Percussive "Libyans" motif associated now and later with dangerous situations

30:56   First half of the main theme, unresolved

31:03	Second statement of first half of the main theme (sequenced at a higher pitch level)
31:10	Consequent theme in its entirety
32:07	Long notes in the high strings as the Peabody family observes the DeLorean in their barn
32:18	Three-note phrase of main theme played on a muted trumpet
33:11	Two statements (slightly different rhythm from the original version) of the first half of the main time travel theme; full Consequent of the main theme as Marty escapes
33:35	Agitated orchestra passage, reminiscent of Doc's exposition theme, is heard as Marty drives
33:55	"The DeLorean Revealed" motif as Marty sees the sign for Lyon Estates
34:04	"Lyon Estates Fanfare"
34:32	"The DeLorean Revealed" theme as Marty looks at the time display in the DeLorean
34:41	Restatement of the "DeLorean" theme cut short when the car will not start
35:15	Marty enters the town square of Hill Valley while "Mr. Sandman" plays; it appears to be sourced from a loud speaker mounted outside of the record store
36:14	Score overtakes the sourced music, long held notes in the high strings when the clock tower strikes ("The Town Square" cue)
36:36	Three-note phrase in muted trumpet, mixed with "Hail to the Chief" from a passing van
37:07	Musical sting when Marty sees the date on a newspaper
37:21	Marty enters the diner; "The Ballad of Davy Crockett" plays in the background; sourced from the jukebox
42:20	Three-note theme in the low brass when Marty is unconscious in Lorraine's house
42:31	Three-note theme played in the flute
42:54	Variant of the Consequent theme (associated with family)
43:00	Music stops with a sting as Marty realizes again that he is in 1955
51:00	Sustained chords when Marty shows Doc the DeLorean
51:17	"The DeLorean Revealed"
51:29	Chord progression from "1.21 Gigawatts" cue
51:34	The same progression is repeated at a higher pitch level
51:54	Large orchestral swell as Doc declares, "It works!"
52:05	"The DeLorean Revealed" moves up in a scalar motion
52:10	Music stops

54:17	Three-note phrase, "1.21 Gigawatts," "The DeLorean Revealed," and Doc's exposition theme from "Einstein Disintegrates," underscore the discussion the bolt of lightning
54:58	Doc's exposition theme continues with the three-note theme, the chord progression
55:36	"The DeLorean Revealed"
55:48	Music stops
1:01:51	High dissonant string passage in background as Marty prepares to convince George to ask Lorraine to the dance using Van Halen music.
1:02:17	Marty plays Van Halen for George
1:03:27	"Rolling" sourced from inside the diner; Marty and George are outside
1:04:01	Marty and George enter the diner
1:05:15	Music stops as Biff enters the diner
1:05:46	"Rolling" starts up again as Marty runs out of the diner
1:05:54	Three-note phrase, repeated
1:06:13	Full restatement of the main theme; repeats in sequence
1:06:33	POV from inside the diner, "Rolling" is playing
1:06:47	Consequent phrase
1:07:05	"Libyans" motif combined with the three-note theme in imitation
1:07:18	Consequent phrase as Marty runs over Biff's car and lands on his skateboard
1:14:56	"The Letter" cue plays as Doc talks about time travel
1:15:38	Three-note phrase in flute as Marty writes a letter to Doc; Consequent phrase in its guise as a theme of resolution, played in the high woodwinds and strings, ascending harp scale
1:16:06	Music stops
1:16:35	Music at the Enchantment Under the Sea dance, sourced from the live musicians
1:17:11	Music from the dance heard from outside of the gym
1:18:24	Back inside the gym; music stops as the band takes a break
1:18:54	"I'll Forever Love You" playing on the car radio
1:20:11	Biff opens the car door, "Libyans" motif continues as Marty is taken away
1:21:05	Jazz music coming from inside the band's car
1:21:29	High string tremolos as George approaches the car; "Libyans" motif appears
1:22:32	Sting as George attempts to punch Biff in the stomach
1:22:37	"Libyans" motif as George struggles
1:23:04	Music stops as George succeeds in stopping Biff

1:23:23	Consequent phrase as the resolution theme
1:23:50	"The DeLorean Revealed" as Marty realizes his siblings have not been restored
1:24:31	Marty and the band play "Earth Angel"
1:25:25	Music of the score encroaches upon the scene as Marty begins to disappear
1:25:51	Three-note phrase sounds
1:26:01	Score and source music combine as "Earth Angel" appears in an orchestrated version
1:27:17	Marty plays "Johnny B. Goode"
1:28:53	Marty's guitar solo
1:29:30	Solo ends
1:29:53	Saxophone song sourced from the dance
1:30:19	Resolution theme as Marty talks to his parents
1:31:07	Fragments of Doc's exposition ("Einstein Disintegrates") as Doc waits for Marty
1:31:50	Percussive cadence as they prepare for time travel
1:32:12	Augmented versions of the three-note phrase and the Consequent/resolution theme (percussive theme continues)
1:33:26	Elements of the "Libyans" motif are added when Doc finds the letter
1:34:00	Xylophone tremolo as the cable from the clock tower becomes detached
1:34:20	"Libyans" motif as Doc enters the works of the clock tower
1:35:16	Three-note phrase and percussive theme
1:35:48	Tremolos
1:36:00	"Libyans" motif continues as Doc tries to re-attach the cable
1:36:32	Three-note phrase as Marty gets the DeLorean ready for time travel
1:37:29	Three-note phrase as car won't start
1:37:40	"Libyans" motif at the clock tower
1:38:03	Three-note phrase in imitation
1:39:00	Time travel theme begins as Marty starts the DeLorean
1:39:13	Theme interrupted when Doc realizes the cable won't reach; "Libyans" motif continues
1:39:42	Time travel theme in augmentation; restated in original form
1:40:22	First half of time travel theme (twice) as Marty drives and Doc attaches the cable
1:41:26	Consequent phrase as Marty drives and the lightning strikes the Clock Tower
1:41:27	Consequent/resolution as Doc realizes they have been successful

1:41:51   Sourced music from a radio as Marty confirms he is back in 1985, "Heaven is One Step Away"
1:43:04   "Libyans" motif is played on the piano as the Libyans pass Marty on their way to Doc
1:43:36   Three-note phrase over percussion
1:44:17   High string tremolos and "The Letter" cue
1:44:31   "The DeLorean Revealed" as Doc blinks his eyes
1:44:43   "The Letter" in the piccolo and in the oboe
1:45:24   Consequent/resolution theme as Doc drops Marty off at home
1:46:09   Consequent theme as Doc travels into the future
1:46:37   Huey Lewis' "Back in Time" plays on Marty's alarm clock
1:47:07   Music stops as Marty discovers the alternate version of 1985
1:49:47   "The Letter" as Marty opens the garage and sees his truck
1:50:33   Doc's exposition motif as he explains they must return to the future
1:51:26   Consequent theme and the preparation for time travel motif play as Doc gets ready to time travel
1:51:42   Credits roll and "Back in Time" plays

Back to the Future II Cue Sheet

00:22   "The DeLorean Revealed"
00:38   Underscore as Marty sees his 4 × 4
01:28   Doc's exposition theme
02:20   Percussive cadence
02:52   drum roll/main theme/credits
04:38   horns honking
05:56   Consequent phrase of main theme
06:50   Three-note theme / Marty steps out of the DeLorean into the future ("The Future" cue)
07:00   Doc's exposition
07:21   Three-note theme/"Libyans"/Military cadence and Consequent/resolution when Doc says, "We've got a mission to accomplish"
10:43   Drum roll "The Future" Hill Valley
11:48   Jaws Cue
12:04   Goldie Wilson III commercial/ synthesizer version of Sousa march
12:42   "Beat It" at Café 80s
13:42   Synthesizer underscore/ might be Goldie's commercial or Cubs commercial from outside

15:12	Wild Gunman cue
15:24	Wild Gunman music
15:42	Goldie Wilson commercial plays outside
17:32	Sting on the word "chicken"
17:54	"Beat It" starts up again as Griff hits television
18:13	"Skateboard Chase" sequence over hoverboard chase
19:20	"Libyans" motif
21:17	Sirens
21:53	Synthesizer music over commercial about Cubs winning World Series
22:14	"DeLorean Revealed"
22:52	"A Flying DeLorean"
23:22	Military cadence/ Doc sees the accident with Griff
23:46	Harp glissando as headline changes/ the chord progression from "1.21 Gigawatts"
24:00	military cadence/ main theme together as Doc says they have succeeded in their plan
24:25	drum hits for Doc's explanation
25:52	dramatic underscore/Doc explains Jennifer could see herself in the future
26:32	Chords from "1.21 Gigawatts"/ Biff finds time machine
30:36	Harp chord like an unarpeggiated "DeLorean Revealed"/ Biff in neighborhood
32:15	Harp chords lead into "Libyans" motif as Biff steals time machine
34:52	Sting for "chicken"
36:31	Future Marty tries to play the guitar
37:08	Low brass hits
37:37	"Libyans" motif as Marty and Doc carry Jennifer back to the DeLorean
41:20	"Alternate 1985" motif as Marty realizes the neighborhood is dangerous
41:49	Broader theme as Marty realizes it is in fact 1985
43:22	"I Can't Drive 55" perhaps sourced from Biff's casino
44:28	Alternate 3-note phrase and reminiscent time travel music for the underscore to Biff's film
46:14	Harp gliss/ flute plays decorated 3-note motif and family theme
46:41	Harp gliss interrupts as Marty realizes he's not where he should be (27th floor!)
47:16	Low brass hits
50:32	"My Father!" cue in graveyard

52:32	long-held notes underscore Marty looking at headline of George's death
53:14	two chords/ Biff steals the almanac
55:32	Music in Clint Eastwood movie (*A Fistful of Dollars*)
56:27	chord progression from "1.21 Gigawatts"/Marty mentions almanac to Biff
58:50	Biff takes out gun/ sinister music becomes generic chase music
1:01:07	Consequent theme as Doc knocks Biff out with DeLorean door
1:01:18	Main theme
1:01:32	reminiscent of military cadence
1:02:25	consequent theme cut off
1:02:38	harp gliss as Doc and Marty arrive in 1955
1:02:50	military cadence
1:04:52	"Mr. Sandman" Marty follows Biff into town
1:09:31	underscore as Biff demonstrates for Griff the accuracy of the almanac
1:10:10	chord progression and underscore continues as Marty realizes he's trapped in garage
1:10:50	military cadence as Marty tells Doc he's trapped; underscore continues as Biff drives to the dance; military cadence returns as Doc tries to free Marty
1:12:13	"Papa Loves Mambo" in Biff's car
1:12:47	"DeLorean Revealed" as Doc sees the set-up for the lightning experiment
1:13:27	"DeLorean Revealed" and "Pair O' Docs" for Doc's conversation with "himself"
1:14:39	"DeLorean Revealed"
1:14:54	"Strolling" at the dance underscores Marty's surveillance of Biff
1:16:31	music fades into background as Biff and henchman go outside
1:18:47	high whining strings, low whining strings, muted brass hits and pizzicato strings as Marty attempts to get the book from Strickland
1:20:05	Strickland is distracted by a car horn playing "La Cucaracha" outside
1:20:11	Three-note motive in sequence
1:20:46	fast moving notes as Marty discovers the Almanac
1:21:34	"Libyans" cue as realizes Biff is about to be hit by George
1:22:09	altered three-note motif in its noble version
1:22:18	sweet version of the consequent phrase
1:22:36	two chords into "Libyans" motif in the high strings, changes to low strings as Marty escapes from Biff's henchmen

1:22:38	Earth Angel with Silvestri underscore
1:24:30	"Jonny B. Goode" at the dance
1:27:39	Next song by the Starlighters
1:28:26	sting for "chicken"
1:29:04	Sting as Biff kicks Marty, underscore has "Libyans" motif as Biff tries to get away from Marty
1:29:46	harp glissandos and hits lead to military-type music as Marty gets into Biff's car
1:32:00	"Libyans" motif as Biff tries to get Marty away from his car
1:33:02	Consequent theme/ cut short as Marty gets almanac but is trapped in tunnel
1:33:21	"Libyans" theme as Biff revs his engine and tried to get Marty
1:34:04	Consequent theme as Marty escapes from Biff and he runs into another manure truck
1:34:39	military cadence and three-note motif as Doc tells Marty to burn the book/main theme mixed in as Marty realizes the future will change ("Burn the Book")
1:36:27	Main theme
1:36:40	Chords from "1.21 Gigawatts"
1:37:42	Underscore as Marty thinks Doc is gone
1:39:12	"DeLorean Revealed" Western Union delivers message ("Western Union")
1:39:55	"The Letter" cue as Marty reads Doc's letter
1:40:17	Consequent theme
1:40:32	Main theme as Doc connects the cable so Marty can go back to the future
1:41:34	Consequent with harp glissando/ different ending as different Marty shows up
1:42:30	Silvestri score from *BTTF III*
1:43:24	End credit music

Back to the Future III Cue Sheet

00:43	"The DeLorean Revealed"
01:01	Main theme as Marty drives down Main Street and lightning strikes the Clock Tower
02:08	Consequent phrase
02:18	Marty reappears, alternate version of the Consequent theme
02:49	Opening logo phrase
03:18	new theme, sweet melody with harp outlining harmony

04:06	Flute and harp song prefigures Clara's music
05:03	"Howdy Doody" opening
06:22	Doc sits on the organ forming dramatic chords
10:49	Short flute notes and string tremolos as Marty and Doc find the time machine in the cave
12:02	High strings underscore
13:31	High tremolos as Doc's dog discovers Doc's grave/ drum roll over minor alternate of three-note theme
15:24	High tremolos as Doc sees a picture of himself from 1885
17:13	Military cadence as they get ready to send Marty back to 1885/ variation of main theme/consequent theme
18:29	Main theme as Marty starts the DeLorean/ consequent theme
19:02	"Indians" cue as Marty enters 1885 and encounters Indians
20:18	Cavalry charge
22:06	Harp glissando as Marty wakes up on McFly farm/ flute plays decorated three-note theme and consequent theme
25:48	Marty holds Will McFly/ harp theme
26:14	New theme as we see Hill Valley for the first time ("Hill Valley")
26:59	Lumbering piano and harmonica music as Marty wanders through town
27:54	Three-note motif played on harmonica as Marty sees the Clock Tower being built
32:10	"Skateboard Chase" music as Buford follows Marty out of the saloon/ new ending with Western theme
32:20	"Hanging" cue as Buford strings Marty up at the courthouse
38:23	"We're Out of Gas" cue as Marty tells Doc the fuel line was torn
38:45	Main western music cue as Marty and Doc see how fast the horses will go
39:19	three-note theme as they try alcohol to run the DeLorean
41:22	Military cadence as Doc explains how they'll use the train to push the DeLorean up to 88 mph
42:35	Reminiscent of "Libyans" cue with Western flavor/ Clara's horses are out of control "It's Clara"
43:40	"At First Sight" cue/ harp glissando into consequent theme/ harp and flute tune
46:26	Drum roll/ Doc realizes he's altered time
50:55	Drum roll and tune as the mayor starts the clock from the Clock Tower
51:39	Acoustic version of "Doubleback" at the Town Festival/underscore to Doc's encounter with Clara/ Doc's dance with Clara/Marty at the shooting gallery

55:00	Fiddle/banjo tune at the dance as Buford arrives/ "Turkey in the Straw"
56:59	"Oh My Darling, Clementine" as Buford dances with Clara
59:17	Sting when Buford asks Marty if he's "yellow"/ drum roll
1:00:51	"Doubleback" acoustic version/over conversation with Seamus and Marty
1:03:07	"At First Sight" cue as Clara and Doc look at the moon
1:05:54	Drum roll and edgy orchestral sounds as Marty draws in the mirror
1:08:27	Sinister variation of three-note theme when Doc tells Marty about the accident in the future
1:08:56	Flute tune/"The Future Isn't Written"/ three-note motif
1:11:40	High tremolos as Doc contemplates what to do about Clara/ visits Clara
1:13:31	Flute plays three-note motif
1:14:50	Saloon piano plays "Camptown Races"
1:16:39	Underscore Marty wakes to find Doc gone
1:17:30	Marty looks for Doc, variation of exposition theme from "Einstein Disintegrates"
1:18:40	Military cadence
1:18:53	Buford rides into town
1:19:03	"Goodbye Clara" as she buys train ticket
1:19:13	"Wake up Juice" cue
1:21:36	Long-held notes as Marty looks at picture/ low chords
1:22:34	High string tremolos/ three-note motif with variations
1:23:39	Sting on "yellow pie-slinger"
1:25:56	"Libyans" cue/ timpani glissando/ pan flute sound
1:27:57	Three-note motif/ sequence/ consequent phrase
1:29:24	Variant of "The DeLorean Revealed" cue/ conversation with Seamus/ "Libyans"
1:30:27	Three-note motif/consequent phrase/train cue
1:30:57	Main theme and variations/ Doc's exposition theme
1:32:28	"A Science Experiment" cue
1:33:21	Three-note cue when train meets DeLorean/ consequent phrase
1:33:46	Military cadence as Doc explains combustion
1:34:08	Clara's theme as she follows the train
1:36:08	Main theme
1:36:59	Variant of "Hill Valley" theme
1:37:56	High string ostinato as Clara declares her love from the train/ "Point of No Return" cue
1:38:59	Consequent phrase as the train reaches 50 mph

1:39:52	Minor version of the "Hill Valley" theme/ "Libyans"
1:40:50	Consequent phrase
1:41:09	Complete consequent phrase as Doc saves Clara/ minor "Hill Valley" theme, two notes of three note theme as the DeLorean hits 88 mph
1:43:29	Three-note phrase in flute (decorated) as Marty tours the wreckage of the DeLorean/ "The Letter" cue
1:44:06	Three-note theme as Marty goes home
1:45:04	"The DeLorean Revealed" as Marty wakes Jennifer/ variant of three-note theme/consequent phrase/ harp glissando
1:46:22	Three-note/ high tremolos/ "Power of Love" coming from Needles' car
1:47:50	"DeLorean Revealed" as the fax erases itself
1:49:10	"DeLorean Revealed"/ consequent theme as Doc and Clara reappear/ "Future Isn't Written Yet"
1:51:20	Consequent phrase/ final ending
1:51:46	End credits

Notes

1. Alan Silvestri, "The Alan Silvestri Interview," *Film Score Monthly* October 1994: 13.

2. Jon and Al Kaplan, "Future Past Perfect," *Film Score Monthly* November/December 2000: 16.

3. Ibid., 17.

4. Ibid.

5. Ibid., 19.

6. Jon and Al Kaplan, "36 Magnificent Movie Music Moments," *Film Score Monthly* March 2003: p. 29.

Works Cited

Kaplan, Jon, and Al. "Future Past Perfect." *Film Score Monthly* November/December 2000: 16.

_____. "36 Magnificent Movie Music Moments." *Film Score Monthly* March 2003.

Silvestri, Alan. "The Alan Silvestri Interview." *Film Score Monthly* October 1994: 13.

7. Back to the Fifties!
Fixing the Future

Elizabeth McCarthy

When asked to describe the kind of film *Back to the Future* was, director Robert Zemeckis replied, "A comedy adventure science fiction time travel
love story."[1] Curiously, what he didn't include in his list was the teen movie,
yet *Back to the Future* certainly can be classed as such. More specifically, using
James Thorburn's description of the Eighties Teen Movie or ETM, we can
see how Zemeckis' film corresponds quite closely with many of the genre's
key plot elements:

> The protagonist wakes up as the opening credits sequence pans his messy bed-
> room. He has breakfast with his annoying younger siblings and uncomprehend-
> ing parents, then goes to school. He arrives at the high school parking lot on/in
> his embarrassing mode of transport and meets up with his equally low-status
> buddy. They walk the halls on the way to class, and see the unattainable object of
> the protagonist's fancy, who is probably hanging out with her cool friends [...] The
> protagonist attempts to interact with the girl, but is humiliated. Lunch in the cafe-
> teria involves kvetching over bad food, the spilling of food or beverages and gen-
> eralized ostracism. After school, our hero goes to his embarrassing part time job,
> and is once again humiliated. [...] The protagonist then makes one last desperate
> bid to win the girl's affection, and succeeds — involving her in a falling in love
> montage. But then ... something happens and they are separated / estranged. But
> then ... the big game/big dance/big competition offers our hero the opportunity
> to prove himself — to the girl, and everyone else who ever looked down on him.
> He wins not only his self-respect, but also the girl, whom he locks in a display
> case and to whom he never speaks again.[2]

As Thorburn acknowledges, not every ETM goes exactly like this, "there
are thousands of permutations, thanks to a genre-approved list of additional
elements that can be added or subtracted."[3] But comparing this outline with
Back to the Future we can see how it has many of the essential ingredients of
the typical ETM — Marty McFly's messy bedroom; mealtime with annoying
family; skateboard to school instead of the coveted 4 × 4 truck ... but here's

where the plot diverges considerably from the ETM schema ... Marty already has the girl of his dreams. Not only that, he also has an eccentric-genius-inventor-friend called Dr. Brown whose latest invention causes Marty to accidentally travel back in time to the year 1955. A considerable divergence from the typical ETM plot one might say, but once *in* 1955 we see the genre's basic plot elements remerge and continue on unabated by the temporal shift; only now, the character who most effectively qualifies as our teen movie protagonist is not Marty but the 1955 version of Marty's father, George McFly. In fact, George has better qualifications for the role than Marty ever had, most notably in his desperate and humiliating bids to gain the attention of the seemingly "unattainable object" of his desire, Lorraine Baines, who is, of course, the future Mrs. McFly. George's "attempts to interact" with Lorraine and his "generalized ostracism" are depicted in various embarrassing scenes in "the halls on the way to class" and during "lunch in the cafeteria," until "the big game/big dance/big competition," in this case The Enchantment Under the Sea Dance, offers George "the opportunity to prove himself— to the girl, and everyone else who ever looked down on him." Admittedly this teen romance plot is played out only as an element of the overarching "adventure science fiction time travel" plot but not to the extent that it is subordinated to it. In fact the outcome of the time travel plot is utterly reliant on the success or failure of George McFly as our protagonist in the teen romance plot. As such, *Back to the Future* has at its heart the same primary concern of all ETMs: The subject of each and every ETM is the sexual romantic ambitions of the protagonist. In coarser terms, "Will our hero bag the cute chick?"[4]

Marty McFly's role in this teen romance plot is, first of all, to act as the obstacle to its success (namely by interfering in the event which should have led to George and Lorraine's meeting and falling in love). His subsequent role is to act as confidant and advisor to his socially and romantically inept young father, a sort of Cyrano de Bergerac figure, only one who accidentally attracts rather than repels the female love interest, thereby remaining an obstacle as well as an aid to the successful resolution of the teen romance plot.

If, as I have been arguing, *Back to the Future* can justly be characterized as an Eighties Teen Movie then exactly what significance can be attached to its split settings of 1955 and 1985 and the division of its teen protagonist into two separate characters? In terms of the film's box-office success, the dual time setting may well have broadened its appeal. As Michael J. Fox has suggested when discussing the popularity of the film:

> I think what made it such an immense hit is that it was cross-generational. Just by the nature of the story, its appeal reached people who remembered the '50s, and interested a whole new generation in the period.[5]

Despite their own box-office success, this idea of cross-generational appeal can hardly be applied to other Eighties Teen Movies like *The Breakfast Club* (1985), *Pretty in Pink* (1986) or *Ferris Bueller's Day Off* (1986), unless of course the older audience members find themselves relating to the parents and/or teachers in these film, which is not all that unlikely considering just how annoying many of these films' teen protagonists are. But if Zemeckis' film does indeed talk to the youth of different eras then it must also be acknowledged that the very idea of youth culture itself is a vague and problematic issue which seems to find its only clear and definitive form in anthropologists' and sociologists' studies.

As deMarrais and LeCompte have pointed out, in their study of American schools, anthropologists and sociologists have debated the existence of a youth culture for many decades. Some argue that, because children grow up and become something other than youth, they are no longer a part of that culture and as such youth culture has no real shape or definition since its members are constantly changing.[6] However, as deMarrais and LeCompte also suggest, it is possible to move into and out of cultures, as long as one achieves the particular characteristics necessary for entrance. In the case of adolescents, several commentators contend that a youth culture may be identified through its development of a specific set of behavior patterns which sets it apart from adults as well as other youth cultures, and that this set of behavior patterns is usually formed around a rebellion against adults and adult institutions.[7] Undoubtedly, these rebellious behavior patterns are more readily definable in some youth cultures and eras than they are in others, primarily due to the extent of their cultural impact and/or their sociopolitical significance — for example, the emergence of rock 'n' roll in the 1950s and the student protests of the 1960s are two noteworthy instances of youth cultures whose fundamental attitudes quite clearly offered a challenge to adults and their institutions.

If such powerful images of rebellion against adults and adult institutions help to define a particular youth culture in a given era then what is particularly interesting about *Back to the Future* (and indeed many other Eighties Teen Movies) is how readily critics have interpreted the film as engaging in a conservative demagoguery which not only complies with but also extols the social vision of that most adult and conservative of institutions — the government. The following is just one of many similar readings which interpret *Back to the Future*'s underlying ideology in this fashion:

> It epitomized the collective yearning for a pristine past that the Reagan years had defined as a core national aspiration. [...] Zemeckis concentrates on Marty's efforts to make the past right (i.e., get his mom and dad to fall in love), much as President Reagan was exhorting the nation to return to its collective past in order to

find its cultural bearings amid an uncertain present. As in Reagan's rhetoric, the past here is a more shining and idealistic time than is the present. [...] As Reagan urged the nation, Marty uses the past to remake the present. At the end of the film, he learns that his intervention into his parents' lives in 1955 has made them happier, more self-fulfilled, and successful in the eighties. In these ways, *Back to the Future* venerates small-town America in terms consistent with the rhetoric of the Reagan presidency (while nevertheless, aiming a few jokes at Reagan for being an actor-turned-president).[8]

This yearning for the past, it is argued, forms part of the neo-conservative agenda of the 1980s. Its impetus being a determination to get over the "cultural crisis of confidence" that Ronald Reagan called the "Vietnam Syndrome" and a nostalgic longing for a time before the 1960s, "a decade synonymous for many neo-conservatives with events — civil rights, multiculturalism and feminism for instance — that signaled a wrong turn in American history."[9] As Graham Thompson suggests, in this sense the 1950s was frequently posited as a time of innocence, at least in neo-conservative terms, "The attempt to recover the 1950s often formed around a rhetoric of contented domesticity and so-called family values of respect, monogamy and simplicity."[10] It also formed around a rhetoric which promoted the dream of unbridled affluence and consumerism.

A number of critics have aligned Zemeckis' film with such neo-conservative rhetoric only to then challenge the comparison's soundness. Referencing the film in their guide to contemporary North American film directors, Allon and Patterson run through its basic plot, describing how Marty is "accidentally sent back in time from a dystopic [*sic*] present to a cheery 1955, [...] and is required to orchestrate his own parent's [*sic*] courtship" in which his father is "taught to stand up for himself and a happy ending is coded through the transformation of Marty's contemporary family into affluent, middle-class folk." However, Allon and Patterson go on to suggest that

> the film, however, is perhaps a little more ambiguous than its detractors might admit. Underlying its neo-conservatism, for example, there is also a somewhat perverse Freudian subtext at work, as Marty finds himself being seduced by his own mother; and, in the case of his mother's alcoholism, there is the suggestion that the supposedly idyllic 1950s actually caused many of the problems of the present.[11]

Thompson also argues that *Back to the Future* challenges the neo-conservative image of an idyllic and unspoiled 1950s America, "At the beginning of the film, the 1950s is depicted as a time when the future for Marty's parents is determined not for the better but for the worse: Marty's mother, Lorraine, is an alcoholic, and his father, George, is Biff Tannen's lackey."[12] And, much like Allon and Patterson, Thompson sees the oedipal subplot as another aspect of the film's challenge to neo-conservative rhetoric:

The determination Lorraine shows in trying to seduce her future son adds a whole new dimension to the accusation that some 1950s men were mummies' boys. The oedipal connotations of this storyline and Biff's attempted rape of Lorraine at the Enchantment Under the Sea dance suggest more complex — and much less chaste — attitudes towards sex and sexuality than those sometimes associated with the 1950s.[13]

Coding a reassuring nostalgia for 1950s America, built "around a rhetoric of contented domesticity and so-called family values of respect, monogamy and simplicity," as a neo-conservative impulse, these critics therefore read *Back to the Future*'s less than perfectly ideal representation of 1955 as evidence of how it defies the conservative rhetoric of the Reagan era:

> *Back to the Future* was the highest earning film of 1985 and provides a reading of the 1950s, and its relationship to the 1980s, which complicates much of this rhetoric despite having been held up as a film that does the job of neo-conservative ideology.[14]

However, on closer analysis, it may be argued that Zemeckis' film does not *complicate* 1980s neo-conservative readings of 1950s America but in fact *extends* its own neo-conservative and ideological framework by interpreting the cultural shifts of the 1950s as the first stages of a "wrong turn in American history"; a wrong turn which would manifest into the social revolutions of the 1960s (for example, the Civil Rights movement and the women's liberation movements).

These cultural shifts in 1950s America find their origins in the overlapping themes of class, race, gender and inter-generational tension, and all of these themes, in turn, are the nub of *Back to the Future*'s subtext. Perhaps the most prevalent of these themes, which underpins the ideological structure of the entire film, is that of class. Long before the Libyans shoot Doc Brown dead and Marty endangers his existence by accidentally traveling back in time, the audience is aware that there is something seriously amiss in Marty's world. Everything seems in place; he has a cool/cute girlfriend, he is in a rock band, he exhibits a healthy teen disregard for school and an equally healthy teen desire for sex and a 4 × 4 truck: "Check out that 4 × 4. That is hot. Someday, Jennifer, someday." Admittedly, he does seem a little insecure about his ability to make it in the music biz but that's the sort of character-building stuff the plot development of an Eighties Teen Movie is all about. But then we meet the McFly family.... While the ETM protagonist is always alienated from his family because they are either too "hands-on" or too "hands-off" or just too annoyingly square to understand him — he is rarely alienated from them because they are from a different social class.[15] Class consciousness and family issues are often features of the ETM but, for the most part, they are manifest in storylines concerned with the theme of love and/or an attraction between teens that are from opposite sides of the tracks, for example, *Pretty in Pink* (1986) and *Some Kind of Wonderful* (1987). In the case of *Back to the Future*, Marty *and* his girlfriend, Jennifer, embody everything the audience of an ETM has come to expect from nice middle-class teen protagonists but when our hero comes home for dinner it is like we have entered some terrible parallel universe where everything is topsy-turvy and somehow Marty McFly belongs to "white trash." The following description of this family meal is taken from the fourth and final draft of Zemeckis' and Bob Gale's screenplay. It is essentially the way the scene appears in the film with only some product placement variations[16]:

INT. AT THE McFLY DINNER TABLE — NIGHT

The McFly family is dining on meat loaf, Kraft macaroni and cheese, Bird's Eye mixed vegetables, and French's instant mashed potatoes.

Marty's mother, LORRAINE, 47, was once very attractive. Now she's OVERWEIGHT, in a rut, a victim of suburban stagnation. She has more food on her plate than anyone else, and a glass of vodka.

Timid GEORGE McFLY, 47, a balding, boring, uninspired man who wears a suit he bought at Sears 4 years ago. He has papers in front of him instead of food: he's doing work Biff gave him. He's also glancing at the TV, which is tuned to a "Honeymooners" rerun.

Sister LINDA, 19, is cute but wears too much eye makeup; brother DAVE, 22, wears a MCDONALD'S UNIFORM and is wolfing down his food.[17]

Without actually using the pejorative term "white trash" this is clearly what the McFly family are coded as in the palpable snobbery of these descriptions — which include the detailed description of the "convenience" food products on the table and the picture of Lorraine as an "overweight" alcoholic (with the word "overweight" capitalized for added emphasis) with piles of food on her plate and a brother in prison ("your uncle Joey didn't make parole again"); the depiction of George as a TV-ogling ineffectual dope, utterly lacking ambition, self-respect or a decent suit and the description of Marty's sister, Linda, as over "made-up" and his brother, Dave, as a fast-food worker, wolfing down his food. The upshot of this entire rendering (which is further enhanced by the *mise-en-scène* of the actual film) unmistakably presents the McFlys as a nightmarish paradigm of a lower class family, whose class is most vividly represented in their sense of taste rather than their financial status.[18] In this way, the film's configuration of Marty's family accurately conveys what recent commentators have defined as a fundamental understanding of class which is aligned to factors that fall outside of pure economics:

As the role of poverty in the determination of social status is soon overwhelmed by the role of tastes and values in American class-consciousness, the label "white trash" is now applied to selective members of the white underclass not because they fall below a certain economic standard, but because they fail to adhere to a certain standard of decorum and taste.[19]

What is equally significant, particularly in terms of *Back to the Future*'s return to the past, is how these value judgments are linked to concepts of family lineage:

Although economics and social demography serve as the defining criterion for the poor white class in the national consciousness, the image has become quickly consumed in tumult of value judgement [sic] and cultural bias that indicts not one's financial status but one's social ancestry.[20]

This is precisely what *Back to the Future*'s time traveling theme reveals. Just as the family meal in 1985 proved to be the scene of embarrassing revelation in terms of Marty's class background, so the family meal in 1955 (with the teenage Lorraine and her family) shows the origins of this background:

INT. DINING ROOM — NIGHT

Marty takes a seat at the dinner table next to Lorraine as MRS. STELLA BAINES, 40 and pregnant, makes the introductions to the KIDS. [...] She hands him a plate of MEAT LOAF. It looks like the same meat loaf he had for dinner in 1985 ... in fact, the whole dinner is the same![21]

In case these directions do not make the link between the 1985 and 1955 dinner scenes explicit enough, the scene also includes that most potent symbol of mindless suburban stagnation — the TV set. This is the family's first TV, Lorraine's father, "gruff SAM BAINES, 45," wheels it into the dining area and, lo and behold, the show being aired is the sitcom, *The Honeymooners*. He sits glued to the screen while drinking a beer. Another link between the 1985 and 1955 dinner scenes is Lorraine's little bother, Joey, referred to in 1985 as "Uncle jailbird Joey"— the joke here being that, even at 11 months old, baby Joey's future is already quite clear. As Lorraine's mother tells Marty, "Joey just loves being in his playpen. He cries whenever we take him out so we just leave him in there all the time." Like one of Cesare Lombroso's "born criminals"[22] (in this case a born *institutionalized* criminal) this child's future is mapped out before him. Cognizant of this future, Marty advises the child, "Get used to those bars kid." However, the concept of recidivism does not seem quite so amusing to Marty by the next installment of the *Back to the Future* trilogy, when it appears to pass through the generational line and the threat of imprisonment looms over his own son, unless, that is, he can get to the future and fix things so this doesn't happen.

The possibility that cycles of behavior go on unbroken from one generation to the next and the anxiety that this possibility provokes pervades the *Back to the Future* trilogy and it forms the basis of the intensely class-conscious portrayal of the meat loaf dinner scenes in the original film. The film's less than ideal picture of the 1950s suburban family is offered as the template for the McFly family in 1985. The affluence of 1950s America is presented here as the beginning of a negative cycle in American society because this affluence has allowed blue collar families, like the Baines, certain "luxuries" which they seem ill-equipped to use "wisely" and/or in moderation. Mr. and Mrs. Baines, as parents and authority figures, mismanage that most precious of family gatherings (meal time). They have turned the image of the plentiful family dinner, idealized so forcefully in paintings such as Norman Rockwell's "Freedom from Want," into a slapdash affair devoid of wholesome food or proper communication. If the family unit is to be held up as the cornerstone of American society and gatherings at the dinner table are an iconic symbol of the American family's togetherness, then the Baines' meat loaf dinner presages a rather dire state of affairs for mid-fifties America. Yet convenience foods and a TV set are only one aspect of this negative representation of blue collar affluence; another is the number of children the Baines have — there is Lorraine (17), Milton (12), Sally (6), Toby (4), Joey (11 months) and another on the way. It seems the Baines' affluence has not only affected their family structure but also its size. The family is clearly a part of America's 1950s baby boom cycle, and as such, Mr. and Mrs. Baines themselves are the progenitors of the era's youth culture with all of its incursive challenges to the social and cultural status quo.

It should of course be noted that the Baines' are indicted as parental failures even before we meet them; most notably in the scene of the McFly's 1985 family dinner, when we discover that their second youngest child, Joey, is a habitual criminal and, that their eldest child, Lorraine, is an unhappy and ineffective wife and mother who suffers from alcoholism and overeating.[23]

Lorraine's character is in many ways the lynchpin to the film's underlying conservatism, particularly its attitude towards women. The films' discomfort with the image of the sexually predatory woman, the bad mother and the dissatisfied woman are all bound up in her representation throughout the trilogy. Lorraine's alcoholism is retrospectively signaled in the first *Back to the Future* in a scene showing her at the age of 17 swigging from a bottle as she sits in a parked car with Marty. Acting as yet another indictment of the Baines' parental skills, Lorraine can, within the remit of American cultural discourses of the 1950s, be labeled a juvenile delinquent. Lorraine's "bad girl" behavior, which includes smoking and drinking and "parking" in cars with boys, allows for a number of comedic role reversal episodes between Marty and his young mother, with Marty admonishing her for her reckless behavior and Lorraine exasperatedly replying, "Marty, you're beginning to sound just like my mother." Naturally, the humor here is intentionally underscored by a serious note, namely that Marty knows Lorraine will develop a drinking problem in later life:

MARTY: No, no. Lorraine, Lorraine, what are you doing?

LORRAINE: I swiped it from the old lady's liquor cabinet.

MARTY: Yeah well, you shouldn't drink.

LORRAINE: Why not?

MARTY: Because, you might regret it later in life.

LORRAINE: Marty, don't be such a square. Everybody who's anybody drinks.

This final remark makes it clear that the interaction in this scene is more than just a commentary on Lorraine's individual predicament and her apparent predisposition to addiction, it also acts as a condemnation of 1950s drinking culture in America and the sense of relaxed sophistication associated with it. Thus Marty's censure of his young mother's actions can be viewed as not only his response to her on a personal level but also a telling denunciation of the blithe attitudes of youth in the 1950s whose disregard for their present would have serious consequences on their future and the future of their children.

Despite the fact that *Back to the Future*'s representation of a defiant 1950s youth culture is more akin to soft-pedaling TV shows like *The Adventures of Ozzie and Harriet* and *Father Knows Best* than it is to psychologically or socially complex films like *Blackboard Jungle* or *Rebel without a Cause*, the youth culture represented in the film nonetheless poses a considerable challenge to Marty McFly's sense of youthful ease and nonchalance. Of course Marty, at times, appears "square" to his young mother because he is in the unique position of having the "wisdom" of prescience which is not usually associated with 17-year-olds. Marty is profoundly concerned about the future not just because he is aware of its negative outcome (e.g. alcoholism, dead end job) but because he quite literally won't exist unless the present (1955) is orchestrated according to a rigid plan (namely the courtship of the teenagers, George and Lorraine, and their subsequent marriage). It may be argued that all of these factors have seriously curtailed any youthful devil-may-care attitude on Marty's part, but the truth is Marty McFly has always been a more controlled and responsible individual than his parents. As James Hay has suggested:

> As an ethnographic narrative, *Back to the Future*'s young protagonist is considerably more mature, sober, and responsible than the 1950s youth that he encounters (or than the adults, introduced at the film's beginning, which the 50s seems to have produced).[24]

The 17-year-old Marty is not only more conscientious and self-controlled than either of his parents in 1955 (both of whom are also 17 years old at this time), he is quite clearly a more sensible and self-possessed person than either George or Lorraine in 1985, when they are both 47 years old. This seems all the more miraculous considering the far from ideal role models his parents

have been. But lest we question this disparity too closely and, more importantly, just in case we start to feel our teen protagonist is a little too indefati-
gably faultless, we are periodically reminded that Marty is human after all
because it seems he has inherited his father's gnawing sense of self-doubt.
However, Marty's lapses of self-belief appear to be more a product of his *fear*
that he may be like his father than any actual indication that he *is* like his
father; when, for example, he worries about rejection from the record company or when accusations of "chicken" unnerve him. As such, Marty's greatest impediment to success is the burden of his father's failure. As his school
teacher, Strickland says: "Why even bother McFly, you haven't got a chance,
you're too much like your old man. No McFly ever amounted to anything in
the history of Hill Valley."

Yet again, we see here the dramatic impetus underlying *Back to the Future*
is the nightmare of biological determinism and, more specifically, the fear
that failure is hereditary. But Marty's will to succeed proves greater than the
weight of this fear. So much so that Marty will not only make a success of
his own life but will (with the aid of Doc and a time-traveling machine) guide
his troubled teen parents towards a far better future than the one they had
made for themselves without his wise and sobering influence.

If this scenario of a self-actualizing and self-governing youth at odds with
his less "mature, sober, and responsible" parents sounds somewhat familiar it
is hardly surprising because Michael J. Fox was already playing this role in
the TV sitcom *Family Ties*. In fact, because Fox was contracted to this hit TV
show, he had to moonlight to work on *Back to the Future*; reporting at Paramount Studios to record *Family Ties* from approximately 10:00 A.M. to 6:00
P.M. and then arriving at Universal to work on *Back to the Future* 6:30 P.M.
to 2:30 A.M.[25] In *Family Ties*, which aired on NBC from 1982 to 1989, Fox
played the hyper-earnest, neo-conservative Alex Keaton, the eldest son of liberal parents who are the products of 1960s counterculture and political
activism. This is how one commentator has described the show:

> Few shows better demonstrate the resonance between collectively-held fictional
> imagination and what cultural critic Raymond Williams called "the structure of
> feeling" of a historical moment than *Family Ties*. [...] this highly successful domes-
> tic comedy explored one of the intriguing cultural inversions characterizing the
> Reagan era: a conservative younger generation aspiring to wealth, business suc-
> cess, and traditional values, serves as inheritor to the politically liberal, presum-
> ably activist, culturally experimental generation of adults who had experienced the
> 1960s.[26]

Working on both character portrayals simultaneously, Alex Keaton by
day and Marty McFly by night, there is more than a touch of uncanny dou-
bling taking place between Fox's two characterizations. At a precursory glance

one might be inclined to notice Alex's and Marty's differences rather than their similarities. Alex Keaton is a suit-and-tie-wearing straight-A college student who dreams of making millions on Wall Street; he wouldn't be caught dead in a down vest, riding a skateboard or playing in a rock band. But these are in many ways superficial differences between the two characters rather than fundamental ones; just because Alex has a Richard Nixon poster on his bedroom wall and Marty has a *Huey Lewis and the News* one on his, doesn't mean they don't have a lot in common ... after all, isn't the show-stealing popularity of Alex Keaton's character in *Family Ties* a testament to the fact that it really was *hip to be square*[27] in 1980s America? As the show's own creator queried, "When else could a boy with a briefcase become a national hero?"[28] Certainly 1980s America can be seen as a decade

> paradoxical by America's usual post–World War II standards, in which youthful ambition and social renovation became equated with pronounced political conservatism.[29]

It should of course be noted that although both Alex's and Marty's parents might be termed baby boomers; they represent very different types of parental figures. Alex Keaton's parents are products of 1960s counterculture while Marty's (being roughly 5–7 years older) are products of 1950s youth culture. Yet, despite these marked differences, both sets of parents find themselves at variance with their teenage sons whose social attitudes and ambitions prove to be more conventional than their own.

Alex and Marty are both, as I have suggested above, more sober levelheaded individuals than their parents — while this is obvious in the case of Alex and his rather chimerical parents, it is equally true of Marty, not only because he is a nonsmoking, tee-totaling, sexually monogamous, sugar-free Pepsi drinker but also because he, like Alex, has a "healthy" dread of failure and a concomitant respect for success and affluence. In this respect the young protagonists of *Back to the Future* and *Family Ties* both embody the zeitgeist of their generation. As one commentator on *Family Ties* has suggested:

> Airing in almost perfect parallel to his administration, from 1982 to 1989, the show captured the new era that Reagan ushered in. Hooked on Reagan's optimism and strength, the Alex Keaton generation was rejecting the counterculture of the 1960s and embracing the wealth and power that came to define the '80s.[30]

Family Ties represented this spirit of the time in scenarios that satirized Alex's ethics; as for example, when Alex reads Robin Hood to his younger brother Andy but changes it so that the hero robs from the poor and gives to the rich and Alex's father observes, "That's not Robin Hood, that's Ronald Reagan." But while these attitudes are the stuff of comedy in the depiction of Alex's character in *Family Ties*, in *Back to the Future*, Marty's discontent with his parents and his desire for a higher standard of living are buried much farther beneath the surface of the narrative and are taken very seriously indeed.

Whatever differences there may be in the underlying politics of these productions, President Ronald Reagan seems to have been a fan of both. He not only declared *Family Ties* his favorite program of the 1980s but also offered to make an appearance on the show.[31] Reagan's admiration for *Back to the Future* (which also makes a few jokes at Reagan's expense but notably only in reference to his actor-turned-president status and not his political policies) is patent in his referencing of the film in his 1986 State of the Union Address:

> And tonight I want to speak directly to America's younger generation, because you hold the destiny of our nation in your hands. With all the temptations young people face, it sometimes seems the allure of this permissive society requires super-human feats of self-control. But the call of the future is too strong, the challenge too great to get lost in the blind alleyways of dissolution, drugs, and despair. Never has there been a more exciting time to be alive, a time of rousing wonder and heroic achievement. As they said in the film *Back to the Future*, "Where we're going, we don't need roads."[32]

Quoting just the final two lines of the above, in his commentary on American culture in the 1980s, Graham Thompson argues:

> This referencing of the film in support of technological progress seems downright ironic when one of the central technological elements of the film — the DeLorean car used by Marty to travel backwards and forwards in time — was one of the biggest hi-tech failures of the 1980s.[33]

But what Thompson fails to take into consideration here is how the entire premise of the *Back to the Future* trilogy is based on turning failure into success, in other words, on *re*invention not invention. Taking this into consideration Reagan's referencing of the film and, indeed, the film's use of the DeLorean car seem highly appropriate. Of course, even before quoting the final lines of the film, Reagan's speech is infused with a spirit which evokes *Back to the Future*; his vision of an era of "rousing wonder and heroic achievement" where the younger generation hold "destiny" in their hands is, in essence, the vision of Zemeckis' film. As is the image of this new generation's "self-control" and successful avoidance of the pitfalls of a "permissive society"; a permissive society which, in Zemeckis' film, is symbolized by the youth culture of the 1950s and the legacy it has left subsequent generations. Above all else, Reagan's belief that the future can be wrought into an ideal place where all of one's hopes and dreams are fulfilled is a belief that runs throughout the *Back to the Future* trilogy. His State of the Union Address ends with the following:

> After all we've done so far, let no one say this nation cannot reach the destiny of our dreams. America believes, America is ready, America can win the race to the future — and we shall. [...]

In this land of dreams fulfilled, where greater dreams may be imagined, nothing is impossible, no victory is beyond our reach; no glory will ever be too great. [...] The world's hopes rest with America's future. America's hopes rest with us. So, let us go forward to create our world of tomorrow — in faith, in unity, and in love. God bless you, and God bless America.[34]

The sentiments expressed here are remarkably in tune with Doc Brown's assertion in the first *Back to the Future* film, "If you put your mind to it you can accomplish anything" and his parting words in *Back to the Future III* "your future hasn't been written yet. No one's has. Your future is whatever you make it. So make it a good one."

When asked, in a 2004 interview, what was the "basic theme" of *Back to the Future* writer, Bob Gale replied:

That you are in control of your own destiny. It's all about personal responsibility. And just because somebody says that something is supposed to be a certain way, it ain't necessarily so. Doc Brown sums it up at the end of *BTTF3* when he says "your future is whatever you make it, so make it a good one."[35]

This is precisely the rhetoric of Reagan's 1986 State of the Union Address and the Reagan administration more generally. As professor of political communication and the modern presidency, Leonard Steinhorn has suggested, "He [Reagan] did communicate a sense of optimism at a time after we lost a war and when we had terrible economic shocks [...] Ronald Reagan comes in and just wants to make people believe we can recapture control of our fate, and that's why he's so warmly remembered."[36] It can quite legitimately be argued that much of *Back to the Future*'s popularity has been based on a similar sense of optimism and reassurance. There is a patent interplay here between the cinema and the economic landscape of the Reagan years; an interplay which, as one commentator has noted, is further "deepened by virtue of Reagan's own very personal ties to acting and show-business."[37]

This sense of limitless possibilities, both in the political and cinematic discourses of the era, is closely aligned to a faith in the "magic" of technology. In his address, Reagan talks of how "physicists peering into the infinitely small realms of subatomic particles find reaffirmations of religious faith"; of how "astronomers build a space telescope that can see to the edge of the universe and possibly back to the moment of creation."[38] He talks of the nation's continued commitment to the space program, to shuttle flights and a space station. He also talks of time-defying travel:

And we are going forward with research on a new Orient Express that could, by the end of the next decade, take off from Dulles Airport, accelerate up to 25 times the speed of sound, attaining low Earth orbit or flying to Tokyo within 2 hours.[39]

Reagan concludes these flights of fancy by observing that "the same technology transforming our lives can solve the greatest problem of the 20th century" in the form of a "security shield [that] can one day render nuclear weapons obsolete and free mankind from the prison of nuclear terror."[40] This almost childlike fascination with technology and faith in its seemingly limitless possibilities which can be found in American political rhetoric of the era runs parallel with a rise, from the late–1970s onward, in what may be termed feel-good fantasy films; films which Robin Wood has labeled the "Lucas-Spielberg Syndrome."[41] Films like *Star Wars*, *E.T.* and *Close Encounters of the Third Kind* are testament to the powerful interplay that existed between cinema and Reagan's vision of a new era of "rousing wonder and heroic achievement." As Wood argues in his essay, "Papering the Cracks: Fantasy and Ideology in the Reagan Era," these films offer a reductionist demagoguery that advocates simplistic solutions to complex social/political problems — whether those problems take the form of the menace of the Evil Empire/Soviet Union (*Star Wars*) or the specter of the dysfunctional/fatherless family (*E.T.*). The special effects in these films are, Wood argues, presented as reassuring magic. As narratives about all-powerful beings that can solve our problems, *E.T.* and *Close Encounters* use this reassuring magic in diegetic form. Other forms of special effects work in a meta-textual manner, demonstrating how the glorious technical advances of New Hollywood cinema can achieve any representation.[42] Both forms of special effects envision a world where complicated social problems will be magically solved by some external source (much as Reagan does in his 1986 State of the Union Address). The special effects magic of the Spielberg-produced *Back to the Future* trilogy works in just this way, with Doc Brown's time-machine acting as the external force which magically raises the McFly family to a more affluent condition by enabling Marty to travel back in time and "cure" George of his ineffectualness as a man; thereby making him a satisfactory male provider, father and husband; which in turn cures Lorraine of her discontent, alcoholism and weight problem; all of which has a knock-on effect on their children and finds Marty rewarded for his trouble with a gleaming 4 × 4 truck.

One of *Back to the Future*'s taglines reads, "Marty McFly just broke the time barrier. He's only got one week to get it fixed."[43] But considering the tremendously successfully renovation that Marty works on his substandard family it would be more appropriate to note that having broke the time barrier our protagonist takes only one week to get his family *fixed*.

The end of *Back to the Future* makes the time-altered McFly family's affluence, success and contentment readily observable, both in the house's décor and the demeanor of the family. An airily and well lit dining area (replete with high-maintenance white sofa and glass-topped table) replaces the dank and cluttered original; healthy food replaces convenience food; a business suit replaces a Burger King uniform; happy, healthy, loving parents replace the dysfunctional originals and Biff, the bullying co-worker, is replaced by Biff, the sniveling lackey. Perhaps somewhat remarkably this "happy" ending is in fact considerably toned down in comparison to the shooting script which makes the McFlys' affluence and success significantly greater. In this version George hasn't just written his first novel but is actually a bestselling author whose latest book has sold 2 million copies (hardcover); the McFlys have a maid named Bertha, and are about to move house:

GEORGE: Well, you won't have to put up with that tiny kitchen much longer.

BERTHA: When will the new house be ready, sir?

GEORGE: Just as soon as they finish painting the tennis court and re-tiling the swimming pool.[44]

The fact that the film version tones down this ending by making the McFlys only moderately affluent (albeit with the potential for greater affluence) may, in part, be due to the filmmakers' concern about giving the film as plausible a happy ending as possible but the more compelling rationale behind the modification of this ending is the filmmakers' fear that the audience will not be able to relate to the McFlys' new affluence if it is too great and may resent rather than admire such a level of prosperity. In other words, an essential ingredient in the feel-good factor of the film's ending is that the audience believes the "newfound" happiness, success and wealth of Marty's family is personally attainable, even without a time machine.

Of course, this kind of feel-good dynamic can be located outside of the movie screen; it also informs the political discourses of the era and is part of the foundational myths of Ronald Reagan's presidency. As one commentator observes, "I think the one area where he [Reagan] had the biggest impact is in the sense he really lived the American-dream narrative, where to make it in America you're a triumphant individual."[45] This American-dream narrative of success through self-belief and self-fashioning is a crucial element in the feel-good factor of Zemeckis' film and one of the most potent symbols of successful self-fashioning is affluence. Paralleling the films of the era with Reagan's presidency, Alan Nadel notes how, "Like Marty, [...] Reagan found approval and self-approval strongly linked to affluence."[46] Indeed, following the plot trajectory of the Horatio Alger myth, rags to riches stories are one of the most popular factual and fictional narratives of 1980s America: "Faith in the almighty market as an engine for upward mobility, and fantasies of class-permeability in general, pervade American cinema in the early 1980s."[47]

These narratives also espouse a faith in the individual's ability to triumph solely by her, or his, own merits ... and a little luck. But, as we have already seen, the narrative of *Back to the Future* is haunted by the fear that the individual cannot escape the burden of the past and, more specifically, that the failures and mistakes of one's forefathers become one's own. In order to counteract this threat to the myth of the self-made man, *Back to the Future*'s protagonist makes a new future for himself by remaking the past. Through "a massive act of rehistoricizing" Marty reconstructs his parents into different people; people who are not failures: "The outcome is that he turns his 1985 parents into people he can like, into people who do not make him ashamed, into people, in other words, who are affluent."[48]

Indeed, as Nadel pertinently observes, when Marty answers his school teacher's jibes about being a failure, "like your old man," by saying "Yeah, well, history is gonna change" he is exactly right; "not because he is going to change the future — make history — but because he is going to change the past — remake history."[49] Marty fixes the future by fixing the past. Thus the myth of the triumphant individual and self-made man remains intact but only by imposing that myth on to the previous generation.

The key to this fixing of the past rests with the remaking of George McFly, the awkward and nerdish protagonist of *Back to the Future*'s teen romance plot. Through the course of his residence in 1955, Marty will guide his young father through a series of events which will make him a more self-confident, dynamic individual; turning George from a loser into a winner and an ideal image of the great white father. The most important adjustment that Marty's tampering in the past makes to George's character is precisely in his role as a teen romance protagonist. This begins with Marty's interference in the event that should have caused Lorraine and George to fall in love. Lorraine says, "Anyway, Grandpa hit him with the car and brought him into the house. He seemed so helpless, like a little lost puppy, my heart just went out for him."

From this description, which Lorraine recounts during the gloomy 1985 meatloaf dinner, it is apparent that her love for George was originally based on a desire to nurture and protect him. Of course, what Lorraine doesn't know is that George was hit by her Grandpa's car because he was otherwise occupied with spying on her through her bedroom window. The upshot of Marty's disruption of this event, and the events that follow, is that that George's desire for Lorraine is channeled into a public display rather than a private one. Instead of sexually desiring her from afar and fortuitously meeting her through a car accident he must now make his desire for her known, first in front of her friends at the malt shop and then at The Enchantment Under the Sea Dance, when he must, not once, but twice, fight off other males in order to prove himself and win her love. While the 17-year-old Lorraine may have been attracted to George's vulnerability the outcome of their marriage (in the original 1985) asserts that this is not the *appropriate* basis for a romantic relationship. On the other hand, once their relationship is played out publicly, with George actively petitioning for Lorraine's affections through embarrassing declarations of love and violent competition with other men, their story of teen romance now fits a normative pattern and the film's happy ending makes it patently clear that this is the perfect foundation for a life-long and fulfilling marriage.

George's desire is now healthy and normal, he has proven himself an adequate male and once this masculinization of Marty's father has occurred, everything else simply falls into place. His nerdish interest in science fiction as a teen is now compartmentalized and channeled into a marketable form of entertainment that will appeal to the masses and make him rich and famous (much like a Lucas or a Spielberg). He is also a shrewd businessman who cannot be cajoled or fooled by underlings, as he explains to Marty, "Some employees will get away with murder if you don't stay on 'em."[50] Lorraine's happiness and self-esteem are, it seems, indistinguishable from her husband's; once George assumes the role of a self-assured, successful and prosperous patriarch who is deserving of respect, she can now respect herself and happily assume the role of the perfect wife and mother. And once these elements are in place, it is simply a matter of course that the McFly children will be happy and successful too. There are other fringe benefits to Marty's meddling in the past:

> In the process of remaking his parents, he also changes the role of the town bully, empowers the future black mayor, and changes the shape of rock n roll by introducing Chuck Berry's cousin to the sound that Berry will claim.[51]

Curiously enough, Marty's tampering with history doesn't appear to have changed him at all. He is the exact same, right down to his clothes and the posters on his bedroom wall, which only adds to the nagging suspicion that he was very nearly perfect all along and just needed a better class of family and a 4 × 4. *Back to the Future Part II* does put forward the possibility that Marty's and Jennifer's own family (in the year 2015) will be less than ideal unless the 1985 Marty can, as Doc puts it, *do something* about their kids. But this still has the intriguing effect of presenting the *1985* Marty (the *real* Marty) as a pretty darn wonderful guy; a guy, who by his own gumption, and with the aid of a time-machine, can sort out the problems of the past, the present and the future.

It should be noted that although the outcome of Marty's meddling in time may be, on the whole, advantageous (at least for himself and the people he cares about), there is, however, a fairly significant difference between his initial interference in fate and his subsequent ones. Marty's first venture in time travel was an accident, as was his unthinking interference in the event that should have caused his parents to meet and fall in love. Thus, his continued intervention into the events of 1955 (in the first film) can be defended on the grounds that he is attempting to get things back on track. The fact that Marty's interference in his young parents' lives actuates a better future for all the McFlys in 1985 may therefore be read as a fringe benefit of his time traveling. However, from the end of the first film onwards, the impetus for both Marty's and Doc's time traveling is expressly to interfere with the course of events in order to "correct" them or, more accurately, in order to make things turn out the way they want them to. Despite Doc's periodic cautioning of Marty about the dangers of tampering with time, the underlying message which is reiterated throughout the trilogy is that interfering with time isn't only a lot of fun it is an invaluable means of securing a desirable present and a successful future.

Most telling of all, perhaps, are the comments made by Doc upon discovering the alternate 1985 that Biff Tannen's tampering with time has created in *Back to the Future Part II*. He tells Marty, "The time machine must be destroyed after we straighten all this out." By "straighten all this out" Doc means get things back to the 1985 that Marty's initially tampering created or, as Nadel phrases it, "after they take appropriate measures to restore the version of the past that made Biff poor and the McFlys rich."[52] Doc even refers to this as "the real 1985." In this sense, Marty's initial tampering is not only acceptable because it made the McFlys affluent, it's more than acceptable; it actually becomes the *real* 1985. The McFlys who existed during the thirty years before Doc unveiled his time machine and prior to Marty's initial intervention into the past are simply a bad dream best forgotten about.

This highly selective rendering of history is just one example of Doc's and Marty's careful monopoly of fate and the exclusive rights they reserve over the altering of time. Despite the fact that Biff's creation of an alternate 1985 is a superb affirmation of Doc's pronouncement that "if you put your mind to it you can accomplish anything," Doc and Marty nonetheless can justify wrenching control of history away from Biff and reinstating their own altered version of it not only because Biff's 1985 turns out bad for the McFlys (with George dead and Lorraine unhappily married to Biff) but also because, in Biff's 1985, the nice middle American town of Hill Valley is blighted by vice and violence.[53] But many other decisions on Doc's and Marty's part appear to be entirely based on their own discriminatory whims. The treatment of Marty's girlfriend, Jennifer is a case in point. At the end of the first film, when Doc reappears to take Marty into the future, the following exchange occurs:

MARTY: No, no, no, look Doc, I just got here, okay, Jennifer's here, we're gonna take the new truck for a spin.

DOC: Well, bring her along. This concerns her too.

MARTY: Wait a minute, Doc. What are you talking about? What happens to us in the future? What do we become assholes or something?

DOC: Oh, no, no, no, no, no, Marty, you and Jennifer both turn out fine. It's your kids, Marty, something has got to be done about your kids.

As "evidence" that, on the completion of the first film, neither he nor Zemeckis had any intention of making a sequel, Bob Gale points to the inclusion of Jennifer in this journey at the close of the film. Apparently, this ending was meant as a joke and not a hint to a future installment "[...] or else we wouldn't have put Jennifer in the car at the end. The first thing we do in *II* is knock her out. She spends the whole movie being carried around."[54] Of course, Gale automatically expects us to understand and accept his meaning here; which is namely that if the filmmakers had intended to make another film they certainly wouldn't have lumbered themselves with the inclusion of a female as a major character. Tampering with history is really a man's job, as is being the hero of a "comedy adventure science fiction time travel" blockbuster movie. And so, in a ludicrous, not to mention chauvinistic, turn of events Jennifer is reduced to a modern-day Sleeping Beauty, remaining unconscious throughout most of *Back to the Future Part II* and *III*.[55] Gale's and Zemeckis' attitude as filmmakers is consequently reflected in the behavior of Doc and Marty. When, at the beginning of *Back to the Future Part II*, Jennifer is traveling with "the boys" in the time machine and excitedly speculates about what she will see in the future (the usual "girl" things like her wedding dress and her house and kids), Doc gets out a gadget and shines it on her face. She falls back, unconscious. Explaining his actions, he tells Marty:

> Relax Marty, it's just a sleep-inducing alpha-rhythm generator. She was asking too many questions and no-one should know too much about their future. This way when she wakes up she'll think it was all a dream.

Of course, the fact that Marty and Doc are continually discovering things about their future and, what's more, tampering with it doesn't appear to be too great an issue. Jennifer, on the other hand, like some modern teenage Eve, must be kept away from knowledge at all cost. This is despite the fact that the impetus for the journey is allegedly to "help" *her* children. It seems Doc has entirely forgotten his comment "This concerns her too" or perhaps he never really meant it; as he explains to Marty, "Don't worry, she's not essential to my plan," to which Marty replies, "You're the Doc, Doc."

Indeed, it is a bitter medicine which Doc administers, for despite Gale's assertion that the basic theme of the *Back to the Future* trilogy is "That you are in control of your own destiny. It's all about personal responsibility," Doc's treatment of Jennifer proffers a very different message. Namely that an individual's power to shape his/her future is by no means a given but is instead closely associated with variables often beyond his/her control; variables which include one's position in relation to various forms of power and authority and the barriers that one may face due to sexual, racial or class discrimination. The ethos of rugged individualism and the dream of equal opportunity which

Back to the Future claims to espouse is that each of us is judged solely on her/his own merits and that, like the Horatio Alger myth, "success in life has nothing to do with pedigree, race, class background, gender, national origin, sexual orientation — in short, with anything beyond our individual control"[56]; as Gale states "just because somebody says that something is supposed to be a certain way, it ain't necessarily so. Doc Brown sums it up at the end of *BTTF3* when he says 'your future is whatever you make it, so make it a good one.'" In promoting this ethos that we each have a fair opportunity to improve our social position, the *Back to the Future* films epitomize the political values of their era. As one analyst of the Reagan administration observes:

> Forget about whatever circumstances you had in life, or the bigotry that may have been visited upon your ancestors. Reagan created this ethos of the triumphant individual, that you're successful because of your own doing. The flip side is that if you're not successful, it's because of you, as well.[57]

This figure of the "triumphant individual" is the crux of what Michael J. Fox has referred to as *Back to the Future*'s "very life-affirming story."[58] But, as the above quote suggests, this positivism, which appears to empower the individual, is based on a blithe disregard for the many socio-cultural, political and economic variables at work which may enable some individuals to peruse their ambitions while hampering others. Despite Doc's parting words to Marty, at the end of *Back to the Future Part III* "your future hasn't been written yet. No one's has," the trilogy itself gives the lie to this vision of personal freedom. Marty's individual freedom to shape his own future is undeniable but the suggestion that this is equally true for everyone certainly is not. Virtually all of the other characters that appear in the trilogy — Jennifer, George, Lorraine, Linda, Dave, Biff Tannen, Mr. Strickland, Clara Clayton — are subjected to a myriad of different possible futures, with little or no control over their own destinies. Their fates are instead the combined result of their genetic predispositions which find them mechanically repeating the behavior of previous generations. Their chances of breaking out of or altering these vicious cycles are utterly reliant on an intervention by forces not only beyond their control but also beyond their understanding or knowledge. The time machine and Marty's and Doc's use of it becomes the magical means by which some are guided towards success and some towards failure. This is hardly the liberating vision of a world where you are in "control of your own destiny." Instead it is a vision of a world where opportunity and success come easily to a select few, who have the ability to manipulate affairs expressly for their own ends while simultaneously subjecting others to discriminatory treatment; thereby ensuring the maintenance of an inequitable status quo. Mirroring the idiom of the Reagan era, *Back to the Future* offsets and deflects attention away from such a grim state of affairs by idolatrizing the concept of individual freedom and liberty. It is by no means insignificant that, in his 1986 State of the Union Address, Reagan chooses to quote the following line from the film, "Where we're going, we don't need roads," because the line presents the future as a place of unlimited possibilities, unfettered by the weight of history or social and economic boundaries. It is in essence the image of the new frontier, the Wild West — the very origin of the American myth of the rugged individualism and freedom. As such, it's of little wonder that Reagan himself (as America's Cowboy President) would find such sentiments in accord with his own self-image or indeed that the final installment of *Back to the Future* finds recourse to the Western to complete its tale of "rousing wonder and heroic achievement." The fact that this freedom is not in reality the prerogative of all Americans is simply disregarded. The future can appear as a blank piece of paper (a blank check) to Marty because he can face it with the knowledge that all has been artfully manipulated so that he has every advantage in life in order to make a success of things in the future. All he need do is borrow a pen and fill in the details.

Notes

1. Robert Zemeckis, *The New York Times Essential Library: A Critic's Guide to the Best Children's Films Available on Video and DVD*, ed. Peter M. Nichols (New York: Times Books, 2003).

2. James Thorburn, "Eighties Teen Movies — Nostalgia, Thy Name is Judd Nelson" (1998), http://www.80s.com/saveferris/essays/thorburn.txt, accessed 1 Mar. 2009. Other elements of the ETM which Thorburn identifies that can be found in *Back to The Future* are — "Advice from buddy" (George McFly getting advice from Marty); "Hatching of improbable scheme" (the plan for George to save Lorraine from a faked assault perpetrated by Marty); "Protagonist demonstrates sensitivity (poetry, short story and/or touching anecdote)" (George's science fiction writing). For more on teen cinema see Thomas Doherty, *Teenagers and Teenpics: The Juvenilization of American Movies in the 1950s* (Boston: Unwin Hyman, 1988), Jon Lewis, *The Road to Romance and Ruin: Teen Films and Youth Culture* (New York and London: Routledge, 1992) and Jonathan Bernstein, *Pretty in Pink: The Golden Age of Teenage Movies* (New York: St. Martin's Griffin, 1997).

3. *Ibid.*

4. *Ibid.*

5. Michael J. Fox, "The Michael J. Fox En-

cyclopedia" on *BTTF.com*, http://www.bttf.com/mjf_bio.htm, accessed 15 Feb. 2009.

6. Kathleen Bennett deMarrais and Margaret D. LeCompte, *The Way Schools Work: A Sociological Analysis of Education* (New York: Longman, 1995), p. 87.

7. *Ibid.*

8. Stephen Prince and Charles Harpole, *A New Pot of Gold: Hollywood Under the Electronic Rainbow, 1980–1989* (Berkeley: University of California Press, 2002), p. 218–19.

9. Graham Thompson, *American Culture in the 1980s* (Edinburgh University Press, 2007), p. 104.

10. *Ibid*, p. 104.

11. Yoram Allon and Hannah Patterson, *Contemporary North American Film Directors: A Wallflower Critical Guide* (London and New York: Wallflower Press, 2002), p. 583.

12. Thompson, *American Culture in the 1980s*, p. 104–5.

13. *Ibid.*, p. 105.

14. *Ibid.*, p. 104.

15. Class consciousness and the theme of upward mobility pervaded the movies of the 1980s in other films such as *Flashdance, An Officer and a Gentleman, Valley Girl* (1983), *All the Right Moves* (1983), *Trading Places* (1983), *Risky Business* (1983), *Class* (1983), *The Break-*

fast Club (1985), *Brewster's Millions* (1985), *Back to School* (1986), and *Down and Out in Beverly Hills* (1986). See Jonathan Bernstein, *Pretty in Pink: The Golden Age of Teenage Movies* (New York: St. Martin's Griffin, 1997).

16. For example, in the film version Marty's brother, Dave, works in Burger King instead of McDonald's. There has been a suggestion that a fifth version of the screenplay may have been written which edited out more scenes and dialogue and generally "tidied" the script up but this has never surfaced.

17. Robert Zemeckis and Bob Gale, *Back to the Future* Screenplay, Fourth Draft — revised 10/12/84 and 10/21/84, Scene 15. Available from "The Daily Script," http://www.dailyscript.com/scripts/bttf4th.pdf, accessed 17 Mar. 2009.

18. This is not to say that the McFly's financial status is irrelevant to the film's portrayal of them, as we shall see at the close of the film, financial success seems to go a long way when it comes to raising Marty's family into a higher class group, but the greatest signifiers of the *original* McFly family's low class status is their lack of taste and decorum rather than their lack of money.

19. Laura Provosty and Douglas Donovan, "White Trash in the Twentieth Century" http://xroads.virginia.edu/~CLASS/AM483_95/projects/trash/trash3.html, accessed 25 Feb. 2009.

20. *Ibid.*

21. Zemeckis and Gale, *Back to the Future* Screenplay, Fourth Draft — revised 10/12/84 and 10/21/84, Scene 55. Available from *The Daily Script*, http://www.dailyscript.com/scripts/bttf4th.pdf, accessed 17 Mar. 2009.

22. See Cesare Lombroso, *Criminal Man* (*L'uomo delinquente*) (1876), trans. Mary Gibson and Nicole Hahn Rafter (Durham: Duke University Press, 2006).

23. As we know nothing of the rest of the Baines children's fates we can only speculate as to their success or failure in 1985. However, in an early draft of *Back to the Future Part II*, Toby in 1967 was depicted as a young man about to turn 18 and looking forward to participating in the Vietnam War so he could "kick some commie butt." At that time, Toby's mother wanted him to go to college, but his father dismissed the idea on account of Toby's low grades.

24. James Hay, "Rethinking the Intersection of Cinema, Genre, and Youth," *Scope*, Oct. 2008, Issue 12.

25. "The Michael J. Fox Encyclopedia" on *BTTF.com*, http://www.bttf.com/mjf_bio.htm, accessed 15 Feb. 2009.

26. Michael Saenz, *The Museum of Broadcast Communications*, http://www.museum.tv/archives/etv/F/htmlF/familyties/familyties.htm, accessed 15 Feb. 2009. Indeed, it may be more accurate to say that it was specifically Alex Keaton's character that captured the "structure of feeling" of 1980s America. Initially the show was supposed to be about Alex's parents, ex-hippies Steve and Elyse, but it was Alex who quickly became the star of the show and the episode plots clearly reflect this as the series was re-centered around Alex.

27. *Huey Lewis and the News* prominently feature on the soundtrack of *Back to the Future* with the songs "Power of Love" and "Back in Time." "Hip to be Square" is the name of one of the band's mid–1980s hits. *American Psycho*'s serial killer protagonist, Patrick Bateman is a big fan of the band and considers "Hip to be Square" their undisputed masterpiece because it celebrates "the pleasures of conformity" and it's so catchy. He plays the song while dancing and then brutally murdering a colleague with an axe. *Back to the Future*'s penchant for middle-of-the-road white rock would continue with *Part II* which featured the song "I Can't Drive 55" by Sammy Hagar, a "cock-rock" whine about the lowering of highway speed limits. *Back to the Future Part III* featured *ZZ Top* as, fittingly enough, a hoedown band at the square dance.

28. Gary David Goldberg, quoted by Saenz, *The Museum of Broadcast Communications*, http://www.museum.tv/archives/etv/F/htmlF/familyties/familyties.htm, accessed 15 Feb. 2009.

29. Saenz, *The Museum of Broadcast Communications*, http://www.museum.tv/archives/etv/F/htmlF/familyties/familyties.htm, accessed 15 Feb. 2009.

30. Stephen Kiehl, "What He Left Behind: From Tom Clancy to Alex P. Keaton, Ronald Reagan's Legacy Extends Beyond the Political and into the Cultural," *Sun Staff*, June 7, 2004.

31. *Ibid.*

32. Ronald Reagan, *Address Before a Joint Session of Congress on the State of the Union*, February 4, 1986, available at *The American Presidency Project*, http://www.presidency.ucsb.edu/ws/index.php?pid=36646, accessed 20 Feb. 2009.

33. Thompson, *American Culture in the 1980s*, p. 104.

34. Reagan, *Address Before a Joint Session of Congress on the State of the Union*, February 4, 1986, available at *The American Presidency Project*, http://www.presidency.ucsb.edu/ws/index.php?pid=36646, accessed 20 Feb. 2009.

35. Bob Gale, "Brain Storm" interviewed by Scott Holleran, *Box Office Mojo* Nov. 18, 2003. Available at http://www.boxofficemojo.com/features/?id=1258, accessed 19 Mar. 2009.

36. Kiehl, "What He Left Behind: From Tom Clancy to Alex P. Keaton, Ronald Reagan's Legacy Extends Beyond the Political and into the Cultural," *Sun Staff*, June 7, 2004.

37. Geoffrey Baker, "Social Mobility in Reagan-era Teen Films: From Inaugural Optimism to the Invention of Generation X," *Americana: The American Popular Culture Magazine*, Sept. 2006, http://www.americanpopularculture.com/archive/politics/reagan_era_films.htm, accessed 15 Mar. 2009.

38. Reagan, *Address Before a Joint Session of Congress on the State of the Union*, February 4, 1986, available at *The American Presidency Project*, http://www.presidency.ucsb.edu/ws/index.php?pid=36646, accessed on 20 Feb. 2009.

39. *Ibid.*

40. *Ibid.*

41. Robin Wood, *Hollywood from Vietnam to Reagan ... and Beyond* (New York: Columbia University Press), p. 144.

42. *Ibid,* p. 148.

43. *Back to the Future* (1985)— Taglines, on the *Internet Movie Database*, http://www.imdb.com/title/tt0088763/taglines, accessed 10 Mar. 2009.

44. Zemeckis and Gale, *Back to the Future* Screenplay, Fourth Draft — revised 10/12/84 and 10/21/84, Scene 229. Available from *The Daily Script*, http://www.dailyscript.com/scripts/bttf4th.pdf, accessed 17 Mar. 2009.

45. Kiehl, "What He Left Behind: From Tom Clancy to Alex P. Keaton, Ronald Reagan's Legacy Extends Beyond the Political and into the Cultural," *Sun Staff*, June 7, 2004.

46. Alan Nadel, *Flatlining on the Field of Dreams: Cultural Narratives in the Films of President Reagan's America* (New Brunswick, NJ: Rutgers University Press, 1997), p. 33.

47. Baker, "Social Mobility in Reagan-era Teen Films: From Inaugural Optimism to the Invention of Generation X," *Americana: The American Popular Culture Magazine*, Sept. 2006.

48. Nadel, *Flatlining on the Field of Dreams: Cultural Narratives in the Films of President Reagan's America*, pp. 76-7.

49. *Ibid.*

50. Zemeckis and Gale, *Back to the Future* Screenplay, Fourth Draft — revised 10/12/84 and 10/21/84, Scene 229. Available from *The Daily Script*, http://www.dailyscript.com/scripts/bttf4th.pdf, accessed 17 Mar. 2009.

51. Nadel, *Flatlining on the Field of Dreams: Cultural Narratives in the Films of President Reagan's America*, pp. 76-7.

52. *Ibid,* p. 81.

53. The nightmare picture of Hill Valley in Biff's altered version of 1985 is one characterized not only by vice, gambling and drive by shootings but also by black neighbors.

54. Bob Gale, from interview on *Back to the Future 4-Disc Ultimate Edition*, Universal, 2005.

55. This treatment of Jennifer's character perfectly reflects the identity politics of "Reaganite" cinema as discussed by Robin Wood, who argues that one of the means by which these films restore the image of the patriarchal white father is by containing ethnic and gendered others. For example, Reaganite films undermine the liberated woman either by the return of women to traditional gender roles, or the complete elimination of them. (Wood, *Hollywood from Vietnam to Reagan ... and Beyond*, pp. 66-7). While the process of "elimination" may be applied to Jennifer, the return of women to traditional gender roles is certainly at work in the "development" of Lorraine McFly's character throughout the trilogy. Further evidence of the trilogy's returning of women to traditional gender roles is the fact that Doc's ideal woman proves to be a schoolmarm from the 19th Century.

56. Harlon L. Dalton, "Horatio Alger" in *Rereading America: Cultural Contexts for Critical Thinking and Writing*, eds. Gary Colombo, Robert Cullen and Bonny Lisle (Boston: Bedford/St. Martin's, 2004), p. 304. See also Harlon L. Dalton, *Racial Healing: Confronting the Fear Between Blacks and Whites* (New York: Doubleday, 1995), Richard Weiss, *The American Myth of Success: From Horatio Alger to Norman Vincent Peale* (New York: Basic Books, 1969) and Jonathan Bernstein, *Pretty in Pink: The Golden Age of Teenage Movies* (New York: St. Martin's Griffin, 1997).

57. Kiehl, "What He Left Behind: From Tom Clancy to Alex P. Keaton, Ronald Reagan's Legacy Extends Beyond the Political and into the Cultural," *Sun Staff*, June 7, 2004.

58. Michael J. Fox, "The Michael J. Fox Encyclopedia" on *BTTF.com*, http://www.bttf.com/mjf_bio.htm, accessed 15 Feb. 2009.

Works Cited

Allon, Yoram, and Hannah Patterson. *Contemporary North American Film Directors: A Wallflower Critical Guide*. London and New York: Wallflower Press, 2002.

Baker, Geoffrey. "Social Mobility in Reagan-era Teen Films: From Inaugural Optimism to the Invention of Generation X," *Americana: The American Popular Culture Magazine*, Sept. 2006, http://www.americanpopularculture.com/archive/politics/reagan_era_films.htm, accessed 15 Mar. 2009.

Bernstein, Jonathan. *Pretty in Pink: The Golden Age of Teenage Movies*. New York: St. Martin's Griffin, 1997.

Dalton, Harlon L. "Horatio Alger" in *Rereading America: Cultural Contexts for Critical Thinking and Writing*, eds. Gary Colombo, Robert Cullen and Bonny Lisle. Boston: Bedford/St. Martin's, 2004.

_____. *Racial Healing: Confronting the Fear Between Blacks and Whites*. New York: Doubleday, 1995.

deMarrais, Kathleen Bennett, and Margaret D. LeCompte. *The Way Schools Work: A Sociological Analysis of Education*. New York: Longman, 1995.

Doherty, Thomas. *Teenagers and Teenpics: The Juvenilization of American Movies in the 1950s*. Boston: Unwin Hyman, 1988.

Fox. Michael J. "The Michael J. Fox Encyclopedia" on *BTTF.com*, http://www.bttf.com/mjf_bio.htm, accessed 15 Feb. 2009.

Gale, Bob. "Brain Storm" interviewed by Scott Holleran, *Box Office Mojo* Nov. 18, 2003. Available at http://www.boxofficemojo.com/features/?id=1258, accessed 19 Mar. 2009.

Goldberg, Gary David. quoted by Saenz, *The Museum of Broadcast Communications*, http://www.museum.tv/archives/etv/F/htmlF/familyties/familyties.htm, accessed 15 Feb. 2009.

Hay, James. "Rethinking the Intersection of Cinema, Genre, and Youth," *Scope*, Oct. 2008, Issue 12.

Kiehl, Stephen. "What He Left Behind: From Tom Clancy to Alex P. Keaton, Ronald Reagan's Legacy Extends Beyond the Political and into the Cultural," *Sun Staff*, June 7, 2004.

Lewis, Jon. *The Road to Romance and Ruin: Teen Films and Youth Culture*. New York and London: Routledge, 1992.

Lombroso, Cesare. *Criminal Man (L'uomo delinquente)* (1876), trans. Mary Gibson and Nicole Hahn Rafter. Durham: Duke University Press, 2006.

Nadel, Alan. *Flatlining on the Field of Dreams: Cultural Narratives in the Films of President Reagan's America*. New Brunswick, NJ: Rutgers University Press, 1997.

Prince, Stephen, and Charles Harpole. *A New Pot of Gold: Hollywood Under the Electronic Rainbow, 1980–1989*. Berkeley: University of California Press, 2002.

Provosty, Laura, and Douglas Donovan. "White Trash in the Twentieth Century," http://xroads.virginia.edu/~CLASS/AM483_95/projects/trash/trash3.html, accessed 25 Feb. 2009.

Reagan, Ronald. *Address Before a Joint Session of Congress on the State of the Union*, February 4, 1986, available at *The American Presidency Project*, http://www.presidency.ucsb.edu/ws/index.php?pid=36646, accessed 20 Feb. 2009.

Saenz, Michael. *The Museum of Broadcast Communications*, http://www.museum.tv/archives/etv/F/htmlF/familyties/familyties.htm, accessed 15 Feb. 2009.

Thompson, Graham. *American Culture in the 1980s*. Edinburgh: Edinburgh University Press, 2007.

Thorburn, James. "Eighties Teen Movies — Nostalgia, Thy Name is Judd Nelson" (1998), http://www.80s.com/saveferris/essays/thorburn.txt, accessed 1 Mar. 2009.

Weiss, Richard. *The American Myth of Success: From Horatio Alger to Norman Vincent Peale*. New York: Basic Books, 1969.

Wood, Robin. *Hollywood from Vietnam to Reagan ... and Beyond*. New York: Columbia University Press, 2003.

Zemeckis, Robert. *The New York Times Essential Library: A Critic's Guide to the Best Children's Films Available on Video and DVD*, ed. Peter M. Nichols. New York: Times Books, 2003.

_____, and Bob Gale. *Back to the Future* Screenplay, Fourth Draft — revised 10/12/84 and 10/21/84, Scene 15. Available from "The Daily Script," http://www.dailyscript.com/scripts/bttf4th.pdf, accessed 17 Mar. 2009.

8. "Mom! You look so thin!": Constructions of Femininity Across the Space-Time Continuum

KATHERINE FARRIMOND

The *Back to the Future* trilogy (1985–1990) appears to provide a wide range of feminine representations, while strategically dividing these representations into the desirable and the undesirable, the authentic and the inauthentic, drawing on a complex relationship between a nostalgic 1950s setting and contemporary concerns about gender. This nostalgia for the 1950s underpins representations of motherhood, premarital femininity, and feminine agency throughout the films. While 1980s constructions of the family on film demonstrate an emerging preoccupation with the role of the father, in these films, representations of motherhood and the female role in the family still occupy a central position.[1] A nostalgic 1950s ideology informs the exploration of this role, in a way which prescribes ideals of appearance, behavior and sexuality, and expresses a desire for a nostalgic past in which the realization of these ideals is the only way of creating and maintaining a society in which an implicitly superior masculinity prevailed.

The time-travel motif in Robert Zemeckis' *Back to the Future* trilogy allows for a series of representations of adult femininity. By shifting the setting across time, rather than space, the films showcase a variety of femininities, as both Lorraine and, to a lesser extent, Jennifer are manifest in various incarnations in keeping with the particular strand of the space-time continuum which they occupy. So, for example, Lorraine is multiply represented as a dowdy middle-aged housewife, a fresh-faced teenager, an energetic and responsive suburban mother, a nurturing grandmother, and a surgically enhanced trophy wife, and Jennifer is multiply seen as both a teenager and as a frustrated housewife.[2] The narrative of the trilogy functions in a way which rejects or valorizes very specific varieties of femininity: of the three 1985 versions of Lorraine, both the frumpy original 1985-Lorraine and glitzy alternate 1985-Lorraine are rejected by adjustments made by Marty and Doc to the space-time continuum, while the carefree, breezy housewife is valorized by her centrality to the happy endings of both the first and third installments of the trilogy, as Marty returns home and reacts with a mixture of joy and relief to his altered family. At the end of the final film he declares "Thank God! You guys are all back to normal!" but they are not, in fact, the family of the trilogy's beginning, but the glossy new-and-improved version from the first film's conclusion, a version he has only encountered for a matter of minutes. This reaction not only confirms the superiority of the final 1985-Lorraine, but Marty's exclamation normalizes this particular model of flirtatious wife and attentive mother, suggesting a crystallization of this ideal of adult femininity. However, 2015-Jennifer's incarnation as frustrated housewife who, in 2015-Marty's words, is prone to "moods" and is "hard to keep track of," is not adjusted in the same way. The trilogy ends with the suggestion that this future has been erased, the implication being that her future self is now likely to undergo a similar positive transformation of Lorraine into an ideal wife and mother.

This time-travel device allows the minutiae of unacceptable feminine behavior and appearance to be exhibited, rejected, and replaced by versions in which aberrations of feminine behavior and appearance have been carefully removed. Marty's various reactions upon encountering another version of his mother provide a key example of the way Lorraine's appearance is judged and appraised across the series. These remarks vary from "you're so thin" on encountering both 1955-Lorraine and the final 1985-Lorraine, to "you're so big," addressed to the surgically enhanced alternate 1985-Lorraine. Thinness here functions as a key indicator of approval, and the contrast with the bloated and lethargic original 1985-Lorraine implies that thinness is not only a symptom of the changes to this final 1985-Lorraine's life, but also a central reason for that approval. Moreover, the alternate 1985-Lorraine may be thin, but she is also "big" having submitted to breast implants at Biff's insistence, and his generalized reference to her "cosmetic surgery" puts the authenticity of her thinness into question. Here, she is presented as inauthentic not only because of her highly visible breast implants, but also because of her bleached hair, ostentatious jewelry and glittery dress, so that the rejection of this image suggests that not only is thinness essential to idealized womanhood, but that this thinness must be authentic, and "natural."

In a series which presents so many different versions of Lorraine, the question of authenticity is essential. The valorization of the revised 1985-Lorraine at the end of the first and third films is due in part to the ascription of authenticity. Marty's declaration that this revised family are "back to normal" authenticates the final 1985-Lorraine, while it de-authenticates the original 1985-Lorraine, who, despite her position as the narrative's earliest version of Marty's mother, is posited as a deviation from the normal and "real" ideal mother. The in-authenticity of both the alternate 1985-Lorraine and the original version posits these characters as temporary malfunctions in the smooth running of history, malfunctions which are eventually amended in order to create the authentic Lorraine of the series' conclusion. The final, authentic, 1985-Lorraine can be seen as the direct continuation of her earlier self, 1955-Lorraine, as final 1985-Lorraine's "natural" thinness and flirtatiousness is aligned with that of the teenage version. While she has visibly aged, this transformation is a comparably minor one, unlike the extreme deviations from the ideally authentic 1955-Lorraine witnessed in the inauthentic original and alternate 1985-Lorraines. The "naturalness" of the progression from teenager to idealized wife valorizes an image of motherhood rooted in a nostalgic 1950s femininity, and posits this image as authentic.

All the films' presentation and subsequent rejection of undesirable femininity is directed specifically toward mothers.[3] By contrast, premarital femininity is presented as almost entirely homogeneous. Lorraine, Jennifer and Clara exhibit very similar characteristics in their premarital stages. While they are all very flirtatious, this attribute is constructed in such a way as to align them with nostalgic 1950s ideals of premarital femininity. As Stephanie Coontz notes, the etiquette of 1950s dating permitted a certain amount of premarital sexual activity:

> "Petting" was sanctioned so long as one didn't go "too far" (although this was an elastic and ambiguous prohibition); a woman could be touched on various parts of her body (how low depended on how serious the relationship was) but "nice girls" refused to fondle the comparable male parts in return; mutual stimulation to orgasm was compatible with maintaining a "good" reputation so long as penetration did not occur.[4]

While these characters are represented as outgoing and flirtatious, these attributes are safely confined within the parameters of the "nice girl," a position explicitly endorsed by the valorized final 1985-Lorraine's approval of Jennifer, and enacted by her own premarital 1955 self. This teenage version of Lorraine, despite her original 1985 counterpart's protestations, is highly flirtatious, takes the lead in pursuing boys, and apparently has some level of sexual experience, suggested by the phrase: "Marty, I'm almost eighteen years old, it's not like I've never parked before." However, this forwardness is countered and regulated by her rejection of Biff's lascivious advances, in scenes in both the first and second films. As he variously grabs at her and makes obscene comments, in the first film she shouts "shut your filthy mouth, I'm not that kind of girl" and in the second, "get your cooties off of me!" These lines firmly locate 1955-Lorraine in the position of "nice" clean girl, who balks at the possibility of being sullied by crude and uncouth sexual advances, suggesting that, although she has "parked" before, her behavior conforms to Coontz's description of acceptable behavior to ensure a "good" reputation. Similarly, despite her forwardness, she declares a conservative belief that "a man should be strong so he can protect the woman he loves." Despite her flirtatiousness, Lorraine's behavior is presented as in line with nostalgic 1950s morality and valorized as such.

Like 1955-Lorraine, Jennifer is also presented as forward and flirtatious; she seems to take as much, if not more, of the initiative in her relationship with Marty as he does, indicated by the original 1985-Lorraine's complaint that "any girl who calls up a boy is just asking for trouble." As this opinion is later revealed to be wildly hypocritical considering the behavior of 1955-Lorraine, and is completely rejected when the authenticated final 1985-Lorraine states that "I sure like her, Marty, she is such a sweet girl," Jennifer's "forwardness" appears to be vindicated. While she intends to stay the night at the lake with Marty, implying premarital sex, this event never occurs, and despite her compliance in kissing Marty in public, she gently removes Marty's hand when it strays too far inside her jacket. As the final 1985-Lorraine puts it, she is a "sweet girl," demure and feminine with just enough agency to retain that sweetness within the boundaries of a nostalgic 1950s morality. Clara, the only non-teenage representation of premarital femininity, is equally forward, pursuing Doc to his workshop in a scene which echoes the 1955-Lorraine's pursuit of Marty, and chasing after him upon realizing she is still in love with him. However, these displays of romantic agency occur within the confines of a courtship which conforms to the films' nostalgic 1950s ideology. Their relationship is clearly framed within a romantic context; "love at first sight" is frequently referred to and their relationship is aligned with that the innocent romance of Marty and Jennifer. Their romantic scene under the stars does not suggest that premarital sex will occur, as the outdoor location, stars, and soft music mark the scene as romantic rather than sexual. This idea is compounded by Doc's explanation for his absence from his own bed: "just taking in the morning air. It's really lovely here in the morning." There is no suggestion that this explanation is not genuine, and his dreamy-eyed meandering clearly places their evening in the realm of the romantic rather than the sexual. Much like Lorraine, Clara is presented as "not that sort of girl" as a result of her altercation with Biff's ancestor, Mad Dog Tannen. As he forces her to dance with him, and makes the lewd suggestion that "I bet there's something you can do that's worth $80," she kicks him hard in the shin in a move that affirms her desire to protect her reputation, and by implication, her virginity.

Outside the representation of their sexuality, all three characters demonstrate a form of agency that nevertheless ultimately needs male support. Jennifer is almost exclusively presented in the public sphere, at school or in various outdoor locations, implying a certain amount of mobility and activity. She also represents a particularly benign form of rebellion: she is occasionally late for school, and her boyfriend is a guitarist with rock star aspirations who she adoringly watches play. However, her role as Marty's cheering squad places her firmly in the position of inactive supportive girlfriend; she displays ultimate passivity by being either sedated, asleep or frozen in time for substantial portions of all three films. This premarital Jennifer is predominantly submissive, and her behavior is safely contained within patriarchal parameters. Clara is arguably the most active and formidable character of the three, as she kicks Mad Dog Tannen in the shins, remonstrates with Doc when she thinks he has lied to her, and leaps from a horse onto a moving train. However, these displays of independence are, like Jennifer's, strictly contained; she still needs to be rescued from both Tannen and the train, and is shown crying into her pillows having fought with Doc. Robin Wood argues of 1970s and 1980s Hollywood cinema:

> Women are allowed minor feats of heroism and aggression (in deference to the theory that what they want is to be able to behave like men): thus Karen Allen can punch Harrison Ford in the face near the beginning of *Raiders* [*of the Lost Ark*], and Princess Leia has intermittent outbursts of activity, usually in the earlier parts of the movies. Subsequently, the Woman's main function is to be rescued by the men, involving her reduction to helplessness and dependency.[5]

This pattern is arguably one which is sustained throughout the *Back to the Future* trilogy. After the police in the future mistake the 1985 Jennifer for 2015-Jennifer and take her home, she becomes trapped in her future house and has to be rescued by Doc. Clara, despite having just leapt from a galloping horse onto a moving train and greeted a huge explosion from the train's furnace with no greater hysteria than a matter-of-fact "golly," suddenly becomes "scared" about inching along the side of the train, and requires the assistance of Doc, to the accompaniment of much high-pitched screaming. Similarly, despite her forthright resistance to his advances, Lorraine twice needs to be rescued from the clutches of Biff, once by Marty, and then, most importantly, by George in the first film's turning point.

The consequences of breaching these idealized parameters for feminine behavior are outlined in the 1955-Lorraine who drinks, smokes, and is most active in her pursuit of male attention. These various characteristics are countered by more conventionally feminine traits; as she needs repeatedly rescuing from a Tannen, and she articulates her belief in the importance of strong men, however, another important factor in the valorization of her passivity over her less feminine traits is the foreknowledge of what will happen as a result of her more active characteristics. Summoning the memory of 1985-Lorraine's incarnation from the beginning of the first film, the characterization of 1955-Lorraine functions as a fore-grounded series of flow diagrams, in which the early indulgence in alcohol that Marty informs her she may regret "later in life" leads to the puffy-faced Lorraine who drinks multiple glasses of neat Vodka for dinner. Similarly her aggressive sexual advances and attraction to young men such as George and Marty because of their passive positions as invalids are intrinsically connected with her subsequent unhappy marriage to a weak and unresponsive husband. These connections betray the series' preoccupation with the superiority of the perceived morality of a nostalgic 1950s. As Fredric Jameson argues of 1980s Hollywood's re-presentation of the 1950s, "[Nostalgia films] restructure the whole issue of pastiche and project it onto a collective and social level, where the desperate attempt to appropriate a missing past is now refracted through the iron law of fashion change and the emergent ideology of the 'generation.'"[6] The series' representation of 1955 appropriates a past which is used to express a concern at contemporary loss of certainty, and specifically, of a fixity of gender by valorizing the "traditional" values of the 1950s. These films present a version of Janice Doane and Devon Hodges' argument that "in the imaginative past of nostalgic writers, men were men, women were women, and reality was real."[7] When Marty expresses his disapproval for 1955-Lorraine's vilified failure to conform to these strictures of gender, her response, "Marty, you're beginning to sound just like my mother," aligns Marty's condemnation of 1955-Lorraine's activities with a particular conception of 1950s morality which the knowledge of her future as original 1985-Lorraine confirms is well-founded, highlighting the dangers of femininity which deviates too far from these moral patterns, and privileging an idealized image of the 1950s.

Lorraine's sexual pursuit of Marty further highlights the dangers of deviating from the films' particular idealized model of young femininity. Andrew Gordon argues that "*Back to the Future* distances us from the incest by making the mother's brazenness and the son's terror laughable."[8] However, the young Lorraine's "brazenness" arguably adds to the dangerous symbols of deviant femininity, an effect that can be seen particularly in the scene following Marty's heroics on a makeshift skateboard, in which bystanders ask "where does he come from?" "yeah, where does he live?" to which Lorraine responds "I don't know, but I'm going to find out." The intensity with which she says this is accompanied by amorous panting and a serious expression on her face which is unsettling and tinged with menace. While the perturbing nature of this shot is due in part to Lorraine's unwitting pursuit of her own son, the sense of danger is arguably enhanced by rather than caused by the specter of the incest taboo. There is a certain single-mindedness about her expression which, even without the incest element, suggests a frightening, and crucially *unfeminine* sense of purpose and unstoppable resolve. The film implies that what is happening to Marty is a re-enactment of George and Lorraine's courtship, as Marty inadvertently and completely took his father's place in the story. This sense is articulated when Marty explains his parents' courtship to Doc: "I guess she felt sorry for him because her Dad hit him with the car... [pause and realization] He hit *me* with the car." This simple replacement of George with Marty in the historical narrative suggests that Lorraine's courtship of George in the original narrative would have been conducted in exactly the same way, and therefore functioned as a contributing factor in the family's future slovenliness. The threat of incest, therefore, works as a tool to strengthen the sense that Lorraine's behavior is dangerous and unacceptable, rather than as the cause of that danger.

Ideal premarital femininity, then, is presented in the trilogy as a homogenized but delicately balanced position, neither too agentive, nor too passive, which ultimately requires a strong masculine presence to dampen any threat of transgression which may lurk within the premarital female body. In presenting premarital femininity as a fixed position, and by rooting this position in a nostalgic image of 1950s morality, the films arguably privilege the stability of gendered identity, and implicitly express concern for the integrity of contemporary femininity. In these films, idealized premarital femininity is presented as a dormant state, one which, no matter what the time period, conforms to the moral codes of a nostalgic 1950s. However, this dormancy is presented as temporary, and imbued with a sense that, unless a suitable masculine influence is exerted in time, destructive behavior may spill over. Premarital femininity is, to an extent, represented as fixed and secure, but, the films suggest, a point will eventually be reached at which this fixity begins to slip, and can no longer be considered "safe"; 1955-Lorraine's agency operates at the boundary of acceptable behavior prescribed by the films' nostalgic 1950s doctrine, and, unless contained, will ultimately become destructive, both to herself, as evinced by the original 1985-Lorraine, and to her family, as substantiated by the social and economic "failure" of Marty's original 1985 family, and by the danger her agency poses directly to Marty in the form of the incestuous threat.

Significantly, both of the rejected images of Lorraine occur in the 1980s, and can only be corrected in an idealized 1950s. As Jameson has discussed, "one tends to feel that, for Americans at least, the 1950s remain the privileged lost object of desire," and in the *Back to the Future* series, the focus of that desire is that of a stable and controlled femininity, from the position of a 1980s in which that stability is perceived to be lost.[9] Although her behavior carries with it the threat of transgression, the 1955-Lorraine is presented as a fixed quantity, whereas her 1980s incarnation is eminently changeable. Gordon argues of the first film: "Marty as omnipotent time traveler goes from the degraded present of 1985 — with its graffiti, homeless drunks sleeping on benches in littered parks, terrorists stalking the streets — to the prelapsarian 1955: spotless, pristine, virginal. But it is a virginity panting to be deflowered."[10] Both 1955-Lorraine and the 1950s are presented in a similar ways in the trilogy: they are both idealized and yet both on the brink of the abyss. Gordon's image of the impatient virgin can be seen in the film as a status which requires concern, rather than applause. November 12, 1955, is a point which Doc describes in the second film as "the temporal junction point of the entire space-time continuum," and the films locate this junction point as one at which nostalgic 1950s values begin to shift towards an unstable contemporary reality. Just as Lorraine's rebellious early drinking will lead to alcoholism later in life, the perceived morality of the 1950s is shifting towards decline. As Lorraine's father pushes the television into the family dining room, declaring "now we can watch Jackie Gleason while we eat!" the echoes of the 1985 in which Marty's father is more fixated on the television than his wife during the family dinner, position the television as a Trojan Horse which brings about a downfall of "family values." 1955 is the site of potential gender disruption; in the original narrative, it contains the events which lead to George and Lorraine's courtship, and the cementing of the relationship dynamic in which conventionally gendered roles are not observed, leading to familial dysfunction.

However, if the 1950s are seen as a point of failure for both morality in general, and femininity specifically, it is also the space for the correction of this failure. In *Back to the Future*, 1955 is presented as a junction point at which gender stability has not quite begun to come undone, as, in Gordon's words "the appropriate crossroads in the past in which to correct things," to prevent the comforting fixity of gender from eroding.[11] The form this cementation takes is literally a realigning of gender along patriarchal lines, thus preserving the values of a nostalgic 1950s: under the influence of a "strong" man, the more transgressive elements of Lorraine's personality are eliminated in a retreat to what Stephanie Coontz describes as "the seeming placidity and prosperity of the 1950s, associated in many people's minds with the relative stability of marriage, gender roles, and family life."[12] While the 1950s are seen in the film as a point of moral collapse, the time travel motif of these films ensure the ability to reinstate traditional gender roles and the attendant morality means that this collapse is potential, rather than determined.

However, despite this fluidity, the three versions of premarital femininity all imply that marriage is inevitable. Marty and Doc's adventures across the space-time continuum entail a series of linear narratives which may be altered or shifted, but never entirely changed, as adult femininity is irrevocably attached to marriage and children. As Doane and Hodges argue, "nostalgic writers locate [the woman's] place in a past in which women 'naturally' function in the home to provide a haven of stability that is linguistic as well as psychic: *nostos*, the return home."[13] The dormant state of premarital womanhood is always replaced by a nostalgic image of marital life and the nuclear family, as Lorraine, Jennifer, and Clara are all represented as moving inevitably towards marriage in the future. For Lorraine this inevitability is concrete, as she will, and must marry George McFly. The married Lorraine at the beginning of the trilogy is the point to which all activity in 1955 looks forward. While a large portion of the first film features her as a teenager, this state is clearly marked as a transient one: for the future to be a happy one, and for the film to have a happy ending, Marty, as protagonist, must return to the world where Lorraine is a wife and mother, creating the implication that Lorraine as mother is both inevitable and appropriate. This imperative toward marriage is still more pronounced in the representation of Jennifer. Unlike Lorraine, Jennifer does not have to marry anyone to restore order, as her adulthood is in the unseen future and so no progeny will be destroyed if she deviates from this path. However, the news from Doc, who tells Marty and Jennifer that in the future "something's got to be done about your kids" sets her path firmly on the path towards an inevitable marriage to Marty, followed by children. On realizing that they are in the future, Jennifer's thoughts automatically turn to what her future wedding, wedding dress, house and children will look like, highlighting a complicity in this imperative, and further strengthening the sense of inevitability about her future status as wife. The representation of Jennifer's family is one which strongly echoes that of Lorraine's at the beginning of the film: a dysfunctional nuclear family, but one which requires some tweaking, rather than complete eradication. This refusal to completely explode the notion of the idealized nuclear family cements the idea that, in the future, Marty and Jennifer's lives will be an improved version of this currently dysfunctional model, and will follow the precedent set by the first film — that of the adjustment rather than drastic alternation of the family. Similarly, the casting of Michael J. Fox as both of Jennifer's children in the second film, and his ancestor, Seamus McFly, in the third, adds to this sense of repetition: history will continue to repeat itself and McFlys will inevitably marry and have children within carefully defined nuclear families, and that the position of wife and mother is central to femininity.

The inevitability of Clara's marriage is presented somewhat differently, as images of her character follow a fairly linear pattern, yet the sense of inevitability is clearly there. The emergence of Emmett with Clara and their two children is foreshadowed by the introduction of Clara in the third film. Doc's tombstone declares that it was "erected in eternal memory by his beloved Clara" despite the 1885-Doc having no idea who she is five days before his death. While the events of the third film mean that history is changed, Doc is saved and the tombstone destroyed, Clara continues on the path toward marriage to Doc, implying that, no matter what else is altered, the marital imperative is both unavoidable and felicitous. This is further emphasized by Clara's first appearance on screen. Having been rescued by Doc from plummeting into a ravine on her runaway wagon, Clara's hat has fallen over her eyes, and she lifts it up and sees him. They appear to fall in love at first sight — both their first sight of each other *and* the audience's first sight of Clara. This positions her from the very beginning as the object of desire for Doc, with whom a romantic conclusion will guarantee a happy ending in the tradition of what Steven Cohan has described as "the heterosexual imperative of romantic comedy," a tradition which offers comforting heteronormative romantic conclusions, thus affirming the fixity of gendered identity.[14] Although the course of history can be adjusted, marriage and motherhood appear to be unshakably the default setting for adult femininity.

Within these representations of inevitable marriage and motherhood, the film is constructed in order that differing versions of motherhood must be amended in order to create the idealized family. The repercussions of deviant models of motherhood are fore-grounded, implying that only the final 1985-Lorraine can produce successful offspring. The original 1985-Lorraine produces Dave, clearly demarcated as an underachiever by his job in a fast food restaurant. Her daughter Linda seems likely to meet the same fate as Lorraine by following her mother's example; settling for a weak and passive man whose inabilities as a husband will lead her to frustrated, bloated alcoholism. While Marty, as the film's protagonist appears better adjusted, he is still flawed and riddled with self-doubt. Similarly, alternate 1985-Lorraine has also produced inadequate children: Marty has apparently been expelled from numerous boarding schools, Linda is a spendthrift with enormous debts, and Dave has been involved in criminal activity and is on probation. 2015-Jennifer's children too are under scrutiny, as it is revealed that she has borne a son who cannot stand up for himself. There is a marked contrast between these representations and final 1985-Lorraine and Clara's idealized families. In Lorraine's case, Dave "always wear[s] a suit to the office," implying greater responsibility, social prowess, and a career more befitting a man of his age. Linda works in a boutique and has a wealth of male admirers. While Clara's family is only presented briefly, and the children are still very young, they are clearly represented as a close and functional group, conforming to patriarchal codes, as Clara stands slightly behind Doc and their children, gazing adoringly at them, having taken her "correct" place within a successful family unit.

This reworked version of the McFlys and the image of Clara's family valorize and prescribe a particular variety of motherhood, one which enjoys a full and loving relationship with the children, as well as being entirely sexually available to the husband. Stephanie Coontz argues that this is a specifically 1950s image of motherhood, derived from a combination of incompatible nineteenth century and 1920s ideals: "the hybrid idea that a woman can be fully absorbed with her youngsters while simultaneously maintaining passionate sexual excitement with her husband was a 1950s invention that drove thousands of women to therapists, tranquilizers, or alcohol when they actually tried to live up to it."[15] Once again, the series wears its celebration of a nostalgic 1950s on its sleeve, as an idealized model of femininity, which must maintain the correct balance between mother and wife, and is celebrated over a series of inadequate models whose failure to achieve this balance has severe consequences for the future. Motherhood operates as the only acceptable feminine identity, and during the first film, the existence of Lorraine's children operates as a crucial indicator of failure or success. In order to prevent himself and his siblings from being erased from history, Marty must guide Lorraine into a relationship with his father, in a scenario which means that the children's reappearance on the photograph of Marty and his brother and sister acts as proof of success, where their absence would denote failure. In this narrative, motherhood is posited as the indicator of a successful mission, a successful narrative conclusion, and, by implication, a successful femininity.

The various changes and corrections made to femininity in the film all highlight the importance of "a good man" as an influential force. Susan Jeffords has argued that the various negative changes to the whole McFly family in the alternate 1985 happen as a result of George McFly's death, that their dysfunction is "the result of a family being cut off from its rightful father."[16] It is arguably this proximity or distance of the female character to a "correct" model of masculinity which affects the female characters in particular throughout the entire trilogy. Lorraine's character is overbearing and unhappy when paired with an emasculated man, is powerless and trapped when she is married to the bullying Biff, and only becomes an ideal mother when paired with the George who has learned to stand up for himself and be a "real man." Nothing about Lorraine's actions has changed in these various scenarios; it is only the influence of a revised masculinity which in turn corrects her femininity. In the first film, after George has punched Biff in the face, providing the turning point of the film, one observer asks "who is that guy?" The response provokes the reaction "*that's* George McFly?" In this scene, a distinct shift in identity occurs in *George*, marked by the onlooker's incredulity, during which he becomes not only Lorraine's rescuer, but embodies the correct model of active manliness to curtail Lorraine's errant behavior, his new found masculinity ensuring that her potentially "destructive" characteristics are kept in check. Similarly, future Jennifer's dissatisfaction and mood swings are tied directly to Marty's inadequacies — Lorraine as grandmother notes that "I think the only reason [she] married him was because she felt sorry for him," directly echoing the pattern of the original, and "incorrect" relationship dynamic between Lorraine and George which resulted in their dysfunctional married life and Lorraine's frustrated alcoholism.

The varying models of femininity that occur because of the alternation of history alter not only as a result of exclusively male activity, but also through attempts to directly change the lives of exclusively male characters. As Jeffords argues:

> What makes these films more than a humorous story about an individual's family history is that the plots tie Marty's life to the character of the entire community in which he live; on his successes and failures depend the fate of all who live in Hill Valley. Underscoring the themes of continuity, Marty's actions take place in relation to his father/great-grandfather/son. Underscoring the theme of revolution, the *Back to the Future* films insist that, indeed, one man *can* change the world.[17]

Not only can one man change the world, the world Marty, Doc, and Biff variously seek to change is an exclusively male one; that of the male lineage Jeffords outlines, with changes to femininity occurring as a by-product of this activity. In the first film, the spectacular changes in Lorraine occur in the process of trying to save Marty's life by making George into a more ideal model of masculinity. Sarah Harwood argues that in 1980s Hollywood film, mothers "react to, rather than initiate narrative development, and their status is defined and legitimized within the text by their relationship to the family and their function as mothers."[18] In the *Back to the Future* series, it is not only mothers who are represented in this way, but female characters in general, and the history-altering motif of the films demonstrates a literal, and unconscious reaction to the forces that affect their lives, the process of which they are not permitted a role. Similarly, the purposeful activity of *Back to the Future II* is equally focused on male characters, with alterations to femininity occurring apparently by accident: the prevention of Marty's son's arrest inadvertently leads to Lorraine's incarnation as plastic glamour-wife as their actions allow Biff to steal the DeLorean and change his past, in stopping Biff from becoming a business tycoon and Doc from being committed, the situation is reversed, and, almost by accident, restores Lorraine to the ideal model of femininity she had been previously. In *Back to the Future III*, Marty's attempts to prevent Doc from being assassinated lead, accidentally, to Clara's rescue from the runaway wagon that was historically doomed to plummet into the ravine, and her subsequent transformation to wife and mother. As a result of this pattern, femininity in the series emerges as an afterthought, and as ultimately and completely passive, as the changes to their characters are merely the peripheral effect of the more important work of correcting masculinity, work that they remain blissfully unaware is occurring. Lorraine, Jennifer and Clara are not responsible for their fates at any point in the series, as events unfold around them they are presented as "to be rescued," or accidentally adapted by alternations to the fabric of time without their knowledge, further emphasizing the idealized passivity propounded throughout the trilogy.

This passivity, and the absence of direct intervention into female histories means that the female characters having a purely symbolic purpose, that their characterization at any given point in the films' various timelines operates predominantly as a highly visible symbol of functional or dysfunctional masculinity. As the alterations to the young George's character are cited in the films as the reason for the transformation of the 1980s Lorraine from dowdy to dynamic housewife, her revision can be seen exclusively as an indication of the success of Marty's efforts in making a man of George, as her idealized adult femininity functions as an indicator of the positive effects that *his* altered masculinity have on a broader scale. Similarly, the shift from this approved version of Lorraine to the glitzy battered woman of the alternate 1985 is shown to occur as a result of the removal of the approved masculinity of George, and the insertion of the bullying would-be rapist Biff. Again, the change occurs without any alteration of character or behavior on her part, and so her revision serves to pass judgment on the varieties of masculinity in question: to stress the importance of the George model, and to condemn the Biff model. The character of Jennifer too serves as an indicator of the proficiency of masculinity in the films. While it is implied that she is frustrated and moody, her future self has very little time on screen, suggesting that it is not her character that is of importance to a scene preoccupied with the future Marty, and Marty Jr. Instead, she functions in the same way as their "rough neighborhood" and broken video-blind, as an indicator that future Marty, as head of the family, is substandard. The reasons for both his and his son's failures are his insecurity and loss of self-control when insulted, which, as the future Lorraine notes, causes "a chain reaction which sent Marty's life straight down the tubes." This creates a similar effect to that of the versions of Lorraine discussed above, that their existence as independent agents, their presence on screen serves primarily to highlight the profound influence of masculinity, and to act as a tool for measuring the desirability of that variety of masculinity and its influence.

In these films, the privilege of altering history is granted exclusively to men. Sean Redmond argues that time travel narratives in science fiction allow for the comforting idea that "if the modern world is one where the individual feels alienated and powerless in the face of bureaucratic structures and corporate monopolies, then time travel suggests that Everyman and Everybody is important to shaping history, to making a real and quantifiable difference to the way the world works out."[19] However, in the *Back to the Future* series, this opportunity is strictly granted to Everyman rather than Everybody. It is only as a result of changes made to male characters which shape history, and the highly conspicuous changes to femininity occur only as collateral, leading to a structure in which masculinity takes precedent and femininity is simply caught up in the tide. Female characters are merely incidental occupants of a space-time continuum, controlled by and preoccupied with masculinity, emphasized by the way in which adjustments to history are made. The DeLorean time machine is presented as a masculine space, a combination of cutting edge style and advanced technology, designed and driven only by male characters, Doc, Marty, and Biff, suggesting that the purposeful alteration of the historical narrative is an exclusively male activity. The only female character to enter this space is Jennifer, who, sitting on Marty's knee fits awkwardly into the space, and encroaching on Marty's space in a way that appears uncomfortable rather than romantic, suggesting that she is an unwelcome and unnecessary presence. As she realizes that they have moved forward in time, she becomes excitable, wondering out loud about her future, as Doc and Marty look on, dismayed and somewhat appalled. Rather than explaining the possible consequences of knowing too much about the future, as he did for Marty, Doc sedates her, claiming that "she was asking too many questions," and that "this way, when she wakes up, she'll think it was all a dream," that he only brought her along because "she saw the time machine and I couldn't just leave her there with that information. Don't worry; she's not essential to my plan." In this scene, Jennifer's presence in the time machine is an annoyance: it is vital that her knowledge is suppressed, and this necessitates her obstructive physical presence in the DeLorean. She is superfluous to Doc's plan, unlike Marty, who undertakes the scheme, and Doc, who is its engineer. Having identified her presence in the time machine as disruptive, Doc then deposits her unconscious body in a litter-strewn alleyway so that he and Marty can go about the important business of changing history.[20] This rejection from the DeLorean and her earlier unwanted presence serves to highlight a consistent ideology in the series: that time travel, and the potential it offers for altering history, is not for girls. Similarly, the other female presence in a time machine is also one of inferior status. Doc's new time machine, unveiled at the end of the third film, is housed in a steam train. Clara is permitted to enter it, but, as the train pulls in, he occupies the position of driver, and operates the controls to open the door, at which point, Clara, who is shown seated behind him, stands up. Here, just as Jennifer was firmly designated as passenger in the DeLorean, Clara too is seen as accompanying, rather than sharing responsibility with Doc. Where she is passenger, Doc is clearly presented as the sole controller of the time machine. As discussed above, Clara occupies a subordinate position to Doc and their sons within the space, as she stands behind them, looking at them adoringly. As Doc speaks to Marty, she is silent, speaking only briefly only in response to Doc's prompt. The nature of the space also dictates her role on board the train. As it is much larger than the DeLorean, it also functions as a domestic, and therefore more feminized space, suitable for children and childcare, and thus, Clara's duty is not to control it, but to travel in it in as dutiful wife and mother. The names of their two sons, Jules and Verne, endow them with a fantastical and scientific aura which implies that they will be trained by Doc, and inherit his legacy. While Doc is able adjust historical events, and, it is suggested, his sons will eventually follow in his footsteps, Clara's is not, suggesting again that Everyman rather than Everybody is responsible for shaping history.

The *Back to the Future* trilogy is predominantly concerned with establishing and maintaining an idealized (patriarchal) society rooted in a nostalgic image of 1950s America, and suggests that the behavior, appearance, and sexuality of women both as potential wives, and as mothers, is central to the stability of this society. The nostalgic 1950s of the series functions as a site of both an absent past to mourn, and a symbol of the changes driving American society toward growing uncertainty surrounding accepted realities. In these films, femininity is influenced and adapted exclusively by masculinity, and therefore can be seen to function most notably as an indicator of the success or failure of masculinity to restore the mythology of a nostalgic past. Despite its multifarious representations of femininity, *Back to the Future*'s premise demonstrates that, although time travel enables Everyman to change history, in Hill Valley, Everywoman is subject entirely to the whims of patriarchal nostalgia.

Notes

1. For more on fatherhood in 1980s film, see Sarah Harwood, *Family Fictions: Representations of the Family in 1980s Hollywood Cinema* (Basingstoke: Macmillan, 1997) 69.

2. Because the film features many different versions of the same characters, I have created a set of terms to create greater clarity in identifying each of these versions: "1955-Lorraine" refers to Lorraine as a teenager from the first and second films, "Original 1985-Lorraine" refers to the dowdy version of Lorraine from the beginning of the first film, "Alternate 1985-Lorraine" refers to the surgically enhanced Lorraine who lives in Biff's penthouse in the second film, "Final 1985-Lorraine" refers to the adjusted version from the end of the first and third films, and "2015-Lorraine" refers to Lorraine as a grandmother in the second film. "Marty" refers to the teenage protagonist of all three films, "2015-Marty" refers to the middle-aged Marty

of the second film, and "Marty Jr." refers to his son. "Jennifer" refers to the teenage Jennifer of all three films, and "2015-Jennifer" refers to the middle-aged Jennifer of the second film. "Doc" refers to the Doc of all three films who introduces Marty to the DeLorean and repeatedly travels through time, and "1955-Doc" refers to the younger Doc of all three films who remains statically in 1955.

3. While the nature of fatherhood does come into question, particularly in the multiple representations of George, and in the position of Doc as symbolic father to Marty, Marty as future father, and the substitution of Biff as potential father, an interrogation of these representations is unfortunately beyond the remit of this article.

4. Stephanie Coontz, *The Way We Never Were: American Families and the Nostalgia Trap* (New York: Basic Books, 1992) 40.

5. Robin Wood, *Hollywood From Vietnam to Reagan ... and Beyond,* rev. ed. (New York: Colombia University Press, 2003) 154.

6. Fredric Jameson, "Postmodernism, or The Cultural Logic of Late Capitalism" in *Postmodernism: A Reader,* ed. Thomas Docherty (Harlow, Essex: Harvester Wheatsheaf, 1993) 75.

7. Janice Doane and Devon Hodges, *Nostalgia and Sexual Difference: The Resistance to Contemporary Feminism* (New York and London: Methuen, 1987) 3.

8. Andrew Gordon, "Back to the Future: Œdipus as Time Traveler" in *Liquid Metal: The Science Fiction Film Reader,* ed. Sean Redmond (London and New York: Wallflower, 2004) 118.

9. Fredric Jameson, "Postmodernism, or The Cultural Logic of Late Capitalism" in *Postmodernism: A Reader* ed. Thomas Docherty (Harlow, Essex: Harvester Wheatsheaf, 1993) 75.

10. Andrew Gordon, "Back to the Future: Œdipus as Time Traveler" in *Liquid Metal: The*

Science Fiction Film Reader, ed. Sean Redmond (London and New York: Wallflower, 2004) 119.

11. Andrew Gordon, "Back to the Future: Œdipus as Time Traveler" in *Liquid Metal: The Science Fiction Film Reader,* ed. Sean Redmond (London and New York: Wallflower, 2004) 116.

12. Stephanie Coontz, *The Way We Never Were: American Families and the Nostalgia Trap* (New York: Basic Books, 1992) 23–4

13. Janice Doane and Devon Hodges, *Nostalgia and Sexual Difference: The Resistance to Contemporary Feminism* (New York and London: Methuen, 1987) 14.

14. Steven Cohan, "'I Think I Could Fall in Love with Him': *Victor/Victoria* and the 'Drag' of Romantic Comedy" in *Terms of Endearment: Hollywood Romantic Comedy of the 1980s and 1990s,* ed. Peter William Evans and Celestino Deleyto (Edinburgh: Edinburgh University Press, 1998) 39.

15. Stephanie Coontz, *The Way We Never Were: American Families and the Nostalgia Trap* (New York: Basic Books, 1992) 9.

16. Susan Jeffords, *Hard Bodies: Hollywood Masculinity in the Reagan Era* (New Brunswick, NJ: Rutgers University Press, 1994) 72.

17. Susan Jeffords, *Hard Bodies: Hollywood Masculinity in the Reagan Era* (New Brunswick, NJ: Rutgers University Press, 1994) 67.

18. Sarah Harwood, *Family Fictions: Representations of the Family in 1980s Hollywood Cinema* (Basingstoke: Macmillan, 1997) 69.

19. Sean Redmond, "The Origin of the Species: Time Travel and the Primal Scene" in *Liquid Metal: The Science Fiction Film Reader,* ed. Sean Redmond (London and New York: Wallflower, 2004) 114.

20. That the actress playing Jennifer (Claudia Wells in BTTF and Elizabeth Shue in BTTF 2 & 3) is changed between films serves as further testimony to the marginalization of Jennifer within the main time travel plot.

Filmography

Back to the Future. Dir. Robert Zemeckis. Universal Studios. 1985

Back to the Future II. Dir. Robert Zemeckis. Universal Studios. 1989

Back to the Future III. Dir. Robert Zemeckis. Universal Studios. 1990

Bibliography

Cohan, Steven. "'I Think I Could Fall in Love with Him': *Victor/Victoria* and the 'Drag' of Romantic Comedy" in *Terms of Endearment: Hollywood Romantic Comedy of the 1980s and 1990s,* ed. Peter William Evans and Celestino Deleyto. Edinburgh: Edinburgh University Press, 1998.

Coontz, Stephanie. *The Way We Never Were: American Families and the Nostalgia Trap.* New York: Basic Books, 1992.

Doane, Janice, and Devon Hodges. *Nostalgia and Sexual Difference: The Resistance to Contemporary Feminism.* New York and London: Methuen, 1987.

Gordon, Andrew. "Back to the Future: Œdipus as Time Traveler" in *Liquid Metal: The Science Fiction Film Reader* ed. Sean Redmond. London and New York: Wallflower, 2004.

Harwood, Sarah. *Family Fictions: Representations of the Family in 1980s Hollywood Cinema.* Basingstoke: Macmillan, 1997.

Jameson, Fredric. "Postmodernism, or The Cultural Logic of Late Capitalism" in *Postmodernism: A Reader,* ed. Thomas Docherty. Harlow, Essex: Harvester Wheatsheaf, 1993.

Jeffords, Susan. *Hard Bodies: Hollywood Masculinity in the Reagan Era.* New Brunswick, NJ: Rutgers University Press, 1994.

Redmond, Sean. "The Origin of the Species: Time Travel and the Primal Scene" in *Liquid Metal: The Science Fiction Film Reader,* ed. Sean Redmond. London and New York: Wallflower, 2004.

Wood, Robin, *Hollywood From Vietnam to Reagan ... and Beyond,* rev. ed. New York: Colombia University Press, 2003.

9. Ronald Reagan and the Rhetoric of Traveling *Back to the Future*: The Zemeckis Aesthetic as Revisionist History and Conservative Fantasy

CHRISTOPHER JUSTICE

In his 1986 State of the Union address, U.S. president Ronald Reagan used the word "future" 16 times. Although not unusual for a president to use *that* word in *that* context, what was peculiar about his oration, spoken only months after the release of Robert Zemeckis' blockbuster *Back to the Future*, was his allusion to the famous trilogy's first installment. Reagan stated, "As they said in the film, *Back to the Future*, 'Where we are going, we don't need roads.' Well, today physicists peering into the infinitely small realms of subatomic particles find reaffirmations of religious faith. Astronomers build a space telescope that can see to the edge of the universe and possibly back to the moment of creation."[1] In those clauses, Reagan deftly merged the awkward bedfellows of popular culture and science to demonstrate the value of a technology-driven future that could revise the past and render new perceptions of tradition and faith. Reagan implied science and technology should no longer serve as instruments for the future, but rather, as tools of the past, because science and technology, in his eyes, precipitate invention and revisionism. As *Time* reporter Richard Stengel commented shortly after Reagan's speech, "For the President, future indicative is past perfect. There were, however, few forward-looking initiatives in his address."[2] In a speech lauded for its futuristic references, Reagan focused mostly on the past. However, science and technology weren't the only weapons Reagan used in his rhetorical arsenal that inspired a nation to proclaim proudly — "It's morning again in America" — in unison with one of his 1984 campaign advertisements.

Like science and technology, Reagan's presidency, too, was a tool of the past because through his political power he restored and revised Americans' ideals of their nation and its history by interweaving them with the future. *Back to the Future* has become a potent cultural artifact representing Reagan's 1980s, for it offers complex snapshots into that decade of revisionist propaganda. The film fundamentally is a Rorschach test that reveals the nostalgic, re-inventive, ironic, and revisionist zeitgeist that dominated Reagan's conservative decade.

As a master of illusion, Reagan understood how to summon this revisionist magic because of his experience and expertise as a mass communicator and media darling. By revising the past, he successfully promoted and solidified the conservative politics of his present. Specifically, through silicon-slick public and media relations, these two core Republican principles — strong anti-terrorism policies and Reaganomics — benefited from Reagan's re-engineering of history. *Back to the Future*'s treatment of these tenets reinforced the revisionist and nostalgic propaganda that defined Reagan's presidency. By distorting present and past political realities, Reagan generated, and *Back to the Future* complemented, a new culture of pathos projecting emotional warmth while ignoring inconvenient social realities. They used those nostalgic feelings to market and fuel their success; not coincidentally, America's 40th president enjoyed *Back to the Future*. However, similar to how those sentimental feelings masked the urgent need for a more critical awareness of Reagan's domestic and foreign policies, the film's popular reception masked its historical and political misrepresentations, and both mistakes cost American culture. As George Orwell once eloquently stated in his classic novel *1984*, "He who controls the past commands the future. He who commands the future conquers the past."[3] During the 1980s (and arguably beyond), Reagan and *Back to the Future* controlled America's past, present, and future.

Reagan's State of the Union address is pivotal in understanding the role American popular culture played in his rhetoric. A close reading of Reagan's words reveals his political intentions. His quotation from the film, "Where we are going, we don't need roads," opens his exposition, which suggests science may have provided evidence that proves the necessity of religious faith and empiricism of creationism. But what exactly is meant by this "roads" metaphor? In the film, "roads" carries literal and figurative meanings. Literally, Doc Brown utters this statement at the film's conclusion in response to Marty's concern that "We don't have enough road to get up to (the speed of) 88."[4] In essence, after much experimentation with his time travel vehicle and its flux capacitor, Doc Brown suggests we won't need roads for his DeLorean. Figuratively, however, Doc Brown's statement means something more prophetic: the old methods of travel are no longer a prerequisite for the new methods of time travel that he, and by extension, science, has unleashed. Doc Brown affirms this universal maxim: through research and development, inventions spur progress, and science, as it has demonstrated for centuries, is the catalyst for replacing obsolete technologies with new ones. Nobody in 1980s American cinema is more credible to make this claim than the ingenious, Einstein-resembling Doc Brown.

That Doc Brown resembles Einstein is not surprising; many portrayals of scientists in popular culture use the Einstein caricature: the lab coat, disheveled gray hair, impressive moustache, and slightly hunched back (Doc at least boasts the first two). However, what is surprising about Doc Brown is his resemblance to Einstein in conjunction with his last name, Brown, which draws comparisons to another great physicist, Wernher von Braun (Braun meaning Brown in German). The two scientists were revolutionary figures in 20th century physics, and each collaborated with their nation's political leaders to further science. Von Braun's contributions eventually led to advances in space travel, another indirect connection to the time travel theme in *Back to the Future*. Winterberg writes,

> It was Albert Einstein who for the first time changed our view of the universe to be a non–Euclidean curved space-time. And it was Wernher von Braun who blazed the trail to take us into this universe, leaving for the first time the gravitational field of our planet earth, with the landing (of) a man on the moon the greatest event in human history.... Both Einstein and von Braun made a Faustian pact with the devil, von Braun by accepting research funds from Hitler, and Einstein by urging Roosevelt to build the atom bomb (against Hitler).[5]

These scientists joined the political discourse of their time to advance scientific theories. While I'm not suggesting Zemeckis collaborated with the American government to make a film supportive of Reagan's policies, I am suggesting the film's many connections to Reagan and his policies are not only beyond coincidence, but more importantly, a reflection of the popular zeitgeist that dominated 1980s America, a cultural climate Reagan governed and narrated with skill. A few examples of these connections should suffice. The speed of 88 is required for the DeLorean to take off and travel back in time; this number also marks the final year of Reagan's presidency. The film begins on a sunny morning, and since it was produced during the 1984 presidential campaign, one in which Reagan's "It's morning again in America" mantra became a popular and effective campaign theme, its relationship to Reagan's campaign slogan is hard to ignore. The film is also set in California, a state Reagan resided in for decades and led as governor. Finally, the film's protagonist, Michael J. Fox, while shooting *Back to the Future*, was also playing Alex P. Keaton in the popular television show *Family Ties*. That Alex was a staunch conservative cast in a stereotypical "yuppie" role who was often at odds with his liberal parents is no secret.

Interestingly, Reagan's reference to this famous quotation uses the same rhetorical logic to reach a dramatically different conclusion. He acknowledges the existence of new technologies but uses them not to replace older technologies or methodologies, but rather, to reinstate, affirm, and legitimize the "old methodologies" of epistemology, faith and tradition. For Reagan, "roads" metaphorically represents a methodology for scientific discovery, namely the scientific method, but his examples of recent scientific discoveries suggest that methodology may be obsolete, or at least misunderstood. For Reagan in 1986, where his administration was going, we didn't need logic, proof, or evidence. What Reagan alludes to is a powerful conservative tenet (at least in the context of American political conservatism since the 1980s): public policy should not solely rely on social, theoretical, or applied science because the scientific method and the logic and reason it embraces are often flawed; public policy must equally be informed by faith, religion, and belief. The contemporary science and research Reagan pointed to in his speech have already proven, in Reagan's estimations, that faith and religious belief are scientifically verifiable and therefore undeniable. Reagan turned reason, logic, and scientific proof against themselves to reveal the power of tradition and belief and assert the values and importance of the past. In essence, the cold, calculating, impersonal reality and methodologies of science have proven the superiority, warmth, and personal legitimacy of traditional beliefs.

However, a closer reading of Reagan's rhetoric reveals how meticulously those ideas were articulated. Reagan was a talented rhetorician, and he and his speechwriters knew these ideas had to be presented carefully. Those "infinitely small realms of subatomic particles" resonate with contradiction: the vastness of infinity modifies "small realms," and within this paradox lurks room for science's re-emergence as the preeminent promulgator of knowledge, one that admittedly to Reagan himself, may be a more viable alternative to faith and religion because of its epistemological veracity. This is an excellent example of how Reagan used the political power of his present to justify how the future, represented in this instance by new technologies, could look backwards and redefine established traditions and beliefs. Ironically, one could argue that if Americans had to explore such miniscule particles for "reaffirmations of religious faith," what does that say about the state of faith in America during Reagan's presidency? Nevertheless, Reagan's use of the word "possibly" in the next clause undermines the assurance that resonates through his claims. In the spirit of Reagan's optimism, anything is possible, including the chance that astronomers might find the moment of creation through a telescope, but also the stark reality that they may not, an option he conveniently fails to emphasize in this address.

Reagan's unique ability to use popular culture as a rhetorical device was a key component of his role as the "Great Communicator." Americans in the 1980s were co-stars in Reagan's drama, but their lives were not screenplays. Nevertheless, they couldn't escape Reagan's storytelling prowess. Reagan's reliance on popular culture was a byproduct of what Yager calls his "narrative intelligence." As someone who saw the world through narrative eyes, it seems logical to use allusions to popular narratives such as films or songs to communicate with a national audience. Yager writes, "Reagan often relied on stories and anecdotes to interpret reality.... Reagan's narrative outlook on reality ... was fundamental to (his) unique ability to articulate a story about America to Americans in the latter half of the twentieth century." Yager believes Reagan's narrative intelligence was a key element of his reputation as the "Great Communicator."[6] By alluding to popular songs and movies, Reagan used simple devices to connect his narrative in complex ways with the common American, and in so doing, retold American history. Heclo adds, "Reagan was devoted to advancing not just a political program, party, or even movement, but a philosophy of history. Reagan did this work in his political life by serving as narrator, a teller of many stories that all served to expound and defend what he regarded as the one American story."[7]

His Strategic Defense Initiative became known as Star Wars to remind Americans of that stark battle between good and evil within not only the popular science fiction film, but also the Cold War; not coincidentally, Reagan once labeled his own personal Darth Vader, the Soviet Union, as the "evil empire." As Stengel reminds us, "Reagan announced that he was pushing ahead with plans for a suborbital airplane, which he dubbed a 'new Orient Express,' that could someday fly at 25 times the speed of sound."[8] Here, Reagan sought to mollify public antagonism against this plan by associating it with the romantic, exotic, and nostalgic images and feelings connected to one of Hollywood's more popular films. Stengel also notes that not only did Reagan use specific allusions to popular culture, but he also used Hollywood's lexicon and concepts to describe "family values." Stengel writes, "His national pep talk (his 1986 State of the Union address) affirmed again and again his belief that 'family and community are the co-stars of this great American comeback.'"[9] When led by a president whose career was launched in the stylish, fictional world of Hollywood, reality is not only subordinate to the illusions of idealism, but also the idealism of illusions.

Nevertheless, Reagan's many critics were throughout the decade able to periodically lift the illusion's veil. A good example of Reagan's misappropriation of popular culture occurred with his misuse of pop singer Bruce Springsteen's hit song "Born in the U.S.A.." As Todd Leopold reports, "The singer wasn't amused by Reagan's appropriation of his work" because the song is ultimately about "the ferocious cry of an unemployed Vietnam veteran."

Springsteen was quoted in *Rolling Stone* magazine as saying, "I think people have a need to feel good about the country they live in.... But what's happening, I think, is that that need — which is a good thing — is getting manipulated and exploited. You see in the Reagan election ads on TV, you know, 'It's morning in America,' and you say, 'Well, it's not morning in Pittsburgh.'"[10]

Notwithstanding Springsteen's rejection of Reagan's revisionist propaganda, the singer represented the minority because the president's masterful use of illusion infiltrated American popular culture throughout the decade. Leopold writes, "The decade's pop culture trafficked in the blur between illusion and reality," and he provides numerous examples of such trafficking including the launching of David Letterman's "irony laden" talk show; "sitcoms that hearkened back to the cozy 1950s" such as *The Cosby Show* (where all African American families have the chance to live like the Huxtables) and *Family Ties* (where 1960s liberals live happily with 1980s conservatives); *Rambo*'s revisionist interpretations of the Vietnam War; the style over substance hits *Miami Vice* and *Dallas*; the computer-generated advertising character Max Headroom, who later (in Britain) mocked the advertising business; and other television shows, films, and popular songs and music videos.[11] Shales writes that *Back to the Future* "almost sums the Eighties up, and that's partly because the movie made time travel a joke, a gag, a hoot. We are not amazed at the thought of time travel because we do it every day." For Shales, the Eighties were "The Re Decade" because of the way popular culture was constantly replayed, reviewed, and recycled; "Television is our national time machine,"[12] he stated.

Due to the ceaseless recycling of popular culture, reality in the 1980s was blurred beyond comprehension and became an illusion itself. Additionally, one could argue Reagan's presidency was based upon illusion because his professional life was built upon symbolic mediation, perception management, and the art of mass communication. Subsequently, he was able to politically capitalize on his illusory self. Interestingly, the same could be said of *Back to the Future* since the three films are chronological shell games that morph different time periods into one narrative, and sometimes, into one scene. Marty frequently fumbles with his present because he must reconcile his knowledge of the future through conversations with people from his past. In one scene, Marty eats dinner with Lorraine's family, which means he is eating dinner with his mother, but they are the same age. When an episode of *The Honeymooners* airs, Marty instantly recognizes it. Defining the present within such a bricolage of images from the past and future is challenging. Gordon writes, "*Back to the Future* demonstrates the reciprocity of contemporary image-making, which cuts across all time lines ... we see video images of the present rerun in the past."[13] At another point, Doc asks Marty, "Do have any concept of time?"[14] For Marty, the answer is rapidly becoming a resounding "no," which is why he so often looks confused throughout the movie. If our collective experience of the film, which is guided primarily by the protagonist's point of view, is equally confused, it should be no coincidence that in the context of Reagan's revisionist, ironic 1980s, so many viewers empathized with Marty. The trilogy's ethos presents history as an irrelevant illusion because history can so easily be revised. Leopold quotes satirist Paul Slansky who "wrote in his diary of the decade, *The Clothes Have No Emperor*, '[My book] is the response of ... an observer whose very sanity was threatened by the ease with which illusion —*an actor is playing the president!*— was embraced as reality.'"[15] Reagan reminded Americans how manufactured reality could be, and *Back to the Future* reminded them how manufactured history was. Not surprisingly, many Americans welcomed those representations because they felt good, dismissed complexity, and ultimately celebrated the present. The duality and contradictions inherent in the film and Reagan's presidency transformed both into illusions that represented different realities simultaneously.

As America's first actor-turned-president, Reagan delivered the country's first "semiotic presidency" with astounding effectiveness. For generations of Americans, mainly older generations familiar with his professional acting career prior to his entry into politics, Reagan's every move as president represented something other than what it was, namely, other than his presidency, policies, or himself: Reagan represented two former lifetimes, his and his "viewers'" during the 1940s, 1950s, and 1960s, times when Reagan was frequently seen in movie theaters and on television sets. With more than 50 films to his credit and two-dozen television appearances, no other American president has been visually experienced so frequently prior to assuming the presidency than Reagan. Since so much of the modern American presidency is experienced through televised or mediated channels, his semiotic resonance was more potent than any other U.S. president's. The familiarity and comfort this extensive media exposure provided Reagan allowed him a degree of popularity impervious to his policies.

The illusions that defined Reagan's professional career as an actor and politician were partly due to the contradictions they generated. In his early 20s, Reagan was a radio sports broadcaster for the radio station WHO in Des Moines, Iowa; as Wagner writes, "Reagan's most notable radio broadcasts were of baseball games he never attended."[16] Reagan was originally a staunch Democrat with a profound admiration for Franklin Delano Roosevelt, but he later turned Republican. As a Democrat and pro-labor fanatic, he became an important public relations spokesman for one of America's largest and most successful corporations, General Electric (GE). Yager writes that Reagan's employment with GE, which started in 1954, was a transformative experience that forced Reagan to work directly with wealthy corporate executives. Reagan learned during this experience that these wealthy men were not all greedy "robber barons." Furthermore, Reagan learned that not all politicians pretending to help disenfranchised citizens harbored angelic intentions. Consequently, his GE career started with him voting as a Democrat, but ended with him changing parties.[17]

Reagan's youthful energy and positivism undermined the reality that he was America's oldest president. His youthful style complemented the substance of his patriarchal, grandfatherly appeal, giving him a unique duality and personality that defied time and chronology. This defiance, for some, assumed mythical dimensions. Ridings and McIver quote journalist and Reagan biographer Lou Cannon, who suggested Reagan's assassination attempt gave him a "mythic" quality.[18] However, his mythic quality had already been cemented prior to this tragedy in most Americans' consciousness because many spent their formative years watching him in larger-than-life roles; after his assassination, his "mythic quality" grew exponentially. If that mythic quality is responsible for his popularity, few can argue Reagan's presidency was not seminal, but the reasons for his political popularity are often overblown by conservatives and underestimated by liberals. His role as America's first semiotic president cannot be overlooked.

As Heclo states, "one must pay as much attention to Reagan's pre-presidential years as to his White House years."[19] Reagan himself was a symbol of America's idealized past — a figure literally emerging from America's collective unconscious who will live into perpetuity on movie, television, and computer screens in dual, contradictory roles: first as an entertainer, and second as president. His many film roles were of wonderfully American characters — humble, hard-working, clean-cut heroes (similar to Marty) — epitomized in his most famous role as George "The Gipper" Gipp in *Knute Rockne All American*. For decades, it was difficult to root against Ronald Reagan the actor, and as president, he capitalized on that popularity and used it to reinvent America, but this penchant for an idealistic and illusory past shaped by conservative ideologies caused problems.

When we idealize, we often overlook reality, ignore complexities, and replace logic with emotion. What feels good becomes good; what feels bad becomes bad. This idealism not only preys upon simplifications, but it celebrates them; it is in this context that one should interpret *Back to the Future* because Zemeckis capitalized on these sentiments. In his review of *Forrest Gump*, another Zemeckis blockbuster, historian Lawrence B. Goodheart writes, "By avoiding controversy and embracing cliché, the movie renders modern history into mass entertainment. Pivotal political and ethical issues are trivialized and transformed into a popular product, an inoffensive commodity of the least common denominator for the greatest number."[20] The same could be said of *Back to the Future*, where history unfolds like an unencumbered red carpet, and the sense of a world outside the small middle-class, white community of Hill Valley is non-existent.

In *Back to the Future*, history is easy to revise because it's presented in simplistic terms. Marty no doubt experiences obstacles when altering his family's history, but his versions of their collective narrative are neatly packaged into a happy ending. Furthermore, history in the film carries no regional, national, social, political, or geopolitical consequences, thus making it easier to process and understand; history has been neutered into nothing more than personal history. When Doc Brown and Marty travel through time, they return to Hill Valley as if trapped in a solipsistic nightmare. Goodheart continues,

> *Forrest Gump* is a superficial and self-indulgent cultural fantasy. Through the Academy Awards, Hollywood honors itself as the arbiter of collective memory. Themes of grief and uplift, sin and absolution, healing and harmony provide a vicarious catharsis from the serious problems of the day. Anti-intellectual and apolitical, *Forrest Gump* promotes a "feel good" narcissism devoid of civic commitment to social issues of power, justice and equity. History merely happens, just as the floating feather fatefully begins and ends the film. Personal preoccupation, not social engagement, is its norm, part of a national malaise that the movie encourages.[21]

Goodheart's words resonate loudly with *Back to the Future*. Marty helps himself and improves his welfare only, not the unfortunate souls he encounters throughout the films. Marty's revising of history does help his family members, but they are ultimately extensions of him. Among the various historical narratives ignored by Zemeckis, the most obvious involve race. For example, the racist barbs launched toward the African American band members by one of Biff's puppets are conveniently ignored. One is also reminded of the third installment, *Back to the Future III*, when Marty hyperspaces onto the Western front in the middle of a U.S. cavalry chasing Native Americans. This major chapter of U.S. history, the eradication of native culture, is rendered as tangential and inconsequential to the film's narrative. The scene's import vanishes as quickly as the horses themselves and is reduced to a simplistic action film trope; the film's treatment of this important chapter in history is brutally dismissive. In fact, most of the third installment's depiction of the American West is subordinated to the personal narratives of Doc and Marty. Again, our collective history is whittled into a solipsistic fantasy.

Another example of Zemeckis's dubious treatment of American history occurs with the film's only overt references to Reagan. In the first installment, a movie poster for *Cattle Queen of Montana* starring Barbara Stanwyck and Reagan appears outside a Hill Valley film theater. Marty then notices their names on the theater marquee. Interestingly, we only experience Reagan in visual terms, but more importantly, we only experience one dimension of his Hollywood career, his role as actor. As former president of the Screen Actors Guild and a major figure in the House Committee on Un-American Activities, Reagan's roles in Hollywood were complicated, and subsequently, his reputation in Hollywood during the late 1940s and early 1950s was controversial. Yager writes, "Reagan increasingly became a polarizing figure in Hollywood at the time of the Conference of Studio Unions strike: Some people deeply despised him, yet others respected and supported him."[22] Although by the mid–1950s Reagan's controversial Hollywood persona had reached its zenith, in the collective narrative that is *Back to the Future*, his Hollywood career has been curiously reduced to one still image. Moreover, *Cattle Queen of Montana*, which was playing in theaters in the mid–1950s, aligns Marty's mission cleverly with Reagan's portrayal of the hired gun Farrell, who as the "knight in shining armor" helps the "damsel-in-distress," Sierra Nevada Jones (Stanwyck), fight a cadre of villains aiming to usurp her land. Marty revises his family's history, and like Reagan in his film, helps save damsel Lorraine from the villainous Biff. While Marty is not seeking to help anyone reclaim their land, he is seeking to reclaim his family's history. Here, Zemeckis draws this interesting parallel between Reagan's role in *Cattle Queen* and Marty's in *Back to the Future*: one's personal history, like one's "real" estate, is a commodity that can be owned, revised, and controlled.

Later in the film, as Marty persuades Doc that he has been transported from 1985 into 1955, Doc seeks evidence of his time travel and asks, jokingly, "Who is president?" When Marty replies, "Ronald Reagan," Doc answers sarcastically and incredulously with another question: "The actor?"[23] As Doc runs outside, he continues his sarcasm by wondering if Jerry Lewis is Vice President, Jane Wyman the First Lady, and Jack Benny the Secretary of Treasury. Superficially, this is a moment of great comedy, one of many in what Ruud calls a "quintessential comedy,"[24] but it reveals the absurdity of Zemeckis's ahistorical tale. In this political fantasy, even the most powerful figures in American government are entertainers. Since Doc is the voice of reason and science, which in Latin means "scientia" or "knowledge," the fact that he questions this possibility suggests it could be accurate. If a scientist with great credibility might believe such a claim, anything is believable. For Zemeckis, history is entertainment, no matter how distorted or fantastical.

As a popular time travel film, *Back to the Future*'s complicated treatment of time reveals its obsession with reinventing history. The film suggests that if one travels through time, that person also travels through history. However, history and time are not synonymous, and experiencing time is not experiencing history. If history is a complex wheel, time represents one spoke in that wheel, and it's arguably the simplest. The complex spokes involve cultural, political, economic, and societal factors that shape historical time periods. Contrary to what the film suggests, history is much more than the raw experience of a clock ticking away seconds; conversely, "preserving" or stopping time is not a historical experience either. The film's visual motif of ticking clocks is juxtaposed against the broken clock tower in the middle of Hill Valley's town square. Marty says to his principal, "Yeah, well history is gonna change,"[25] as if to warn us that our history might be rewritten too (by Reagan and his political allies). Later, a lady in charge of the mayor's preservation efforts urges Marty to donate money to maintain the broken clock. By doing so, presumably, Marty will also be preserving the town's history. He rejects that plea, which foreshadows his desire to control history and rewrite it according to his own narrative preferences, something Reagan did for eight years as president. Preserving history was popular throughout the 1980s as Reagan and the conservative movement frequently sought to resuscitate images of America's past and instill those values in contemporary society to transform it, like Hill Valley, into a time when Main Streets thrived, schoolboys smiled, and families inspired.

Unfortunately, the idealism fueling such idealized pasts also preys upon clichés, stereotypes, and caricatures, and *Back to the Future*'s characters are laced with such traits. George McFly is the Nerd: gullible, tight, and obsequious, he is the classic "unhip" 1950s dad who writes science fiction stories. His wife, Lorraine, is the Homemaker: overweight, exhausted, and sexually pure, she is the classic overly protective mom who dips the vodka bottle when nobody's looking. Doc Brown is the Mad Scientist: asexual (for two of the films), eccentric, frazzle-haired, and sloppy, he'll do anything for science, loves his gadgets, and experiments impetuously. And Biff is the Bully: hulking, thuggish, and beer drinking, he is the archetypal suburban antagonist. Gordon believes the film's stock characters, along with its "stock premise (time travel, the subject of so many movies and TV shows) and its star, Michael J. Fox, borrowed from a successful sitcom" reflect deliberate decisions by the filmmakers to "to tame the potentially touch[y] subject of incest."[26] However, Gordon overemphasizes the role incest plays in the film, and while his point is useful, it risks underemphasizing many of the film's overtly political themes, particularly as they relate to affirmations of Reagan's policies. What is troubling about Zemeckis's film is that it suggests the only way to transcend stereotypes is through fantasy. Once we are labeled stereotypically, *Back to the Future* suggests, the only panacea available is the fictional solution of time travel or fantasy. Likewise, history cannot be penetrated without fantasy and delusion. Of course, stereotyping is not uncommon in Hollywood, and the industry is based on the commodification of stereotypical images. Nevertheless, when stereotypes are as abundant and one-dimensional as they are in *Back to the Future*, and when they are cast in a narrative that fundamentally seeks to reinvent history, they become dangerous conventions.

Goodheart concludes his diatribe against the Zemeckis aesthetic with these lines, which again are strikingly interchangeable with *Back to the Future*:

> This modern fable with its myth of an earlier golden age mirrors the conservative political appeal of Ronald Reagan during the 1980s and the continued attraction for his successors during the 1990s. Burdened with personal debt, frustrated with a decline in real earnings, frightened of job layoffs, fearful of crime in the streets, alarmed at black rage, confused about cultural change, cynical about politics, and confounded about the Vietnam War, many white voters have turned rightward. President Reagan recalled "the good old days," a blend of fact and fiction, in which all was right with America, images not unlike those from the movies in which he acted. In their evocation of national innocence and individual salvation, *Forrest Gump* and Ronald Reagan share a common mentality, one of escape and delusion. The theme of "back to the future," as Zemeckis would have it, makes for mediocre movies, poor politics, and bad history.[27]

Of course, not much was right with Reagan's good old days, just as little was "right" with Marty's experience of the 1950s. Stengel wrote, "His reference to the movie *Back to the Future* was fitting: his image of the future, a peaceful era of happy families in tight communities, harks back to his vision of an idealized past."[28] However, that vision, too, was an illusion, which is why Marty returned to the 1950s to fix his family's history. In Zemeckis's 1955, teenagers smoke not only cigarettes but marijuana; they drink liquor at high school dances; bullies like Biff rule the high school campus; young girls such as Lorraine are essentially raped in parking lots; and racism is prevalent. Nevertheless, a clever Hollywood script quickly fixed those problems with an illogical, and as Goodheart suggests, "delusional" happy ending. For Reagan and Zemeckis, history is a tool for the present, and if entertainment can help us overlook those sobering realities, all is good, and the self-indulgent giddiness reigns.

Perhaps the most unexpected element in Zemeckis' portrayal of 1955 is its flirtation with incest. Gordon writes, the "film succeeds because it deftly combines two current and oddly connected American preoccupations — with time travel and with incest — and defuses our anxieties about both through comedy."[29] But why are our anxieties about this topic defused? If Reagan and others enjoyed this film because of its Rockwellian depiction of 1950s America, they must have overlooked its blatant treatment of incest because Reagan and his conservative followers must have disapproved of frivolously dismissing such important social matters. As Gordon notes, "The desire, guilt, and fear are still attached to the incest taboo, but the audience is comfortable with those feelings because we get a momentary comic bonus from them."[30] Historically, the 1950s were an anxious period for many reasons, and one was the decade's understanding and exposure to sexual deviance and promiscuity, which partly surfaced due to emerging counterculture movements, Alfred Kinsey's 1948 publication "Sexual Behavior in the Human Male," and other factors. By treating the 1950s comically, and by alluding to that decade within the context of the 1980s' political framework, Reagan was able to govern his political future by blending present political realities with narratives of the past distorted by media images. By providing a momentary relief from such taboos, viewers were given the opportunity to re-engage with them through humor and with a revived vigor, something Reagan and his Republican peers supported given their fundamentalist stances toward homosexuality and the growing AIDS virus.

Much of Reagan's narrative was inspired by his religious beliefs. Heclo writes, "his political career expressed a historical and philosophical worldview that was Christian in a very traditional American sense."[31] Given that Reagan was a potent symbol himself and that he often narrated his version of American history through archetypal symbols and religious imagery, he may have found a kinship in Zemeckis's use of religious symbols (or vice versa). Richardson explains many such images including the Twin Pines Mall, which she believes offers an allusion to "the mythic Garden of Eden where it is said God planted the 'tree of the knowledge of good and evil.'"[32] Not coincidentally, in this mall parking lot, the good guys (Doc and Marty) fight the bad guys (the Libyans). Richardson also notes the film's uses of fire and light, both of which have numerous connotations to Biblical stories; the frequency of circular objects, particularly the circular object on Marty's shirt, which she argues reflects the unity of time and the "oneness," in Jungian terms, of developing a unified psyche by conjoining past, present, and future into a timeless sense of spiritual euphoria; and the pervasive themes of heroes (Marty, who saves the damsel in distress) and gods (Doc, who can control and manipulate time).[33]

Of course, not much was right with Reagan's 1980s either, particularly in the realm of foreign policy and terrorism. Reagan's presidential legacy, especially in the context of his anti-terrorism policies, has peculiarly escaped scrutiny in the post–9/11 era. Many critics argue that his anti-terrorism blunders allowed terrorist groups to thrive. Bovard writes, "Though Reagan spent his entire time in office warring against terrorism, far more American civilians died in terrorist attacks at the end of his reign than at the beginning. Yet terrorism lost none of its political value as a hobgoblin. The Reagan administration almost totally escaped bearing responsibility for its failures to deliver promised protection to Americans."[34] But *Back to the Future* provided the illusion of protection. One of the trilogy's most politically charged scenes occurs early in the first installment when Libyan nationals attack Marty and Doc Brown at the Twin Pines Mall. Interestingly, this scene launches the *Back to the Future* trilogy, and subsequently, draws parallels to Reagan's presidency. Both the film's plot and Reagan's presidency are fueled by the need to combat an evil enemy. Reagan's decades-long opposition to Communism, and Marty and Doc's stand against the Libyan terrorists initiate Reagan's and Zemeckis's odyssey. More importantly, the Libyan terrorists are depicted as cold-blooded killers. Their actions are despicable: they fire automatic weapons upon unarmed civilians and want to steal radioactive plutonium. Just as Reagan framed Communism as a threat to the soul of American democracy, Zemeckis achieved the same impact with *Back to the Future*: these terrorists, because their terrorism unfolds on American soil in a shopping mall parking lot, are a threat to the soul of American democracy: capitalism. As the Libyans chase Marty around the parking lot, the looming presence of JC Penney's white logo reminds us of capitalism's overbearing innocence. For Zemeckis, this is a simple war of good vs. evil against an enemy that can be stereotyped too easily. The Libyans' arrival is tuned to the militaristic beats of the film's soundtrack. Doc labels them with a definite article — "*the* Libyans" — because they've already been introduced (But by whom? How many viewers will remember the news story about the plutonium theft during the film's first minutes? Or have they been introduced in some other capacity?). Furthermore, we forget that Doc Brown admittedly stole the plutonium from these Libyan nationals, thus making him a criminal as well.

Zemeckis' portrayal of these Libyans is more caricature than anything else. Shaheen writes, "On the silver screen the Muslim Arab continues to surface as the threatening cultural 'other.' Fear of this strange 'faith' keeps some people huddled in emotional isolation."[35] The Libyans appear on screen momentarily, and they don't appear again until the film's conclusion. They have no depth or complexity, and we hardly see their faces. Constantly moving and firing weapons, they appear in a flurry and thus are dehumanized because they are more the embodiment of terrorist "motion" than terrorists themselves. Interestingly, they are also disconnected from Libya and the Middle East. Shaheen writes, "Unsightly Arab Muslims and prejudicial dialogue about them appear in more than two hundred movies that otherwise have nothing at all to do with Arabs or the Middle East ... Libyans, especially, are a favorite target."[36] However, the degree to which Zemeckis simplifies these individuals is proportionate not only to their overall complexities as people, but also to the complexities that defined U.S.-Libyan relations during Reagan's presidency.

In this important scene, Zemeckis conveniently paints a narrow picture of U.S.-Libyan relations in the 1980s. One of Reagan's most public allies, the

Soviet Union's Mikhail Gorbachev, supported Libyan dictator Muammar Qaddafi.[37] U.S. naval ships during the early 1980s conducted military exercises in the Gulf of Sidra, but Qaddafi argued the waters belonged to Libya; in August 1981, U.S. and Libyan combat planes exchanged fire due to this dispute.[38] Notwithstanding how "the Libyans" are depicted as evil incarnate in *Back to the Future*, Bovard has examined the circumstances surrounding the 1986 U.S. bombing of Libya. He quotes Neal Koch, who in 1986 served as The Pentagon's counterterrorism chief, and who explained a major reason why Libya was bombed: "Libya was simply considered the easiest target among terrorist-supporting nations."[39] In other words, "the Libyans" were the weakest and least ruthless of Middle Eastern terrorist-supporting states. About the U.S. bombing of Libya, Bovard continues: "One F-111 bomber dumped its load on a residential neighborhood, also damaging the French embassy. The Pentagon postponed admitting responsibility for several days even though a weapons officer on the F-111 immediately sent word about the mistake. Libya said the raid killed more than 30 people and wounded almost 100."[40] Although Libyans are portrayed as terrorists in the film, their role can be reversed: in reality, average Libyans perceived Americans as terrorists because the U.S. military bombed their neighborhoods. Essentially, the conflict that spawns the trilogy's narrative is nothing more than jingoistic propaganda.

Beyond foreign and anti-terrorism policies, Reagan's economic strategies, known widely as Reaganomics, created watershed economic change. Ehrman explains how Reagan's policies established a new era in corporate takeovers and mergers. He writes, "The Reagan administration's greatest, and most far-reaching, success was in the deregulation of the market for corporate control — the actual ownership of large corporations."[41] Low corporate stock prices, deregulation, poor corporate management, inflation, and the emergence of a junk bond market led by Michael Milken allowed numerous companies to merge. According to Ehrman, "In 1980, some 1,500 mergers, worth $32 billion, had taken place. The figures then climbed through the Reagan years, with the number of deals peaking at almost 4,400 in 1987, and their value topping off at $226.6 billion the next year."[42] The film's visual design, especially as conveyed in Hill Valley's town square, supports this concept of corporate conglomerates because the sets resemble a giant advertisement. Corporate logos and small business advertisements are ubiquitous, and viewers initially struggle to decipher the differences between small businesses such as The Bluebird Hotel and large corporations such as JC Penney or Texaco. Ultimately though, in comparison to the small business advertisements, the more prominent corporations and their popular logos are more identifiable, so they visually "take over" and consume our attention. Since they blend together to form one giant corporate impression, the entire *Back to the Future* landscape appears as an advertisement not for any one company or business, but for American capitalism, as if it was owned by one monolithic mega-corpora-tion. In *Back to the Future II*, this notion is personalized through Biff, who symbolizes this phenomenon of corporate takeovers since he "owns" so much of Hill Valley, including Marty's mom.

Another major economic trend that surfaced during the Reagan years was a sharp rise in consumer spending in various markets. Ehrman writes, "for most Americans the 1980s was a time of rising living standards ... Amer-icans went on a shopping spree in the 1980s as retail sales, adjusted for inflation, rose by a third from 1980 to 1988." He later adds, "These consumers sought greater variety in their choices, embraced new products, and demanded higher quality in the goods they purchased."[43] Nowhere is this more explicit than in the rampant product placement that pervades the three films. The Merriam-Webster Online Dictionary defines "product placement" as "the inclusion of a product in a television program or film as a form of paid adver-tisement."[44] Interestingly, Steven Spielberg's *E.T.* is credited as a pioneering film in the history of product placement. As a result of the movie, the pop-ularity of Reese's Pieces soared[45]; given Spielberg's role in *Back to the Future*, it should be no surprise that product placement weighed heavily in Zemeckis' film. Among the various brands featured in the trilogy are Calvin Klein, Pepsi, Tab, BMW, Ford, Nike, the NFL, Burger King, Budweiser, Gibson guitars, and many others. In fact, one ambitious soul counted more than 100 prod-uct brands placed in at least one of the trilogy's films.[46] However, these prod-uct placements represent two problematic trends: 1) they're an early reminder of the growing corporatization and conglomeration of the entertainment industry, a movement that ultimately corrupts the aesthetic objectives of cin-ematic art; and 2) they exploit consumers' original purchasing intentions. Since the 1980s, Federal Communications Commission laws have required advertisers to disclose their commercial intentions to consumers; rampant product placement such as the kind that appears in *Back to the Future* would in 2008, without such disclosures, be illegal.

Another market that benefited from Reagan's economic policies was the housing and construction market, and Zemeckis's film portrays this housing explosion as inconsequential. Ehrman reports, "The changes in housing and consumption took place against a landscape that was being transformed ... census data shows that the growth rates of the outer suburbs were as great, or greater, than those of the older suburbs had been in the 1950s."[47] Since we only witness Hill Valley in snapshots, those from 1955 and in 1985, we never experience this suburban growth's costs or the transitions it caused. Zemeckis conveniently fast forwards and rewinds these two depictions of Hill Valley to serve his narrative needs as if they are before and after photographs; nothing is seen or experienced during the interim between 1955 and 1985, so we never learn about this sprawl's environmental and ecological ramifications; the impacts it inevitably had on local schools; the economic impact it had on local businesses; or its many other effects. However, Zemeckis does reveal the downside of this suburban sprawl through his portrayal of the shopping mall, which serves an important purpose. "The number of malls and shopping centers in the United States increased (in the 1980s) by two-thirds," Ehrman writes.[48] But at what cost? Zemeckis seems intent on offering warning signs. Although the town square in Hill Valley remains a potent source of civic life in 1985, the looming mall, depicted at night in the darkness as a lonely place where criminals congregate, serves as a harbinger of that square's demise. Spreading civic life onto a town's outskirts is what suburbs do, and the film suggests Hill Valley's civic center may be deteriorating. The Libyans move into the town square by the film's conclusion, and much corruption is depicted within the friendly confines of Hill Valley including violence, racism, drug use, and rape. As Yeats warned, "Things fall apart; the centre cannot hold; Mere anarchy is loosed upon the world,"[49] or in the case of *Back to the Future*, on the suburbs.

Nevertheless, this is one of Zemeckis's lone forays into seriously critiquing Reagan's policies. For most of the first installment, and certainly the trilogy's majority, the good behind Reagan's policies is affirmed. The popularity of entertainment mediums also blossomed during the 1980s with the rapid spread of cable television, video games, MTV, music videos, electronic media, cell phones, VCRs, DVDs, and computer technologies. As an extension of the first installment's obsession with product placements, many entertainment products are also exposed including Jules Verne novels; Chuck Berry, Huey Lewis, Eric Clapton, Etta James, and Lindsey Buckingham songs; *The Honeymooners* reruns; and the films *Cattle Queen of Montana*, *Tarantula*, and others, to name a few. The film is a glorification of mass media entertainment and a celebration of the style-over-substance ethos that dominated the 1980s. Nowhere is this more apparent than in Zemeckis's decision to feature the DeLorean automobile.

When asked why he chose this particular vehicle, Doc Brown says, "The way I see it, if you're gonna build a time machine into a car, why not do it with some style?"[50] That statement exemplifies Reagan's 1980s. The DeLorean itself was the epitome of style, but it was also saddled with various mechanical problems. Its creator, John Z. DeLorean, was also an eccentric, glamorous auto entrepreneur who became a symbol of corporate corruption in the 1980s. Although he was acquitted of each charge, three separate incidents sealed his reputation. According to *The New York Times*, the company that produced the vehicle "fell into financial trouble and was the subject of a British government investigation into financial irregularities." Additionally, "DeLorean was arrested and charged with conspiring to obtain and distribute 55 pounds of cocaine." In "another trial, in Detroit, on fraud charges ... a grand jury accused him of siphoning off about $9 million that investors had put into his auto company."[51] Often in *Back to the Future*, narrative decisions appear stylish and appealing, but when one digs deeper, one finds a sordid back story highlighting the film's inability to distinguish itself from the ironic zeitgeist that shaped it.

Like many films, *Back to the Future*'s popularity is due more to the historical, political, and social context in which it surfaced than its own aesthetic merit. However, that is not always a bad characteristic. If art is an inspiring reflection of the historical context that produced it, then *Back to the Future* is a precious cinematic relic. Indistinguishable from many of the policies Ronald Reagan promoted throughout his presidency, Zemeckis through *Back to the Future* articulated those policies by affirming their value. However, if art's purpose is to challenge the status quo, redirect our attention, and cultivate more critical stances toward our politics, society, and culture, *Back to the Future* leaves us with more questions than answers. What purpose did Zemeckis's conformist tendencies promote? Would *Back to the Future* have been as successful if Reagan wasn't president during its release? At what point does a film's success become a sign of its weaknesses? The film is very entertaining but only because by showing us Reagan's misguided follies, it also reveals its own. In a decade of decadent irony, that perhaps may be *Back to the Future*'s most enduring contribution. Hopefully, this collection will begin to address the eye-opening dearth of scrutiny aimed at this profoundly successful film. *Back to the Future* certainly deserves more, if for no other reason, to understand the confusing and complex decade in American culture known as the 1980s.

Notes

1. Ronald Reagan, *Address Before a Joint Session of Congress on the State of the Union*, http://www.presidency.ucsb.edu/ws/index.php?pid=36646.

2. Richard Stengel, "Back to the Future, Again," *Time*, February 17, 1986, http://www.time.com/time/magazine/article/0,9171,960654-3,00.html.

3. George Orwell, Quoteland.com, http://www.quoteland.com/author.asp?AUTHOR_ID=190.

4. *Back to the Future*, DVD, directed by Robert Zemeckis (1985; Los Angeles, CA: Amblin Entertainment / Universal Pictures, 1985).

5. Friedwardt Winterberg, *Abstract: T9.00004: Albert Einstein and Wernher von Braun — the two great German-American physicists seen in a historical perspective*, http://meetings.aps.org/Meeting/APR08/Event/83897.

6. Edward M. Yager, *Ronald Reagan's Journey: Democrat to Republican* (Lanham, MD: Rowman & Littlefield, 2006), 91.

7. Hugh Heclo, "Ronald Reagan and the American Public Philosophy" in *The Reagan Presidency: Pragmatic Conservatism & Its Legacies*, eds. W. Elliot Brownlee & Hugh Davis Graham (Lawrence: University of Kansas Press, 2003), 18.

8. Stengel, "Back to the Future, Again," *Time*, February 17, 1986, http://www.time.com/time/magazine/article/0,9171,960654-3,00.html.

9. *Ibid.*

10. Todd Leopold, "Analysis: The Age of Reagan," *CNN.com*, June 16, 2004, http://www.cnn.com/2004/SHOWBIZ/06/16/reagan.80s/index.html.

11. *Ibid.*

12. Tom Shales, "The Re Decade," *Esquire*, March 1986: 67–68.

13. Andrew Gordon, "Back to the Future: Œdipus as Time Traveler," *Science Fiction Studies*, 14 (1987): 373–374.

14. *Back to the Future*, DVD, directed by Robert Zemeckis (1985; Los Angeles, CA: Amblin Entertainment / Universal Pictures, 1985).

15. Leopold, "Analysis: The Age of Reagan," *CNN.com*, June 16, 2004, http://www.cnn.com/2004/SHOWBIZ/06/16/reagan.80s/index.html.

16. Heather Lehr Wagner, *Great American Presidents — Ronald Reagan* (Philadelphia: Chelsea House Publishers, 2004), 33.

17. Yager, *Ronald Reagan's Journey*, 45.

18. William J. Ridings Jr. and Stuart B. McGiver, *Rating the Presidents: A Ranking of U.S. Leaders, From the Great and Honorable to the Dishonest and Incompetent* (Secaucus, NJ: Carol Publishing Group, 1997), 260.

19. Heclo, "Ronald Reagan and the American Public Philosophy," 18.

20. Lawrence B. Goodheart, "*Forrest Gump* and the Myth of American Innocence," *Journal of American Studies of Turkey*, 2 (1995), http://www.bilkent.edu.tr/~jast/Number2/Goodheart.html.

21. *Ibid.*

22. Yager, *Ronald Reagan's Journey*, 25.

23. *Back to the Future*, DVD, directed by Robert Zemeckis (1985; Los Angeles, CA: Amblin Entertainment / Universal Pictures, 1985).

24. Jay Ruud, "Back to the Future as Quintessential Comedy," *Literature Film Quarterly*, 19 (1991).

25. *Back to the Future*, DVD, directed by Robert Zemeckis (1985; Los Angeles, CA: Amblin Entertainment / Universal Pictures, 1985).

26. Gordon, "Back to the Future: Œdipus as Time Traveler," 374.

27. Lawrence B. Goodheart, "*Forrest Gump* and the Myth of American Innocence," *Journal of American Studies of Turkey*, 2 (1995), http://www.bilkent.edu.tr/~jast/Number2/Goodheart.html.

28. Stengel, "Back to the Future, Again," *Time*, February 17, 1986 http://www.time.com/time/magazine/article/0,9171,960654-3,00.html.

29. Gordon, "Back to the Future: Œdipus as Time Traveler," 372.

30. *Ibid.*, 375.

31. Heclo, "Ronald Reagan and the American Public Philosophy," 20.

32. Elizabeth A. Richardson, "Back to the Future: Yang-Yin=0, Yang+Yin+1," *Extrapolation*, 29 (1988): 132.

33. *Ibid.*, 133–137.

34. James Bovard, *Terrorism Debacles in the Reagan Administration*, http://www.fff.org/freedom/fd0406c.asp.

35. Jack G. Shaheen, "Hollywood's Muslim Arabs" in *A Community of Many Worlds: Arab Americans in New York City*, eds. Kathleen Benson and Philip M. Kayal (New York: Museum of the City of New York; Syracuse: Syracuse University Press, 2002); 192.

36. *Ibid.*, 196.

37. John Patrick Diggins, *Ronald Reagan: Fate, Freedom, and the Making of History* (New York: W.W. Norton, 2007), 362.

38. *Ibid.*, 236.

39. Bovard, *Terrorism Debacles in the Reagan Administration*, http://www.fff.org/freedom/fd0406c.asp.

40. *Ibid.*

41. John Ehrman, *The Eighties: America in the Age of Reagan* (New Haven: Yale University Press, 2005), 96.

42. *Ibid.*, 97.

43. *Ibid.*, 121.

44. Merriam-Webster Online Dictionary, 11th ed., s.v. "product placement."

45. Jay Newell, Charles T. Salmon, and Susan Chang, "The Hidden History of Product Placement," *Journal of Broadcasting & Electronic Media*, 50.4 (December 2006): 575–594.

46. Product Database — Craig's OUTATIME Back to the Future Website, http://www.bttf.20m.com/database.htm

47. Ehrman, *The Eighties*, 144.

48. *Ibid.*

49. William Butler Yeats, "The Second Coming," *The Norton Anthology of Poetry*, 3d ed., eds. Alexander W. Allison, Herbert Barrows, Caesar R. Blake, Arthur J. Carr, Arthur M. Eastman, and Hubert M. English,

Jr. (New York and London: W.W. Norton, 1983), 520.

50. *Back to the Future,* DVD, directed by Robert Zemeckis (1985; Los Angeles, CA: Amblin Entertainment / Universal Pictures, 1985).

51. Danny Hakim, "John Z. DeLorean, Father of Glamour Car, Dies at 80," *The New York Times,* March 21, 2005, http://www.nytimes.com/2005/03/21/business/21delorean.html?pagewanted=1&_r=2&oref=slogin.

Works Cited

Back to the Future. Dir. Robert Zemeckis. California, USA: Universal Pictures, 1985.

Back to the Future II. Dir. Robert Zemeckis. California, USA: Universal Pictures, 1989.

Back to the Future III. Dir. Robert Zemeckis. California, USA: Universal Pictures, 1990.

Bovard, James. *Terrorism Debacles in the Reagan Administration,* http://www.fff.org/freedom/fd0406c.asp.

Cattle Queen of Montana. Dir. Allan Dwan. Montana and California, USA: Filmcrest Productions, 1954.

The Cosby Show. Created by Bill Cosby. California, Georgia, and New York, USA: NBC, 1984.

Dallas. Created by David Jacobs. California and Texas, USA: Lorimar Television, 1978.

The David Letterman Show. Dir. Bruce Burmester and Hal Gurnee. New York, USA: NBC, 1980.

Diggins, John Patrick. *Ronald Reagan: Fate, Freedom, and the Making of History.* New York: W.W. Norton, 2007.

Ehrman, John. *The Eighties: America in the Age of Reagan.* New Haven: Yale University Press, 2005.

Family Ties. Created by Gary David Goldberg. California, USA: Paramount Television, 1982.

Forrest Gump. Dir. Robert Zemeckis. California, South Carolina, North Carolina, Montana, etc., USA: Paramount Pictures, 1994.

Goodheart, Lawrence B. "*Forrest Gump* and the Myth of American Innocence," *Journal of American Studies of Turkey,* 2 (1995) http://www.bilkent.edu.tr/~jast/Number2/Goodheart.html.

Gordon, Andrew. "Back to the Future: Œdipus as Time Traveler," *Science Fiction Studies,* 14, 1987. pp. 372–385.

Hakim, Danny. "John Z. DeLorean, Father of Glamour Car, Dies at 80," *The New York Times,* March 21, 2005, http://www.nytimes.com/2005/03/21/business/21delorean.html?pagewanted=1&_r=2&oref=slogin.

Heclo, Hugh. "Ronald Reagan and the American Public Philosophy" in *The Reagan Presidency: Pragmatic Conservatism & Its Legacies,* eds. W. Elliot Brownlee & Hugh Davis Graham. Lawrence: University of Kansas Press, 2003.

The Honeymooners. New York, USA: Jackie Gleason Enterprises, 1955.

Knute Rockne All American. Dir. Lloyd Bacon. Indiana, USA: Warner Brothers Pictures, 1940.

Leopold, Todd. "Analysis: The Age of Reagan," *CNN.com,* June 16, 2004, http://www.cnn.com/2004/SHOWBIZ/06/16/reagan.80s/index.html.

Miami Vice. Created by Anthony Yerkovich. Illinois, Florida, California, etc., USA: Universal TV, 1984.

Murder on the Orient Express. Dir. Sidney Lumet. England, France, Turkey: EMI Films, 1974.

Newell, Jay, Charles T. Salmon, and Susan Chang. "The Hidden History of Product Placement," *Journal of Broadcasting & Electronic Media,* 50.4. December 2006.

Orwell, George. Quoteland.com, http://www.quoteland.com/author.asp?AUTHOR_ID=190.

Rambo: First Blood. Dir. Ted Kotcheff. British Columbia, Canada: Elcajo Productions, 1982.

Reagan, Ronald. *Address Before a Joint Session of Congress on the State of the Union,* http://www.presidency.ucsb.edu/ws/index.php?pid=36646.

Richardson, Elizabeth A., "Back to the Future: Yang-Yin=0, Yang+Yin+1," *Extrapolation,* 29 (1988).

Ridings Jr., William J., and Stuart B. McGiver. *Rating the Presidents: A Ranking of U.S. Leaders, From the Great and Honorable to the Dishonest and Incompetent.* Secaucus, NJ: Carol Publishing Group, 1997.

Ruud, Jay. "Back to the Future as Quintessential Comedy," *Literature Film Quarterly,* 19 (1991).

Shaheen, Jack G. "Hollywood's Muslim Arabs" in *A Community of Many Worlds: Arab Amer-*

icans in New York City, eds. Kathleen Benson and Philip M. Kayal. New York: Museum of the City of New York; Syracuse: Syracuse University Press, 2002.

Shales, Tom. "The Re Decade," *Esquire*, March, 1986.

Star Wars. Dir. George Lucas. Guatemala, Tunisia, England, California, etc.: Twentieth Century–Fox Film Corporation, 1977.

Stengel, Richard. "Back to the Future, Again," *Time*, February 17, 1986 http://www.time.com/time/magazine/article/0,9171,960654-3,00.html.

Tarantula. Dir. Jack Arnold. California: Universal International Pictures, 1955.

Wagner, Heather Lehr. *Great American Presi-*dents — *Ronald Reagan*. Philadelphia: Chelsea House Publishers, 2004.

Winterberg, Friedwardt. *Abstract: T9.00004 : Albert Einstein and Wernher von Braun — the two great German-American physicists seen in a historical perspective*, http://meetings.aps.org/Meeting/APR08/Event/83897.

Yager, Edward M. *Ronald Reagan's Journey: Democrat to Republican*. Lanham, MD: Rowman & Littlefield, 2006.

Yeats, William Butler. "The Second Coming," *The Norton Anthology of Poetry*, 3d ed. Eds. Alexander W. Allison, Herbert Barrows, Caesar R. Blake, Arthur J. Carr, Arthur M. Eastman, and Hubert M. English, Jr. New York and London: W.W. Norton, 1983.

10. "This is what makes time-travel possible": The Generation(s) of Revolutionary Master Signifiers in *Back to the Future*

MICHAEL WILLIAMS

This article deploys the French psychoanalyst Jacques Lacan's work on the modalities of discourse in order to explain the meta-theme of *Back to the Future* (Robert Zemeckis, 1985). In brief, the meta-theme of the film is the failed generation of what Lacan calls the "master signifier" in the lineage of the McFly family. For Lacan the master signifier — like any signifier — is that which represents a subject to another signifier.[1] However, in the case of the master signifier this mark represents the crystallization of the identity of the subject in question — the specific desire, idiosyncratic sensibility, and peculiar aesthetic of the subject (whether an individual person or a generational cohort). As Lacan says: "It says that it is at the very instant at which S_1 intervenes in the already constituted field of the other signifiers, insofar as they are already articulated with one another as such, that, by intervening in another system, this \$, which I have called the subject as divided, emerges."[2] Lacan's point is that the subject — as alienated, as divided, as lacking, as desirous — comes into being as the master signifier. The generation of the master signifier for each subject is a project that not only secures the identity of the subject in question (the specific desire, idiosyncratic sensibility, peculiar aesthetic) but also guarantees the continuity of the generations in time. Lacan's point is that there must be a dominant master signifier of the elder generation (the S_1) that, from the perspective of the younger generation, appears antiquated (the S_2). In the tussle between the generations the S_1 (or S_2) succumbs to reinvention by the next generation. The succession of the generations, then, is a continuity of displacement of master signifiers that represent the subject (whether an individual person or a generational cohort) to another signifier.

Lacan explains the necessary conditions for the generation of the master signifier — of the displacement of master signifiers between the generations — in terms of the four discourses as theorized in his *Seminar XVII* (1969–1970). The four discourses that Lacan outlines are the discourse of the master, the discourse of the university, the discourse of the hysteric, and the discourse of the analyst.[3] To briefly explicate the four modalities of discourse: the master's discourse articulates from the position of the master signifier (the S_1) in relation to the antiquated knowledge (the S_2) in the production of enjoyment (a — or the object of desire) and the repression of the split in the subject ($); the discourse of the university articulates from the position of the antiquated knowledge (the S_2) in relation to enjoyment (a) in the production of the hysterical subject ($) and the repression of the master signifier (the S_1); the hysteric's discourse articulates from the position of the split subject ($) in relation to the master signifier (the S_1) in the production of the antiquated knowledge (the S_2) and the repression of enjoyment (a); and the analyst's discourse articulates from the position of enjoyment (a) in relation to the hysteric in ($) in the production of the master signifier (the S_1) and the repression of the antiquated knowledge (the S_2).

In concrete terms, the dominance of the discourse of the master produces an enjoyable resistance among the repressed hysterics — a rebellion that is a prerequisite for the production of the new master signifier of the subject in question (whether an individual person or a generational cohort). The reign of the university discourse entails the predominance of conventional wisdom and produces a hysterical subject alienated from his master signifier — a situation that both conditions and obstructs the generation of the master signifier, of the production of any new knowledge. As Lacan puts it: "What leads to knowledge is — allow me to justify this in the more or less long term — the hysteric's discourse."[4] The hysteric's discourse engages the master signifier and produces a canonical body of knowledge in the repression of enjoyment — a effluvium of creativity that invents a university discourse unto itself (for example, the engagement between Freud and the hysterics produced the twenty-four volumes of the science of psychoanalysis, an S1 at the time, perhaps an S2 today). Lacan intimates this knowledge that is produced on the side of the analyst in relation to the discourse of the hysteric: "That one, the second on the blackboard, is the hysteric's discourse. It's not obvious straightaway, but I will explain it to you."[5] Lacan as analyst will "explain" — or: publish — the knowledge that he (and Freud) gathered in their engagements with the discourse of the hysteric. Lacan cogently articulates this productive relationship between analyst and hysteric: "Freud extracted its master signifiers from the hysteric's desire."[6] Finally, the analyst's discourse engages the hysteric in the production of the new master signifier and represses the antiquated knowledge of the canon — a project that displaces the old (the S2) with the new (the S1). Lacan describes the function: The analyst says to whoever is about to begin — 'Away you go, say whatever, it will be marvelous.'"[7]

The generation(s) of the master signifiers is the key to the development of the subject — how is such generation possible in the Lacanian schema? How must the four discourses be manipulated in order to produce the master signifier for the subject in question — whether an individual person or a generational cohort? In brief, what is required is the convergence of two discursive functions: the function of the discourse of the master and the function of the discourse of the analyst. The master provokes enjoyable resistance (such as the student's rebellion against his parents and teachers) and the analyst provokes the master signifier (such as the student's clandestine slam poetry or secret punk band). Not only is this convergence of master and analytic discourses necessary in the enjoyable production of the identity of the subject in question (individual person or generational cohort) but the very life of the next generation (the S_1 of the younger generation) requires the antiquated knowledge (the S_2 — the former master signifier, the former S_1) of the elder generation. This is the reason that the seemingly conservative master's discourse (the agent of the master signifier) and the university discourse (the agent of the canon of knowledge) are fundamentally constitutive of the seemingly radical hysteric's discourse (the agent of the split subject) and the analyst's discourse (the agent of enjoyment). The kids can only rebel — and invent the future — in the presence of the tradition. In the absence of the tradition — what Lacan would call the university discourse — the convergence of enjoyable resistance (aroused by the authority of the master) and the production of the master signifier (instigated by the silence of the analyst) ceases to transpire. The effect of such a bungled transmission of tradition — of the convergence of enjoyable resistance and the generation of the new master signifier in the displacement of the S_2 by the S_1 — is nothing less than suspended history. The failure of the elder generation's master signifier obstructs the production of the younger generation's master signifier. In the absence of the generation of the master signifier the generations themselves cease to reproduce.

"I'm just not very good with confrontations": The Aura of Paternal Failure

What does the master signifier — its generation, displacement, and reinvention — have to do with *Back to the Future*? It is my contention that the meta-theme of the film — failed paternity in the figure of a hapless George McFly — underscores the fundamentality of the master signifier — its generation, displacement, and reinvention — in the success of the subject in question (individual person or generational cohort) and the continuity of history in time. The master signifier cannot be produced in the absence of the hystericization of the subject's desire. This is the purpose of the master: "What the hysteric wants," Lacan says, "is a master."[8] Lacan continues: "This is absolutely clear — so much so that you have to wonder whether this isn't where the invention of the master began."[9] The subject must be hystericized — desirous of an object from which he is split — in order to properly produce the master signifier. A hysteric (in consultation with an analyst) without a desire — however inchoate, undecided, and unformed — is no hysteric at all. It is the silent work of the analyst to elicit the master signifier in the place of the hysteric's rants and raves. The trouble with George McFly — and so for his family, Marty included — is that his desire remains latent, repressed, and veiled: George's desire is not yet hystericized to the point at which the enjoyable resistance of the hysteric is analytically channeled into the production of the new master signifier. The repression of the master signifier — its latent and not manifest form — in George's psyche is visible in the scene in the school cafeteria in 1955 when George refuses to let Marty read his latent master signifier: "stories, science fiction stories." His reason for refusing to share his creativity (his master signifier, his S_1) is the same as his son's wariness to send the demo tape of his band (his master signifier, his S_1) to the record label: "I just don't think I could take that kind of a rejection." In the absence of a master that will hystericize the desire of either George or Marty — either father or son — the production of the identity (specific desire, idiosyncratic sensibility, peculiar aesthetic) of the subject in question remains latent, repressed, veiled, and finally unfulfilled. The analyst cannot perform his silent magic without the rabble-rousing of the master's discourse. As Lacan articulates: "this master's discourse has only one counterpoint, the analytic discourse, which is still so inappropriate."[10] Lacan continues: "the psychoanalytic discourse is quite precisely located at the opposite pole from the master's discourse."[11]

The Oedipus complex conditions the possibility of the proper hystericization of desire — and it is no coincidence that the climax of the film involves an Oedipal scenario between mother and son in the parked car outside of the Enchantment Under the Sea dance. The McFly men are not properly Oedipalized — the importance of which is to stave off the risk of psychosis across the social body. As Lacan writes in his *Seminar III* (1955–1956): "in order for there to be reality, adequate access to reality, in order for the sense of reality to be a reliable guide, in order for reality not to be what it is in psychosis, the Oedipus complex has to have been lived through."[12] George and Marty have not "lived through" the Oedipus complex — the hystericization of their desire by which they experience and internalize lack as the condition of desire itself. What is the effect of such botched Oedipalization? Ultimately, the effect is the aporetic structure of failed paternal authority that saturates the McFly household. In the terms of Lacan's vernacular, we would say that the paternal metaphor — the substitution of the father's law for the mother's desire — has failed.[13] In such a situation the risk of psychosis is great, and, more pressingly, the failure of the generation(s) — of both the creation of the master signifier and the production of the next generation — portends the collapse of the identity of the subject in question.

"Hey Dad, George — hey, you on the bike!": From Father/Son to Brother/Brother

The plot of the film reproduces the infantile Oedipus complex within a teenage context. The film re-contextualizes the infantile Oedipus complex in high school. The plot repositions the players in the complex (George, the father, Lorraine, the mother, Marty, the son) as friendly members of the same cohort, of the same generation. The brilliant horror of the time-travel genre consists of this displacement of the generational differences and hierarchies that otherwise mark the distinction between parents and children. The ideal reader of the psychoanalytic text is the child even if the actual reader of such work is the adult. The trouble that Marty and George encounter as they attempt to (re)unite George and Lorraine is that son and father find themselves in competition, from Lorraine's perspective, for the same woman, the mother, as in the original scene of the Oedipus complex itself. Rather than desirous Oedipalized subject the film depicts Marty as desired not-yet Oedipalized object of his mother's desire. The trick of the flick is the displacement of Lorraine's desire from the improper object, Marty, to the proper object, George. The crucial point, however, is that George must be adorned with the phallic signifier (the signifier of desirability) in order to garner Lorraine's desire — and such an adornment, such phallicization in the production of the master signifier, is only possible in the event of the *hystericization* (provocation of desire) and the *analysis* (solicitation of the master signifier) of George. The two processes — the hystericization by way of the master's discourse and analysis by way of the analyst's discourse — are constitutive: "the analytic practice is, properly speaking, initiated by this master's discourse."[14] What George needs is a master and an analyst — and, unfortunately for both him and Marty, he has neither.

The disruption of the generational differences in the teenage Oedipus complex makes possible the revolutionary couplet: namely, that father and son play on the same team as brothers. It is this disruption of the generations that, paradoxically, makes possible the hystericization and analysis — and phallicization — of George as object of Lorraine's desire. Rather than a rivalry for the mother, the father and the son, George and Marty, seek to defend the father (and the family, by synecdoche) from the threat of castration in the figure of the murderous, desirous, jealous child: namely, Biff. The time-travel genre conditions the transformation of the father/son relationship into a brother/brother relationship — a shift in the power dynamics that renders them, George and Marty, teammates rather than rivals. Indeed: Marty's interventions in 1955 during the week between the red letter day in science and the night of the Enchantment Under the Sea dance strive to (re)unite the two lovers, despite the inconvenience that Marty's interference renders him, rather than George, the object of Lorraine's desire. The latent truth of the Oedipus complex is revealed in this exchange of roles from father/son to brother/brother: that the friendly brothers, unlike the querulous pair of father and son, agree to suspend the rivalry in order to preserve the family, the social unit. As Freud theorizes the suspension of primal violence in his *Totem and Taboo* (1913): "The patriarchal horde was replaced in the first instance by the fraternal clan, whose existence was assured by the blood tie."[15]

Marty's return to the past introduces the accidental possibility that the coordinates of his family's life — namely, the success of paternity — could be reconfigured and readjusted such that, to invoke Doc's words: "everything will be fine." The intervention of Doc's time-machine introduces the possibility of the radical "passage of the act" — the reconfiguration of the coordinates that define the situation, the historical archive, the dominant university discourse that utters the reality of castration: "No McFly has ever amounted to anything in the history of Hill Valley." Marty's rejoinder to Strickland's barb foreshadows the vehicle, the instrument, of the reconfiguration of the historical archive: the DeLorean, the flux capacitor, and something with a bit more kick — plutonium! The coordinates of the social order that require reconfiguration are the signs of paternal failure that I have outlined: the aura of potential rejection — "I just don't think I could take that kind of a rejection" — that animates both George's and Marty's relationship to their own emergent master signifiers: in George's case, the science fiction stories, and in Marty's case, the punk band "The Pinheads." Marty cannot act — produce his master signifier in full confidence — until his father reclaims paternal authority through the production of his own master signifier, the science fiction stories that embody the confidence required to confront a bully like Biff. These two factors — the production of the master signifier embodied in

George's first novel and the playfully stern riposte to his former rival: "Now, Biff, don't con me"—animate the conclusion of the film, as a testament to the successful reconfiguration of the coordinates of Hill Valley that Marty's haphazard—if serendipitous—interventions in 1955 produce.

"What's a rerun?":
The Original Ritual Gone Awry

Marty's initial attempt to reassemble his family's existence consists of both a regression and a progression: although Marty usurps his father's position—"he hit *me* with the car"—he also obstructs the attribution of the flaccid—almost pansy—phallic mark that animates Lorraine's initial ambivalent desire for George: "He seemed so helpless, like a little lost puppy, and my heart just went out to him." The philosopher Slavoj Zizek explains the presence of the absence of the phallic attribution: "This signifier—Lacan calls it the 'empty signifier'—is the signifier of symbolic castration: a signifier whose very *presence* marks the constitutive *absence* of the feature in question."[16] Linda, Lorraine's daughter, adds the supplement to the mother's explanation: "Yeah, mom, you've told us this story a thousand times, you felt sorry for him..."— what Doc refers to as the "Florence Nightingale effect." In this exchange— of Marty for George, of Lorraine's (future) son for her (future) husband—the original ritual, that of the little lost puppy's being struck by the father's automobile, that of the fantasy as the scene of desire (and, as it is for George and Lorraine, ambivalent desire, a desire animated by pity, the worst of human traits according to Nietzsche), the original ritual goes awry. Marty's first attempt at a retroactive initiation of paternal success for the McFly clan positions the son, Marty, rather than the father, George, as the object of Lorraine's desire—but a desire animated by a vibrant sexuality ("that is your name, isn't it, Calvin Klein?—it's written all over your underwear") rather than an ambivalent regret. Although the substitution of Marty for George activates Lorraine's vibrant sexuality, it also sustains, unbeknownst to either her or her son, the effect of mommy-gator that suffocates the identities and desires of both Marty and George. As Lacan says: "A huge crocodile in whose jaws you are—that's the mother."[17] As the son, Marty, says to his mother, Lorraine, back in good old 1955: "where are my pants?" Mother to son: "Over there— on my hope chest."

The ritual undone—and gone awry—invites Marty as cohort (brother, lover, other) to not only reposition the two destined lovers, George and Lorraine, in a truly desirous rather than regrettably pitiable amorous economy but also to displace Biff, the subject whose prowess as the bully of Hill Valley high school and as the supervisor at George's office renders him a phallic rival for authority in the McFly household. One of the conditions that makes it possible for George to assume phallic authority and to protect his family from the tyranny of Biff in the alternative 1985 (the trajectory after Marty's hap-hazard — if serendipitous — interventions in the original 1955) is that the desire of Lorraine (as future mother) in 1955 — her orientation, attitude, and approach toward Biff, that is to say, her speech in relation to the authority of George (as future father) — is steadfast and clear: she wants nothing to do with Biff, as she says of his sexual advances in the school cafeteria in 1955: "Get your meat-hooks off of me!" Even if George, busy transcribing his science fiction stories during lunch in the cafeteria, misses Lorraine's rebuff to Biff, Marty listens to the words and, in recognition of both his own desire (to redo the ritual gone awry at the Baines' residence by way of the future kiss between these two Earth Angels at the Enchantment Under the Sea dance) and his mother's desire (to be rid of Biff), confronts Biff twice: once in the cafeteria, interrupted by Strickland, and again in Lou's Diner, when he lands the punch by unfortunately upstaging his father, George, in his memorable line: "Yes, yes, I'm George, George McFly, I am your density, I mean, your destiny." Despite George's best — if awkward — efforts, Lorraine finds herself enthralled by Marty, Calvin Klein, who she deems: "Isn't he a dream-boat?"

Despite the disjointed second-order narrative that Lorraine and George offer of their original meeting — "it was the night of that terrible thunderstorm, remember George?" — the spectator of their relationship circa the original 1985 must wonder: what transpired to submit George to such intense subju-gation? — to the pathetic if adorable father of a restless clan? Lorraine's plaint to Marty that a "man should be strong, so he can stand up for himself and protect the woman he loves" bespeaks the second-move of a double-gesture that comprises the revolutionary "passage of the act" if not in psychoanalysis then at least in the power of love. The first move in this passage is the hys-tericization of desire — that the subject lacks, that an object beyond the sub-ject may fill the hole in this lack, in this case Lorraine — the master's production of George's hysterical desire; the second move consists of the active defense of this love, the literal knock-out of Biff, as in the scene of the date-rape in the parking lot outside of the high school on the night of the rhyth-mic ceremonial ritual — the analyst's solicitation of George's master signifier. What we can gather, then, of the original 1955 is that George performed his passive desire for Lorraine ("the Florence Nightingale effect" — Lorraine's father hits the peeping-tom George with the car) without the revolutionary "pas-sage of the act" (the knock-out of Biff — George hits Biff with his fist) that would reconfigure the coordinates not simply of the love between George and Lorraine but also of the entire town of Hill Valley. As a chick at the dance yells to George after he knocks-out Biff: "Have you thought about running for class president?" This interval between the hystericization of his desire (George as peeping-tom of Lorraine before being knocked-out by her father's car) and the defense of that love in the analytical production of his master signifier (George as a man who knocks-out Biff) — what we may term, following *Huey Lewis and the News*, the power of love — marks the transition from George as hapless loser to George as the author of *A Match Made in Space* — his first novel that Biff in the alternative 1985, cloaked in the sweat-suit of a simpering slug, rushes into the house as he interrupts putting on the second — nay, first — coat of wax on the BMW. The power of love, then, consists of two necessary moves: the hystericization of desire and the invention of the new master signifier. The power of love is nothing less than the movement of history. As Lacan puts it: "And the master subsequently appears only as the instrument, the magnificent Cuckold of history."[18]

Doc and the McFly men share subjugation to the dominant discourse of Hill Valley — what Lacan calls the discourse of the university. The university discourse, as Lacan theorizes, produces hysterics — it works to hystericize, that is to say, manifest, the desires of the divided subjects who remain alienated from their objects of desire. It is this object — the master signifier that will establish and consolidate the identity-desire of the subject in question — that interests the analyst. As Lacan writes: "everything that interests us analysts as knowledge originates in the unary trait" — in the master signifier.[19] Marty's encounter with Principal Strickland and Huey Lewis — the speakers of the university discourse in Hill Valley — activate Marty's desire. The university discourse prepares the divided subject for an encounter with the master whose canonical master signifier (the S_2) produces the pleasurable and enjoyable resistance of the next generation of a new master signifier (the S_1) in consultation with the analyst. The hystericization of Marty's desire requires the engagement with the master — of the S_2 that provides the antiquated master signifier (for Marty, his father's science fiction stories — which have yet to manifest!) as an anchor for his new master signifier (for Marty, the punk band, "The Pinheads" — whose demo tape may or may not be sent to the record label). The paternal failure manifests most acutely at this juncture. George's failed power of love — his unconsummated hystericization and postponed analysis — makes it impossible for him to provide an S_2 (the antiquated master signifier, the science fiction stories — which have yet to manifest!) for his son to reconfigure — like father, like son: "I just don't think I could take that kind of rejection." In the absence of the S_2 Marty can neither successfully hystericize his desire with a master nor confidently produce his own master signifier in analysis. Like his father, George, Marty as slave, as student, as son, needs — but lacks — the master, the teacher, and the father. This absent legacy disturbs the hystericization of Marty's desire and the invention of his master signifier.

The hystericization of desire is properly *historical, generational,* and *paternal*— it is only by way of a fluxed-out time-machine that desire can be hystericized from within the stasis of the cohort. The father is absolutely fundamental to the development of the future master signifiers that comprise the continuity of history. Indeed, the father, for Lacan, is the source of invention and innovation: "This implies that in the word 'father' there is something that is always in fact potentially creating."[20] Even if Marty's desire finds hystericization by the university discourse of Hill Valley (best spoken in the critical words of Principal Strickland and a disguised Huey Lewis), Marty's identity cannot succeed — the invention of his master signifier cannot flourish — in the absence of the hystericization and analysis of his father, George. The father's own desire conditions the possibility of the son's "passage of the act" in the creation of the new master signifier that reorganizes the coordinates of the dominant symbolic order. This explains the purpose of Marty's haphazard mission in 1955: to hystericize George's desire (as master) in order to analyze him in the production of his master signifier (as analyst); this double task — the condition of the power of love — should (re)unite his parents and (re)condition his very existence. Marty's intervention must analytically solicit George's master signifier — his phallic attribute — that would animate Lorraine's vibrant sexuality beyond mere pity and regret ("the Florence Nightingale effect") and toward torrid desire and passion. In brief, Marty's adventures in 1955 seek to make possible his own Oedipalization.

"Give me a milk — chocolate": The Original Ritual Gone Aright

The shenanigans in 1955, then, must succeed in the hystericization and analysis of George's desire — and, as a significant effect, the invention of his son's own identity. The scene that depicts the hystericization of George's desire (already slightly manifest by Lorraine's natural beauty) is the sequence in which Marty dons Doc's hazardous waste facemask and poses as Darth Vader to the sounds of Van Halen. The next morning George finds Marty to seek his advice in asking Lorraine to the Enchantment Under the Sea dance because, in his words, "Darth Vader came down from the planet Vulcan and told me that if I didn't ask Lorraine out to the dance that he would melt my brain." The immediate hystericization of George's desire is performed by his own son — albeit in the guise of an other-worldly alien who threatens his father with death if he fails to perform his proper duty.

The second-move of the power of love after the hystericization of his desire is the invention of the master signifier — the phallic attribute — that will garner Lorraine's desire. After performing the role of master to his own father Marty must transition to the role of analyst — to the role of directing his father's rebellious hysteria into the invention of a proper master signifier (one of which remains visible but latent in 1955: the science fiction stories). The talented analyst's trick is to let this master signifier speak: to allow it the time and the space to manifest itself in all its glorious invention. As Lacan says of the analyst's role: "If the analyst doesn't speak, what might become of this swarming production of S_1's? Many things, surely."[21] However, rather than refrain from speech Marty as zealous analyst offers his father, George, a pick-up line: "I am your destiny" — a line that George himself finally botches on delivery to Lorraine. As analyst Marty overreaches in his solicitation of the master signifier of George as hysteric. The proper work of the analyst must transpire more subtly and silently. As Lacan memorably describes the work of the analyst: "The question is to put oneself in a position where there is someone whom you have taken charge of with respect to his anxiety, who wishes to come and hold the same position that you occupy, or that you do not occupy, or that you barely occupy, who wishes to come to know how you occupy it, and how you do not occupy it, and why you occupy it, and why you do not occupy it."[22] Despite their conjoined and collective effort — that father and son, George and Marty, play for the same team as brothers rather than as Oedipal rivals — the pair of analyst (Marty) and hysteric (George) fail to invent the father's proper phallic attribute. The time-travel genre has certainly reversed the roles of analyst and hysteric, for the film positions the son as the (failed) analyst to his father as (unanalyzed) hysteric.

If Marty's sloppy analytical endeavors to solicit George's master signifier fail, then the reason is clear: George's desire awaits analysis not by Marty nor by Lorraine — but by the sadistic cruelty of the bully of Hill Valley: namely, Biff. As an overzealous analyst who strives to artificially orchestrate rather than spontaneously elicit the master signifier from George as analysand Marty concocts a date-rape scenario in which George will interrupt Marty's unwanted sexual advances toward Lorraine and save her chastity for George as future husband. In the actual scene the misplacement of Biff for Marty — the exchange of the Oedipal rival, Biff, for the analyst, Marty — allows George to activate and manifest his identity-desire in the manifestation of the master signifier. If the tangible form of George's master signifier is his future text, *A Match Made in Space,* then the auratic form of this master signifier is the majestic knock-out of Biff on the night of the Enchantment Under the Sea dance.

The proper scene of (psycho) analysis in the film transpires in the parked car. The exchange of Biff for Marty — of the bully for the dream-boat — substitutes two characters for the single position of the analyst of George, namely, the position that will evoke the master signifier in the place of George McFly as hysteric. It is the simple — if often botched — function of the analyst to provoke the appropriate response from the analysand — to produce the organic master signifier that defines the identity and desire of the subject in question. If it were Marty in the car with Lorraine, then the historical knock-out of Biff — the revolutionary "passage of the act" that reconfigures the coordinates of the symbolic order of Hill Valley — would never transpire. This absence in the historical archive would preserve the dominant university discourse ("No McFly has ever amounted to anything in the history of Hill Valley") and assure the continued subjugation of the McFly clan. This necessity — that Biff be positioned in the right place at the right time in order to solicit the proper hysterical action from George and the appropriate reaction from Lorraine — demonstrates that the truly historical "passage of the act" does not consist of a mere transferential displacement to any fictional representative of the hysteric's historical past, such as an anonymous analyst. Rather, the truly historical "passage of the act" requires that the manifestation of the desire be directed — like the energy of the 1.21 gigawatts of electricity that Doc will "channel into the flux capacitor" — at the real person from the hysteric's historical present. The truly revolutionary "passage of the act" in psychoanalysis requires that the analysand assume his hysterical identity-desire (master signifier) not in relation to a substitute in a mock transference with an analyst; rather, the reconfiguration of the coordinates of the symbolic order require that the libidinal energy, like the lightning bolt that strikes the clock tower at 10:04 P.M., be channeled at the precise locus of the subject in question.[23] It is either "destiny" or "density" — or a bit of both, for sure — that Biff, the right man, is in the right place, at the right time, for the knock-out that provokes, in the second gesture of the power of love, the reconfiguration of the coordinates of the symbolic order of Hill Valley.

The hystericization of George's desire in the provocation of enthusiastic energy (by way of Darth Vader and the planet Vulcan) and the analysis of George's desire in the invention of the master signifier (by way of knocking-out Biff) conditions Marty's assumption of his own identity and desire in the form of a master signifier. Like his father before him — or at the same time as him, given the time-travel genre — there are two necessary and constitutive positions that a potentially hysterical Marty must confront in the assumption of his Oedipal identity and desire: the master's discourse and the analyst's discourse. Whereas in the normal domestic routine the father would articulate the master's discourse, the S_2 to be displaced by the son's S_1, in the McFly household, the S_2 is absent from the person of the father, George. In order for the coordinates of the McFly family to be reconfigured — like a truly historical "passage of the act" in psychoanalysis — a master must produce the enjoyable resistance and revolutionary abandon in the subject whose engagement, as an hysteric, with an analyst, produces the new master signifier. The criticisms of Principal Strickland and a veiled Huey Lewis perform a nascent hystericization of Marty's desire. However, Marty's emergent hysteria is suffocated by the mother's omnivorous desire that threatens to overwhelm him.[24] Marty's master — the force that hystericizes his desire — is fundamentally existential, the situation in which he finds himself: namely, at the crossroads of his own potential death. It is the bizarre time-travel situation in which he must (re)unite his parents that finally hystericizes Marty's desire — and to forge his own master signifier that detaches himself from the Oedipal triangle with his parents.

If Marty's desire is hystericized by the existential situation, then what accounts for the analysis of his desire, the channeling of his desire into the invention of his master signifier? This force of analysis — the source of the provocation of the master signifier — is nothing less than destiny and density — and Doc's apparatus that sends Marty "back — to the future!" in order to save his family from the fate of middle-class dreariness. The effect of this hystericization and analysis — if not the cause — manifests during his showboat (if lip-synched) performance of "Johnny B. Goode" at the Enchantment Under the Sea dance. This performance marks the passage from a nascent identity and emergent desire — suffocated by the psychotic dysfunction of a failed paternity ("the Florence Nightingale effect") by way of an Oedipal rival, Biff, and an indifferent mother, Lorraine — to a rocked-out identity and vocalized desire unleashed on the stage at the dance. This passage is only possible once the (re)union of Marty's parents is consummated, on the dance floor, with the kiss of the two destined Earth Angels. The successful assumption of Marty's identity as rock-star (even if the blues riff in B is stolen from Chuck Berry) requires that the phallic attribute be properly positioned: namely anchored, as an S_2 for Marty, on the person of George, his father. It is destiny and density that makes possible the emergence of Marty's master signifier, the rocked-out rendition of "Johnny B. Goode" (itself an antiquated S_2 from Chuck Berry). As he plays his electric guitar not only are his parents and siblings rescued from historical obliteration but his master signifier sings.

"When this baby hits 88 MPH you're going to see some serious shit": Doc(s) as the Perverse Masterly Analysts

However, to turn to a crucial question: how has the destiny and density of this fortuitous arrangement been achieved? Who is the masterly analyst who elicits Marty's successful adventures in 1955? In brief: Doc, as the perverse masterly analyst — the role that seeks to reconfigure the proper players in the appropriate positions. Insofar as Doc performs the duties of the master he does not desire to know; indeed, he desires that the system work. As Lacan says, "A real master, as in general we used to see until a recent era, and this is seen less and less, doesn't desire to know anything at all — he desires that things work."[25] Who can forget Doc's gleeful bellow — "It works! I've finally invented something that *works!*" — when Marty shows Doc the time-machine hidden behind the billboard for the future Lyon Estates? Moreover, Doc's desire as analyst is to entice the analysand to discover his desire — his master signifier — such that he becomes a subject of desire in the social economy of lack. Doc's position, like the flux capacitor, fluctuates between two poles: first, that of the position of the master who provokes enjoyable resistance to the status quo (hystericizes the desire of the subject in question); and second, that of the analyst who inspires the hysteric's own master signifier (Oedipalizes the subject in question). Doc's delicate dance between the position of the master and the position of the analyst — amidst the context of the university discourse, the historical archive of Hill Valley — masquerades Doc's true position: as masterly analyst of perversity. As such, Doc enjoins the masterly provocation of rebellious energy with the analytical invention of the new master signifier within the field of enjoyment. Lacan hopes that the slaves, the students, and the hysterics "will be captivated by the revelation of this truth that they are the ones who make history, and that the master is only there to get the show on the road."[26] The perverse masterly analyst makes this historical movement possible — and enjoyable at the same time. The pervert, after all, is the figure who seeks the greatest pleasure imaginable. The time-machine is this masterly analyst's mechanism — a device that invites Marty to perform the impossible: to rewrite the historical narrative of the McFly family, to reconfigure the empirical archive of Hill Valley, to redo the infantile Oedipus complex, and to redress the (re)union of the two lovers — and to return home safely to an alternative 1985. If Marty and George are ultimately amiable brothers rather than rivalrous father and son, then Doc figures as an outside friend, as well, one whose invention, the time-machine, makes possible the triumph over the traumas and the rituals that we, as brothers and sisters, members of the same cohort, never quite get over: namely, the high school experience in all its full alma mater regalia.

My analysis of the film applies to the economy of political revolution, as well. A comparison of the two great scientists of the twentieth century — Sigmund and Emmett — demonstrates the revolutionary potential of perversity: namely, of the enjoinment of the discourse of the master and the discourse of the analyst. Doc as the inventor of time-travel mirrors Freud's own role as the inventor of the nascent science of psychoanalysis. Doc provokes the resistance of his detractors (Principal Strickland, for one) and conditions the possibility of the master signifiers of both George and Marty with his invention of the time-machine. Freud, too, performs the role of the perverted masterly analyst — as the masterful initiator of the enjoyable resistance of the dissenters of psychoanalysis, such as the shocked Victorians who refused to accept the sexuality of precocious children (known as a form of repression by Freud), and as the analytic solicitor of the master signifiers (the rants and raves of the hysterics). As Lacan describes, this productive relationship between analyst and hysteric; "The analyst who listens is able to record many things. With what your average person today can state, if he pays no attention to anything, one can compile the equivalent of a small encyclopedia."[27] However, absent from the compilation of this "small encyclopedia" is the factor of *enjoyment—* that which the master provokes — as the seeds of the rebellious invention of the little red book of the subject in question (whether an individual person or a generational cohort). This is the reason that analysis must mime mastery: the effect of the discourse of the master is the effluvium of revolutionary abandon, the very scene of the production of the master signifiers of an alternative society of enjoyment. This movement (of history, of invention, of hysteria, of master signifiers) is infinite, for whereas the analyst's discourse produces the master signifier in the place of the hysteric — the nascent identity and emergent desire that defines the hysteric's subjectivity — the hysteric's discourse produces the canonical body of knowledge in the place of the analyst — the twenty-four volumes that comprise the playbook of the psychoanalytic corpus. As Lacan puts it: "It's on his [the analyst's] side that there is S_2, that there is knowledge."[28] The antiquated knowledge (the S_2, the embodiment of the discourse of the university) conditions the next generation's reconfiguration of the tradition. The arrangement of the players in such a way that this reconfiguration — nothing less than revolution — is possible constitutes the art of the perverse masterly analyst.

The different eccentricities of the two scientists — the Brownian pate of wild white hair and the Freudian puff of smoke — indicate a nonetheless common historical movement: of a return to the traumatic past on the way to the reconstruction of the future. Doc's time-machine returns to the original 1955 in order to rectify the paternal failure that mars the future McFly household. Freud's science of psychoanalysis excavates the trauma of the patient's historical past in order to ameliorate the symptoms of the future.

It is peculiar — and revolutionary — that neither the Freudian science of psychoanalysis nor the Brownian sciences of time-travel have legacies. Freud's discovery of the unconscious and Doc's invention of the time-machine do not themselves emerge from a tradition, an aged S_2. The two inventions — the

Freudian unconscious and the Brownian flux capacitor — emerge from nothing, no legacy, no heritage, no family; they are literally creations out of nothing, magical rabbits pulled from otherwise empty hats. As Doc puts it: "I
remember it vividly, I was standing at the edge of my toilet hanging a clock,
the porcelain was wet, I slipped, hit my head on the edge of the sink, and
when I came to I had a revelation, a vision, a picture in my head, a picture
of this, this is what makes time-travel possible — the flux capacitor!" The scene
of the discovery of the flux capacitor — an image of the tripartite structure of
the Oedipal complex, no less — consists of the blow to the head that, as a
trauma, an encounter with the real, revolutionizes the coordinates of both
science and Hill Valley. As for Freud, his creation of the unconscious broke
with the tradition of neuropsychology and the Western tradition of modern
philosophy that centered the subject around consciousness. Like Doc's invention of an originary S_1 outside of an historical lineage of an aged S_2, Freud's
invention of the unconscious is purely his own, a fundamental break with the
humanist tradition. The two fathers, then, Freud as the father of the science
of psychoanalysis and Brown as the father of time-travel, lack the paternal
legacy, the aged S_2, which conditions the emergence of the S_1. The invention
of the time-machine and the discovery of the unconscious represent the dimension of the Lacanian real itself. As Lacan puts it in *Seminar I* (1953–1954):
"the real, or what is perceived as such, is what resists symbolization absolutely."[29] This resistance to symbolization marks both inventions: the flux
capacitor simply fluxes without further scientific explanation and the unconscious easily signifies beyond any rationality. This real returns to the same
place, the place of an originary invention, out of nothing, that functions as,
in Derridean terms, *différance,* the non-originary origin whose deferred presence is only visible in the trace — the trace of the burned rubber from the wheels
of the DeLorean and of the trace of the significance of the opaque dream.[30]

"I figured — what the hell": The Generation(s) of Revolutionary Master Signifiers

Although Freud and Doc invent their respective master signifiers outside
of the text, their positions as the perverted masters of their respective univer-
sities (Hill Valley and the psychoanalytic circle) require the other (of the slave
to the master, of the student to the teacher, and of the hysteric to the analyst)
in order to mobilize — manifest, reveal, exhibit — their master signifiers. In the
absence of these necessary functionaries the originary S_1 fails to flourish. For
the S_1 to properly function — that is, for it to consolidate an emergent identity and desire personally, interpersonally, even generationally — it must find

affirmation— the kind that George receives from his brotherly son, Marty, in pursuit of Lorraine in 1955 — from an "other" that confers authority onto the S_1 that defines the emergent identity and desire of the personal, interpersonal, even generational economy. However, this other is neither strictly master nor solely analyst. Although both Freud and Doc invent their technologies outside of historical necessity the relevance of their inventions requires the affirmation conferred by the authority of the pervert. The perverse affirmation approximates the supportive analyst whose advice to his hysteric — "'Off you go, say everything that comes into your head, however divided it might be, no matter how clearly it demonstrates that either you are not thinking of else you are nothing at all, it may work, what you produce will always be admissible'" — affirms the production and deployment of the hysteric's new master signifier of her emergent identity-desire with the addition of the imperative of enjoyment.[31] The master's role is to provoke enjoyable resistance in the other; the analyst's role is to direct this effluvium in the direction of the production of the hysteric's own master signifier. The pervert's role is to affirm the revolution — to enjoy the resistance, to enjoy the effluvium, to enjoy the creativity: to enjoy sadistic destruction and to enjoy masochistic pain — the very conditions of the revolution, the emergence of the new master signifier outside of the text, beyond historical necessity. Indeed: the philosophical equivalent of this perverse figure is the Nietzschean future philosopher who deconstructs the old values (the S_2) and reconstructs the revolutionary values (the S_1). What is required of Freud and Doc — and of all revolutionary subjects whose enjoyable resistance has been activated by the master and whose master signifier has been elicited by the analyst — is a lateral affirmation — not from the elder master nor from the elder analyst — but from the brother of the same aesthetic cohort — George's Marty and Marty's Jennifer and Doc's Marty and Freud's Breuer. In other words: the revolution — the generation of the new master signifier — requires comrades — requires the generation.

The position — or discourse — of the pervert superimposes the master signifier (the agentic position in the discourse of the master) and enjoyment (the agentic position in the discourse of the analyst). As Lacan puts it: "Let's see what is at work here in the analyst's discourse. It is he, the analyst, who is the master. In what form? This is what I shall have to reserve for our subsequent meetings. Why in the form of object a?"[32] What is "at work" in the discourse of the analyst is precisely perversion: namely, the collusion of the discourse of the master (the production of enjoyable resistance) and the discourse of the analyst (the production of the master signifier). The reason that the "form" that the master takes is that of the analyst (the object a) is that "at work" in the discourse of the analyst is the revolutionary production of the master signifier — that is to say, of the enjoyable generation (the product of the discourse of the master) of the S_1 of the new order (the product of the discourse of the analyst). The union of enjoyment and the generation of the master signifier define the revolution — and the aesthetic of the pervert. The problem — but also solution — is that the discourse of the analyst produces its own S_2 in the place of truth. As Lacan puts the question: "What does the position of S_2 in the place of truth offer us now?"[33] In short: it installs the regime of the university discourse — but it also conditions the revolutionary hystericization of the next generation (of master signifiers). Needless to say: the revolution — the perverse union of enjoyment (the production of the discourse of the master) and the production of the new master signifier (the production of the discourse of the analyst) — the revolution reproduces the form of the regime that it seeks to upset, namely, the university discourse. As Lacan notes: "in seeking to escape from the university discourse one implacably reenters it."[34]

This revolutionary dynamic is performed differently in the film and in psychoanalysis. In *Back to the Future* George needs Marty's romantic advice — as George says of Marty's counsel: "I'm writing this down, this is good stuff" — in order to win Lorraine's heart as the condition of the authorship of *A Match Made in Space*, the signifier of the revolution in the McFly household. Marty needs Jennifer's encouragement — as Jennifer says of his demo tape: "But you're good Marty, you're really good" — to coax him into sending the demo tape of the revolutionary band "The Pinheads" to the record label. Doc requires Marty to see if those bastards can do 90 MPH in order to activate Doc's invention — Doc's S_1, the time-machine — after his measly pistol fails to protect him from the bazooka gun of the Libyans. More pointedly: Doc needs Marty to provide the torn-and-taped note — "your friend in time, Marty" — that allows Doc to witness his own revolutionary invention. In Freud's case he needs Breuer as his partner in perversion to respond to his letters and to co-author the early revolutionary work, *Studies in Hysteria,* in 1892. The revolution requires the perverse deuce — at least. Intercourse is revolution; masturbation is not.

In the scene of the revolution the pairs of comrades are ultimately perverts. The pervert represents the father who wields creative and affirmative love rather than reactive and negative castration. The brotherly pervert, then, suspends the traditional law of the father without the risk of psychotic function. It is the perverse revolutionaries — the brothers — and the sisters — that embody the future, by way of a return to the past, in the affirmation of the creation of the master signifiers that sing in the wake of the subject's slavish engagement with the master and hysterical engagement with the analyst. The perverse brothers and sisters — those who enjoy despite the guilt and the shame after the murder of the primal father — affirm — the ecstatic "yes, yes": the

Nietzschean affirmation, the Derridean affirmation, the Joycean affirmation — all in the name of a revolution in the social order, the "passage of the act," the reconfiguration of the coordinates of the symbolic order.[35] In the traditional revolutionary scene it is the younger generation whose enjoyable resistance and hysterical creation is provoked by the elder generation of masters and analysts. In this conventional economy the younger generation (the counterculture) pits itself against the elder generation (the culture of the masters and the analysts). However, in the time-travel genre, in *Back to the Future,* the masters and the slaves, the analysts and the hysterics, are not generationally separated; Doc's invention bridges the gap between the generations and invites the younger and the older generation to cavort as the same cohort. Indeed: this is precisely the upshot of the teenage Oedipus complex — the son (or daughter) is no longer the rival to the father (or mother); rather, the two are on the same side, members of the same team — oriented toward the same goal of the "passage of the act" in the revolutionary reconfiguration of the social order. Marty's interventions on behalf of his father (and, by extension, his mother) symbolize the revolutionary potential of the cross-generational reduction of the younger and the elder into the same cohort of good old 1955. Even as he feigns — rather unsuccessfully — the roles of master and analyst to his father, George, Marty is ultimately the perverse brother, the comrade to his nerdy dad, as they work to revolutionize the history of Hill Valley.

How, then, does Doc embody the role of the perverse masterly analyst? What ultimately makes Doc — cloaked in a white lab coat with shaggy dog Einstein by his side — the consummate pervert? It is Doc's sacrifice — he literally loses his life, shot in the chest by the barrage of bullets fired by the Libyans — that marks him as the masterly pervert, as that subjective position that sacrifices all, including life itself, for the sake of the revolutionary enjoyment of the other. As Zizek describes the will of the perverse position, "The imperative of a pervert, on the contrary, is to work for the Other's enjoyment, to become an object-instrument of it."[36] It is Doc's death — his martyrdom — that marks him as the revered perverted masterly analyst: the revolutionary party leader — a Lenin of sorts. As Lacan says of the analyst: "This is knowledge of which he who is prepared, in advance, to be the product of the pyschoanalysand's cogitations, that is, the psychoanalyst, makes himself the underwriter, the hostage — insofar as, as this product, he is in the end destined to become a loss, to be eliminated from the process."[37] Nevertheless, Doc's ultimate sacrifice succumbs to the necessities of the franchise: namely, that he survive the barrage of gunshots for the sake of the sequels. More to the point, however, is that Marty's intervention on behalf of Doc's life makes possible the self-affirmation of Doc's own master signifier: the DeLorean. Marty's interference (the note that warns Doc of the terrible tragedy on the night that

Marty goes back in time) in Doc's ultimate sacrifice (his death at the hands of the Libyan nationalists) reduces Doc from martyr — the perverse masterly analyst, the party leader — to simply the brotherly pervert, the comrade-in-arms. The trick of the time-travel genre is that the perverse economy deconstructs the hierarchical generational structures between master and slave, teacher and student, hysteric and analyst, leader and follower — even bourgeois and proletarian — such that all of the subjects — all of the citizens of Hill Valley, even Mayor Goldie Wilson — are perverse brothers of the revolution. Even the father — the loathsome figure who threatens the emergent generation with castration for their self-enjoyment — revolts against the university discourse. As Marty says to his father, chasing after him on the way to the revolution: "Hey Dad, George — hey, you on the bike!" If not a DeLorean pimped out with a flux capacitor, then a bicycle with a bell will do the trick — that is, the project of the revolutionary generation(s) of master signifiers. After all, even if the master signifier is new, the revolution is not: your mom sat in a parked car with a boy once, too.

Notes

1. Lacan's dictum that the signifier represents a subject to another signifier derives from his deployment of Saussurian structuralist linguistics to psychoanalysis. It is a non-idealized materiality (the signifier) that represents the subject (that object that finds representation through the signifying chain) to another signifier. Lacan's point is two-fold: first, the subject does not represent itself— it is a non-idealized materiality (the signifier) that represents the subject in the subject's place; and second, the subject (embodied in the non-idealized materiality of the signifier) is represented for another signifier, for the signifying chain itself. The upshot is that the subject is fundamentally split, divided, and alienated from his representation.

2. Jacques Lacan, *Seminar XVII* (New York: W.W. Norton, 2007), p. 15.

3. *Ibid.*

4. *Ibid.*, p. 23.

5. *Ibid.*, p. 21.

6. *Ibid.*, p. 129.

7. *Ibid.*, p. 52.

8. *Ibid.*, p. 129.

9. *Ibid.*

10. *Ibid.*, p. 87.

11. *Ibid.*

12. Jacques Lacan, *Seminar III* (New York: W.W. Norton, 1997), p.198.

13. In psychoanalysis the function of the paternal metaphor consists of not only the separation of the child from the mother — to make space for a displacement of the mother's desire for the child and to make possible the inauguration of the child's desire for an identity apart from the mother — but also of the coordination of a system of oppositional pairs that organize a symbolic order based in convention and custom. Lacan's account of psychosis suggests that the lack in the place of the father — the failure of the paternal function, the absence of the name-of-the-father — wrecks havoc on the social order for three interrelated reasons: first, the failure of the father to displace the mother's desire from her son as maternal phallus to another object impedes the development of the differentiated identity and separated desire of the child; second, the absence of the displacement of the mother's desire and the botched individuation of the child from the mother hinders the provocation of enjoyable resistance to the status quo of the state (what Lacan refers to as the university discourse) in the hystericization of the child's desire; and third, in the absence of the hystericization of the child's desire this improperly Oedipalized child cannot engage with an analyst who, in his proper role, solicits the subject's new master signifier that defines his identity, desire, and even generational cohort.

14. Lacan, *Seminar XVII*, p. 152.

15. Sigmund Freud, *The Standard Edition of the Complete Psychological Works of Sigmund Freud* (London: Hogarth Press, 1966), vol. 13, p. 148.

16. Slavoj Zizek, *For They Know Not What They Do* (New York: Verso, 2002), p. xxi.

17. Lacan, *Seminar XVII*, p. 112.

18. *Ibid.*, p. 171.

19. *Ibid.*, p. 46.

20. *Ibid.*, p. 95.

21. *Ibid.*, p. 35.

22. *Ibid.*, p. 163.

23. This brief interpretation demonstrates the limitations of the practice of psychoanalysis. In the traditional scene of the transference the analyst embodies the object of desire and the "subject supposed to know" of a figure from the analysand's historical past. The wager of psychoanalysis is that the transferential analysis of the analysand's desire in relation to the analyst as character from the analysand's historical past will relieve the symptom. However, if we want to pass beyond the mere relief of the symptom, and if we want to reconfigure the coordinates of the symbolic order in the truly historical "passage of the act," then the analysis of desire and the generation of a new master signifier require that the subject that the subject in question be the right subject, in the right place, at the right time.

24. In Lacanian terms we could say that Marty's mission in 1955 consists in the transition from being his mother's absent phallus (an object of desire rather than a desirous subject of lack) to having his own phallus (a desirous subject of lack with a master signifier that garners the other's desire).

25. *Ibid.*, p. 24.

26. *Ibid.*, p. 172.

27. *Ibid.*

28. *Ibid.*

29. Jacques Lacan, *Seminar I* (New York: W.W. Norton, 1988), p. 66.

30. Derrida's infamous neologism *différance* refers to the processes of differentiation (spatialization) and deferral (temporalization) that define the field of signification. In Derrida's textualized universe the ultimate origin and final destination of signification are always already displaced — differentiated and deferred — such that even the trace of the signifier resists determinate signification.

31. Lacan, *Seminar XVII*, p. 107.

32. *Ibid.*, p. 35.

33. *Ibid.*, p. 36.

34. *Ibid.*, p. 64.

35. Jacques Derrida, A Derrida Reader, ed. Peggy Kamuf (New York: Columbia University Press, 1991), p. 592.

36. Zizek, p. 271.

37. Lacan, *Seminar XVII*, p. 38.

Bibliography

Derrida, Jacques. *A Derrida Reader.* Ed. Peggy Kamuf. New York: Columbia University Press, 1991.

Freud, Sigmund. *The Standard Edition of the Complete Psychological Works of Sigmund Freud.* Transl. James Strachey. London: Hogarth Press, 1966.

Lacan, Jacques. *Seminar I.* New York: W.W. Norton, 1988.

_____. *Seminar III.* New York: W.W. Norton, 1997.

_____. *Seminar XVII: The Other Side of Psychoanalysis.* New York: W.W. Norton, 2007.

Zizek, Slavoj. *For They Know Not What They Do.* New York: Verso, 2002.

11. Showdown at the Café '80's: The *Back to the Future* Trilogy as Baudrillardian Parable

RANDY LAIST

The cultural and critical significance of Jean Baudrillard, the French theorist of hyperreality, is becoming increasingly acknowledged in the wake of his recent death. Indeed, since the mid–1970s, when he first articulated the thesis that contemporary life takes place in a mode of being that is no longer "real" in any traditional sense, the world has only become more Baudrillardian. A Gulf War that "did not take place," as Baudrillard controversially announced; a year 2000 that will not arrive; a "War on Terror" waged in the name of an emptily rhetorical "freedom"; Baudrillard must have felt that the reality was copying itself after his own model of hyperreality. But looking back, the 1980s is certainly the definitive Baudrillardian period, the decade in which Baudrillard's characteristic style would take shape and also the decade in which the culture caught up with his vision in an undeniable way. The Reaganization of politics, the Star-Warsization of movies, a junk bond economy; the texture of the period is saturated with echo effects and simulations of simulations. The extent to which we are still in Baudrillard's world in the 21st century is the sense in which we are still in Baudrillard's 80's. It is the extent to which, not only did the 1980s not end, but all of history retrospectively became "museumified" in the Café 80s. As Baudrillard himself explains, "At some point in the 1980s, history took a turn in the opposite direction.... We are faced with a paradoxical process of reversal, a reversive effect of modernity which, having reached its speculative limit and extrapolated all its virtual developments, is disintegrating into its simple elements in a catastrophic process of recurrence and turbulence."[1] The proliferation of commodities, advertising, nuclear weapons, and other vectors of hyperreality has reached a saturation point beyond which temporality itself becomes derealized. Baudrillard is fond of quoting Elias Cannetti's observation that "as of a certain point, history was no longer *real*. Without noticing it, all mankind suddenly left reality."[2] Baudrillard explains that "this point is also the end of linear time, and all the marvelous inventions of science fiction for 'going back in time' are useless if time no longer exists."[3]

Saying that time machines are useless is another way of saying that time travel is a common feature of everyday experience. Welcome to the world of Marty McFly, the 1980s teenager who invented rock and roll and who is his own eponym. *Back to the Future*, the highest grossing movie of 1985, is a kind of allegory of the Baudrillardian flattening of history into an ahistorical precession of signs which are their own original referents. Marty actually becomes a father figure to his own teenage father and simultaneously brings into being a looping continuity between the American 1950s and 1980s that undermines classical conceptions of cause and effect. In the process, Marty reveals for the audience a vision of a vanished America that is more likely ruled over by Oz than by Eisenhower. Marty travels into the cinematic past, a kind of alternative fictional American history which has magically, under the influence of Ronald Reagan's cinematic charisma, replaced the historical past as the "real" one. In the two sequels, director Robert Zemeckis and writer Bob Gale seem to become much more self-conscious about the centrality of the theme of hyperreality to the *Back to the Future* paradigm. Whereas the Marty of Part One traveled into a cinematic representation of the mythical 1950s, Marty of Part Two actually enters the movie *Back to the Future* Part One and sneaks around in its margins. In Part Three, Marty is shot right into a movie screen into an Old West that is simultaneously and reciprocally a crucible of both American mythology and post-war American cinema. Although the differences between the various time periods represented are played for laughs, the more fundamental impression is of an eternal recurrence of stock characters and ready-to-hand sentiment, lame jokes which echo repeatedly throughout all possible iterations of the past and future, and a heavy-handed narrative structure; in short, all of history is bound together by its cinematic hyperreality.

Time in Baudrillard's universe is extremely ductile, because the very structure of hyperreality makes a hash out of linear, Enlightenment temporality. In "The Precession of Simulacra," Jean Baudrillard summed up the ontological mood of the 1980s with his paradoxical assessment that the contemporary environment had become one characterized by "a real without origin or reality: a hyperreal."[4] The possibility of a copy without an original relies on a conception of time as a Möbius strip rather than an arrow, a closed orbit of possibilities repeating themselves with only superficial variations for all time past and future. William Bogard explains that "Many of Baudrillard's texts produce this paradoxical sense of time inversion and reversal, of histories written before their events (but which none the less are not prophesies), of pasts inhering in presents and futures in pasts. This is because Baudrillard adopts in his writing style the temporal frame of simulation, which is *repetition in advance*."[5] Bogard foregrounds the strangeness of this temporality in his assessment that "simulation is like a miracle, for only a miraculous technology could revive the past in the present (and project it endlessly into the future).... The miracle produces a cyborg time-traveler."[6] Doc Brown's DeLorean is a kind of shuttle that runs back and forth through time and weaves a condition of hyperreality. The kind of time that the DeLorean allows Marty to travel around in is extremely ambiguous. The rules of time-travel in the *Back to the Future* movies do not follow any rigorous science-fiction logic. At the end of *Future One*, Marty returns to a 1985 which has been altered by his 1955 interventions; the 1985 he leaves is the 1985 future of a past he has not affected (1985a), and the 1985 to which he returns is 1985b, the post-time travel present. But there are also indications that 1985a was always already 1985b. The most obvious suggestion in this direction is Marty's own tautological naming. More outrageously, Marty's accomplishments also include encouraging the local black person to run for mayor and inspiring Chuck Berry to invent Rock n Roll. Marty not only returns to, but has always lived in a world which is an uncanny echo of itself. In Part Two, when Biff steals the time machine in 2015 to travel back to 1955 to give the sports almanac to his younger self, the 2015 to which he returns should be the post–Biff Co 2015, if the movies were concerned with that kind of consistency. But the *Future* movies aren't supposed to make that kind of sense, because they are only superficially about time. Marty is less a traveler in time than a traveler in hyperreality, exploring the kind of world that exists in the wake of the reversal of history.

Roger Ebert wrote of *Back to the Future* that it "resembles Frank Capra's *It's a Wonderful Life* more than any other conventional time-travel movies. It's about a character who begins with one view of life and reality and is allowed, through magical intervention, to discover another."[7] *Future Two* certainly goes on to exploit more deliberately the cinematic allusion to the famous Capra film, but the difference between George Bailey's narrative and Marty McFly's is instructive. Unlike George Bailey (or Dorothy Gale), it is not Marty's "view of life" that is altered by his magical experience, but reality itself. Rather than learning to appreciate the humble values of home and family, Marty's happy ending involves the alteration of his family to make them more consistent with his initial view of life. Nothing changes too radically at the end of *Future One*; George and Lorraine still get married, live in the same house, and produce three kids, but they have a more upscale décor in their living room, they have preppier clothes and hairstyles, and they have a BMW in the driveway instead of a junker. They've even bought Marty the Toyota truck that he's always dreamed of having. It is a utopia of commodities, and it is the brave new reality made possible by the dream of time travel. Reagan waves his magic wand and the gritty drabs and earth tones of the 1970s are replaced with the shiny chrome surfaces of a neo–50s, as if history could be rewired to bypass the 1960s and 1970s and create a seamless loop from the era of post-war economic prosperity to the era of simulacral Reaganomic prosperity. This is the magical effect implicit in Baudrillard's description of "Reagan's smile — the culmination of the self-satisfaction of the entire American nation — which is on the way to becoming the sole principle of government."[8]

Marty's successful resolution at the end of *Future One* is his success in altering not only the details of reality, but moreover of the very nature and texture of reality. What "happened" to the members of Marty's family who existed in 1985a? Have they become, as in Doc's dire formulation, "erased from existence?" In *Future One*, the implication is that Marty returns to people who have always been the way they are. They have changed not in the temporal sense of being one way and then becoming another, but in the hyperreal sense of always having been changed and having no memory or history of having been otherwise. In *Future Two*, however, Doc advances a different hypothesis about what "happens" when they change the future. When Marty protests that it's wrong to leave Jennifer and Einstein the dog in the post–Biff Co 1985c, Doc explains that they are not abandoning 1985b Jennifer to a hopeless future as a homeless, amnesiac victim of street thugs as would appear to be the case. Rather, when Marty and Doc change the past, the new reality (or is it the old reality?) will take shape around Jennifer and she will be none the wiser. In this version, reality is subject to a radical catastrophism. At any given moment, the McFly family might be one thing, with one way of dressing and one history of either subservience or dominance in relation to Biff, and then the next moment, something has re-tinkered their past and now they are, and feel themselves always to have been, living in a completely different world as completely different kinds of people. In the wake of Marty's time-traveling, all of reality has become artificialized, ephemeralized, and torn loose from "nature." Instead of reality, there is a proliferation of alternate realities and an implosion of any differentiation between illusion and reality. All of existence takes on the nature of Baudrillard's fourth stage of simulation: "It has no relation to any reality whatsoever: it is its own pure simulacrum."[9]

The kind of history Marty travels through is a simulacral history. He travels to the midpoint of decades —1985, 1955, 2015, and 1885 — as if to hook up with that period at its highest, most essential point, so he is not so much in 1985 or 1955 as he is in "the 80s" or "the 50s." The condition of hyperreality is made possible in large part by the kind of realist metaphysics that imparts an illusion of identity to such abstractions as the zeitgeist of a time period. However contrived and artificial the stereotypical image of the Reagan-Huxtable 1950s may be, this illusion is nevertheless real in its effects when this manufactured image becomes the basis for a political culture. In fact, the manufactured model may very well be said to be *more* real, *more* persuasive, *more* influential in the way it informs cultural self-understanding than the so-called historical reality of the 1950s "themselves" (whatever that may mean). By making a period of time the starting point for historical understanding, a repeatable, empty, mathematical value becomes the foundational reality. Anything that happens over the course of that ten-year span is reduced to a secondary status as "filler." Decades are always already empty values, so VH1 can produce an endless series of shows about popular culture called "I Love the 80s" or "I Love the 70s" in a way that would not be possible within a style of history that prioritized social or political events; "I Love the Civil Rights Era" or "I Love the Cold War." The self-conscious artificiality of Marty's 1980s and of his parents' 1950s seems to represent an underlying acknowledgement that Marty isn't actually traveling through time at all, but through a parody of hyperreal time which only *seems* to pass. The clock tower that dominates the civic life of Hill Valley has been frozen in place for thirty years, and in the streets of the town, the same people are surrounded by the same advertisements for the same things. The teens go to the same school, suspended in an eternal state of concern about bullies and girls, people drink the same brand of soda and watch the same television shows, and the mayor's campaign slogan still promises "progress." As in the transition from 1985a to 1985b, the only things that change in Marty's transition from 1985 to 1955 are the clothes, the style of music, and the color of the mayor's face.

Robert Zemeckis, whose movies tend to resemble elaborately produced television shows, is true to form in the *Future* movies which, with their intimate ensemble of returning characters, reliance on running gags and taglines, and flat visual style, seem to strive for a televisual effect. The casting of Michael J. Fox as the anchor character certainly reinforces this impression. As Alex P. Keaton of *Family Ties*, Fox emblematizes in his clean-cut conservativism a kind of fusion of Eddie Haskel and George Will, the essence of the 1980s understanding of itself as a reversal of the Keaton parents' 1960s and 1970s radicalism and the "return" to that ideal of a "50s" which we remember from reruns of old television shows. The person of Michael J. Fox himself signifies a televisual circuit between the image of the 1950s and the image of the 1980s, just as surely as does the figure of Ronald Reagan. "No wonder your president has to be an actor," marvels 1955 Doc. "He has to look good on television!" Television is where hyperreal history takes place (or rather, doesn't take place), and Marty himself and his temporality constitute a vision of history as television show. Ebert complained of *Future Three* that "this movie's West is unfortunately a sitcom version that looks exactly as if it were built on a back lot somewhere."[10] But Hill Valley has always looked like a movie set sealed under a *Truman Show* dome, outside of "real" history. Even the paradoxical name of the town seems to indicate a blatant, absurd, self-conscious fictionality. When Marty is introduced, accordingly, it is not as a person, but as a collection of "80s" signifiers — his Nike sneakers, then his skateboard, then his denim togs, his blow-dried hair, and his Van Halen guitar. It is not until after Marty reenacts the iconic 1980s Memorex advertisement (Is it live or is it Memorex? — a fitting slogan for the hyperreal) that he raises his 1980s shades and we see that it is Alex P. Keaton under all that 1980s stuff. He is a self-referring 1980s teen, signifying himself as an accumulation of commodities. Baudrillard might have had Marty in mind when he described "the skateboarder with his walkman ... everywhere ... you find the same blank solitude, the same narcissistic refraction."[11] When Marty skateboards to school during the opening credit sequence, we see that Marty's whole 1980s world is actually a collage of corporate logos and 1980s advertisements, and the booming presence of Huey Lewis gives the entire scene a music video feel (complete with aerobic dancers) — or is it a Mountain Dew commercial? — that confirms that Marty lives in a world that is entirely simulacral, entirely televisual, ahistorical, and self-referential.[12] Time travel is as easy in this kind of temporality as changing channels on your television set or pressing rewind or fast forward on your VCR remote. It involves nothing more drastic than redecorating the set and recostuming the locals.

Doc's demonstration of how to operate the time machine in fact recalls the procedure for programming a VCR.[13] Baudrillard also appeals to the metaphor of the programmable VCR as emblematic of hyperreal temporality when he writes, "Can you, by setting the video recorder for the same time on the previous day, resuscitate yesterday's programme? [Sic] Can we, by reversing the digital clock at Beaubourg, turn the century around to run backwards? ... But there is not even any need [to do so]: the turnaround of history has already taken place."[14] Bogard's commentary is even more explicit in his suggestion that the VCR is the "clock" of hyperreal time. "Within the envelope of the repeated past, simulation produces other 'miracles'; time in general, any-time-whatever, is reproduced on its screen — future, past, present, all can be repeated or played back, and, moreover, this can be done at variable speeds (fast forward, slow motion, reverse motion, freeze frame, stop time)."[15] The way Doc describes it, time travel sounds a lot like watching the History Channel. "Say you want to *see* the signing of the declaration of independence! Or *witness* the birth of Christ!" Doc's failure to take cognizance of the 20th Century truism that the presence of the observer might influence what he observes suggests that he is thinking of his time machine as an extension of television technologies. One of the 1980s gadgets that Marty carries in the time machine back to 1955 is a camcorder, so that in the same way that Marty watches replayed Honeymooners episodes from 1955 in 1985, Doc can watch his 1985 death on television in 1955. Television and recorded video weave these two time periods into a mutual contemporaneity in their ability to transform linear temporality into a bank of images that can be summarily accessed, replayed, or filed away. William Irwin Thompson, writing in the Baudrillardian mode, posits that "if you grew up with fifty channels on your TV set, or Hypercard stacks in your personal computer, then the past is not a text that moves from left to right with everything dated in linear fashion from B.C. to A.D."[16] As a faithful representation of the TV generation, Marty is much cooler than Doc when it comes to dealing with the condition of hyperreality. Whereas Doc seems to be constantly falling apart into an aghast panic about the catastrophic effects time travel might have on reality, Marty slides supplely through all the hazards his adventures present him with, balletically negotiating logical paradoxes and tight schedules with a grace that confirms that hyperreality is his natural habitat. To the extent that Marty has any superpowers in the past, it is his ability to existentially merge with his trove of video memories; he borrows the identity of "Darth Vader from the planet Vulcan," he copies the bullet-proofing trick from *A Fistful of Dollars*, he even benefits from his familiarity with *Back to the Future Part One*. He merges so easily with these media images because he's already a post–VCR subject. The time machine is not only a metaphor for the VCR, but a representation of how the culture of the VCR affects temporality by inducting us into a hyperreal condition of eternal repeatability.

Doc's time machine also combines the technologies of the automobile and the nuclear bomb into its metaphor for hyperreal temporality. The automobile is a particularly prominent apparatus in Baudrillard's writing. His 1988 book, *America*, is largely a meditation on the phenomenology of driving in America. "Driving is a spectacular form of amnesia. Everything is to be discovered, everything to be obliterated."[17] The centrality of the car to American culture is not so much a material fact as an ontological condition of detachment and circulation. The disrelation between the world of the road and the world of the driver is evocative of that between the television viewer and the television show. As Bryan S. Turner explains in his reading of Baudrillard, "The car screen and the TV screen have a number of things in common. The passenger, like the viewer, is passive, indifferent, entertained and perhaps over-stimulated by the flashing trivia of the landscape and the scene."[18] Both technologically mediated forms of disrelation are symptomatic of a general condition in which everything circulates, everything is exchangeable, and everything is divorced from the kind of stability characteristic of classical, realist modes of temporality. Human beings become subject to the same transvaluation as their ambient commodities; Baudrillard's own "restless circling through the highways of America parallels the circling of the sign in the sign economy."[19] Marty's frustration about the totaling of the family car and his consumer desire for the Toyota truck are both rerouted into his acquisition of the ultimate automobile, one that allows you to drive transversely through your own life, to drive past yourself, as Marty does at several points in the trilogy. Doc's DeLorean is the fulfillment of the hyperreal possibility for which the regular automobile is a metaphor.

As for Marty's exclamation that "this sucker's nuclear," Baudrillard explains that "The nuclear is the apotheosis of simulation."[20] In the suspended aggression of the Cold War, Baudrillard finds one of his most evocative metaphors for the condition of hyperreality. "The nuclear, behind the presumed risk of explosion, that is to say of hot catastrophe, conceals a long, cold catastrophe, the universalization of a system of deterrence."[21] If the conventional treatment of nuclear material in science-fiction movies from *Them* to *The China Syndrome* has been to portray the nuclear as potentially apocalyptic, *Back to the Future* domesticates nuclear technology by bringing it into the circulatory system of transvalued commodities. The Libyans' fissionable material is exchanged for pinball machine parts and the nuclear reactor is replaced with a Mr. Fusion just as harmlessly as the conventional ovens of 1955 become the microwave ovens of 1985. Rather than signifying a coming apocalypse, Doc's use of nuclear technology opens the door to a hyper-universe in which we might say along with Baudrillard, "What will happen will never be the explosion, but the implosion."[22] Doc's apocalyptic warnings of what could happen if the paradoxes become too blatant — "a chain reaction that could disrupt the fabric of the space-time continuum and destroy the universe!" — is repeatedly invalidated throughout the movies. Doc's nuclear apprehensions are suggestive of the traditional kind of apocalypse characteristic of linear time. But Marty's rambunctious unconcern with paradox is a symptom of a kind of apocalypse that has become hyperreal along with everything else. Marty's redirection of nuclear technology from the doomsday mode to the hyperreal mode emblematizes Baudrillard's announcement that "the apocalypse is finished, today it is the precession of the neutral."[23] Rather than a movement toward a transcendent finale, history resembles the flat expansiveness of a temporality characterized by the slogan, "To be continued...."

The flattening of history is analogous to and coextensive with a flattening of psychological processes and existential values. Marty's journey into the dimension of hyperreality resolves what had conventionally been considered the deep mysteries of sex and death into nonissues. The oedipal content of *Future One* is a nod at Freudian depth psychology, hidden forces, and secret meanings, but Marty replays the Oedipal crisis as a cartoon. Andrew Gordon's thesis that *Back to the Future* succeeds as a family movie despite its incest theme because it "diffuses out anxieties about [incest] through comedy"[24] is another way of saying that *Future* takes the subject of incest and empties it of its psychological resonance. Marty's situation hardly merits such a grandiose term as "Oedipal." The most interesting aspect of the treatment of the Oedipal plotline is how lightly it's treated, as a sitcom scenario rather than a Freudian trauma. If there were any indication that Marty was attracted by the prospect of sleeping with the girl who will someday be his mother, we would be in different territory, or if there were any indication that Lorraine is attracted to Marty because she senses unconsciously in Marty the dark possibility of a taboo sexual encounter, we could justify describing the movie in Freudian terms. But Marty is basically asexual in the style of 1980s (and 1950s) cinematic heroes; the nature of his psychology was theorized in Burbank, not Vienna (observe the variously misogynistic techniques employed to keep the character of Marty's girlfriend out of the story as much as possible). And although Lea Thompson brings a simmering sexuality to her performance as 1955 Lorraine, the climactic Oedipal moment is diffused instantaneously upon the discovery that incest is naturally unsexy. The primitive taboos must have been redundant all along; the Oedipal situation is not a deep conflict, but merely the set-up for a series of comic situations.

In the dimension of hyperreality, Baudrillard explains, "the true Oedipal problem for everyone [is] not so much to free yourself from the parental triangle as from your virtual double."[25] For people who are named after themselves, who are parental figures to their own parents, and who preside over the circumstances of their own conception — that is to say, for the hyperreal subject who is a copy without an original — the crisis is not one of origins but of proliferating duplication. At the end of *Future One*, Marty spies on his 1985b self, the self who has presumably grown up in the life our Marty has just usurped. What will be the fate of 1985b Marty? Whose life will he usurp? In *Future Two*, the problem of multiple realities, the risk of people seeing their doubles, and the narrative superimposition of the sequel and the original movie all represent the hyperreal preoccupation with reiteration and potentially infinite seriality. (Who is to say there are not hundreds more "Martys" crawling around in the shadows of all of the *Future* movies?) The DeLorean is not only a VCR, automobile, and nuclear bomb, it is also a cloning machine. To Baudrillard, the clone represents a prosthetic extension of the individual that turns the "original" individual into a faceless member in a series. Unlike twins, who have a mythic resonance, "cloning enshrines the reiteration of the same: 1 + 1 + 1 + 1, etc."[26] Rather than a copy of an original, the process of cloning turns both participants into interchangeable units. Which is the "real" Marty, 1985a or 1985b? The same ambiguity enters the texture of reality itself: what is the "real" history, a or b? As Ebert pointed out in his review of *Future Two*, "How does [Doc] know that the 'real world' of the first movie was not itself an alternate time line?"[27] In hyperreality, all timelines are alternate and all individuals are their own autochthonous clones. "One is never the ideal or mortal mirage of the other, they can only be added to each other, and if they can only be added, it means that they are not sexually engendered and know nothing of death."[28] To be sure, in addition to replacing sexually charged Oedipalism with an asexual mode of human replication, Marty and Doc also use the time machine as an instrument for eliminating the possibility of death. Doc's violent death at the beginning of the first movie is reconstituted as a simulacrum of death by the end of the movie, and the plot of *Future Three* entirely revolves around the objective of using the time machine to keep Doc from dying. Death is impossible in hyperreal temporality. "Death no longer has a stage, neither phantasmatic nor political, on which to represent itself, to play itself out, either a ceremonial or a violent one."[29] There are no beginnings and no endings in hyperreality, only the infinite precession.

Pauline Kael captured this insubstantial dizziness in her observation that *Future Two* "seems to be on a treadmill in a void. And yet the construction keeps you going — it's like a frenzied daydream that you don't want to break off."[30] Kael's image is a perfect depiction of Baudrillardian precession, a free-floating circulation characterized by "a principle of instability and vertigo."[31] Once Doc and Marty have opened the Pandora's Box of hyperreality, they inhabit a new kind of reality from which there is no going back. Marty's attempt to restore the "natural" narrative of history in which his parents marry and have kids is extremely similar to the attempts Baudrillard describes to "restore" The Cloisters from New York City to France or to "return" the Tasaday tribe to their natural habitat. Moving the medieval monastery from the shores of the Hudson back to its "original" locale in Europe is an attempt to conceal the new condition of hyperreal circulation under an illusion of consistency, but the Cloisters rebuilt in France is just as artificial as the Cloisters rebuilt in Manhattan, perhaps even more so because the French Cloisters represents an outright denial of (hyper)reality. Likewise, the attempt described by Baudrillard on the part of concerned anthropologists to "protect" the Tasaday by strictly controlling their contact with the outside world creates an illusion of the Natural which is in fact an artfully designed and ceaselessly regulated effect. By going back in time and manipulating the course of events, Marty has cut history loose from nature; it is now an artificial construct, an illusion that has to be tirelessly maintained. Doc's return at the very end of

Future One signifies that the preservation of the illusion of history is now a full-time job. For Doc and Marty, all of history past and future is laid out in front of them as something to be tinkered with, visited and revisited, but no longer actually inhabited. They live out Baudrillard's thesis that "our societies have all become revisionistic: they are quietly rethinking everything, laundering their political crimes, their scandals, licking their wounds.... We no longer make history. We have become reconciled with it and protect it like an endangered masterpiece."[32]

One of the effects of the 4-year gap between the filming of *Future One* and *Future Two* is that, by 1989, the 1980s have already become "the 80s." Marty is no longer an ultra-contemporary archetypal American teen; by 1989, he's a throwback to an earlier time and has to be dressed in period costume. Having spent a week in a very stereotyped atmosphere representative of "the 50s," Marty returns to 1985 to discover that the present has been periodized. The time traveler returns to a present that is just another time in the circulatory flux of fads and fashions. *Future Two* makes the irony of this situation very explicit in its depiction of 2015. As in 1955 and 1985, the advertisements, the town layout, and the social relationships are all exactly the same. The writers have to invent absurd fads ("All the kids in 2015 wear their pants inside out!") to come up with a parallel for the (equally absurd, we recognize in retrospect) fashions of the 1950s and 1980s. In retrospect, Marty's signature down vest and denim jacket have become signifiers not of his "coolness," but of his 80s-ness. The accumulation of 1980s stuff in the window of an antique shop suggests that what binds us to our moment in history is nothing more substantial than an accumulation of future curiosities; what separates one era from another in hyperreal temporality is only the shape of our junk. The inclusion in the window of a Roger Rabbit doll, a reference to another Zemeckis production, metanarratively indicates that Marty himself is a character in an 1980s Zemeckis production; that might just as well be a Marty McFly doll in the antique case. They may as well be playing "The Power of Love" in the Café 80s. In the same way that 1985 has become "the 80s," Marty has become "Marty." More so than arguably any other sequel in movie history, *Future Two* is, as Deason Howe put it, "exhaustive with self-reference."[33] Gag for gag, Marty's experiences in the Café 80s recapitulate his experiences in what we can retronymically identify as the Café 50s. The sequence of Marty's skateboard escape from Griff and his thugs is so reliant on the audience's memory of the parallel sequence in *Future One* that it is almost as if we have already gone back into the first movie before the plot literally takes us there. As a result of his immersion into the hyperreal condition of traveling transversely through time, Marty is no longer rooted in any historical or psychological identity. *Future One*'s spontaneity becomes *Future Two*'s nostalgia for *Future One*'s spontaneity, and Marty's field of possibilities as a character is narrowed down to a finite repertoire of stunts and quips which we have already seen him perform and utter. In the exhaustion of his possibilities, Marty's identity becomes simulacral; he is a copy of his previous cinematic incarnation.

Baudrillard describes hyperreality as "infinitely self-referential,"[34] so what is there for a hyperreal movie plot to do but to "roll around on itself" like Baudrillard invites his own writing to do.[35] Janet Maslin's observation that *Future Two* "isn't an ordinary sequel; It is as if the earlier film had been squared"[36] expresses the unique implosion of narrative that the movie orchestrates. The most surreal leg of Marty's adventures is his shadowy participation behind the scenes of *Future One*. The scenario has something in common with similar situations in movies such as *The Purple Rose of Cairo* or *Last Action Hero* in which human beings pass through the movie screen portal into movie-world, except with the Borgesian twist that the movie that Marty passes into is his own. He was always already a movie character, so there is no disruption of ontological registers. As a hyperrealized character in a hyperreal world, Marty enjoys completely free mobility across his two-dimensional cosmos. The DeLorean is not only a VCR, a car, a nuclear bomb, and a cloning machine, but also a movie camera which performs the task of projecting Marty into cinematic space. In *Future Three*, the writers might have tried to give us *Back to the Future* cubed, in which Marty returns to various scenes in *Future Two*, but their decision to deposit Marty in the Old West represents a more subtle form of the same maneuver. Rather than going back into his own movie, the DeLorean brings Marty into the heart of American cinema itself. The movie character becomes a self-conscious embodiment of his own movie-ness.

As if to clarify this reading of their trilogy, Gale and Zemeckis set the time travel sequence at the beginning of *Future Three* in the parking lot of a drive-in movie theater. This scene is among the wittiest in the trilogy, playing very openly and very metanarratively on the peculiar kind of action hero Marty has become. The drive-in is decorated in a Western motif, but the surrounding Monument Valley landscape expresses Baudrillard's appraisal that "it is not the least of America's charms that even outside the movie theaters, the whole country is cinematic. The desert you pass through is like the set of a Western."[37] Baudrillard describes the phenomenological uselessness of seeking "to strip the desert of its cinematic aspects in order to restore its original essence."[38] The American desert is Baudrillard's supreme vision of an American reality that is always already cinematographic in its perceptual being. Doc and Marty are not in a movie theater in the desert, they are in a world that is a perfect fusion of Nature and Art; a reality that is fundamentally cinematic. When Doc instructs Marty to "drive right toward that screen at 88 miles per hour," he is sending Marty not so much from the present into the past, not even from one kind of reality into another, but only from one genre (science fiction) into another (Westerns), the equivalent of moving from one movie theater into another. All the while, our real locality is in hyperreal America, which is itself only a copy of its cinematic self-representation. The rampaging band of Indians painted on the drive-in mural become "real" when Marty breaks through to 1885, but they are only "real" insofar as Marty has entered into the same kind of cinematic unreality as they. Marty has always relied on his familiarity with movie culture as one of his staple characteristics (Darth Vader from the planet Vulcan), but in the sequels, Marty's character and environment both become more densely allusive to cinematic models. In Part Two, Marty mysteriously introjects Jim Stark's touchiness about being called chicken from *Rebel Without a Cause*, and Part Three becomes an inexhaustible game of spot-the-reference. Mad Dog Tannen brandishes a silver-handled whip like the one wielded by Liberty Valance, Doc shoots Marty's noose in a reference to *The Good, The Bad, and the Ugly*, the dance sequence between Doc and Clara is a nod to *My Darling Clementine*.[39] Marty does a Travis Bickle [from Martin Scorsese's *Taxi Driver*] impersonation in a mirror, toying with the depthless variety of available cinematic personae, and wins the day by mimicking the finale of *A Fistful of Dollars*. If an ironic loop of self-referentiality was established in the first movie by the indication that Marty was named after himself, in *Future Three*, Marty fits into his cinematic environment by adopting the pseudonym Clint Eastwood. Whereas the first movement peels Marty away from his personal history and makes him his own simulacrum, the second anachronistic self-naming locates Marty as a composite personality of filmic images: American teenager as human VCR.

In "repeating" many of the same gags and escapades from the 20th and 21st centuries in 1885, Marty exemplifies Baudrillard's aphorism that "history reproducing itself becomes farce. Farce reproducing itself becomes history."[40] Marty's proactive repetitions of his own and other movies magically insinuate themselves into the documents of history, creating a total situation in which American history has become saturated with cinematic influences just as irreversibly as the American landscape has. The 20th century understanding of the late 19th century American West has evolved through the medium of cinema. This cinematic understanding, in turn, is so potently a factor in the political behavior of Americans that it actually serves the function of "real" history. Clint Eastwood *does* travel back in time to write our history for us, his time machine powered by the hyperreal imagination in which "history is our lost referential, that is to say, our myth. It is by virtue of the fact that it takes the place of myths on the screen."[41] Marty travels into a kind of reality which is at once history, myth, and cinema, but if we laugh at the absurdity of Marty's situation, it is only because we recognize a comic variation on our own daily experience as hyperreal citizens. Simultaneously, we can distance ourselves from Marty's predicament, turning off the DVD player to return safely to the "real" world, where time is not so chaotically intermixed and where identity really is rooted in a history of things that have happened and will always have happened. The depiction of Marty's hyperreal adventures as a cartoonish fantasy deters us from recognizing the extent to which our everyday lives are hyperreal. In this sense, the installation of *Back to the Future: the Ride* in Universal Studios at Disneyland is particularly fitting, Disneyland being the Baudrillardian epicenter of this kind of deterrence. "Disneyland is presented as imaginary in order to make us believe that the rest is real, whereas all of Los Angeles and the America that surrounds it are no longer real, but belong to the hyperreal order and to the order of simulation."[42] *Back to the Future: the Ride* zaps the rider into the *Future* movies in the same way that Marty was zapped into his own movie. Strapped into the motion simulator, you chase Biff into 2015, into the Ice Age, into the Jurassic period, and then step out blinking into the California sun, under the impression that the ride is over. We are Marty waking up, as he does in all three movies, with the falsely reassuring impression that we have been dreaming. But here we are, safe and sound, back in good old ... hyperreality!

Notes

1. Jean Baudrillard. *The Illusion of the End.* Chris Turner, tr. Stanford: Stanford University Press, 1994. 10–11.

2. Jean Baudrillard. *Fatal Strategies.* In *Jean Baudrillard: Selected Writings.* Mark Poster, ed. Stanford: Stanford University Press, 2001. 188–209. p. 193. *Illusion of the End,* 1.

3. *Fatal Strategies,* 194.

4. Jean Baudrillard. *Simulacra and Simulations.* Sheila Faria Glaser, tr. Ann Arbor: University of Michigan Press, 1994. 1.

5. William Bogard. "Baudrillard, Time, and the End." In *Baudrillard: A Critical Reader.* Douglas Kellner, ed. Oxford: Blackwell, 1994. 313–33. 316.

6. *Ibid.,* 318–9.

7. Roger Ebert. "Back to the Future." 7/3/85. http://rogerebert.suntimes.com/apps/pbcs.dll/article?AID=/19850703/REVIEWS/507030301/1023.

8. Jean Baudrillard. *America.* Chris Turner, tr. London: Verso, 1988. 34.

9. *Simulacra and Simulation,* 6.

10. Roger Ebert. "Back to the Future Part III." 5/25/90. http://rogerebert.suntimes.com/apps/pbcs.dll/article?AID=/19900525/REVIEWS/5250301/1023.

11. *America,* 34.

12. In a rare convergence of popular movie culture and literary culture, the top-grossing movie of 1985, *Future One,* and the National Book Award Winner of 1985, Don DeLillo's *White Noise,* both portray the contemporary American landscape in similar, Baudrillardian terms.

13. The comparison between Doc's DeLorean and a VCR is the subject of a joke in *Back to the Future: the Ride,* when the digital time readout of the damaged DeLorean blinks 12:00 to indicate that it needs to be reset.

14. Jean Baudrillard. *Fragments.* Emily Agar, tr. London: Verso, 1997. 93.

15. Bogard, 319.

16. William Irwin Thompson. *The Ameri-*

can Replacement of Nature. New York: Doubleday, 1991. 36.

17. *America*, 9.

18. Bryan S. Turner. "Cruising America." In *Forget Baudrillard*. Chris Rojek and Bryan S. Turner, eds. London: Routledge, 1993. 146–61. 153.

19. Chris Rojek and Bryan S. Turner. "Introduction: Regret Baudrillard?" In *Forget Baudrillard*. Chris Rojek and Bryan S. Turner, eds. London: Routledge, 1993. ix–xviii. xii.

20. Jean Baudrillard. *Simulations*. Paul Foss, Paul Patton, and Philip Beitchman, tr. New York: Semiotext(e), 1983. 58.

21. *Simulacra and Simulation*, 53.

22. *Ibid.*, 55.

23. *Ibid.*, 160.

24. Andrew Gordon. "*Back to the Future*: Œdipus as Time Traveler." In *Liquid Metal: The Science Fiction Film Reader*. Sean Redmond, ed. London: Wallflower Press, 2004. 116–25.

25. *Fragments*, 119.

26. *Simulacra and Simulation*, 97.

27. Roger Ebert. "Back to the Future Part II." 11/22/89. http://rogerebert.suntimes.com/apps/pbcs.dll/article?AID=/19891122/REVIEWS/911220301/1023.

28. *Simulacra and Simulation*, 97.

29. *Ibid.*, 164.

30. Pauline Kael. "Back to the Future Part II." http://www.geocities.com/paulinekaelreviews/b1.html.

31. Jean Baudrillard. *The Transparency of Evil*. James Benedict, tr. London: Verso, 1993. 107.

32. *The Illusion of the End*, 22–3.

33. Desson Howe. "Back to the Future Part II." *Washington Post*, 11/24/89. http://www.washingtonpost.com/wp-srv/style/longterm/movies/videos/backtothefutureiihowe.html.

34. Jean Baudrillard. *The Perfect Crime*. In *Jean Baudrillard: Selected Writings*. Mark Poster, ed. Stanford: Stanford University Press, 2001. 266–75. 268.

35. Jean Baudrillard. *Cool Memories*. In *Jean Baudrillard: Selected Writings*. Mark Poster, ed. Stanford: Stanford University Press, 2001. 223–30. 225.

36. Janet Maslin. "Back to the Future Part II." *New York Times*. 11/22/89. http://movies.nytimes.com/movie/review?_r=1&res=950DE3D8153EF931A15752C1A96F948260&partner=Rotten%20Tomatoes&oref=slogin.

37. *America*, 56.

38. *Ibid.*, 69.

39. This last allusion is insightfully explicated in an article by Fred Erisman: "The Night Christopher Lloyd Danced with Mary Steenburgen." *Journal of Popular Film and Television*. 20.1, 1992. 29–33.

40. *Fragments*, 93.

41. *Simulacra and Simulation*, 43.

42. *Ibid.*, 12.

Works Cited

Baudrillard, Jean. *America*. Chris Turner, tr. London: Verso, 1988.

_____. *Cool Memories*. In *Jean Baudrillard: Selected Writings*. Mark Poster, ed. Stanford: Stanford University Press, 2001.

_____. *Fatal Strategies*. In *Jean Baudrillard: Selected Writings*. Mark Poster, ed. Stanford: Stanford University Press, 2001.

_____. *Fragments*. Emily Agar, tr. London: Verso, 1997.

_____. *The Illusion of the End*. Chris Turner, tr. Stanford: Stanford University Press, 1994.

_____. *The Perfect Crime*. In *Jean Baudrillard: Selected Writings*. Mark Poster, ed. Stanford: Stanford University Press, 2001.

_____. *Simulacra and Simulations*. Sheila Faria Glaser, tr. Ann Arbor: University of Michigan Press, 1994.

_____. *Simulations*. Paul Foss, Paul Patton, and Philip Beitchman, tr. New York: Semiotext(e), 1983.

_____. *The Transparency of Evil*. James Benedict, tr. London: Verso, 1993.

Bogard, William. "Baudrillard, Time, and the End." In *Baudrillard: A Critical Reader*. Douglas Kellner, ed. Oxford: Blackwell, 1994.

Ebert, Roger. "Back to the Future." 7/3/85. http://rogerebert.suntimes.com/apps/pbcs.dll/article?AID=/19850703/REVIEWS/507030301/1023.

_____. "Back to the Future Part II." 11/22/89. http://rogerebert.suntimes.com/apps/pbcs.dll/article?AID=/19891122/REVIEWS/911220301/1023.

_____. "Back to the Future Part III." 5/25/90. http://rogerebert.suntimes.com/apps/pbcs.dll/article?AID=/19900525/REVIEWS/5250301/1023.

Erisman, Fred. "The Night Christopher Lloyd Danced with Mary Steenburgen." *Journal of Popular Film and Television*. 20.1, 1992.

Gordon, Andrew. "*Back to the Future*: Œdipus as Time Traveler." In *Liquid Metal: The Science Fiction Film Reader*. Sean Redmond, ed. London: Wallflower Press, 2004.

Howe, Desson. "Back to the Future Part II." *Washington Post*, 11/24/89. http://www.washingtonpost.com/wp-srv/style/longterm/movies/videos/backtothefutureiihowe.html.

Kael, Pauline. "Back to the Future Part II." http://www.geocities.com/paulinekaelreviews/b1.html.

Maslin, Janet. "Back to the Future Part II." *New York Times*. 11/22/89. http://movies.nytimes.com/movie/review?_r=1&res=950DE3D8153EF931A15752C1A96F948260&partner=Rotten%20Tomatoes&oref=slogin.

Rojek, Chris and Bryan S. Turner. "Introduction: Regret Baudrillard?" In *Forget Baudrillard*. Chris Rojek and Bryan S. Turner, eds. London: Routledge, 1993.

Thompson, William Irwin. *The American Replacement of Nature*. New York: Doubleday, 1991.

Turner, Bryan S. "Cruising America." In *Forget Baudrillard*. Chris Rojek and Bryan S. Turner, eds. London: Routledge, 1993.

12. "Doing it in style": The Narrative Rules of Time Travel in the *Back to the Future* Trilogy

JENNIFER HARWOOD-SMITH AND
FRANCIS LUDLOW

Introduction

In *Back to the Future Part II*, the ulterior motives of Michael J. Fox's character, Marty McFly, provoke Doc Brown to provide an explicit justification for the invention of his time machine. This occurs when Doc discovers Marty's intent to use future knowledge contained in *Gray's Sports Almanac 1950–2000* for monetary gain. Doc Brown (Christopher Lloyd) in an archetypal portrayal of the almost-mad inventor-scientist, and despite the mandatory eccentric veneer of his delivery, his words hold weight and even move into the profound.

> The intent here is to gain a clear perspective of humanity. Where we've been, where we're going, the pitfalls and the possibilities, the perils and the promise and perhaps even an answer to that universal question: Why?

Doc's speech suggests a considered treatment of time travel in the *Back to the Future* trilogy, regardless of its comedic focus, Hollywood mass appeal and blockbuster status, often the death knell for the serious examination of any topic. The trilogy as a whole has received little academic attention, with only the first film read at all, variously as an Oedipal text,[1] or "a nostalgic call to arms for a return to the heady days of the American dream."[2] David Wittenberg has "no objection, in principle, to this scantiness"[3] of attention and appears surprised that the first film might sustain more than one reading. This chapter presents a reading of the concept of time travel in the trilogy, with reflection on the trilogy's use of time travel as a narrative device, an approach not seriously attempted before. Brief consideration is given to two other 1980s films that adopt time travel as a central concept and narrative device to provide a counterpart to the *Back to the Future* trilogy. These are *The Terminator*, directed by James Cameron, 1984, and *Bill and Ted's Excellent Adventure*, directed by Stephen Herek, 1989.

Time travel as a science fiction trope was well established by 1985 and *Back to the Future's* release. Paul Coates suggests the emergence of cinema is itself linked to the emergence of time travel narratives, in that cinema is not only a time machine in showing images of past events, but with editing, scenes can be made out of sequence and reordered to linearity.[4] The depiction of time travel in film and its employment as a narrative device is not, therefore, inherently new or innovative; however we argue that the trilogy is undeservedly neglected in its contribution to science fiction's exploration of time travel and its use as a narrative device.

A distinction between many TV series or films that feature time travel and the *Back to the Future* trilogy is its treatment of time and events occurring therein as changeable. In *Back to the Future*, a person's life and the events of which it comprises are not locked into history, an unusual perspective when compared with most scientific thought, philosophy and literature. In Irwin Allen's 1966–67 TV series *The Time Tunnel* and Terry Gilliam's 1995 film *Twelve Monkeys*, the past is unchangeable. Travelers may return and influence the past, but a traveler's actions simply form part of an already-established past. These works explore the response of philosophers such as Paul Horwich,[5] David Lewis,[6] Nicholas Smith,[7] and others,[8] to the traditional argument that time travel must be impossible, because otherwise events in our past could be changed from those we have sound knowledge of. In the view of Horwich and company, the past may be *affected* or *influenced*, but it cannot be changed. There cannot be two pasts; one before the actions of the time traveler, and one after. Only one unchangeable past exists. Actions taken by a time traveler to the past have already been taken, regardless of whether the traveler leaves for *our past* from *our future*. Such thinking leads ultimately to the notion of the closed causal time loop, where a traveler's influences may contribute directly to the cause of past events he seeks to alter, leading to his return to the past. These concepts have enthralled philosophers interested in freewill, predestination and paradox, and have enthralled filmmakers and authors who attempt to portray the sequence of events in closed causal time loops.

Manfred Nagl comments on the perception that "strong stereotyping, reduction to a few themes and basic models, as well as thoroughgoing plagiarism rate as characteristics of SF film."[9] The engine for ideas in science fiction is widely recognized to be the short story, but this medium has far less audience than science fiction film. If science fiction is serious in its oft-stated goal of communicating ideas of the potential of science and technology to affect society, then the role in delivery of concepts to significant audiences in film must be recognized. What of those who would confine the trilogy to the realms of fantasy or science fantasy due to its departure from an immutable timeline? The term "science fantasy" is often employed in commenting negatively upon works, the misconception being that they are inferior in freedom from adherence to currently-plausible science. Without entering a debate on the status of the *Back to the Future* trilogy (and time travel stories in general) as science fiction or science fantasy, the guidance given by respected author David Gerrold to prospective authors of science fiction and fantasy is worth quoting: "Go ahead, make something up! Anything. After all, this is fantasy, right? Wrong. The audience *still* wants to believe ... and believability comes from the recognition of an internally consistent system of logic."[10] If the filmmakers have achieved anything in their trilogy, it is a world in which time travel stays faithful to consistent rules and logic.

Joe Haldeman states that "most time travel stories are about narrative structure — whether the author is aware ... or not."[11] The potential logical complexities underlying causal chains of events in works premised on closed time loops has resulted in many fascinating and intricately narrated works of film and literature. In employing a concept of time in which past events are changeable, the makers of the *Back to the Future* trilogy could be accused of opting out of the challenge presented by closed causal time loops arising from travel to an unalterable past, and indeed, of ignoring most thinking on the subject. To those for whom adherence to science is important in evaluating the merits of science fiction,[12] this might be detrimental to evaluation of the trilogy (as the majority of scientists and philosophers who accept time travel to the past as a possibility subscribe to the idea that time travelers may influence, but not change the past), while others do not believe in the possibility of travel to the past at all.[13] John Barrow notes that a "worry about the analysis of time travel is the exclusion of ... quantum mechanics ... it is far less restrictive about what can happen in the world ... instead of telling us that a given cause has a particular effect ... there is a whole array of different possible outcomes with different possibilities."[14] In Hugh Everett's 1957 "many worlds" interpretation of the probabilistic nature of quantum mechanics, if a glass falls, there exists a world where it breaks and one where it does not. A traveler may return to the past and intervene in events, but in doing so exists in an alternate universe. That from which the traveler originates is one in which she did not intervene. Thus, the traveler's past is not really changed.[15] In any case, as discussed below, no conclusive evidence exists to suggest the filmmakers employed the "many worlds" concept in their trilogy.

Avoiding the strictures of an unalterable past may be an avenue to a lazy treatment of time travel, but a changeable past offers scope for narrative invention and intricacy if treated well. Indeed, an entire subgenre of science fiction branded "alternate history" concerns itself with resolving in intricate detail potential consequences of changes to past events, tending "to cluster around particularly dramatic and colourful [sic] junctures of history, with World War II and the American Civil War as particular favourites [sic]."[16] Nor is this confined to science fiction. Historians have analyzed consequences of changes to key historical events under various "what if?" scenarios.[17] The *Back to the Future* trilogy is, if somewhat unusual, at least therefore in good company, even if it does focus more on the personal than the global.

Care has clearly been invested in the treatment of time and time travel in the trilogy. This is evident even in the small details. Timekeeping is important. At no point does Doc describe an event without at least giving its date, and where he knows it, the specific time.[18] Marty is constantly checking his watch, though it never seems to work correctly. The first film begins with the ticking of multiple clocks and the climactic moment comes when the clock (in the clock tower) in the town square is struck by lightning and will never work again. In 2015 the symbol for the courthouse is a clock with a lightning strike, and scenes in 1885 occur around the construction of the same clock. Michael Klastorin and Sally Hibbin note "Doc doesn't pay much attention to fashion, yet he is a man whose clothing constantly changes with the times. His shirts sometimes reflect things to come. In *Part III*, when Marty prepares to take the DeLorean from 1955 to 1885, Doc's Hawaiian shirt just happens to be emblazoned with lariats and cacti."[19] Thus, even when characters are not directly referencing time, it is omnipresent throughout the films. We also see Richard J. Gott,[20] and Paul J. Nahin,[21] use the trilogy to illustrate time travel concepts. This is further testament to careful treatment of time travel in the trilogy. C. J. Henderson remarks of the first film that "time travel is obviously a theoretical science at best, but it's amazing how many filmmakers get even the most basic concepts regarding it fouled up. Here the science is tightly thought out."[22] This is ironic, given that *Back to the Future* relies on its own internal narrative logic, not external science.

Klastorin and Hibbin state that director Robert Zemeckis and co-producer Bob Gale "always hoped to make a movie about time travel, a subject that had fascinated them both since childhood."[23] The care of the filmmakers in treating time travel and the consistency with which they track forward changes made in the past belies Harlan Ellison's accusation that "the lofty time paradox possibilities are reduced to the imbecile level of sitcom"[24] in the first movie. It also belies George Mann's statement that the first film "doesn't stand up to a great deal of analysis."[25] Though the second and third films are often seen as weaker,[26] they contribute much to the concept of time travel in the trilogy, enhancing and exploring the ideas employed in the first film. Jonathan

Cowie and Tony Chester remark that "the SF really got going in *Back to the Future II*."[27] It is true in making the first film, Zemeckis and Gale intended it to stand alone, with no sequels planned.[28] However, it is unfair to view the final two films as motivated simply by financial interests after the success of the first.[29] All three work successfully together and are properly seen as "a set-piece and make for one of the best time travel romps on the big screen."[30] Full appreciation of the concept of time travel developed in *Back to the Future* requires consideration of all three films. This also applies to the use of time travel as a narrative device.

In addition to being science fiction, the *Back to the Future* trilogy is also comedy, and, despite its comic veneer, presents its main characters with numerous moral challenges, dealing with Marty's conflicting views of his mother and family, his tendencies towards greed and altruism, and what these commingled qualities lead to when coupled with the challenges and opportunities presented by a time machine. It is the greed/altruism dichotomy in Marty's character that we focus upon when examining the use of time travel as a narrative device in the trilogy. Finally, against claims that the trilogy's portrayal of the 1950s is idealized, it can be remarked that it deals with race, bullying, burgeoning sexuality, and attempted rape, and thus cannot be considered *that* idealized.

"We're going to do it, so we've done it already" vs. "It will be done once we have done it; it has not happened before"

Andrew Gordon remarks that the 1980s was a decade filled with time travel films.[31] Of the plethora of such films in the 1980s, *The Terminator* and *Bill and Ted's Excellent Adventure* are chosen for comparison with *Back to the Future*. All three films enjoyed enormous success upon release, were originally stand alone with sequels added afterwards and have attained cult popularity years after release. *Terminator* and *Bill and Ted's* time travel narratives are an interesting example of what *Back to the Future* rejected in favor of a changeable timeline, and are therefore worth some examination.

Perhaps the more iconic, and more successful in terms of franchising, is *The Terminator*. The closed causal loop of the film is created for the specific purpose of ensuring the continued existence of John Connor by his father traveling from the future to protect and impregnate his mother (John Connor is, in terms of dates of birth, older than his father). *The Terminator* resolves one of the larger issues of time travel, namely Arthur C. Clarke's remark that "however unpleasant our age may appear to the future, surely one would expect scholars and students to visit us, if such a thing were possible...."[32] Associated with this is the question why, if there are travelers from the future in the present, we do not see them? *The Terminator* does away with any subtlety on the part of the time travelers. The end of the world is coming, and their respective missions, Kyle Reese's to save Sarah Connor and the Terminator's to kill her, are both so urgent as to require them to abandon any subterfuge. Sarah Connor is also sufficiently unimportant to her contemporaries that the events of *The Terminator* are not likely to incite any great investigation, so society as a whole fails to realize what is happening. The narrative leads inevitably to a dystopia, a brutal war with heavy losses on both sides. However, the journey into the past is already a part of the established timeline, representative of Lawrence Sklar's "self causing events."[33] John Connor's assertion that "there is no fate save what we make" is belied by his part in his own conception, which is not his own idea, but rather what he has been told he will and must do to save mankind. This is the primary difference between *The Terminator* and *Back to the Future*; the past is immutable.

The secondary difference lies in the greed/altruism dichotomy of time travel narratives. In immutable timelines, the outcomes of greed and altruism are fixed; any moral questions these outcomes raise are undermined because no matter what is done, the timeline cannot change. This raises the issue of freewill versus predestination. Arguably, an immutable timeline involves both, in that events result from the actions of individuals, whose actions essentially lock events so that they cannot be changed. Even though John Connor is destined to send his father back in time, he does so not primarily from greed, but from altruism towards the human race. He has no guarantee of the human race's survival and freedom if he does not create himself. Kyle Reese credits John Connor with saving humanity, with being the core of the resistance, and John Connor is raised with this knowledge. Without John Connor, *Terminator* implies, the human race is doomed.

Bill and Ted's Excellent Adventure also involves a closed causal loop. Twice the viewer sees Ted, from two different angles, remind his younger self to wind his watch; however Ted still forgets. The future society of *Bill and Ted* know they must insert someone into the past to bring about their present, but there is no indication they believe this involves changing history. In fact, the film starts with the council telling Rufus that Bill and Ted are about to be separated, and that this must be prevented. For them, the preservation of history is imperative, and nothing that they do will change it, merely ensure it.

The greed/altruism dichotomy takes on a slightly different meaning from *The Terminator*, in that it involves the creation of a utopia, and not the creation of the means to survive a dystopia. The future society is founded on such principles as "Be Excellent to Each Other" learned from Bill and Ted. By ensuring this present, they are preserving utopia for mankind. The presumption in both films is that the timeline, though immutable, is the best possible timeline, and that even if it could be changed, it would be detrimental to mankind. *Back to the Future* challenges this idea by introducing a changeable, malleable timeline that moves like a river, with alterations to its course resulting not in the destruction of the timeline, but a slightly different one.

A final point of interest about time travel in *The Terminator, Bill and Ted's Excellent Adventure* and *Back to the Future* is the notion of causality beyond the linear, a causality related to local personal, rather than linear time. Many scientists and philosophers struggle with non-linear (i.e. circular) causality. Jonathan Harrison could not escape the fact that the result of time travel, that is, the presence of people in the past, preceded the cause, that is, the building of the time machine.[34] For some theorists the maintenance of linear causality is an obsession.[35] Works of fiction featuring time travel tend towards predication upon non-linear personal causality. John Connor's father is born after John Connor, and Rufus ensures his own existence long before he is born, as does Marty McFly. Personal causality is a staple of series such as *Doctor Who*, which depends upon acceptance that Doctor visited the end of the universe prior to his visit to Pompeii, despite the linear order of events. Time travelers must reject linear causality, and embrace personal causality for their universe to make sense. From the perspective of an outside observer, moving through linear time and observing linear causality, the above events are out of sequence and effect precedes cause (it could almost be compared to watching a film being made; everything is out of order. However, if the person watching the finished film is compared to a time traveler, to them it makes sense).

For *The Terminator* and *Bill and Ted's Excellent Adventure*, time is immutable, and the travelers exist in the past before (in terms of linear time) they are born in the future. As the timeline is unchangeable, the struggle between greed and altruism is never really resolved, and outcomes are fixed. With changeable timelines, the greed/altruism dichotomy takes character development further than in immutable timelines. For example, in *Terminator 3*, John Connor goes from a drifter with no ambition to taking responsibility for the human race. This, arguably, does not result from any internal struggle within John. Rather, it results because it has always done so, John knows he has no choice and has been raised to be capable of his role. In the *Back to the Future* trilogy, Marty's choices are not made until he makes them, and he must determine the resolution of his conflicting tendencies to greed and altruism. Given this distinction, Marty McFly is arguably a more interesting character than John Connor can ever be, since Marty has the opportunity to grow beyond what he is told he will be.

"It hasn't happened until it has happened"

The core premise of the *Back to the Future* trilogy is that time is changeable, but exceptions are noted where Marty's influence may predate his first travel to the past. These involve Marty's apparent inspiration of character Goldie Wilson to become Mayor and his inspiration of Chuck Berry in inventing rock and roll. The films provide insufficient proof to say definitively whether these are closed causal loops or if Marty's influences coincide with already-occurring events. Indeed, Goldie's statement that he is going to night school and going to make something of himself, before Marty says anything to him, indicates that his path to being Mayor was already underway. However, Bob Gale states: "it wasn't a foregone conclusion ... that 1955 was the year [to which Marty returns but] ... was important because we wanted Marty to invent rock and roll...."[36] Thus, we may infer the intention to create some closed causal loops, engaging in what Paul J. Nahin terms "the central puzzle of time travel."[37] Another reading of this is that the filmmakers temporarily ignored consistency to the concept of a changeable timeline in the trilogy for the sake of a gag.

The above aside, time is changeable in *Back to the Future*, and the internal structure of the films constantly reinforces this. What Marty or Doc do when time traveling has not happened until they do it. This allows Marty engage in the most-discussed aspect of time travel: auto-infanticide. Nicholas Smith says that "auto-infanticide makes time travel more improbable than impossible."[38] However, for worlds in which time is malleable, the potential for auto-infanticide makes time travel more inadvisable than anything else. If a many worlds view is adopted, a traveler might not return to their own past, but to an alternate past, and therein kill a child identical to them but not-them, the completion of this act being one aspect differentiating the timeline of the universe in which they now exist. It may be tempting to read the trilogy as employing the many worlds concept, if only to satisfy those whose rating of a work of science fiction, and its classification *as* science fiction,[39] depends upon use of plausible science. Some aspects of the trilogy might suggest a many worlds concept. One such is Doc's description of older Biff's changes to the past (upon stealing the DeLorean in *Part II*) as creating an alternate 1985. However, it should be remembered that as far as Doc can see, there are alternate worlds; as the viewer, it is possible to see that there are no alternate worlds, merely changes to a single timeline. Old Biff's return to his original future implies that he could not have generated an alternate future, because that would have been the only place he could have ended up. The reasoning behind his ability to return to that future and Marty and Doc's inability to do the same later on in the second film is discussed later.

A reading without reference to many worlds is possible and incorporates the evidence of the films more fully. One key aspect is the handling of doubles. When Doc and Marty enter alternate 1985s (at the end of the first film, the middle of *Part II*, and end of *Part III*) no doubles are seen, though Marty and Doc have, apparently, existed and been involved in events up to their re-entry to the timeline after traveling. Thus, when Marty first returns from 1955 he does not discover another in his place, though his family has changed radically and he has existed alongside them. Nor are any doubles seen in the alternate 1985 in *Part III*. When Marty and Doc travel to Bifftastic 1985 in *Part II* doubles are absent, but Biff and Lorraine believe Marty is in boarding school, while a newspaper shows Doc in a mental institute. The trilogy leaves open the existence of doubles of Marty and Doc in the alternate 1985s but implies there exists only one Marty and Doc. Indeed, the Marty we see starting his journey in the first film is the Marty we follow to the end. This absence is confirmation that a many worlds concept is not adopted in the trilogy, as an alternate Marty and Doc would exist in each alternate world or timeline. Though we see other characters markedly different when the timeline is altered, the implication is that these are not doubles of characters existing simultaneously in other timelines, but *the same characters in a single changeable timeline* altered by different events and experiences.

The doubles that are seen in the trilogy (e.g. two Martys witnessing Doc shot at the end of the first film, both on-stage at the dance in 1955 in *Part II*) are the *same* Marty at an earlier stage in his adventures in his own personal time. Even older Marty in 2015 is not a true alternate Marty or double but an older version of the same time-traveling Marty further along the timeline established by his own actions in 1955 in the first film; however, it is not the future of the Marty who travels in time in the second film. 2015 Marty is eventually negated by the personal growth that younger Marty goes through, which will be explored later. It is therefore misleading to describe each 1985 visited by Marty as an *alternate* 1985 or alternate timeline, but more correctly as an *altered* 1985 on a single malleable timeline.

This raises an important question: if only one Marty exists in a single changeable timeline, how does Marty survive or experience the changes he makes to the timeline? Marty returns in the first film to 1955 and causes changes leading to a situation where he will not be born (i.e. he, not George, is hit by Lorraine's father's car). This clearly represents an instance of inadvertent auto-infanticide. Time is not immutable and Marty must remedy the situation. He cannot rely upon the fact that he exists *now* to ensure that he *will* be born, as one might in a past that is unchangeable (wherein Marty's actions in the past would already form part of the timeline leading to his birth). Thus, Marty must act to ensure his existence, as his fading from his family photograph explicitly depicts.

Nor does Marty's involvement in ensuring his own birth imply the existence of a closed causal loop wherein his actions in 1955 result in his birth, growing up, and ultimately his travel from 1985 to 1955 to ensure his birth. Instead, history is changeable and Marty was born before having any influence on the past. Thus, while Marty's remedial actions ensure he will again be born, his very presence in the past means he cannot ensure his life will unfold exactly as before traveling to the past. In returning to 1985 Marty and his family have had different experiences leading to different outcomes, such as George McFly's success as an author. Marty is technically part of this, having, from the perspective of the non-time travelers, lived an improved life. It may be argued, therefore, that Marty has not fully prevented auto-infanticide, since the events and experiences comprising the identity of the Marty we know from the original timeline have no longer occurred. Yet the Marty we follow from the first film retains his memories of the original timeline. Presumably the act of time travel protects Marty (and Doc) from changes in the timeline and allows them to re-enter in the state they left. *The Butterfly Effect* (2004) directed by Eric Bress and J. Mackye Gruber addressed this by generating new memories in the traveler's mind when changes in the past created new events and experiences. It should be noted, however, that in *The Butterfly Effect*, the two time travelers in the film do not physically travel in time; rather, their older consciousnesses take control of their younger bodies and change events in the past. In the *Back to the Future* trilogy, the memories and experiences of alternate events remain lost or unaccounted for, perhaps because the act of the time travel is physical and not mental.

As time travel in the trilogy does not involve true alternate universes, time itself is changeable. This is an important break from general time travel theory because until Marty goes back to 1955 he has never been in 1955. One might object that in the first film when Marty returns from 1955 to 1985, he sees his slightly younger self travel to 1955. This might appear to contradict the notion that Marty's actions in the past change an already-established timeline. The films' use of instantaneous changes to items from the future solves this problem succinctly. There is no need for Marty to continually return to 1955 to ensure the existence of the altered 1985. As seen from the instantaneous return of Marty and his siblings to the photograph, once events are definitely going to happen, they are essentially locked into the timeline. As soon as the Libyans attack, Marty is definitely going to travel back in time;

thus, the altered 1985 does not begin with Marty's return to it, but rather several minutes before Marty time travels at all. Therefore, the older Marty can arrive at the scene of the Libyan attack and still see his younger self traveling back. This is further reinforced by the fact that Marty traveled through time after the changes to his family's history were set. Because a few hours passed between his changing his past (including his father standing up to Biff), Marty ends up traveling behind the wave, so he re-enters the timeline in the new 1985, and not the original one. In fact, what the older Marty is witnessing, from the altered 1985, is the last remnant of the original 1985 collapsing around the trip to the past (as a result of this, Doc is actually dead right up until the younger Marty has traveled through time). Because Marty travels back several minutes before he left, what he is witnessing is an action that no longer exists, but for it to no longer exist, it must have happened in the first place. A good analogy for this is to think of the changes of the timeline moving like a river, with Marty's escape in the DeLorean to the past as a rock being submerged by the river. Even when the new timeline has, for all intents and purposes, covered up that original event, the event still happened at some point in the timeline, despite its invisibility. Hence, Doc survives the shooting by the Libyans, something that does not happen before Marty's first travel to 1955 where he warns Doc of the attack.

Support for the idea of changes moving forward in time comes from the photograph of Marty and his siblings shown at key moments in the first film. When Marty interrupts his parents' first meeting by preventing George's collision with Lorraine's father's car, he and his siblings do not pop out of existence immediately, but fade slowly from the picture. This implies that changes to the established timeline (that sees Marty's birth) are gradual and propagate through time. Until changes are absolutely going to happen, inertia maintains the original timeline to a point. Marty's existence remains enough of a *possibility* throughout most of the first film to allow him to continue to exist; as soon as Marty's birth starts to become sufficiently improbable, Marty begins to disappear. When Marty's efforts lead directly and indirectly to George and Lorraine's kiss at the dance, he and his siblings will definitely be born, and their return to the picture is much faster than their disappearance, when their existence was doubtful but still possible. The notion of changes in the timeline moving like a wave is reinforced in *Part II*, where the older Biff from 2015 steals the DeLorean and gives his younger self the Almanac in 1955. Because time travel is instantaneous while changes to the timeline are not, older Biff returns to the 2015 from which he departed. The delay in this case — as Biff is a character that would use the Almanac without qualms — is most likely because older Biff leaves soon after giving younger Biff the Almanac. Younger Biff is skeptical of its authenticity until that evening, when he compares it to sports results on the radio. Since older Biff leaves before this, he returns to 2015 ahead of the changes that are moving like a wave through time; thus his disappearance, similar to Marty's partial disappearance in the first film, is a result of changes to the timeline catching up to him. Older Biff has thus engaged in a form of incomplete auto-infanticide. The experiences that comprise older Biff's character no longer occur, and in consequence older Biff ceases to exist as a distinct identity, replaced by Biff in the Bifftastic timeline.

Marty and Doc travel from 2015 back towards the wavefront, meet it, and end up in Bifftastic 1985. It can be surmised that Marty and Doc did not experience Bifftastic 2015 because of how soon after older Biff's alteration they left. As with Marty's return to the improved 1985 in the first film, neither Marty nor Doc have memories from the radically altered Bifftastic timeline (prior to their first experiences of it upon arriving in 1985). Marty still remembers the first timeline (from which he originally departs to 1955 after Doc's shooting) and does not recall events like his father's death in the Bifftastic timeline, while Doc remembers the second (wherein he survives shooting) and does not remember events such as his confinement to an asylum. Once in Bifftastic 1985, Marty and Doc cannot return to 2015 to prevent older Biff stealing the Almanac or DeLorean because, unlike older Biff, they are now behind the wave of changes and unable to bypass it. Their only option is to return to the past before older Biff's changes and counteract them there.[40] Whether they can head into the future and bypass the Bifftastic future by jumping centuries ahead, and therefore passing the wavefront is an interesting debate; however since such an action would not be helpful to them in repairing the past, it is unexplored.

In the second film, as in the first when Marty ensures his birth, the restoration of the timeline is near instantaneous, with the matchbox Marty took from Bifftastic 1985 changing moments after the Almanac is destroyed in 1955, and both the newspaper articles kept by Marty and Doc changing also. When Marty and Doc save Clara in 1885, in the third film, Marty is again protected from remembering the changed timeline. He remembers the canyon where Clara died as Clayton Ravine, though we know at the end of the third film it is now Eastwood Ravine owing to Marty's (i.e. "Clint Eastwood's") presumed death with the destruction of the hijacked train in 1885. Like the changes of the first two films, preventing Doc's death at the hands of Mad Dog Tannen has an immediate effect upon the picture of Doc's tombstone. Thus, the system of potential changes as opposed to definite changes, as seen in the first film, is consistently maintained throughout the trilogy.

A traveler who prevents their own birth raises the specter of a paradox in which they both have and have not existed to destroy themselves. This is deemed impossible in worlds where the timeline is immutable. But the timeline is not immutable in *Back to the Future* and we can speculate on another possibility — the outcome should Marty fail to ensure his own birth. Assuming that events of the night of the Enchantment Under the Sea dance that lead to George and Lorraine's kiss are not banana skins created by a universe attempting to maintain the events of the original timeline,[41] and assuming the filmmakers were willing to let their hero lose, then Marty could fail to bring his parents together. If so, changes to the timeline would move forward into the future to 1985, to the night where Marty should be traveling back to ensure these changes. Since Marty no longer exists to make the journey, the wavefront would stall, as it were, and, without Marty's interference, a new wavefront begins in 1955, overwriting Marty's alterations and reasserting the original timeline. However, since Marty once more exists to travel into the past, and presumably does so again, he again inadvertently destroys himself, *provided that he acts precisely as he did the previous time he traveled back*. This means that, in Hill Valley at least, two versions of the same thirty years are constantly looping. Neither version of the timeline is capable of moving beyond the act or non-act of time-travel in 1985 because it is that which restarts the loop. Marty might therefore pop in and out of existence countless times before he repairs the timeline and ensures his birth, assuming he *can* act differently each time around. This kind of repeating loop does not happen in *Back to the Future*, however, the speculation about it happening, and the consequences in the specific narrative logic of the films, does raise some interesting questions.

Since the act of time travel in the trilogy does not in itself produce paradoxes, the filmmakers suggest the potential for a different universe-destroying paradox. In a world where a traveler may meet his future self in a timeline altered by his previous actions, or meet his past self in the process of time traveling, he will, according to Doc Brown, either pass out from shock or generate a temporal paradox that will destroy at least the Milky Way. When younger Jennifer meets her future self, both pass out. It appears the rule about time travel not having happened until it has happened applies to the future too; older 2015 Jennifer has not time traveled, and cannot recognize her younger self as a time traveler. Nor has younger Jennifer any clear idea of what has happened to her, and both faint from shock upon seeing each other. This implies that if there is to be a universe-destroying paradox, it might be generated by the meeting of two versions of the same person, *both of whom are in the process of time traveling*.

If younger Marty and 2015 Marty met, both would recognize the other as time travelers, as 2015 Marty has lived in a timeline affected by his own travel to 1955 in the first film, something he would certainly recall. But he would have no memory of traveling to 2015 as this has not happened until it happens in *Part II*. Younger Marty is here meeting his future self in the first altered timeline established by his first trip to 1955. The meeting of a version of Marty that will definitely continue to exist, and a version that will be replaced as a result of the younger Marty's new journey to the future has the potential for creating a paradox. One such result could be 2015 Marty's attempting to prevent 1985 Marty from returning to the past, realizing that the presence of this time traveler will cause an alteration similar to that which happened to his parents (given 2015 Marty's life, it does seem likely that he might encourage changes instead). However, this is less likely, as the older Marty will simply be absorbed/altered by changes traveling forward in time. When Marty returns to 1955 in *Part II*, he must avoid his younger self, since Marty's second incursion into the past did not happen in the first film, and in consequence he risks interacting in events in his local or personal past, which leads to the likeliness of him changing his *personal time traveling* past, a far more dangerous feat than changing his personal future.

Once one does not interfere in their personal past and the younger self does not recognize the older self, some interaction can happen. When older Doc meets younger Doc in 1955 in *Part II*, he manages to hide his identity, even though both spend time in conversation. He does not interrupt younger Doc's preparations to harness the lightning strike to send Marty back to 1985 in the first film. Traveling to 1885 is certainly easier for Marty and Doc, in that they do not risk encountering their past selves. What might happen if Marty or Doc interfered in their own personal past is debatable, but would likely result in their fading from existence as their younger counterparts make different decisions leading to a paradox where the actions of Marty or Doc are influenced by future selves who cease to exist because of their own influences. Whether any of this is possible or not, as Nichols, Smith and Miller remark, "time travel is mysterious."[42] This would appear to hold whether the past is fixed or changeable, the timeline linear or circular. The complexities of time travel are not lost on the filmmakers. As Zemeckis remarks of *Part II*, "we were in a situation that was very unique because we had the opportunity to do a sequel to a movie that's about time travel and time paradox ... we could do something ... you could never do under any other circumstance ... to go into the first movie in the second movie from a different angle. That excited me and ... *Back to the Future II* is one of my most interesting movies ... certainly the strangest movie I've made."[43]

It remains to comment on the technicalities of time travel in the trilogy, and its relation to that in *The Time Machine*, the influence most clearly cited by the filmmakers. Veronica Hollinger states that *The Time Machine* is the story "that first applied technology to time travel and ... remains the most influential time-travel story ever written."[44] As in *The Time Machine*, the original concept for the machine in *Back to the Future* was a stationary object. Zemeckis relates that "the time machine went through a lot of variations ... a refrigerator we thought of at one point ... as the story developed and we started to think ... if you ... were to build a time machine ... that you'd be foolish not to make it mobile and to take it with you...."[45] This explains why the time machine is built into a DeLorean, but not why it must move to enable time travel. Time travel is inextricably linked with velocity in Einstein's universe. Thus, someone traveling faster than light will reach their destination before light from their original position. Regarding the significance of the DeLorean attaining 88 mph to allow time travel, Bob Gale remarks, "why 88 miles per hour, what's so special about that? It's easy to remember that's all, there's no special significance...."[46] Despite this, the fact that the DeLorean must move to enable time travel avoids the problems associated with time travel in a stationary position, as with *The Time Machine*, where, among other difficulties, the time machine could reform just before the lever was pulled for the original trip, thus paradoxically destroying itself before its journey.[47] Furthermore, references throughout the trilogy, including the naming of Doc's dog, Einstein, imply awareness of the significance of movement in time travel.

Gale states that "in discussing ... what was time travel going to look like, we started coming up with ... all kinds of ideas. What is the space time continuum going to look like when Marty's in the DeLorean ... and at a certain point Bob [Zemeckis] and I looked at each other and said ... we don't need any of that stuff. Time travel should be instantaneous. This is a story about people; it's not a story about hardware. The hardware is just what we use to make it believable."[48] The technical aspects of time travel in the trilogy thus impart little more about the concept employed, but do serve as an excellent plot device. Because time travel is dependent upon getting the DeLorean to 88 miles per hour and generating 1.21 gigawatts of electricity, in 1955 Marty and Doc must find a way to generate the electricity they need. In *Part II*, Doc has solved both problems using a fusion generator and a hover conversion, but in 1885, Marty and Doc have no way to get the DeLorean to travel at 88 miles per hour since the gas tank ruptured and there is no way for them to make suitable gasoline for the car's engine. Thus, the films integrate not only the nature of time into their narrative structure, but also the technicalities of time travel in the trilogy, rather than using these simply to provide special effects shots at the expense of story.

Time travel is punishing for the DeLorean; as it powers up, lighting crackles all over it, its wheels leave burning trails when it starts to move through time, and its exterior is freezing when it re-enters the timeline. Something invariably happens to it, whether it be the starter failing, the gas tank getting ruptured or the time circuits acting up. The DeLorean suffers for time travel, eventually getting destroyed by a train upon its final re-entry to 1985. It would seem that the risks that accompany the lives of time travelers do not leave time machines unscathed and indeed, the changes to the timeline itself may be responsible for the generally decrepit state of time machines (not just the DeLorean, but Bill and Ted's phone box, whose time circuit is held together by chewing gum, and Doctor Who's consistently malfunctioning TARDIS). Time travel may be permissible in the world of *Back to the Future*, but it would seem the Universe does not intend to make it easy.

Greed, Altruism and Growing Up

In discussing time travel as narrative device in the trilogy, we must concentrate upon how situations arising from time travel drive the development of Marty's character. Because a changeable timeline allows the possibility of *accidentally* initiating auto-infanticide, characters are placed in extreme situations that allow for personal growth. This is where the greed/altruism dichotomy appears in the trilogy. Marty's desire to ensure his existence in the first film is motivated mostly by self-interest. Nowhere does Marty explicitly say he wants to restore the timeline for his brother and sister. His concern with his family photograph only becomes pronounced when he himself begins to vanish. None of the McFlys at the start of the first film appear happy, with the exception of George and Dave, both in dead-end jobs and more concerned with lives devoid of stress than achievement. In some ways, it shows a lack of character when Marty leaves behind the former version of his family with such ease upon creating the improved 1985 at the end of the first film. While the McFlys might be happier for changes in the timeline, only Marty has truly escaped the autoinfanticidal consequences of time travel with his identity intact. Marty's family changes due to his actions, but these changes are not of their own volition. Nor might they willingly submit to them if a choice were presented. Marty is arguably selfish for preferring the "improved" version of his family to that which raised him, along with his increased material wealth.

For the first film, Marty is essentially a selfish character, doing whatever it takes to return to 1985, manipulating those around him to ensure his existence, even if he is unaware (and thus not motivated) by the fact that his future is greatly improved by his actions. This self interest is offset by his affection for Doc (despite, or perhaps because of Doc's slightly "nutty" status) and when, upon seeing George in danger, his instinct is to save him, putting his own existence at risk not just from Lorraine's father's car but the change introduced in the timeline. He is proud of his father upon discovering his creativity in writing, but this reveals how little he knew of his father before going to 1955. However, it is in fact Marty's initial self interest that helps make the *Back to the Future* trilogy engaging. By placing this flaw in Marty's character, he has the opportunity to grow. If not for time travel, Marty might have remained emotionally stunted and frustrated.

In the second film, Marty's greed combines with the negative possibilities of time travel when he purchases the sports almanac to win at gambling, leading to Doc's succinct line: "I didn't invent the time machine to win at gambling; I invented the time machine to travel through time." Marty's greed leads directly to the creation of the Bifftastic reality (a post apocalyptic present, rather than future) and the death of his father. The Bifftastic world is hell not only for Marty, but for everyone in Hill Valley.

An interesting side note is to examine the 2015 Marty as the inevitable result of greed. His selfishness loses him his livelihood, and it would be interesting to contemplate how he would react to meeting his younger time-traveling self, and whether, like Biff, Marty would try to change the past to make his own life better. The implication is that 2015 Marty has learned no lessons from his life, and so would have the wrong influence on his younger self. However, 2015 Marty is not developed enough as a character to make those judgments, and might influence his younger self to preserve his own past, even at the expense of the future he'd dreamed of.

Nineteen eighty-five Marty's guilt over his actions results not just in determination to retrieve the almanac at any cost, but his prompt destruction of the almanac, saving not just himself, but everyone he knows and loves from a future where Biff is in power. As the films progress, Marty's greed is tempered by growing altruism for others. At the start of *Part III* it is revealed that Doc will die just days after he writes the letter delivered to Marty by Western Union. Marty decides immediately to go back in time to save Doc, in the face of Doc's explicit instructions that he return to 1985. He even faces Mad Dog Tannen, a far worse substitute for Biff, to make sure Doc will not be killed. At the climax of the trilogy, Marty does not prevent Doc from leaving with Clara, even though Doc will be gone from his life. Nor, when Doc appears with his train/time machine, does he try to convince him to stay. Invariably we learn that time travel in the trilogy is about the traveler's responsibility to the overall timeline as opposed to their personal gain, even if change is unavoidable. Marty's struggle with greed and altruism is most fully developed in parts *II* and *III* of the trilogy. At the end of the first film, Marty's struggles are not resolved, yet his adventures are rewarded by material gain and a family of whom he can be proud. Robert Zemeckis comments that "you gotta look at that ending in historical context, it's a very eighties ending ... there were a couple of reviews that came out of Europe that keyed in ... on the idea ... how can these filmmakers equate this kind of happiness with ... material possessions."[49] In contrast, both sequels bring something real to Marty's development as a character by resolving issues raised by the first film.

Time travel helps rid Marty of another flaw: hotheadedness. This is a disadvantage in all three films. Had he not repeatedly fought Biff and impressed Lorraine, she might not have become infatuated with him. If he were inclined to think things through, he would not have prevented George being hit by Lorraine's father. Admittedly, his reaction in saving George was probably too quick to think through, but by the last film he judges situations more carefully. A tendency to jump into situations headlong helps save his son from prison and allows him to acquire the hoverboard in the second film, but becomes a liability twice more. In 2015 he loses his job when challenged to break the law by Needles, who calls him a chicken. Lorraine's conversation with Marlene reveals Marty's aggressive reaction to being called a chicken ruined his life when he becomes involved in a drag race that, interestingly, occurs on the day in 1985 he first went back in time (keeping in mind that while Marty time traveled the night before, he did so after midnight). When Marty could have run away from Biff outside the dance in 1955, he allows himself to be provoked and loses the almanac to Biff once more, having to chase after him for it. However, the incident with Biff in 1955 is the first time Marty acknowledges he should not allow himself be bothered by someone calling him a coward. This is not long-lived; only days later Marty is provoked by Mad Dog Tannen and ends up getting dragged through 1885's Hill Valley by a horse.

But rather than any changes made to the past, it is ultimately the lessons Marty learns upon his adventures that save his future. When provoked by Needles into a drag race at the end of *Part III*, Marty recreates his future by refusing to participate and grows as a character that the audience can both relate to and respect.

Time travel as a narrative device is also one of the more entertaining ways to tell a story, with lots of inside jokes. Uncle Joey's joy in his playpen is only funny if the viewer, like Marty, is aware that he will end up in jail (no alterations to the timeline seem capable of preventing this, though he might not be in jail in the altered 1985 of the first film, as Joey's situation is not revealed). Lorraine's father calling Marty's parents idiots and admonishing Lorraine not to have a child like him is hilarious only because we know Lorraine is Marty's mother. Few time travel stories that mix 1950s and 1980s can resist portraying the disbelief of 1950s characters at Ronald Reagan's presidency in the 1980s.[50] Lorraine's drinking, smoking and overt sexuality are laughable in contrast to her older self's prudishness. George's repetition of Marty's fear of rejection allows the viewer to see that George has influenced Marty, albeit negatively. Marty's recognition of Goldie Wilson as future mayor of Hill Valley is amusing not just because we know Goldie will be, but because of Marty's absolute shock at seeing his mayor so young. When George balls up his fist and hits Biff, it is all the more stirring after the image of his future self impotently balling up his fist as he explains to Marty how he could not stand up to Biff. The Cafe '80s in *Part II* is amusing to 1980s viewers because of its bizarre depiction of 1980s culture. Anything involving the clock tower is laced with insider knowledge on the part of the viewer. As a narrative device, therefore, time travel seems destined to amuse the viewer, if not the participants.

Conclusion

David Lowenthal remarks that "five reasons for going ... back dominate time-travel literature: explaining the past, searching for a golden age, enjoying the exotic, reaping the rewards of temporal displacement and foreknowledge, and refashioning life by changing the past."[51] The *Back to the Future* trilogy explores all of these and is a work from which much can be read. As C. J. Henderson states: "*Back to the Future* is more than it seems on the surface. As a science fiction movie it deserves an A+."[52] Although *Terminator* espouses the creed that there is "no fate but what we make," it is in the *Back to the Future* trilogy that this concept is truly realized. Marty McFly remakes his family's past, his own present, and his and Doc's future. There is a sense of optimism in the trilogy and even the dystopia of *Part II* does not dispel this. Indeed, it informs the viewer that no matter what mistakes they make in life, there is a way back, that the world can be rescued from the consequences of greed by courage and selflessness. Marty's reward in the end is not only an improved life, happier for him and his family, but self-growth. This secures his own future more than any changes he makes to the past; when he grows enough as a character to resist, without foreknowledge of the outcome, involvement in the drag race with Needles in *Part III*, avoiding the consequences blamed for his failure to fulfill his potential as a musician in 2015. When the fax Jennifer brought from the future goes blank, his future is unknown, but brighter than before.

This reading of *Back to the Future* is one which has focused on the internal consistencies of the work, rather than trying to apply the realities of time and physics to it. It is a brief analysis of only one facet of the many themes and ideas presented in the films. The possibility of further readings, not just in terms of time travel but in many other areas, highlights the trilogy's complexity as a work of science fiction, something many critics have declined to notice. In the end, *Back to the Future* is, like most art, an attempt to re-present the universe we live in, where people learn from their mistakes and try to correct them, and in doing so, grow into better people. Like most art, the films seek not only to inform, not only to make us believe in something that is not truly there, but also to entertain. As Marty says "Great Scott" and Doc Brown says "Heavy" [in *Part III*], we see that perhaps what *Back to the Future* shows best is what a sense of humor the universe has.

Notes

1. Andrew Gordon, "Back to the Future: Œdipus as Time Traveler," *Science Fiction Studies*, 14 no. 3 (1987), 372–385; Martin M. Winkler, "Oedipus in the Cinema," *Arethusa* 41 (2008), 67–94; David Wittenberg, "Oedipus Multiplex, or, The Subject as a Time Travel Film: Two Readings of *Back to the Future*," *Discourse*, 28 nos. 2 and 3 (2006), 51–77.

2. George Mann, *The Mammoth Encyclopedia of Science Fiction* (London: Constable & Robinson, 2001), 337. Mark Cousins, *The Story of Film* (London: Pavilion Books, 2004), 390, suggests *Back to the Future* represents the "new optimistic decade of the 1980s," part of "Reagan's triumphant consensus," in which America had had enough of the self-critical films of the 1970s.

3. Wittenberg, 51.

4. Paul Coates, "Chris Marker and the Cinema as Time Machine," *Science Fiction Studies*, 14 no. 3 (1987), 307–315, 307.

5. Paul Horwich, "On Some Alleged Paradoxes of Time Travel," *The Journal of Philosophy*, 72 no. 14 (1975), 432–444.

6. David Lewis, "The Paradoxes of Time Travel," *American Philosophical Quarterly*, 13 (1976), 145–152.

7. Nicholas, J. J. Smith, "Bananas Enough for Time Travel?" *The British Journal for the Philosophy of Science*, 48 no. 3 (1997), 363–389.

8. See also, Paul J. Nahin, *Time Machines: Time Travel in Physics, Metaphysics, and Science Fiction* (New York: American Institute of Physics, 1993); Paul, J. Nahin, *Time Travel: A Writer's Guide to the Real Science of Plausible Time Travel* (Cincinnati: Writer's Digest Books, 1997); Richard J. Gott, 2001, *Time Travel in Einstein's Universe: The Physical Possibilities of Travel Through Time* (London: Phoenix, 2002); and Ryan Nichols, Nicholas D. Smith, and Fred Miller, *Philosophy Through Science Fiction: A Coursebook with Readings* (Abingdon: Routledge, 2009).

9. Manfred Nagl, "The Science-Fiction Film in Historical Perspective," *Science Fiction Studies*, 10 no. 3 (1983), 262–277, 263.

10. David Gerrold, *Worlds of Wonder: How to Write Science Fiction and Fantasy* (London: Titan Books, 2001), 24.

11. Joe Haldeman, "Story Time," *Science Fiction Studies*, 30 no. 3 (2003), 540–543, 541.

12. Such as, Paul J. Nahin, *Time Machines* and *Time Travel*.

13. Stephen Hawking, "The Chronology Protection Conjecture," *Physical Review*, 46D (1992) 603–611; Larry Niven, "The Theory and Practise of Time Travel," in Dick Allen and Lori Allen, eds., *Looking Ahead: The Vision of Science Fiction* (New York: Harcourt Brace Jovanovich, 1975), 363–372.

14. John D. Barrow, *Impossibility: The Limits of Science and the Science of Limits* (London: Vintage, 1999), 206.

15. For discussion, see Nahin, *Time Travel* and *Time Machines*; Gott; John Gribbin, *In Search of Schrodinger's Cat: Quantum Physics and Reality* (London: Bantam, 1984); Mary Gribbin and John Gribbin, *Time Travel for Beginners* (London: Hodder Children's Books, 2008); Michio Kaku, *Parallel Worlds: The Science of Alternate Universes and Our Future in the Cosmos* (London: Allen Lane, 2005).

16. Bruce Sterling, "Science Fiction," in *Encyclopedia Britannica, Standard Edition* (Chicago: Encyclopedia Britannica, 2009).

17. Andrew Roberts, ed., *What Might Have Been: Leading Historians on Twelve "What Ifs" of History* (London: Weidenfeld and Nicolson, 2004).

18. The only instance where Doc Brown does not give the exact time of an event is in the first film, where he is describing how he came up with the idea of the flux capacitor. This lapse is likely due to the head injury he sustained, and his period of unconsciousness.

19. Michael Klastorin and Sally Hibbin, *Back to the Future: The Official Book of the Complete Movie Trilogy* (London: The Hamlyn Publishing Group, 1990), 37.

20. Gott.

21. Nahin, *Time Machines.*

22. C. J. Henderson, *The Encyclopedia of Science Fiction Movies: From 1897 to the Present* (New York: Checkmark Books, 2001), 25.

23. Klastorin and Hibbin, 9.

24. Harlan Ellison, "Harlan Ellison's Watching," *The Magazine of Fantasy and Science Fiction*, 70 no. 1 (1986), 84–93, 88.

25. Mann, 337.

26. David Gritten, *Halliwell's The Movies That Matter: From Bogart to Bond and All the Latest Releases* (London: Harper Collins, 2008), 45, states the second film as "the weak link in this generally splendid trilogy ... overstuffed with ideas, some of which misfire."

27. Jonathan Cowie and Tony Chester, *Essential SF: A Concise Guide* (London: Porcupine Books, 2005), 32.

28. Klastorin and Hibbin, 10, quote Gale: "when we made Back to the Future, the original ending was merely a joke ... no one had any thoughts of a sequel at the time, and we figured it was appropriate for the heroes to go flying into the proverbial sunset and off to a new adventure."

29. John Costello, *The Pocket Essential Science Fiction Films* (Harpenden: Pocket Essentials, 2004), 107, states: "I wouldn't bother with the third for-cash-only outing."

30. Cowie and Chester, 32.

31. Gordon.

32. Arthur C. Clarke, *Profiles of the Future: An Inquiry into the Limits of the Possible* (London: Victor Gollancz, 1999), 120.

33. Lawrence Sklar, "Comments on Malament's 'Time Travel in the Gödel Universe,'" *PSA: Proceedings of the Biennial Meeting of the Philosophy of Science Association*, 2 (1984), 106–110, 107.

34. Jonathan Harrison, "The Inaugural Address: Dr. Who and the Philosophers or Time-Travel for Beginners," *Proceedings of the Aristotelian Society, Supplementary Volumes*, 45 (1971), 1–24.

35. John Travis, "Could a Pair of Cosmic Strings Open a Route Into the Past?" *Science*, 256 no. 5054 (1992), 179–180, 179, quotes MIT astrophysicist Alan Guth as stating that physicists have a "deep-seated belief that things should be causal."

36. *Back to the Future* (1985) Feature Commentary with Robert Zemeckis and Bob Gale (Los Angeles: Universal Studios, 2007).

37. Nahin, *Time Machines*, 127.

38. Smith, 364.

39. See, Carl D. Malmgren, "Towards a Definition of Science Fantasy," *Science Fiction Studies*, 15 no. 3 (1988), 259–281, for discussion of the definition of works concerning time travel as science fiction versus science fantasy.

40. Doc does question why it happens to be November 5 1955 to which they again return, speculating that it is a "temporal junction point for the entire space time continuum." This particular date could have been chosen by older Biff for one of three reasons: First, he was unwittingly drawn back there because Marty's original visit and intrusion into the timeline at that point made it a temporal junction point for the entire spacetime continuum. Second, he could have remembered that day particularly well as the day he got decked by George McFly, something that undoubtedly humiliated him for years to come. Thirdly, as the DeLorean's time circuit was on the fritz, it might have been the first date to appear when he switched the time circuit on.

41. Larry Niven's 1978 story, "Rotating Cylinders and the Possibility of Global Causality Violation," first published in *Microcosmic Tales*, depicts the universe taking pre-emptive action to stop civilizations constructing machines capable of time travel, to prevent violations of linear causality.

42. Nichols, Smith, and Miller, 216.

43. *Back to the Future Part II: Making the Trilogy* (Los Angeles: Universal Studios, 2007).

44. Veronica Hollinger, "Deconstructing the Time Machine," *Science Fiction Studies,* 14 no. 2 (1987), 201–222, 201.

45. *The Making of Back to the Future. Back to the Future Trilogy* (Los Angeles: Universal Studios, 2007).

46. *Back to the Future* (1985). Feature Commentary with Robert Zemeckis and Bob Gale. (Los Angeles: Universal Studios, 2007).

47. For discussion, see Nahin, *Time Machines.*

48. *Back to the Future* (1985). Making Trilogy: Chapter 1 (Los Angeles: Universal Studios, 2007).

49. *Back to the Future* (1985). Feature Commentary with Robert Zemeckis and Bob Gale (Los Angeles: Universal Studios, 2007).

50. Among others, Stephen King notably reused this trope for a joking aside in *The Dark Tower* series.

51. David Lowenthal, *The Past is a Foreign Country* (Cambridge: Cambridge University Press, 1985), 22.

52. Henderson, 25.

Bibliography

Barrow, John D. *Impossibility: The Limits of Science and the Science of Limits.* London: Vintage, 1999.

Clarke, Arthur C. *Profiles of the Future: An Inquiry into the Limits of the Possible.* London: Victor Gollancz, 1999.

Coates, Paul. "Chris Marker and the Cinema as Time Machine." *Science Fiction Studies,* 14 no. 3 (1987), 307–315.

Costello, John. *The Pocket Essential Science Fiction Films.* Harpenden: Pocket Essentials, 2004.

Cousins, Mark. *The Story of Film.* London: Pavilion Books, 2004.

Cowie, Jonathan, and Tony Chester. *Essential SF: A Concise Guide.* London: Porcupine Books, 2005.

Ellison, Harlan. "Harlan Ellison's Watching." *The Magazine of Fantasy and Science Fiction,* 70 no. 1 (1986), 84–93.

Gerrold, David. *Worlds of Wonder: How to Write Science Fiction and Fantasy.* London: Titan Books, 2001.

Gordon, Andrew. "Back to the Future: Œdipus as Time Traveller." *Science Fiction Studies,* 14 no. 3 (1987), 372–385.

Gott, Richard J. *Time Travel in Einstein's Universe: The Physical Possibilities of Travel Through Time.* London: Phoenix, 2002.

Gribbin, John. *In Search of Schrodinger's Cat: Quantum Physics and Reality.* London: Bantam, 1984.

Gribbin, Mary, and John Gribbin. *Time Travel for Beginners.* London: Hodder Children's Books, 2008.

Gritten, David. *Halliwell's The Movies That Matter: From Bogart to Bond and All the Latest Releases.* London: Harper Collins, 2008.

Haldeman, Joe. "Story Time." *Science Fiction Studies,* 30 no. 3 (2003), 540–543.

Harrison, Jonathan. "The Inaugural Address: Dr. Who and the Philosophers or Time-Travel for Beginners." *Proceedings of the Aristotelian Society, Supplementary Volumes,* 45 (1971), 1–24.

Hawking, Stephen. "The Chronology Protection Conjecture." *Physical Review,* 46D (1992) 603–611.

Henderson, C. J. *The Encyclopedia of Science Fiction Movies: From 1897 to the Present.* New York: Checkmark Books, 2001.

Hollinger, Veronica. "Deconstructing the Time Machine." *Science Fiction Studies,* 14 no. 2 (1987), 201–222.

Horwich, Paul. "On Some Alleged Paradoxes of Time Travel." *The Journal of Philosophy,* 72 no. 14 (1975), 432–444.

Kaku, Michio. *Parallel Worlds: The Science of Alternate Universes and Our Future in the Cosmos.* London: Allen Lane, 2005.

Klastorin, Michael, and Sally Hibbin. *Back to the Future: The Official Book of the Complete Movie Trilogy.* London: The Hamlyn Publishing Group, 1990.

Lewis, David. "The Paradoxes of Time Travel." *American Philosophical Quarterly,* 13 (1976), 145–152.

Lowenthal, David. *The Past Is a Foreign Country.* Cambridge: Cambridge University Press, 1985.

Malmgren, Carl D. "Towards a Definition of Science Fantasy." *Science Fiction Studies,* 15 no. 3 (1988), 259–281.

Mann, George. *The Mammoth Encyclopedia of Science Fiction.* London: Constable & Robinson, 2001.

Nagl, Manfred. "The Science-Fiction Film in Historical Perspective." *Science Fiction Studies,* 10 no. 3 (1983), 262–277, 263.

Nahin, Paul J. *Time Machines: Time Travel in Physics, Metaphysics, and Science Fiction.* New York: American Institute of Physics, 1993.

_____. *Time Travel: A Writer's Guide to the Real Science of Plausible Time Travel.* Cincinnati: Writer's Digest Books, 1997.

Nichols, Ryan, Nicholas D. Smith, and Fred Miller. *Philosophy Through Science Fiction: A Coursebook with Readings.* Abingdon: Routledge, 2009.

Niven, Larry. "The Theory and Practise of Time

Travel" in Dick Allen and Lori Allen, eds., *Looking Ahead: The Vision of Science Fiction.* New York: Harcourt Brace Jovanovich, 1975.

Roberts, Andrew, ed. *What Might Have Been: Leading Historians on Twelve "What Ifs" of History.* London: Weidenfeld and Nicolson, 2004.

Sklar, Lawrence. "Comments on Malament's 'Time Travel in the Gödel Universe.'" *PSA: Proceedings of the Biennial Meeting of the Philosophy of Science Association,* 2 (1984), 106–110.

Smith, Nicholas J. J. "Bananas Enough for Time Travel?" *The British Journal for the Philosophy of Science,* 48 no. 3 (1997), 363–389.

Sterling, Bruce. "Science Fiction" in *Encyclopædia Britannica, Standard Edition.* Chicago: Encyclopædia Britannica, 2009.

Travis, John. "Could a Pair of Cosmic Strings Open a Route Into the Past?" *Science,* 256 no. 5054 (1992), 179–180.

Winkler, Martin M. "Oedipus in the Cinema." *Arethusa* 41 (2008), 67–94

Wittenberg, David. "Oedipus Multiplex, or, The Subject as a Time Travel Film: Two Readings of *Back to the Future.*" *Discourse,* 28 nos. 2 and 3 (2006), 51–77.

Filmography

Back to the Future. Dir. Robert Zemeckis, Universal Studios, 1985.

Back to the Future Part II. Dir. Robert Zemeckis, Universal Studios, 1989.

Back to the Future Part III. Dir. Robert Zemeckis, Universal Studios, 1990.

Bill and Ted's Excellent Adventure. Dir. Stephen Herek, Orion Pictures, 1989.

The Terminator. Dir. James Cameron, Orion Pictures, 1984.

About the Contributors

John Exshaw is a freelance writer. He is a regular contributor to *Cinema Retro* magazine, and is the review columnist for *Boxing Monthly* magazine. His work has also appeared in *Sight & Sound, The Bram Stoker Society Journal, The Times, The Sunday Times, The Irish Times, The Independent, The Guardian,* and *The Irish Independent.*

Katherine Farrimond is a doctoral student at Newcastle University where she also teaches courses on literature and film. Her research interests include feminist theory, and intersections of sexuality, femininity and the body in Hollywood film.

Lucy Fife Donaldson is a PhD student in the Department of Film, Theatre and Television at the University of Reading, researching performance in the post-studio horror film, with particular focus on the materiality of performance and its relationship to elements of film style.

Christine Lee Gengaro is an assistant professor of music at Los Angeles City College and has a PhD in music history from the University of Southern California. She worked on the *Journal of the American Musicological Society,* led the online music journal *Resonance,* was the 2008 program book editor for the Aspen Music Festival, and has been an annotator for numerous concert series.

Andrew Gordon is a professor of English and director of the Institute for the Psychological Study of the Arts at the University of Florida. He is co-author, with Hernan Vera, of *Screen Saviors: Hollywood Fictions of Whiteness,* and co-editor, with Peter Rudnytsky, of *Psychoanalyses/Feminisms.* He is also author of *An American Dreamer,* about Norman Mailer, and *Empire of Dreams,* about Steven Spielberg.

Jennifer Harwood-Smith is a graduate of the University of Limerick and Trinity College Dublin, and is preparing for a PhD on world-building in science fiction. The 2006 winner of the James White Award, she has been published in

Interzone magazine, contributed two chapters to *Battlestar Galactica: Mission Accomplished or Mission Frakked Up?*, and is currently writing a novel.

Christopher Justice teaches writing, literature, film, and journalism at the University of Baltimore. He has recently written about the sexploitation films of Edgar G. Ulmer, travel in Michael Haneke's films, and radicalism in Joseph H. Lewis's *Gun Crazy*. His monthly column "The Tackle Box" in *PopMatters* explores the confluence of fishing and popular culture.

Randy Laist received his PhD in 2009 from the University of Connecticut. He is the author of *Technology and Postmodern Subjectivity in the Novels of Don DeLillo*, the editor of a forthcoming book of critical essays on the television show *Lost*, and has published articles on Melville, Kafka, Mailer, and YouTube.

Francis Ludlow lectures in the Geography Department, Trinity College Dublin, and teaches a speculative fiction writing course to gifted teenagers in Dublin City University. He has published numerous articles, book reviews and interviews, and works on the magazine of science fiction, fantasy and horror *Albedo One*. He is co-editor with Roelof Goudriaan of the story collection *Emerald Eye*.

Stephen Matterson teaches American literature in the School of English, Trinity College Dublin, and has published widely on many aspects of American literature, with a notable emphasis on poetry and on 19th century writing.

Elizabeth McCarthy holds a PhD from Trinity College Dublin, where she currently teaches. She has written on the vampire body; the guillotine in the French Revolution; and post–World War I American advertising. She has also co-edited with Kate Hebblethwaite the book *Fear: Essays on the Meaning and Experience of Fear*. She is co-founder and co-editor of the online *Irish Journal of Gothic and Horror Studies*.

Bernice M. Murphy is a lecturer in popular literature in the School of English, Trinity College Dublin. Her book *The Suburban Gothic in American Popular Culture* was published in 2009 and her edited collection *Shirley Jackson: Essays on the Literary Legacy* was published by McFarland in 2005. She is co-founder and co-editor of the online *Irish Journal of Gothic and Horror Studies* and has published articles on Stephen King and on suburban-set zombie narratives.

Sorcha Ní Fhlainn teaches American literature, cinema and the gothic at Trinity College Dublin, where she received a PhD. She has written on horror cinema, vampirism, the slasher genre under Reagan and postmodernism, and edited the collection *Our Monstrous (S)kin: Blurring the Boundaries Between Monsters and Humanity*.

Michael Williams is an assistant professor in the Department of Liberal Arts at Berklee College of Music. He received a BA from Swarthmore and a PhD in visual and cultural studies from the University of Rochester. He has written on psychoanalysis, philosophy, feminism, and film. His current project involves an exploration of the ontology of the cartoon character.

Index

Index